Protection of Human Life at Sea in International Law

The law of the sea imposes a long-established duty to rescue persons in distress, which connotes one of the most important tools in safeguarding safety of life at sea. Other rules of international law, namely, international human rights and refugee law also come into play in drawing the legal parameters for the conduct of rescue operations.

Amid the thousands of people undertaking perilous sea journeys in search of safety, European legal responses have primarily focused on the securitization of migration. This book exposes the human rights violations that may be perpetrated against migrants attempting to cross the Mediterranean and strongly advocates for the development of a framework for operationalizing the protection of human rights – and life – at sea. It combines theory and practice in which philosophical theories of rights are applied to create a framework for legal analysis and the development of practical legal standards. The study presents an innovative evaluation of selected judgments of the European Court of Human Rights and other international human rights bodies pertaining to complex questions of extraterritorial jurisdiction and a State's human rights obligations towards persons in distress at sea.

The book will be of interest to all those engaging with migration and security studies, international human rights scholarship, international law of the sea, refugee and migration law and legal philosophy, whether generalist or specialist.

Dr Aphrodite Papachristodoulou is Research Fellow at the Irish Centre for Human Rights, University of Galway where she completed a two year Post-Doctoral Fellowship focusing on AI Technologies in Maritime Border and Migration Management. She holds a Law degree from the University of Southampton, a Master of Laws in Maritime Law from University College London (UCL), and a PhD in Law from University College Dublin. Dr Papachristodoulou publishes on international law issues including migration, extraterritorial human rights jurisdiction, maritime security and border technologies, and teaches at universities across Europe, including the University of Cyprus. She is a consultant to a number of national and international governmental and non-governmental organizations, and serves as Management Committee Member of the COST Action BlueRights (CA23103)(representing Cyprus).

Law and Migration

Series Editor Satvinder S. Juss, King's College London, UK

Migration and its subsets of refugee and asylum policy are rising up the policy agenda at national and international level. Current controversies underline the need for rational and informed debate of this widely misrepresented and little understood area.

Law and Migration contributes to this debate by establishing a monograph series to encourage discussion and help to inform policy in this area. The series provides a forum for leading new research principally from the Law and Legal Studies area but also from related social sciences. The series is broad in scope, covering a wide range of subjects and perspectives.

Other titles in this series:

Persecution, International Refugee Law and Refugees
A Feminist Approach
Mathilde Crépin

Human Rights and The Revision of Refugee Law
Romit Bhandari

Refugees, Democracy and the Law
Political Rights at the Margins of the State
Dana Schmalz

Inside Asylum Appeals
Access, Participation and Procedure in Europe
Nick Gill, Nicole Hoellerer, Jessica Hambly and Daniel Fisher

Protection of Human Life at Sea in International Law
Rescuing Maritime Migrants
Aphrodite Papachristodoulou

For more information about this series, please visit: www.routledge.com/Law-and-Migration/book-series/LAWANDMIG

Protection of Human Life at Sea in International Law

Rescuing Maritime Migrants

Aphrodite Papachristodoulou

Routledge
Taylor & Francis Group
LONDON AND NEW YORK

First published 2025
by Routledge
4 Park Square, Milton Park, Abingdon, Oxon OX14 4RN

and by Routledge
605 Third Avenue, New York, NY 10158

Routledge is an imprint of the Taylor & Francis Group, an informa business

British Library Cataloguing-in-Publication Data
A catalogue record for this book is available from the British Library

Library of Congress Cataloging-in-Publication Data
Names: Papachristodoulou, Aphrodite, author.
Title: Protection of human life at sea in international law : rescuing maritime migrants / Aphrodite Papachristodoulou.
Description: Abingdon, Oxon [UK] ; New York, NY : Routledge, 2025. | Series: Law and migration | Includes bibliographical references and index.
Identifiers: LCCN 2024061075 (print) | LCCN 2024061076 (ebook) | ISBN 9781032940083 (hardback) | ISBN 9781032940090 (paperback) | ISBN 9781003568537 (ebook)
Subjects: LCSH: Boat people—Legal status, laws, etc. | Refugees—Legal status, laws, etc. | Illegal immigration. | Emigration and immigration law. | Law of the sea. | International law and human rights.
Classification: LCC KZ6530 .P37 2025 (print) | LCC KZ6530 (ebook) | DDC 341.4/86—dc23/eng/20250111
LC record available at https://lccn.loc.gov/2024061075
LC ebook record available at https://lccn.loc.gov/2024061076

ISBN: 978-1-032-94008-3 (hbk)
ISBN: 978-1-032-94009-0 (pbk)
ISBN: 978-1-003-56853-7 (ebk)

DOI: 10.4324/9781003568537

Typeset in Galliard
by Apex CoVantage, LLC

In loving memory of my grandfather, Αντώνης Παπαντωνίου . . .

Contents

Preface

This volume reconnoiters in depth how legally enforceable the value of human life at sea is and how this often ends as the unspoken victim of that perennial clash of titans – the undisputed right of every sovereign state to the inviolability of its frontiers and to control the entry of non-nationals, of the one part, and, of the other, the fundamental human right of every person to life and not to be subjected to inhuman and degrading treatment. The immanently historic phenomenon of migration seems to erode the certainty of both these values. Conflicts born of large-scale movements of people put unbearable stresses on ethical and legal hierarchies. They upset human cravings for symmetry, for neat frontiers between legal and illegal.

The visionary Hugo Grotius, in his 1609 Freedom of the Seas, codified the first principles of maritime law. The protection of human life at sea found no place in that huge pioneer architecture.

Geographers teach us that water occupies over 70 percent of the terrestrial surface and less than 30 percent consists of land. And yet, human ingenuity has, over the centuries, engineered the protection of human life on *terra firma* in an overabundance of different ways, starting with basic criminal and civil norms and leading to more or less cast-iron regional and international conventions. On land, ever more compellingly, sophisticated and enforceable norms safeguard human life, but protection of that same human life and rights at sea sadly remains a jurisdictional and juridical Cinderella.

Dr. Aphrodite Papachristodoulou did not turn a deaf ear to the wailings wafting from this normative black hole. Her amazing research, her determination, her passion for law as ultimate justice has produced a bible that codifies the dogmas of the faith in the supremacy of human rights, the manual for the safeguards of life at sea, threatened as they are by the ever more unrelenting movements of persons fleeing from massacre or in search of a more meaningful future.

The buildup of this book shows what tools for human rights already exist in the arsenal, and how to exploit them. To borrow a phrase from the US Supreme Court justices, perhaps the aim is to discover a right to be rescued at sea in the penumbral fringes of established legislation. There is, or there should be, plenty of protection at the migrant's or asylum seeker's point of departure and at the point of arrival, but, so far, only the Papachristodoulou dialectics in between.

The soft universality of human rights should, of itself, posit the widest application of extraterritoriality in the jurisdiction of human rights enforcers and tribunals. Personally, I have been a vocal advocate of extraterritorial jurisdiction in the enforcement of human rights when my voice counted for anything. Though some advances have undoubtedly been registered, these have mostly been timid, hesitant and contested. Half-hearted protection – hampered, undermined and mocked by populist phobias – hardly replaces the robust bastions of established legislation and the bold case law of a proactive judiciary.

Political will remains the last resource to rely on. Generally, policy makers are more concerned with deterring migrants from leaving and with making landings as unattractive as possible than with fostering the basic humanity of the migrant and the asylum seeker. The increasing numbers of migrants lost at sea remain a lethal testament to this well-crafted state inertia. Note: crafted and crafty share a common lexical root.

I predict the author's research will turn out to be fundamental and indispensable to political thinkers, students, academia, the judiciary, legal historians and, perhaps mostly, to those lawyers and barristers who care.

Giovanni Bonello served as Judge of the European Court of Human Rights, 1998–2010

Acknowledgments

I wish to extend my heartfelt gratitude to all those who offered me assistance in the research and writing of this study. Many of the ideas in this book took shape in my doctoral thesis, written whilst I held the National University of Ireland (NUI) Fellowship in International Law at University College Dublin. I would like therefore to first note my deep appreciation for the unwavering guidance offered by my doctoral supervisor, Professor Richard Collins, Dean of Internationalisation and Engagement in the Faculty of Arts, Humanities and Social Sciences at Queen's University Belfast. I am forever grateful for his endless support and encouragement throughout my research journey. It is indeed a privilege to have the support of such a kind and generous person. I also owe a weighty debt of gratitude to my two final examiners, Professor Joseph McMahon, Full Professor of Commercial Law at University College Dublin, and Established Professor Siobhán Mullally, Director of the Irish Centre for Human Rights at the University of Galway and the UN Special Rapporteur on Trafficking in Persons, for their helpful comments made during and after the *viva* and for their consistent support and encouragement. I owe a profound thanks to Professor Mullally, who was my mentor during my two-year NUI Post-Doctoral Research Fellowship and has bestowed on me a wealth of knowledge.

The University College Dublin, where I pursued my PhD, and the University of Galway, where I conducted my Post-Doctoral research, deserve my gratitude for generously providing me access to research facilities and resources which allowed this work to come to fruition. This research was partly funded by the A.G. Leventis Foundation and the National University of Ireland. I am grateful for their support and trust in the quality of my research.

This study would not have been possible without the wisdom, insights and continuous support of my colleagues at the University College Dublin: Dr. Liam Thornton, Professor Suzanne Kingston, Professor Suzanne Egan, Dr. Graham Finlay and Professor Imelda Maher. I also benefited greatly from attending research workshops on the philosophy of human rights convened by Professor John Tasioulas, Director of the Institute for Ethics in AI at the University of Oxford, who was a source of much inspiration. I acknowledge an intellectual and personal debt of gratitude to him for illuminating discussions about the proliferation of rights and migration.

I was privileged to have the opportunity to present parts of this book and related papers, at various stages of development. Chapter 2 contains a much altered and extended version of a previous article, 'Mediterranean Maritime Migration: The Legal Framework of Saving Lives at Sea' (2020) 20 UCD Law Review 87–112, while portions of Chapters 4 and 5 appeared as 'The Recognition of a Right to be Rescued at Sea in International Law' (2022) 35(2) Leiden Journal of International Law 1–20, albeit significantly updated.

Lastly, I would like to say some words to those warmest to my heart: my family and friends. Special thanks go to my family, my mother, Maria Papantoniou, my father, Giorgos Papachristodoulou and my brother, Athos Papachristodoulou, for their love and unreserved support in my endeavors. I would also like to express my gratitude to my grandma, Aphrodite Papantoniou, whom I have spent most of the Covid-19 period (2020–2021) with, for always taking the best care of me – you were my sanity in difficult times. Finally, I would like to thank my second family, my closest friends for support when despair would otherwise have set in: Linda Mallouride, Pavlina Theodoulou, Maria A. Anastasi, Xristina Georgiou, Andia Stylianou, Maria Panaseti, Konstantina Maragkou, Encarnita Ioannou, Vasileia M. Anaxagorou and Penny Theodorou. Above all, I want to thank you for filling my life with love and everyday joy. This book is dedicated to my beloved grandfather, Antonis Papantoniou. He had left this world before I embarked on my doctoral journey, but I am sure that he watches over me from above. He is the driving force behind my unwavering passion for the field to which I have dedicated myself. His influence, starting from a very young age, has profoundly shaped the way I perceive philosophy and the law, imbuing me with a powerful perspective; his words will always echo in my mind, 'You will become a judge one day', and this sentiment continues to resonate within me. Here's to the next project.

Aphrodite Papachristodoulou
Cyprus

Abbreviations

ACHPR	African Charter on Human and People's Rights
ACHR	American Convention on Human Rights
ASR	International Law Commission, Articles on the Responsibility of States for Internationally Wrongful Acts with Commentaries, Yearbook of the International Law Commission, 2001, vol. II
CAT	Committee Against Torture
CJEU	Court of Justice of the European Union
CoE	Council of Europe
CRC	Convention on the Rights of the Child
CSDP	Common Security and Defence Policy
ECHR	European Convention for the Protection of Human Rights and Fundamental Freedoms
ECtHR	European Court of Human Rights
EEZ	Exclusive Economic Zone
EU	European Union
EU Charter	Charter of Fundamental Rights of the European Union
EUBAM	EU Border Assistance Mission (Libya)
EUNAVFOR MED	European Union Naval Operation Against Human Smugglers and Traffickers in the Mediterranean
FRA	EU Agency for Fundamental Rights
FRONTEX	European Agency for the Management of the Operative Cooperation at the External Borders of the Member States of the European Union
GLAN	Global Legal Action Network
HRC	UN Human Rights Committee
IACHR	Inter-American Court of Human Rights
IACmHR	Inter-American Commission of Human Rights
ICCPR	International Covenant on Civil and Political Rights
ICESCR	International Covenant on Economic, Social and Cultural Rights
ICJ	International Court of Justice

ILC	International Law Commission
IMO	International Maritime Organization
IMO MSC	Maritime Safety Committee
IOM	International Organization for Migration
ITLOS	International Tribunal for the Law of the Sea
LCGN	Libyan Coast Guard and Navy
MRCC	Italian Maritime Rescue Coordination Centre
MOAS	Migrant Offshore Aid Station
MOU	Memorandum of Understanding
MSF	Médicins San Frontières
NATO	North Atlantic Treaty Organization
NGOs	Non-governmental organizations
OHCHR	Office of the United Nations High Commissioner for Human Rights
PACE	Parliamentary Committee of the Council of Europe
RCC	Rescue Coordination Centre
Refugee Convention	Convention Relating to the Status of Refugees, as amended by Protocol Relating to the Status of Refugees
Salvage Convention	International Convention on Salvage
SAR	Search and Rescue
SAR Convention	International Convention on Maritime Search and Rescue
Smuggling Protocol	Protocol against the Smuggling of Migrants by Land, Sea and Air Supplementing the United Nations Convention against Transnational Organized Crime
SOLAS	The International Convention for Safety of Life at Sea
UDHR	Universal Declaration of Human Rights
UK	United Kingdom
UN	United Nations
UNCAT	UN Convention Against Torture and Other Cruel, Inhuman or Degrading Treatment or Punishment
UNCLOS	United Nations Convention on the Law of the Sea
UNGA	UN General Assembly
UNHCR	United Nations High Commissioner for Refugees
UNCESCR	UN Committee on Economic, Social and Cultural Rights
UNTS	UN Treaty Series
US	United States of America
VCLT	Vienna Convention on the Law of Treaties

Introduction

The Predicament of Migration by Sea

Today, people imagine a world of anthropologically confined societies, each enjoying their own culture and ethnos.[1] Since antiquity, however, the default position has been the opposite, as illustrated by the story of the Greek mythical figure of *Europa*, with intense cultural and social interaction and the existence of traditions and institutions among all communities. In fact, the origins of the word Europa signal the very fact that it was not European at the outset. It was *Europa*'s displacement (*Europa* being a Phoenician princess), meaning, her abduction (movement) from her homeland, Phoenicia (today, this area stands for Syria–Israel), by the Greek God Zeus in the guise of a bull (this is understood as a metaphor for 'ship') to another place, Greece, which gave birth to the name of Europe.[2] It can be argued that Europe's mythological counterpart, *Europa,* shaped migration as it exemplified a tangled yet sophisticated link between Europe's continent and the volatile regions of the Muslim world, and particularly migration at sea. The pivotal significance of the geographical configuration of the Mediterranean Sea – bounded by three continents in all – ties these regions together. Relatedly, prior studies have substantiated the belief that the story of *Europa* came to be acknowledged as a performative product of migration through the Mediterranean over the years.[3]

By definition, migration is a source of human mobility that is best described as a geographical phenomenon conceptualized by the movement of people

1 Jeremy Waldron, 'Cosmopolitan Norms' in Seyla Benhabib, *Another Cosmopolitanism* (Robert Post ed, Oxford: Oxford University Press 2006) 98 fn 19.

2 On a discussion of the mythical figure of Europa and its association with the European Union see Ian Manners, 'Global Europa: Mythology of the European Union in World Politics' (2010) 48(1) Journal of Common Market Studies 67–87.

3 Almut-Barbara Renger, 'Tracing the Line of Europa: Migration, Genealogy, and the Power of Holy Origins in Ancient Greek Narrative Knowledge and Cultural Memory' (2014) 25(3) History and Anthropology 357.

DOI: 10.4324/9781003568537-1

across State borders and spaces.[4] In fact, migration to control or set entry requirements in a State or group of States, like the European Union (EU), equally has a geographical dimension. As Étiene Balibar has argued, borders create various forms of legal and irregular migration by differentiating between the terms of movement and residence based on citizenship and reasons for migration.[5] In Europe, third-country nationals who do not carry the apposite visa documentation to secure legal entry are often forced to seek unauthorized access via dangerous migration routes – the most well-known being the sea.

Migration is not new, but in a world of increasing armed conflict, rapid climate change and degradation, natural disasters as well as technological advancements, it has reached a new proportion. Indeed, it is the scale of it that has brought it to the forefront. Contemporary migration in the form of irregular movement by sea has received global attention in the last decades, not only for the economic, political and social issues it raises but also for raising the specter of threats to life and the person, and thus of effective human rights protection of migrants. The perils of the sea for human beings that choose to set sail upon it are obvious enough. However, these dangers are particularly pronounced for those trafficked or smuggled across the sea.[6]

Today, more than ever, migrants and refugees[7] travel in the same boats trying to reach European shores by resorting to the only apparent (nonlegal) avenue: irregular, lengthy and perilous sea crossings in unseaworthy and barely functional boats. Smuggling and trafficking networks provide the means of securing such transit,[8] namely, 'flagless' or 'stateless' vessels, which makes the whole experience even more treacherous. For this reason, the term 'illegal' migrant is overly employed in studies, as the vast majority of seaborne migrants

4 Jukka Könönen, 'Legal Geographies of Irregular Migration: An Outlook on Immigration Detention' (2020) 26(5) Population, Space and Place <https://onlinelibrary.wiley.com/doi/full/10.1002/psp.2340>.

5 Étiene Balibar, *Politics and the Other Scene* (London: Verso 2002); See also Hannah Arendt, *The Origins of Totalitarianism* (Cleveland: The World Publishing Company 1951) 296.

6 For an analysis on the vulnerabilities of trafficked persons who are victims of egregious abuse, but in the absence of access to legal protection and securing migration status, they also become irregular migrants, see Siobhán Mullally, 'Migration, Gender, and the Limits of Rights' in Ruth Rubio-Marín (ed), *Human Rights and Immigration* (OUP 2014) 145–146.

7 A refugee is a person who 'owing to well-founded fear of being persecuted for reasons of race, religion, nationality, membership of a particular social group or political opinion, is outside the country of his nationality and is unable or, owing to such fear, is unwilling to avail himself of the protection of that country; or who, not having a nationality and being outside the country of his former habitual residence as a result of such events, is unable or, owing to such fear, is unwilling to return to it' as per Article 1A(2) of the 1951 Convention relating to the Status of Refugees (adopted 28 July 1951, entered into force 22 April 1954) 189 UNTS 139 (Refugee Convention) and its 1967 Protocol relating to the Status of Refugees (31 January 1967) 606 UNTS 8791.

8 Report of the Special Rapporteur on the Human Rights Council on Extrajudicial, Summary or Arbitrary Executions, UN Doc. A/72/335, 15 August 2017, at [43].

do not carry the appropriate travel documents.[9] Yet, in a daring attempt to flee and reach a 'safer' haven, they nonetheless seek an (illegal) entry to a State in order to seek protection. Still, many of them *never succeed* in arriving at the physical borders of a State. The risk of death associated with migration by sea is especially high due to drowning, malnourishment, suffocation, dehydration, starvation, unsanitary conditions and violence.[10]

In the powerful words of Hannah Arendt, 'once they had left their homeland they remained homeless, once they had left their state they became stateless; once they had been deprived of their human rights they were rightless, the scum of the earth'.[11] The statement symbolizes the current disdain for migrants' plight attempting to cross the Mediterranean Sea from the Middle East and North Africa in their quest to reach Europe. Against this background, the core principle of saving lives of persons in distress at sea is of critical importance for safeguarding the right to life under international human rights law. Apart from being a long-standing and fundamental tradition of seafaring, this humanitarian norm is also incorporated as a legal duty of the search and rescue (SAR) system under the international law of the sea.[12] Arguably, the attention of preventing deaths that occur once people embark on perilous sea journeys has been deflected to the protection of borders and, in particular, policies which increasingly focus on external border management and remote surveillance control. Accordingly, the EU and its Member States have drawn migration control policies, concluded bilateral, unilateral and multilateral forms of cooperation with third countries and fortified borders in a manner that shifts the focus of humanitarian efforts towards preventing migration flows at *all* costs – even one's life.

Over the course of drafting this book and tracing the situation in the Mediterranean region, the conditions for migrants continuously deteriorated amidst a drastic reduction of SAR capacity in the Mediterranean by the European States and a worrisome increased reliance on aerial surveillance technologies in order to enhance third-countries' capacity to prevent exit and intercept migrant boats

9 In the absence of a universally accepted definition for the term 'migrant' in international law, this book adopts the IOM's definition, which is arguably the most encompassing: 'An umbrella term, not defined under international law, reflecting the common lay understanding of a person who moves away from his or her place of usual residence, whether within a country or across an international border, temporarily or permanently, and for a variety of reasons. The term includes a number of well-defined legal categories of people, such as migrant workers; persons whose particular types of movements are legally-defined, such as smuggled migrants; as well as those whose status or means of movement are not specifically defined under international law, such as international students'. IOM, 'International Migration Law No 34, Glossary on Migration' (IOM, 2019) <https://publications.iom.int/system/files/pdf/iml_34_glossary.pdf>.

10 Bríd Ní Ghráinne, 'Left to Die at Sea: State Responsibility for the May 2015 Thai, Indonesian and Malaysian Pushback Operations' (2017) 10 Irish Yearbook of International Law 7.

11 Arendt (n 5) 267.

12 United Nations Convention on the Law of the Sea (adopted 10 December 1982, entered into force 16 November 1994) 1833 UNTS 397 (UNCLOS), Art 98.

(pull-back practice). This study observes however that 'it is not geography or the lack of surveillance capacity that poses limits to rescue but lack of human engagement and indifference to human suffering. Many could have been rescued had fellow beings *not ignored* their pleas for help'.[13] On 14 June 2023, the second deadliest shipwreck on record in the Mediterranean since 2015 occurred in the open waters of Greece near the tourist island of Pylos. The International Organization for Migration (IOM) has calculated that in total, approximately 750 people were traveling on the *Adriana* boat, of whom 104 survived the wreck, 78 were recorded dead and the rest (approximately 600) are feared dead. As unpalatable as this may seem, this is a case where migrants called for help, several actors witnessed and came in close proximity with the migrant boat in question and yet, all parties involved chose to remain *inactive*. Against this understanding, the key question becomes whether international human rights treaties apply in cases of nonperformance of SAR operations. A plethora of troubling issues surrounds the Pylos shipwreck, which are examined in Chapter 2 in the context of contemporary State practices in the Mediterranean.

As a consequence, images of migrant boats stranded on shores, images of migrants drowning in shipwrecks, images of children washing up dead on European coasts have become recurring features of the weekly news cycle. The IOM has recorded more than 30,522 migrant disappearances and deaths in the Mediterranean Sea since 2014. Reflecting on more recent data, in 2023 there were more than 3,041 migrant disappearances and deaths in the whole Mediterranean region compared to 2,411 in 2022. This represents an 11 percent increase in mortality rates in 2023, while in 2022 there was an 18 percent increase from 2021,[14] despite a sharp reduction in the number of sea crossings. Emphatically, the loss of life during sea crossings reveals poignant weaknesses in the international legal frameworks governing protection of human life at sea.

This book explores the phenomenon of irregular migration by sea by analyzing State practices in the Mediterranean that fall short of complying with

13 Tugba Basaran, 'The Saved and the Drowned: Governing Indifference in the Name of Security' (2015) 46(3) Security Dialogue 206 (emphasis added).

14 These figures were generated by the author on the basis of data taken from the IOM's Missing Migrant Project, which collects the most comprehensive figures on the region; <https://missingmigrants.iom.int/data>. The data was analyzed using descriptive statistics to determine mortality rates, comparing the annual number of attempted crossings with the actual number of deaths/missing persons. It needs to be noted that relying on data presumptions on the number of migrants that have died or gone missing in the process of migration to Europe, regardless of their legal status, presents an acute challenge to the reliability of these datasets, as many migrant fatalities around the world go unrecorded; hence the data are not fully complete. As such, the data can sometimes be under-inclusive and may not represent the actual number of migrant fatalities at sea. In this vein, the IOM has stressed that migrant deaths tend to be 'underreported or sometimes unrecorded' by virtue of a number of unconfirmed invisible shipwrecks recorded on maritime migration routes to Europe (in 2020 particularly). Notwithstanding this inevitable difficulty, these are the most reliable sources of data that we as researchers can use in order to analyze the effect of European policies on the human rights of migrants.

relevant international standards. These include abandonment at sea, negligently handling distress information, push-backs by a proxy third actor, privatized *refoulement* in connection with aerial *refoulement* and floating detention centers. The widely documented experiences of irregular migrants illustrate the broader reality that they routinely see their human rights violated. For this reason, I describe the status quo as a prolonged *humanitarian crisis at sea*.[15] This forms the *prima facie* basis for the European situation becoming the point of departure of the analysis, as the unfolding events in the Mediterranean over the past two decades present a regional example of a broader global issue – the many apparent gaps in protection of the human rights of migrants.

Human Rights at Sea

The protection of people at sea has long escaped the attention of international lawyers and academics alike, notwithstanding the intrinsic international character of the sea and the different nationalities of the people to be found aboard vessels and platforms. Maritime migration cases are now increasingly being brought before human rights bodies, like the United Nations (UN) Committee Against Torture (CAT), the UN Human Rights Committee (HRC or Committee) or the European Court of Human Rights (ECtHR or Strasbourg Court or Court), where victims of alleged human rights violations or the relatives of those victims seek redress for violations that occur at sea.[16] Safeguarding human rights at sea has historically been overlooked, since only in the past 15 years has it started to garner attention in light of the increased human presence at sea and the subsequent poignant rights breaches in the context of migration control.[17] Irini Papanicolopulu, in this regard, has argued that the law may apply incompletely, inefficiently or even incorrectly at sea.[18]

15 The terms 'European refugee crisis' and 'European migration crisis' have often been used interchangeably in academic scholarship, politics and by the media referring to the period starting in 2015 where over one million people arrived in Europe seeking protection and resettlement. This was the greatest mass movement since World War II. However, referring to these migration movements as 'migration' or 'refugee' crisis has been much contested in human rights, political and social discourses. The reason that I prefer to employ the term 'humanitarian crisis at sea' is because it is terminology that shows that the rights of refugees and migrants, either in the form of refugee asylum protection or, more broadly, the universal human rights and freedoms that should be enjoyed by everyone regardless of legal status, are exponentially violated.

16 Anna Petrig, *Human Rights and Law Enforcement at Sea: Arrest, Detention and Transfer of Piracy Suspects* (Brill, Nijhoff 2014); Efthymios Papastavridis, 'The European Convention of Human Rights and Migration at Sea: Reading the "Jurisdictional Threshold" of the Convention under the Law of the Sea Paradigm' (2020) 21(3) German Law Journal 418–421.

17 Sofia Galani, 'Port Closures and Persons at Sea in International Law' (2021) 70(3) International and Comparative Law Quarterly 605; Selive Trevisanut, 'Search and Rescue Operations at Sea' in André Nollkaemper and Ilias Plakokefalos (eds), *The Practice of Shared Responsibility in International Law* (CUP 2016) 432.

18 Irini Papanicolopulu, *International Law and the Protection of People at Sea* (Oxford: OUP 2018) 8.

At this stage, it is important to examine why human rights become susceptible at sea. The pertinent question in international law is whether individuals are subject to the sovereignty of a State, which encompasses the territorial sea and vessels bearing the State's flag, or whether the State is exercising effective control over individuals outside its *terra firma*. Central to the latter is the traditional understanding that States have human rights obligations primarily within their territorial borders, where they exercise jurisdiction or sovereignty.[19] In the context of irregular migration by sea, most, if not all, maritime incidents occur on areas beyond the territorial jurisdiction of any sovereign State, that is, the high seas.[20] As will be expounded in Chapter 2, the legal regime of the high seas is traced back to 1609 by Grotius, who first published his *Mare Liberum*, articulating 'the freedom of the high seas' concept which survives to this day.[21] This book explores the notion of human rights jurisdiction in the high seas commons, where States ordinarily do not enjoy sovereign control and where humans, in the absence of a normative relationship with a duty-bearer (and the protection from their home countries), in practice, cannot enjoy protection of their rights. It has been argued that 'the high seas remain one of the few places on earth not subject to a national sovereign legal order, which could be said to make the legal framework rather thin, both legally and, especially, institutionally'.[22]

Intriguingly, human rights treaties remain silent concerning maritime law issues. For example, neither the International Covenant on Civil and Political Rights (ICCPR)[23] nor the European Convention on Human Rights (ECHR or Convention)[24] refers to the maritime space. Similarly, the United Nations Convention on the Law of the Sea (UNCLOS),[25] the 'Constitution of the

19 *Legal Consequences of the Construction of a Wall in the Occupied Palestinian Territory* (Advisory Opinion) [2004] ICJ Rep 136 para 109, 112 (*The Wall* case); See also *Hirsi Jamaa and Others v Italy* (*Hirsi*) App no 27765/09 (ECtHR, 23 February 2012) para 178.

20 It is vital to stress that distress incidents, border controls and maritime interceptions occur not only on the high seas, which is the area beyond the 200 nautical miles from a State's coastal baseline, but from just outside the 12 nautical miles territorial sea; this is known as the Exclusive Economic Zone (EEZ). Briefly, in the EEZ, States have sovereign jurisdiction over the exploration and exploitation of marine resources and certain economic activities, but for the purposes of SAR, this area is treated as if it is the high seas. Article 58 (2) of UNCLOS is important in this respect as it sets out the continuance of high seas freedoms in the EEZ, insofar as they are not incompatible with the EEZ regime. This is further examined in Chapter 2.

21 Hugo Grotius, *Mare Liberum* (Indianapolis: Liberty Fund 2004).

22 Tanja E Aalberts and Thomas Gammeltoft-Hansen, 'Sovereignty at Sea: The Law and Politics of Saving Lives in Mare Liberum' (2014) 17 Journal of International Relations and Development 459–460.

23 International Covenant on Civil and Political Rights (adopted 16 December 1966, entered into force 23 March 1976) 999 UNTS 171 (ICCPR).

24 Convention for the Protection of Human Rights and Fundamental Freedoms (adopted 4 November 1950, entered into force 3 September 1953) 213 UNTS 222.

25 United Nations Convention on the Law of the Sea (adopted 10 December 1982, entered into force 16 November 1994) 1833 UNTS 397 (UNCLOS).

Oceans',[26] fails to recognize human rights explicitly within its *de facto* wording, as it was never meant to be a human rights convention. In turn, UNCLOS, like most international treaties, is primarily concerned with attributing rights and obligations to States, in this case in the maritime context. In this vein, Bernard Oxman is among the legal commentators who has recognized that several UNCLOS provisions relate to human rights principles and tries to advance specific community interests associated with '"affirmative" human rights'; one of them being the duty to render assistance to those in distress at sea without discrimination.[27] Relatedly, Sophie Cacciaguidi-Fahy, among various scholars, contends that the concept of the duty to render assistance at sea 'is an ideal of maritime ethics based on the respect for human life and its dignity'.[28]

Evidently, the underlying purpose of the duty to rescue is the protection of human life at sea; hence it can be perceived as the operational obligation stemming from – or, at the very least, sharing an affinity with – the right to life in international human rights law.[29] As a result, these two areas of law shall not be treated as distinct since the one gives voice to the other.[30] There is ample scholarship on the application of human rights treaties at sea,[31] pointing out that the law of the sea pursues the protection of human rights indirectly. For this reason, as Papastavridis – convincingly, I contend – posits, the ECtHR

26 Richard A Barnes and Jill Barrett (eds), *Law of the Sea: UNCLOS as a Living Treaty* (British Institute of International and Comparative Law 2016); Sofia Galani, '"Human Rights at Sea" Challenges for Shipping' (2018) <https://safety4sea.com/human-rights-sea-challenges-shipping/>.

27 Bernard Oxman, 'Human Rights and the United Nations Convention on the Law of the Sea' (1997) 36 Columbia Journal of Transnational Law 404. See also, Felicity G Attard, *The Duty of the Shipmaster to Render Assistance at Sea under International Law* (Queen Mary Studies in International Law, Brill Nijhoff 2020) 193–194, Art 98 of UNCLOS.

28 Sophie Cacciaguidi-Fahy, 'The Law of the Sea and Human Rights' (2007) 2(9) Panóptica, Vitória 1, 20; For other similar argumentation, see Papanicolopulu (n 18) 6; UNCHR, 'UNHCR and IOM Appeal to European Leaders to Tackle Mediterranean Deaths' (2018) <https://www.unhcr.org/cy/2018/10/17/unhcr-and-iom-appeal-to-european-leaders-to-tackle-mediterranean-deaths/>; Mark Pallis, 'Obligations of States towards Asylum Seekers at Sea: Interactions and Conflicts between Legal Regimes' (2002) 14 International Journal of Refugee Law 329, 335.

29 See also Seline Trevisanut, 'Is There a Right to Be Rescued at Sea? A Constructive View' (Questions of International Law, Zoom-In, 23 June 2014) <http://www.qil-qdi.org/is-there-a-right-to-be-rescued-at-sea-a-constructive-view/>.

30 This was confirmed in the Geneva Declaration on Human Rights 2019, 'there can be no safe and secure legal order for the seas and oceans, if human rights are not enjoyed by all people at sea'. See, Human Rights at Sea, 'Geneva Declaration on Human Rights at Sea (Version 1, 5 April 2019)' <https://gdhras.com/wp-content/uploads/2019/07/HRAS_GENEVA_DECLARATION_ON_HUMAN_RIGHTS_AT_SEA_April_2019-Version1-FINAL-LOCKED.pdf>.

31 See, e.g., S Cacciaguidi-Fahy, 'The Law of the Sea and Human Rights' (2007) 2(9) Panóptica, Vitória 1; B Oxman, 'Human Rights and the United Nations Convention on the Law of the Sea' (1997) 36 Columbia Journal Transnational Law 399; T Treves, 'Human Rights and the Law of the Sea' (2010) 28(1) Berkeley Journal of International Law 1.

'should take the legal contours of the law of the sea into serious account when deciding upon cases relating to the latter'.[32] In this context, the duty to rescue is being increasingly raised before human rights bodies, with its normative content starting to shape international human rights law.

Interpretation of Treaties in International Law

The legal regimes of the international law of the sea and human rights law have begun to be synthesized by the judiciary, by claims either under the dispute settlement provisions of UNCLOS (e.g., before the International Tribunal of the Law of the Sea [ITLOS] or another arbitral tribunal) or alternatively, human rights bodies (e.g., the ECtHR) that are asked to examine violations of maritime duties and, alternatively, the applicability of human rights obligations extraterritorially.

In approaching the task of interpretation, human rights bodies have recognized the applicability of the rules of treaty interpretation contained in the Vienna Convention on the Law of the Treaties 1969 (VCLT).[33] The classical starting point is Article 31 of the VCLT; paragraph 1 *inter alia* prescribes: 'A treaty shall be interpreted in *good faith* in accordance with the *ordinary meaning* to be given to the terms of the treaty in their context and in the light of its *object* and *purpose*'.[34] In this manner, legal interpretation is advanced in line with the object and purpose of a treaty and ideally serves the teleology of a legal provision.[35] Additionally, Article 31(3)(c) provides that treaty provisions need to be read in light of States' other international obligations; this is also recognized as the principle of 'systemic integration', which requires treaties

32 Efthymios Papastavridis, 'European Convention of Human Rights and the Law of the Sea: The Strasbourg Court in Unchartered Waters?' in Malgosia Fitzmaurice and Panos Merkouris (eds), *The Interpretation and Application of the European Convention of Human Rights: Legal and Practical Implications* (Queen Mary Studies of International Law 2013) 121.

33 United Nations, Vienna Convention on the Law of Treaties (23 May 1969, entered into force 28 January 1980) 1155 UNTS 331 (VCLT); See also, Suzanne Egan, 'The Doctrinal Approach in International Human Rights Scholarship' (2017) UCD Working Papers in Law, Criminology & Socio-Legal Studies Research Paper No. 19/17, 12 <https://papers.ssrn.com/sol3/papers.cfm?abstract_id=3082194>.

34 (emphasis added). This is known as the principle of effectiveness or teleological approach. Arguably, the most famous example of its use is the extrapolation of the principle of non-refoulement from the provision of Art 3 of the ECHR. See *Soering v United Kingdom* (1989) 11 EHRR 439, para 87, where the ECtHR highlighted that the Convention is an instrument for the protection of individual human beings (hence, adopting a teleological *pro-homine* approach).

35 Ibid; See also analysis by Velerio de Oliveira Mazzuoli and Dilton Ribeiro, 'The Pro Homine Principle as an Enshrined Feature of International Human Rights Law' (2016) III The Indonesian Journal of International & Comparative Law 77; Alain Pellet, Tenth Report on Reservations to Treaties, Addendum, International Law Commission, Fifty-seventh session, UN Doc A/CN.4/558/Add 1 para 81 <https://legal.un.org/ilc/documentation/english/a_cn4_558.pdf>.

to be interpreted with reference to their 'normative environment'.[36] Ergo, all standalone treaties should not be read in isolation from one another but instead implemented in harmony with other canons of international law.[37]

Relatedly, UNCLOS is read as a constitutional treaty as it reaches outwards to other treaties and international instruments to shape the meaning of its provisions.[38] Analogously with the interpretative tool provided in the VCLT, Article 293 of UNCLOS provides a specific norm prescribing that judicial bodies addressing UNCLOS disputes 'shall apply this Convention and other rules of international law not incompatible with this Convention'. As argued by Petrig and Bo, this provision not only provides for systemic integration but also works as a 'gap-filling' instrument that is particularly relevant in substantive human rights clauses.[39] In this regard, the concept of 'considerations of humanity' has been regularly employed by the ITLOS to protect human rights that might be at stake during maritime activities.[40] As Sofia Galani has argued, like the ECHR, UNCLOS is a living instrument 'and, as such, it has been subject to evolutionary interpretation that reflects the need to protect human rights at sea'.[41] It must nonetheless be stressed that individuals cannot initiate a dispute or bring a claim under the dispute settlement provisions of UNCLOS as it provides only for interstate proceedings.[42] For this reason, human rights alone cannot be the subject of litigation before UNCLOS dispute settlement bodies, and any recognition of rights should take place in international human rights law.

In accordance with the rules of treaty interpretation, this study opines for a *pro-homine* (human first) approach to irregular migration by sea,[43] which

36 Campbell McLachlan, 'The Principle of Systemic Integration and Article 31 (3)(c) of theVienna Convention' (2005) 54(2) International and Comparative Law Quarterly 284.

37 See, e.g., Jane McAdam, 'Interpretation of the 1951 Convention' in Andreas Zimmermann (ed), *The 1951 Convention Relating to the Status of Refugees and Its 1967 Protocol: A Commentary* (OUP 2011) 83; Michelle Foster, *International Refugee Law and Socio-Economic Rights: Refuge from Deprivation* (CUP 2007) 42; Papastavridis, 'European Convention of Human Rights and the Law of the Sea' (n 32) 121.

38 See Preamble of UNCLOS. It reads *inter alia* 'aware of the historic significance of this Convention as an important contribution to the maintenance of peace, justice and progress for all peoples of the world'.

39 Anna Petrig and Marta Bo, 'The International Tribunal for the Law of the Sea and Human Rights' in Martin Scheinin (ed), *Human Rights Norms in 'Other' International Courts* (CUP 2019) 355.

40 *The M/V 'Saiga' (No 2) (Saint Vincent and the Grenadines v Guinea)* (Judgment of 1 July 1999) ITLOS Reports 1999, 10, para 155.

41 Galani (n 17) 618.

42 For clarification purposes note that Part XI of UNCLOS concerning seabed dispute settlement allows a number of relevant legal persons to bring disputes ('natural or juridical persons'), see in particular Art 187.

43 Arguably a teleological interpretation reflects and recognizes the *pro-homine* principle as it addresses the human person in the context of international human rights law. For a thorough study of the pro-homine principle, see, Marie-Bénédicte Dembour, *When Humans Become*

allows norms to be interpreted as extensively as possible for the individual and, by contrast, as restrictively as possible when a norm imposes limits on the enjoyment of human rights.[44] The ECtHR has recognized the *pro-homine* principle in its case law by reiterating the importance of international human rights law as 'an instrument for the protection of individual human beings' through a teleological interpretation of the ECHR.[45] As has been maintained, the purpose of this human-centered approach is to advance norms in situations where the status of an individual is under threat.[46] In this study, the matter of concern is the protection of human *life*, which prompts us to deliberate whether the time is ripe to recognize a right to be rescued at sea vested in individuals.

Against this understanding, the teleological *pro-homine* approach together with the principle of systemic integration allows courts to interpret the existing right to life as encompassing an implicit right to be rescued at sea. This, also called the 'derivation' strategy, is another interpretative tool for identifying 'new' human rights from existing ones by virtue of recognizing previously 'unarticulated aspects of old human rights'.[47] Accordingly, the teleological approach to treaty interpretation has been at the heart of the jurisprudence of the ECtHR, the African Commission and domestic courts alike, as well as EU law where it has been perhaps most famously applied.[48] As Takele Soboka

Migrants: Study of the European Court of Human Rights with an Inter-American Counterpoint (OUP 2015) 1–32. On *the pro-homine* principle, see also Hèléne Tigroudja, 'La Cour Interaméricaine des Droits de l' Homme au Service de l' "Humanisation du Droit International Public" – Propos Autour des Récents Arrêts et Avis' (2006) 52 AFDI 617; Mazzuoli and Ribeiro (n 35) 77. For example, one can also trace this approach in various environmental cases; see *inter alia* the Irish High Court case, *Friends of the Irish Environment (FIE) v Ireland* [2019] IEHC 747, where the court ruled that the Constitution protects a 'right to environment' and highlighted for the first time the existence of 'an unenumerated personal constitutional right' to an environment consistent with the *human dignity* and well-being of citizens at large (para 241).

44 Hayde Rodarte Berbera, 'The Pro Personae Principle and Its Application by Mexican Courts' (2017) 4(1) Human Rights Review 9; Lucas Lixinski, 'Treaty Interpretation by the Inter-American Court of Human Rights: Expansionism at the Service of the Unity of International Law' (2010) 21(3) European Journal of International Law 588.

45 *Wemhoff v Germany*, App no 2122/64, A/7 (ECtHR, 27 June 1968) para 8.

46 Samanta Kowalska, 'Pro Homine Principle: An Axiological Compass in Interpretation Norms in the Field of Human Rights' (2021) 16 The Age of Human Rights Journal 216.

47 Kerstin von der Decken and Nikolaus Koch, 'Recognition of New Human Rights: Phases, Techniques and the Approach of "Differentiated Traditionalism"' in Andreas von Arnauld, Kerstin von der Decken and Mart Susi (eds), *The Cambridge Handbook of New Human Rights: Recognition, Novelty and Rhetoric* (CUP 2020) 13.

48 For instance, see, *Artico v Italy* (1980) 3 EHRR 1, para 33. *In casu*, the ECtHR identified rights and positive obligations of states not specifically contained in the Convention, which can be described as one of those moments of judicial activism. In particular, the Court highlighted that the Convention is intended to guarantee not rights that are 'theoretical or illusory' but rights that are 'practical and effective'. Accordingly, the Court derived a right to legal representation from the right to a fair trial. The ECtHR frequently emphasizes this needs and shows to be adopting a robust teleological approach to interpretation together with the

Bulto points out, a teleological approach is employed *inter alia* 'to promote the objectives for which the rule of law was designed and to fill legal gaps in a given legal order'.[49] Pursuant to this, the right to life will be interpreted in line with its object and purpose in a manner that is responsive to the dangers that migrants face during irregular sea crossings.

Aims, Theoretical Framing and Approach

The book aims to mobilize a concentrated international effort to combat narratives of migrant 'rightlessness' at sea. While it might be true to a great extent that migrants face difficulties in asserting rights when found at sea because they become de facto stateless and hence are unable to establish their identity and nationality status, this does not render them *ipso facto* 'rightless'. Notwithstanding scholars have frequently employed this term to show how international law can create spaces 'in which humans are rendered *rightless*'.[50] Conversely, I support that human rights analysis needs to focus on the *rights* of (potential) victims, otherwise, it would be impossible to redress those human rights abuses. Similarly, I view human rights as pre-political, possessed by all simply in virtue of their humanity.[51] Ergo, I employ an interest-based account of human rights which justifies holding (yet-to-be) others under duties to respect, protect and fulfil certain human rights based on values of universal human interests and human dignity – the equal worth of every human being.[52]

derivation approach, which is sometimes though subject to critique. Yet, the positive impact of such expansive interpretations of the Convention can only benefit migrants' precarious stage at sea; The African Commission on Human and People's Rights has done so by identifying certain 'unenumerated' rights in the ACHPR, see for instance *Serac v Nigeria*, A.Comm. No. 155/96, 2001; See also analysis by Suzanne Egan, 'The Doctrinal Approach in International Human Rights Scholarship' (2017) UCD Working Papers in Law, Criminology & Socio-Legal Studies Research Paper No. 19/17, 12 <https://papers.ssrn.com/sol3/papers.cfm?abstract_id=3082194>.

49 Takele Soboka Bulto, 'The Emergence of the Human Right to Water in International Human Rights Law: Invention or Discovery?' (2011) 12 Melbourne Journal of International Law 10.

50 Itamar Mann, 'Maritime Legal Black Holes: Migration and Rightlessness in International Law' (2018) 29(2) The European Journal of International Law 347, 348 (emphasis added); See also Adel-Naim Reyhani, 'Absolute Rightlessness Sur Place through Excessive Externalisation – The case of Libya' (2019) European Yearbook on Human Rights 133–157.

51 This view associates with John Tasioulas' theory and writers such as Jeremy Waldron, Amartya Sen and Seyla Benhabib. For Tasioulas' relevant works, see *inter alia*: John Tasioulas, 'On the Nature of Human Rights' in G Ernst and J-C Heilinger (eds), *The Philosophy of Human Rights: Contemporary Controversies* (Berlin: De Gruyter 2012) 17–59; John Tasioulas and Effy Vayena, 'Just Global Health: Integrating Human Rights and Common Goods' in Thom Brooks (ed), *The Oxford Handbook of Global Justice* (OUP 2020).

52 John Tasioulas, 'Saving Hunan Rights from Human Rights Law' (2019) 52 Vanderbilt Journal of Transnational Law 1179; On migration by sea and the universal values under threat by migration policies, see in particular, Siobhán Mullally, 'Migrant Crisis: It's a Question of Human Rights – Not Charity' (Irish Times, 3 September 2015) <https://www.irishtimes.com/opinion/migrant-crisis-it-s-a-question-of-human-rights-not-charity-1.2339237>.

Notwithstanding the promised universality of human rights,[53] protection often falls short in the actual experiences of irregular migrants as will be evidenced in this book.

The analysis in this book approaches these issues by unpacking the following key question: *how can a human-rights-based approach buttress the protection of human life in the context of irregular migration by sea?* To best explore the deleterious effect of migration and border management policies, I focus on the area where migrants attempt to flee and cross the Mediterranean and end up in a distressed situation on the high seas. From an international law standpoint, the location of a vessel is of utmost importance as it serves as a critical factor in establishing the relevant rights and obligations of the concerned State(s) and individuals. Whilst this book explores the spiralling loss of life in the Mediterranean region, it does not seek to establish or attribute responsibility for purported human rights violations, but rather builds on the current situation to contextualize this crisis in order to justify stronger human rights standards and a reconsideration of States' extraterritorial human rights obligations.

The arguments put forth in this book are based on a comprehensive analysis of existing legal practice and scholarly literature discussing the implications of migration and external border management at sea on the rights of migrants. The analysis offers a combination of theory and practice in which philosophical theories of rights are applied to create a framework for legal analysis and the development of practical legal standards. Driven by an ambition to fill the vacuum of human rights protection at sea created by policy stratagem, my analysis adopts a *pro-homine* reading of the duty to render assistance which prioritizes the human person and endows a correlative 'right to be rescued at sea' to individuals. This aspect of the argument is most notably influenced by the legal–philosophical theory of rights by the American jurist Wesley Newcomb Hohfeld,[54] which provides the conceptual basis for the recognition of 'new' rights in the international sphere. The normative justification for the right to be rescued at sea finds voice in Hohfeld's correlativity scheme for delineating the legal relationship between rights and duties and demonstrates that a right to be rescued at sea *ought to be recognized* as the logical correlative of the duty to render assistance at sea. The Hohfeldian rights model provides a *sui generis* theory, which is a rich lode for analysis of international legal relationships.[55] Arguably, any legal analysis on the recognition of rights should start by reference

53 This is extensively documented in Marie-Bénédicte Dembour and Tobias Kelly (eds), *Are Human Rights for Migrants? Critical Reflections on the Status of Irregular in Europe and the United States* (Routledge 2011).

54 Wesley Newcomb Hohfeld, 'Some Fundamental Legal Conceptions as Applied in Judicial Reasoning' (1913) 23 Yale Law Journal (YLJ) 16 (Hohfeld 1913). Then, the second article is Wesley Newcomb Hohfeld, 'Fundamental Legal Conceptions as Applied in Judicial Reasoning' (1917) 26 YLJ 710 (Hohfeld 1917).

55 John R Morss, 'The Legal Relations of Collectives: Belated Insights from Hohfeld' (2009) 22(2) LJIL 289, 305.

to Hohfeld's scheme as it stands to be the backbone to all major contemporary jurisprudential discussions.[56] This is so because his model portrays the different concepts of four basic types of rights and shows how rights and other kinds of normative positions relate to one another. In fact, many rights today can be seen as bundles of Hohfeldian rights.[57] In order to gain a clearer understanding of Hohfeld's project, it is a useful precursor to realize and at the same time accept that his framework is of a definitional nature providing a 'neutral' model of rights, rather than an attempt to work out an empirical analysis.[58]

More specifically, Hohfeld espoused a theory of legal relations that was mainly set out over the course of two seminal articles published in 1913 and 1917: *Fundamental Legal Relations as Applied in Judicial Reasoning*. Although his work is more than one hundred years old, it still remains persuasive and is undoubtedly useful in present-day legal thought and in understanding legal relationships.[59] By observing the vexing meaning of the word 'right' and likewise, its wide-ranging inclusiveness covering all legal relations, Hohfeld wished to limit its 'chameleon-hued' character to a definite and appropriate meaning, as the word rested on uncertainty, often causing ambiguities and misuse when applied in judicial reasoning.[60] As a result, he espoused that legal rights can be divided into four groups of legal relations according to type, which he labelled as 'incidents': claim-right (or simply, right), privilege, power and immunity.[61] Each incident is said to have a specific, unique opposite and a specific, unique correlative. As such, the principal aim of separating and narrowly defining these four legal interests into distinct individual forms was to provide a tool for the analysis of legal problems in which rights and duties were to be distributed; a preliminary step to the solving of legal problems.[62]

Hohfeld in his first pair of jural correlatives, right–duty, sought to articulate a narrow and proper meaning for the word 'right' with reference to its

56 Pierfrancesco Biasetti, 'Infinite Regress and Hohfeld: A Comment on Hillel Steiner's "Directed Duties and Inalienable Rights"' (2015) 126(1) Ethics 140; Liora Lazarus, Benjamin Goold, Rajendra Desai and Qudsi Rasheed, 'The Relationship between Rights and Responsibilities' (2009) 18/09 Ministry of Justice Research Paper Series <https://commons.allard.ubc.ca/fac_pubs/153/>.

57 For instance, see, Jack Clayton Thompson, 'The Rights Network: 100 Years of the Hohfeldian Rights Analytic' (2018) 7(28) Laws 7, where Thompson claims '[a]ll rights must comprise at least one of the Hohfeldian incidents'; Walter Wheeler Cook, 'Hohfeld's Contributions to the Science of Law' (1919) 28(8) YLJ 721.

58 Cook (n 57) 723.

59 Luca Fiorito and Massimiliano Vatiero, 'Beyond Legal Relations Wesley Newcomb Hohfeld's Influence on American Institutionalism' (2009) 45(1) Journal of Economic Issue 199.

60 Hohfeld 1913 (n 54) 31, 35; See for instance *Lonas v State* (1871) 3 Heisk. (Tenn.) 306–307, in the words of Mr. Justice Sneed 'It is said that the words rights, privileges and immunities, are abusively used, as if they were synonymous. The word right is generic, common, embracing whatever may be lawfully claimed'.

61 Michael K Addo, 'Does Hohfeld Still Matter' (1997) 29 Bracton Law Journal 7.

62 Thompson (n 57) 28.

correlative relation, duty, and he used the term 'claim-right', which signifies that a right is an affirmative claim against another.[63] The terminology employed by Hohfeld, 'correlative', plainly means that the existence of one term, *right*, assumes the existence of the other term, *duty*, and vice versa. Therefore, correlativity essentially has to do with what one party, be it a State or a natural person, can expect of another. For instance, we can trace how this correlativity between a right and a duty behaves in the legal system by taking the following example: the State has a duty to abstain from arbitrarily killing individuals in their jurisdiction, and accordingly the individual has the correlative right to life.[64]

Furthermore, Immanuel Kant's moral philosophy, particularly in *The Metaphysics of Morals*,[65] supports the above correlative relation, which assumes that a duty implies a correlative right, in the following passage: '[the man] is obligated to acknowledge, in a practical way, the dignity of humanity in every other way. Hence, he is subject to a duty based on the respect he must show every other man. . . . Every man has rightful claim to respect from his fellow man'.[66] From the Kantian account, it can be concluded that the correlativity between rights and duties is not only logically supported, but also serves as an imperative tool for human rights to be able to uphold the dignity of a person. More specifically, the Kantian understanding of duties giving rise to correlative rights is the idea 'that their performance is *owed* to another, who may *claim* this performance from specific duty-bearers as her *due*'.[67]

The case made in this book supports the theorization of a right to be rescued at sea that is not only based on Hohfeld's analytical scheme of relations but also underpinned by a Kantian respect for the inherent dignity of a person. Together they provide a robust justification for the courts to start a jurisprudential inquiry by identifying a right to be rescued as correlative to the duty to render assistance at sea. Thereafter, the emphasis shifts to establishing the facts of each case, including the risk to life of the migrants adrift at sea and what the State knew or ought to have known in the circumstances. In other words, the first issue is the identification of the right, before then determining whether it has been violated on the facts. Against this Hohfeldian backdrop, the courts can delve into an analysis of extraterritoriality and shape the normative contours of this right by engaging with the methods of treaty interpretation.

63 Hohfeld 1913 (n 54) 33; See, also, Allan D Cullison, 'A Review of Hohfeld's Fundamental Legal Concepts' (1967) 16(3) Marshall Law Review 559.

64 Ibid; *Rights and Law Analysis and Theory* (Hart Publishing 1997) 2.

65 Ibid; Immanuel Kant, *The Metaphysical Principles of Virtue: Part II of the Metaphysics of Morals* (James Ellington trans., Indianapolis 1964) 132.

66 Ibid.

67 Eric Boot, 'Judging Rights By their Duties: A Kantian Perspective on Human Rights' in Larry Krasnoff, Nuria S Madrid, Paula Satne (eds), *Kant's Doctrine of Right in the 21st Century* (University of Wales Press 2018) 47.

Based on this theoretical framework, this book supports that Hohfeld's correlativity scheme provides judges with an analytical tool to support a normative argument that structures a right to be rescued at sea within the existing right to life. Undeniably, the time is ripe for such development in order to deal with the systemic deficiencies of the legal frameworks surrounding the protection of human life at sea and, respectively, to help strengthen compliance with international obligations in an effort to minimize future human tragedies.

It shall be acknowledged that the discussion on the recognition of a right to be rescued at sea was first introduced by Seline Trevisanut in 2014, who sketched the legal basis for recognizing such a right.[68] Since then, there has been little, if any, further attention paid to exploring in-depth how this right can become positive law; hence it remains neglected within academic literature. Consequently, Chapter 4 builds on Hohfeld's correlativity scheme in order to proclaim the existence of a right to be rescued at sea, as well as the avenues in which this right can become fully recognized (binding law).

While the geographical scope of human rights obligations is determined by the concept of jurisdiction within the treaty in question, it is by now clear that the territorial scope of international human rights law is undergoing systematic obstruction. At present, the means by which States acquire jurisdiction over migrants at sea have significantly departed from the 'accepted' spatial or 'territorial' and personal or 'state agent authority over individuals' types of extraterritorial human rights jurisdiction. What remains unclear is how jurisdiction can accommodate cases in the context of maritime migration, where 'effective' control over an individual's rights does not happen spatially or personally. Given that this concept of jurisdiction over migrants at sea remains underdeveloped and inherently unpredictable, the book challenges existing concepts of how States can acquire jurisdiction extraterritorially and provides a refined reading of jurisdiction under the international human rights framework to overcome a stumbling block to the protection of migrants. For this reason, I argue that human rights jurisdiction has to be reoriented or rethought fundamentally to incorporate contemporary manifestations of State power that, if and when exercised, can amount to effective control, triggering a State's human rights obligations. When discussing jurisdiction in international human rights law, it is imperative to comprehend that jurisdiction is about the relationship between the State and the individual(s). Therefore, the analysis in Chapters 5 and 6 will present an evaluation of selected judgments of the ECtHR and the HRC pertaining to such complex questions of jurisdiction

68 Trevisanut (n 29); See also Efthymios Papastavridis, 'Is There a Right to Be Rescued at Sea? A Skeptical View' (Questions of International Law, Zoom-In, 23 June 2014) <http://www.qil-qdi.org/is-there-a-right-to-be-rescued-at-sea-a-constructive-view/>; Reference to the right to be rescued at sea has also been made by Vassilis P Tzevelekos and Elena Katselli Proukaki, 'Migrants at Sea: A Duty of Plural States to Protect (Extraterritorially)?' (2017) 86 Nordic Journal of International Law 432.

and State extraterritorial human rights obligations towards persons in distress at sea.

In this light, by placing the human being at the core of the duty to render assistance, the analysis embraces a functional concept of jurisdiction by advocating that the recognition of a right to be rescued at sea will offer fertile ground for judicial experimentation to reconcile the challenges that migrants face during sea crossings. Arguably, such a human-rights-based approach is justified by the need to redress the situation of migrants' vulnerability at sea.[69] For the sake of clarity, it is vital here to explain what I mean by a *functional* concept of jurisdiction in this book. The term *functional* is understood from a capacity perspective, that is, a State's potential (power) to affect the human rights of individuals (that are relevant in the circumstances), if and when a State is in a position to do so. To a great extent my understanding of a functional approach to jurisdiction is shaped by the concurring opinion of Judge Bonello in *Al-Skeini and Others v the United Kingdom*, arguing:

> Jurisdiction is neither territorial nor extraterritorial: it *ought to be functional* – in the sense that when it is within a State's authority and control whether a breach of human rights is, or is not, committed, whether its perpetrators are, or are not, identified and punished, whether the victims of violations are, or are not, compensated, it would be an imposture to claim that, ah yes, that State had authority and control, but, ah no, it had no jurisdiction.[70]

Evidently, Judge Bonello places strong emphasis on the State's power to ensure adherence to human rights obligations. In a similar manner, my understanding of a State's power – capacity – to determine the material course of events in a given situation can amount to an exercise of 'effective' control. Crucially, this concept is not restricted to scenario types of effective control over persons (in other words whether that power physically manifests). Whilst understanding jurisdiction as functional adheres to broader notions of human rights universalism, this does not ignore the fact that jurisdiction needs to have clear parameters, otherwise it would impose disproportionate burdens on States that might have a chilling effect. Nonetheless, it is supported that a truly functional approach to jurisdiction should apply in all situations in which the duty of protection can realistically be complied with. Evidently, the quest for a unified understanding of extraterritorial human rights jurisdiction is an important one.

69 On 14 March 2023, the UHCHR published its training guide No. 26 'Towards a Human Rights-Based Approach to Migration'. See here <https://www.ohchr.org/sites/default/files/documents/publications/Towards-Human-Rights-Based-Approach-Migration-Training-Guide.pdf>.

70 *Al-Skeini and Others v the United Kingdom*, App no 55721/07 (ECtHR, 7 July 2011) Concurring Opinion of Judge Bonello, para 12 (emphasis added).

Against this backdrop, Yuval Shany highlighted that international human rights law 'has struggled to define a standard for determining the extraterritorial applicability of its norms that would reconcile the universality of humanitarian norms, on the one hand, with the centrality of borders in delineating State powers and responsibilities under international law, on the other hand'.[71] Amidst the escalating phenomena of abandonment at sea and contemporary push-back practices,[72] the Strasbourg Court needs to continue adjusting the parameters of human rights jurisdiction to ensure that the ECHR remains a 'living instrument' that is 'interpreted in the light of present-day conditions' and guarantees rights that are 'practical and effective' for all individuals including migrants.[73] As Upendra Baxi powerfully posits, 'there is also reason why we must think and act with hope for a world where human rights talk and practice include migrants'.[74] This book has been written throughout years in which European migration policies have been in upheaval, and it forms an attempt to contribute to the debate about a viable concept of human rights jurisdiction and extraterritorial obligations, with the goal of advancing the protection of human life at sea for irregular migrants.

Structure of the Book

The narrative arc of the book begins by introducing the system of international refugee protection along with the role of human rights law in complementing this framework, with a focus on the *non-refoulement* principle and the right to seek asylum. By doing so, Chapter 1 aims to depict the challenges irregular migrants face during cross-border maritime crossings and provide an explanatory analysis of what the legal problem is in this context. To answer this question, it explores the events that led to the European 'migration' or 'refugee' crisis and sheds light on key EU policy events and European State practices from 2015 to 2023 in the Mediterranean Sea, with particular focus on the Central Mediterranean route. The reason for this focus – migrant crossings, largely from Libya and other North African countries including Tunisia, Algeria and Egypt to Italian or Maltese coasts – is because it is considered the most dangerous migrant

71 Yuval Shany, 'Taking Universality Seriously: A Functional Approach to Extraterritoriality in International Human Rights Law' (2013) 7(1) Law & Ethics of Human Rights 47.

72 Nick Vaughan-Williams, *Europe's Border Crisis: Biopolitical Security and Beyond* (Oxford: OUP 2015) 60.

73 *Hirsi* (n 19) para 174; The 'living instrument' doctrine which upholds this interpretative task was first articulated in *Tyrer v the United Kingdom*, App no 5856/72 (ECtHR 25 April 1978) para 31. For a detailed discussion on the ECtHR's approach in interpreting the Conventions' provisions, see Niko Krisch, 'The Open Architecture of European Human Rights Law' (2008) 71(2) The Modern Law Review 183; See also See also Itamar Mann, Humanity at Sea: Maritime Migration and The Foundations of International Law (Cambridge: Cambridge University Press 2016) 3–4.

74 Upendra Baxi, 'Afterword: The Struggle for Sans-Papiers Human Rights' in Dembour and Kelly (n 53) 223.

route in the world, and accordingly, the purpose is to observe how States have tackled migration flows in that area. Instead of making this argument in abstract, the chapter provides some descriptive statistics from quantitative data analyzed to better understand and assess the current situation with respect to the risk of dying in the Mediterranean Sea. By doing so, this chapter sheds light on the discernible impact of the policy framework on migrants' human rights (and *life*), which is vital to fathom before turning the attention to the relevant legal regimes safeguarding the protection of human life at sea.

Chapter 2 aims to elucidate *why* the international law of the sea framework suffers in implementation by identifying the ambiguities in the law surrounding maritime rescues at sea. It first introduces the legal duty to rescue, as embodied in a variety of overlapping treaty regimes and customary international law. These treaties regulate maritime SAR, namely, UNCLOS, the International Convention for the Safety of Life at Sea 1974 (SOLAS);[75] the International Convention on Maritime Search and Rescue 1979 (SAR Convention)[76] and the International Convention on Salvage 1989 (Salvage).[77] A doctrinal analysis of these instruments will reveal the problematic areas of the law that need clarification and amendment in light of treaty gaps and deficiencies in the SAR operational framework, as well as the lack of compliance with the duty to save lives at sea informed by contemporary practice. This is first exhibited through a meticulous discussion of the *Tampa* affair, reflecting on its implications for the law of the sea, human rights and refugee law. Such an in-depth analysis will help to demonstrate that the gaps in treaty law are the overarching reasons that give leeway to political expediency, mainly due to the still unresolved issue of disembarkation. In addressing the conceptual obstacles that center upon the meaning of a 'place of safety', 'disembarkation' and 'distress', the chapter then critically analyzes the secondary literature (case studies concerning the Mediterranean Sea) to prove the dysfunctionality of the mechanisms in question, which thereby greatly contribute to the large number of lives lost at sea, giving rise to unparalleled human rights concerns.

Having surveyed various contemporary manifestations of State power in the Mediterranean, along with the fragmented law of the sea framework, the book switches focus to the realm of international human rights law. In doing so, Chapter 3 highlights the inextricable link between the duty to render assistance at sea as enshrined in the law of the sea instruments and the right to life as enshrined in all major human rights instruments. Much of what has been discussed thus far raised questions as to the nature and scope of the right to life as well as its capability of being secured on the high seas. This chapter sheds light on the former by evaluating the obligations endowed on

75 International Convention for the Safety of Life at Sea, 1974, as amended, 1184 UNTS 278 (adopted 1 November 1974, entered into force 25 May 1980).
76 International Convention on Maritime Search and Rescue, 1979, with annexes, 1405 UNTS 97 (adopted 27 April 1979, entered into force 22 June 1985).
77 International Convention on Salvage, 1989, UKTS 93 322.

States to safeguard the right to life as they have been developed by judicial and quasi-judicial bodies, while the latter is examined in Chapter 5. Hence, in this chapter it is assumed that jurisdiction is established in all the cases to be observed, as my primary concern is to examine the scope and extent of positive obligations, including actions and omissions, arising from the right to life. My analysis focuses mainly on the ECtHR's rich case law in developing the scope of substantive and procedural obligations which emerge from the right to life and situates this right in the maritime migration domain. The reason for the principal focus of the ECtHR's jurisprudence on the right to life is twofold: 1) the European Convention on Human Rights is the human rights convention with the closest geographical relation for the matter under consideration; 2) the Strasbourg Court has developed the most prosperous case law in this context and is considered an authoritative international body interpreting the Convention rights. The underlying aim of this chapter is to examine the factors and analytical issues that will trigger a State's positive obligations to secure the right to life so as to revisit this at a later stage.

The remaining analysis in the book seeks to answer the question *how* international human rights law can remedy the challenges individuals face in distress at sea by invoking a normative, human-rights-based approach that allows the restructuring of the right to life in a manner that sustains a 'new' right to be rescued at sea[78] that is international in scope and application.

Chapter 4 builds on Hohfeld's theory and applies it to the human rights context, by developing a critical, counterfactual framework that allows for the intellectual justification of an individual right to be rescued at sea. The chapter proceeds to a jurisprudential analysis of pertinent case law to demonstrate how Hohfeld's model, and in particular the correlativity scheme, works in – and advances – practice. As Hohfeld's theory is silent as to the identification of the right-holder or the duty-bearer, this chapter further examines the normative grounds that can accommodate this right by introducing Onora O'Neill's theory of human rights, the so-called 'claimability objection', which undeniably presents a powerful challenge to the correlative recognition of rights. Accordingly, this chapter explores diverse accounts from contemporary rights theorists like John Tasioulas, Kathryn Sikkink, Amartya Sen, Jeremy Waldron and Seyla Benhabib who provide distinctive and detailed responses to the claimability question by employing a more robust account of human rights, attentive to the

78 A caveat is in order. Sometimes in this book, I refer to the right to be rescued at sea as a 'new' right. However, it is not my intention to mean that it is a 'new' right in the sense that it never *existed* before as a normative value or a moral right. Instead, I employ the adjective 'new' because its existence has not yet been recognized. As such, the use of the terms *recognizing* or *proclaiming* a 'new' right concerns the *discovery* (not the creation) of a new reality in light of evolving challenges in human rights protection in the specific context of jurisdiction in the maritime space. See also earlier work, Aphrodite Papachristodoulou, 'The Recognition of a Right to Be Rescued at Sea in International Law' (2022) 35(2) Leiden Journal of International Law 1–20.

underlying interests and values they protect. In doing so, the chapter moves beyond the philosophical debates which allows us to justify the existence of a right to be rescued at sea, to consider the practical phases of recognition (how a right becomes fully recognized) as well as the techniques for achieving this end.

Having shown how this 'new' right can enter its normative sphere, Chapters 5 and 6 study the pivotal framework of jurisdiction and demonstrate how a right to be rescued at sea can become realizable by first delving into the history of the case law on extraterritoriality. The structure of the argument in Chapter 5 is three-pronged. The first section pauses to reflect on the notion of jurisdiction in human rights law, exploring its meaning and scope *qua* threshold criterion for safeguarding human rights. In turn, it explains its association, if any, with related yet dissimilar notions of jurisdiction in international law. The second section explores how judicial and international expert bodies have interpreted extraterritorial jurisdiction, both in general settings and in the maritime space. The third section dissects the HRC's decision in the *A.S.* cases regarding the right to life and examines the normative consequences of a functional approach to jurisdiction. Arguably, this focus turns into a case study as this is the most recent development dealing with the concept of State jurisdiction in an extraterritorial setting, precisely in the context of SAR operations. By scrutinizing the implications of the decision and various factual scenarios that can arise on the high seas, this chapter puts forward a proposal as to how jurisdiction should be interpreted in human rights law.

Closing, Chapter 6 returns to the question of operationalizing the protection of life at sea and provides clear insights into the novelty and vitality of a right to be rescued at sea in conjunction with the functional jurisdiction model. It then demonstrates that the recognition of this right will gain legal shape by instigating a process of specification and definition that helps close accountability gaps and remedy inconsistencies in the existing law, promoting a coherent development of international human rights law. The chapter then culminates in an analysis of a pending migration-related case before the ECtHR, *S.S. and Others v Italy*,[79] and reflects on the implications of functional reading of jurisdiction by the ECtHR. The book ends with a reflection on potential avenues for further inquiry and raises key questions on the increasing use of surveillance technology in external border management.

A note: This book considers legal and policy developments on European border management and migration case law that had taken place up to 10 October 2024, unless stated otherwise. Some of the reflections that follow are not entirely new and have been previously documented in my earlier work, academic publications or articles in the press. Where applicable, specific references are provided. These ideas have not been reproduced *verbatim*; rather, I have endeavored to engage with them in retrospect, now with the passing of some time. This is particularly relevant in instances where these thoughts were originally written at the same time as the unfolding events.

79 *S.S. and Others v Italy*, App no 21660/18 (ECtHR, communicated on 26 June 2019).

1 Irregular Migration in the Mediterranean Sea

'Europe, the cradle of human rights idealism and the birthplace of the rule of law, [should] cease closing its doors to people in despair who have fled from arbitrariness and brutality'.[1] Amidst the evolving migration landscape in the Mediterranean region, the words of Judge Pinto de Albuquerque in his concurring opinion in *Hirsi Jamaa and Others v Italy* (*Hirsi*) serve as an emblematic representation of the European approach to irregular migration crossings by the sea. On the one hand, Europe professes to live up to this high moral and ethical standard. On the other hand, Europe is largely driven by the securitization logic;[2] a logic that labels issues as '*extreme* security' that must be *urgently* dealt with because they pose a *danger* to a community.[3] In this way, treating the act of migration as a 'threat to national security' makes it legitimate to require ad-hoc arrangements, policies and practices that, however, fail to comply with the relevant international standards.

This stance on migration was largely exacerbated by geopolitical regional changes, chiefly the aftermath of the Arab Spring in 2011, which has caused the 'biggest transformation of the Middle East since decolonization' and produced a revolutionary migration wave across the North African regions, forcing millions of people to flee in the face of horrendous violence and atrocities.[4] As a result, the upsurge in the smuggling of arms along with proliferation of irregular migrants arriving at Europe's shores has led to the adoption of dehumanizing policies, which have deflected the attention from the protection of *persons* to the securitization of *borders* through *inter alia* border surveillance technology to detect these phenomena. In this light, Siobhán Mullally argues

1 *Hirsi Jamaa and Others v Italy*, App no 27765/09 (ECtHR, 23 February 2012) Concurring Opinion of Judge Pinto de Albuquerque.

2 UN, 'Europe and the Refugee Crisis: A Challenge to Our Civilization' <https://www.un.org/en/academic-impact/europe-and-refugee-crisis-challenge-our-civilization>.

3 Clara Eroukhmanoff, 'Securitisation Theory: An Introduction' (E-International Relations, 14 January 2018) <https://www.e-ir.info/2018/01/14/securitisation-theory-an-introduction/>.

4 Laura Bacon, 'To What Extent Can the Right to Asylum Be Limited by a State's Sovereign Right to Control Its Borders? A Comparative Assessment of the Lawfulness of European National Asylum Law and Procedure' (2016) 22 Auckland University Law Review 70.

DOI: 10.4324/9781003568537-2

that the irregular migrant who is likely to claim international protection poses a 'significant challenge' to a State's right to secure its borders, marked by an unwillingness to accept the *other* in its territory.[5]

It is indubitable that the phenomenon of irregular migration by sea is considered, fundamentally, a State sovereignty challenge. Policies that focus on tackling migration are not new and have always played a key role in 'protecting' a State's sovereign claims to control their borders as well as monitor admittees. Accordingly, the governments of the Central Mediterranean (like Italy and Malta), especially those most affected by migratory flows in virtue of geographic proximity to the countries of origin in North Africa – including Tunisia, Algeria, Libya and Egypt – have strengthened their border control and adopted migration policies that project an extraterritorialization of European borders.[6] Such practices have stretched the concept of State sovereignty even beyond the territorial limits of a State to countries of origin and transit, hence creating a 'foreign border', which will keep migrants as far as possible from European shores and subjected to dire consequences.[7] As Guild asserts, the process of externalizing migration has moved 'from the border of the sovereign state into which the individual is seeking to enter to within the state of origin'.[8] This has resulted in an outright contradiction between human rights declarations and States' border management policies, highlighting how the 'Westphalian model of state sovereignty is in crisis'.[9]

As unpalatable as it might be to even say, the Mediterranean Sea has become a maritime graveyard, with thousands of people drowning each year in an effort to reach European shores. Whilst migrant deaths at sea occur across the globe, the Central Mediterranean route, in particular, presents currently the world's deadliest migrant route, with per capita death rate rising each year.[10] Nonetheless, the number of migrant crossings has fallen starkly since 2016, making the relative increase in the mortality rates particularly unsettling. This decrease can be attributed to several factors, including EU measures to control migration flows, the abandonment of thousands of migrants at sea, and

5 Siobhán Mullally, 'Migration, Gender, and the Limits of Rights' in Ruth Rubio-Marín (ed), *Human Rights and Immigration* (Oxford: OUP 2014) 146.

6 Violeta Moreno-Lax, '*Hirsi Jamaa and Others v Italy* or the Strasbourg Court versus Extraterritorial Migration Control?' (2012) 12(3) Human Rights Law Review 574; See also Thomas Gammeltoft-Hansen, 'Extraterritorial Human Rights Obligations in Regard to Refugees and Migrants' (2021) in Mark Gibney Gamze Erdem Türkelli, Markus Krajewski and Wouter Vandenhole, *The Routledge Handbook on Extraterritorial Human Rights Obligations* (1st edn, Routledge, Routledge International Handbooks Series 2021) 153.

7 Maarten Den Heijer, *Europe and Extraterritorial Asylum* (Hart Publishing 2012) 5.

8 Elspeth Guild, 'The Borders of the European Union' (2004) 7 Tidsskriftet Politik 34.

9 Seyla Benhabib, *The Right of Others: Aliens, Residents, and Citizens* (CUP 2004) 4.

10 Aphrodite Papachristodoulou and Richard Collins, 'Pulling Back Navies and Pushing Back Migrants: Questioning the EU's Legal Responsibility in the Mediterranean Sea' (2018) UCD Working Papers in Law, Criminology & Socio-Legal Studies, Research Paper No. 01/2020, 13–15 <https://papers.ssrn.com/sol3/papers.cfm?abstract_id=3548637>.

an almost absolute retreat from search and rescue (SAR) operations. This chapter primarily focuses on the response of Europe's frontline States in the Central Mediterranean region, which depicts the most alarming humanitarian situation.

On top of this humanitarian crisis at sea, the Covid-19 outbreak had substantial implications on access to asylum procedures, as Europe was no longer considered a 'safe' haven. Consequently, it presented the perfect pretext for the EU and its Member States to not only seal their borders to migrants but also to circumvent international obligations in the Mediterranean space. Border closures (including seaports and airports), internal border controls and travel bans are some of the broader measures adopted by governments, either to internally protect their resident population or to prevent third-country nationals from entering their territory, with the primary aim being to flatten out the growth of infection rates. The right of irregular migrants to seek international protection was severely curtailed, and those more fortunate that managed to get rescued ended up indefinitely in *floating detention centers*.[11] Alas, the effect of pandemic-motivated measures to alleviate heightened pressures at external borders manifest, at their heart, an expansion of the sovereign powers of States that primarily challenges well-established customary norms and international human rights obligations. As one might have expected, the pandemic has to some extent disrupted migrant flows in the Mediterranean, however, it did not bring them to an end, as people kept trying to reach Europe on barely functional boats in a daring attempt to seek international protection.

In light of the above discussion, this chapter aims to demonstrate the need to revisit the legal frameworks governing protection of life at sea by unraveling the tactics that the EU and its Member States have employed in the current quagmire, using statistical evidence to highlight the humanitarian impact of European policy choices and extraterritorial practices. Before proceeding, a caveat is in order. Firstly, whilst the following analysis will take account of the overarching policy focus of the EU in its management of its external borders, particularly across the Mediterranean, my primary concern is the operational shifts in the Central Mediterranean route. Overall, between the period of 2014–2023, there were four active operations in the Central Mediterranean aimed at the protection of maritime security. The EU's naval Operation EU-NAVFOR MED Operation *Sophia* (Operation *Sophia*) (2015–2020), which was replaced in March 2020 with the military Operation *Irini*,[12] and Frontex's 'Joint Operation *Triton*' (2014–2018), which was replaced in February 2018

11 Aphrodite Papachristodoulou, 'Migrants at Sea Amid the Coronavirus Pandemic: The Perfect Pretext for Endorsing Respect for Human Rights' (2021) European Yearbook of Human Rights 283.

12 Council of the EU, 'EU Launches Operation IRINI to Enforce Libya Arms Embargo' (31 March 2020) <https://www.consilium.europa.eu/en/press/press-releases/2020/03/31/eu-launches-operation-irini-to-enforce-libya-arms-embargo/>.

with Operation *Themis*, are the two main operations currently operating in the Central Mediterranean route. In addition, there are two more active operations in other parts of the Mediterranean: Frontex's Joint Operation *Poseidon* in the Eastern Mediterranean (2006–present), which carries border surveillance mostly along the Greek sea borders with Turkey, and Frontex's 'Joint Operation *Indalo*' in the Western Mediterranean (2007–present), that carries surveillance and SAR primarily from North West Africa to Spain. Whilst this book does not make specific mention of these other operational frameworks, as will become apparent, policy initiatives aimed at one Mediterranean Sea route will necessarily impact migrant flows and death rates in another.

1. International Refugee Law and Human Rights Law: The *Non-Refoulement* Principle and the Right to Seek Asylum

This section briefly introduces the relevant legal frameworks providing the protections for individuals who have fled their homes to seek asylum and, respectively, outlines the rights and responsibilities of States, before setting the scene for the maritime migration landscape that will tie these elements together.

Dating back to 1982, the Supreme Court of the United States in *Nishimura Ekiu v United States*, provided the following:

> It is an accepted maxim of international law, that every sovereign nation has the power, as inherent in sovereignty, and essential to its self-preservation, to forbid the entrance of foreigners within its dominions, or to admit them only in such cases and upon such conditions it may see fit to prescribe.[13]

The above quote reflects the basic assumption of international law that a State has primary authority over its territory and population by way of its sovereignty and may for this reason decide if and how it allows non-nationals to enter its territory.[14] At the same time, international human rights law recognizes the right to leave any country, including one's own; however, it does not grant a corresponding right to enter another State's territory.[15] Conse-

13 *Nishimura Ekiu v United States* [1982] 142 U.S. 651, Gray J., 659.

14 See also *Saadi v the United Kingdom*, App no 13229/03 (ECtHR 29 January 2008); *Chahal v the United Kingdom*, App no 22414/93 (ECtHR, 15 November 1996). For further discussion see, e.g., Vincent Chetail, 'The Transnational Movement of Persons Under General International Law – Mapping the Customary Law Foundations of International Migration Law' (2014) in Vincent Chetail and Céline Bauloz (eds), *Research Handbook of International Law and Migration* (Cheltenham: Edward Elgar Publishing 2014).

15 Stefanie Grant, 'Irregular Migration and Frontier Deaths: Acknowledging a Right to Identity' in Marie-Bénédicte Dembour and Tobias Kelly (eds), *Are Human Rights for Migrants? Critical Reflections on the Status of Irregular in Europe and the United States* (Routledge 2011) 57.

quently, individuals who enter without permission do so unlawfully and, in turn, States' have sovereign authority to remove those who are irregularly in its country. The development of the Convention Relating to the Status of Refugees 1951 (Refugee Convention)[16] is of critical importance in this context as it provides a humanitarian exception to this general rule.[17] The most powerful principle of refugee protection is the principle of *non-refoulement*, prohibiting measures that cause refugees to be returned (or pushed back) to territories where they will likely face persecution. The *locus classicus* of the principle is enshrined in Article 33 of the Refugee Convention, which stipulates:

> No Contracting State shall expel or return ("refouler") a refugee in any manner whatsoever to the frontiers of territories where his life or freedom would be threatened on account of his race, religion, nationality, membership of a particular social group or political opinion.[18]

The obligation provides that States should refrain from returning *refugees* to a place where their life or liberty would be at risk.[19] It also incorporates not only direct *refoulement*, but also indirect or chain *refoulement*, in other words, where the refugee is returned to an interim country notwithstanding the reasonably foreseeable fact that the State is likely to return him or her to their country of origin.[20] The principle applies indirectly through Article 3 of the European Convention on Human Rights (ECHR or Convention),[21] as well as to the EU specifically in Article 19(2) of the Charter of Fundamental Rights (EU Charter or Charter)[22] and is by now a well-accepted principle of customary international law.[23] The only exception to the principle is provided in Article 33(2) which refers to instances where the refugee poses a threat to national security or where he or she has been convicted of particularly serious crime.

16 Convention Relating to the Status of Refugees (adopted 28 July 1951, entered into force 22 April 1954) 189 UNTS 137 (Refugee Convention).

17 The significance of the Convention in terms of international law is simply demonstrated by the fact that 142 states are currently parties to both the Convention and its Protocol.

18 Refugee Convention, Art 33.

19 Richard Barnes, 'Refugee Law at Sea' (2008) 53(1) International and Comparative Law Quarterly 62.

20 Douglas Guilfoyle, *Shipping Interdiction and the Law of the Sea* (CUP 2009) 223.

21 Convention for the Protection of Human Rights and Fundamental Freedoms (adopted 4 November 1950, entered into force 3 September 1953) 213 UNTS 222.

22 The Charter of Fundamental Rights of the European Union, OJ 2012 C326/02, Dec. 7, 2000 (EU Charter or Charter).

23 See, e.g., Seline Trevisanut, 'The Principle of Non-Refoulement at Sea and the Effectiveness of Asylum Protection' (2008) 12 Max Planck United Nation Yearbook 215; Guy Goodwin-Gill and Jane McAdam, *The Refugee in International Law* (3rd edn, Oxford: OUP 2011) 345–354.

At first glance, it can be observed that the scope of Article 33 allows for a conditional protection, applying only to refugees. The apparent difficulties that arise from this interpretation are twofold: 1) persons increasingly travelling by vessels at sea are both asylum seekers (possibly refugees) and migrants (economic, environmental or for other reasons), such that there is mixed migration by sea, as explained in the Introduction; and 2) persons will not be recognized as refugees until they have successfully entered a State where their claims can be then assessed;[24] as such, in the maritime space, all persons should be treated in an equal manner.

One way in which the limitation entrenched in the Refugee Convention can be overcome is by making a closer inspection of the international human rights regimes, which provide for the prohibition of torture. This would reveal that the scope and content of the principle vary under international refugee law and international human rights law.[25] In contrast to the Refugee Convention, the principle of *non-refoulement* is much broader in scope in international human rights law. Article 3(1) of UN Convention against Torture, and other Cruel, Inhuman or Degrading Treatment or Punishment (CAT)[26] enshrines this principle and provides that 'no person' shall be returned; as such, it is evident that it does not entail the 'refugee' prerequisite for the prohibition of return to apply, as persons may not (yet) adhere to that legal status but may still face serious human rights violations.[27] As Lauterpacht and Bethlehem note, the obligation of *non-refoulement* 'protects both refugees and asylum seekers' and as such it applies irrespective of whether their 'refugee' status has been formally assessed.[28]

Moreover, the *non-refoulement* principle also applies to rejection at the frontiers of States. This appears to conflict with the general principle in international law that States have the right to control the entry of non-nationals into their territory and their stay therein, allowing States to reject asylum seekers at the border or close their borders in the event of a mass influx of

24 Dublin III regulation establishes that the responsibility for dealing with an asylum seeker's application falls on the country of first entry. See Regulation (EU) No 604/2013 of the European Parliament and of the Council of 26 June 2013 establishing the criteria and mechanisms for determining the Member State responsible for examining an application for international protection lodged in one of the Member States by a third-country national or a stateless person (recast), OJ L180/31 (29 June 2013).

25 Elihu Lauterpacht and Daniel Bethlehem, 'The Scope and Content of the Principle of Non-Refoulement: Opinion' in Erika Feller, Volker Türk and Frances Nicholson (eds), *Refugee Protection in International Law: UNHCR's Global Consultations on International Protection* (CUP 2003).

26 CAT Art 3(1): 'No State Party shall expel, return ("refouler") or extradite a person to another State where there are substantial grounds for believing that he would being danger of being subjected to torture'; Suffice to mention, that the widespread adoption of UNCAT, with 165 Contracting State parties, proves the universal legal nature of the doctrine.

27 Chantal Marie-Jeanne Bostock, 'Legal Obligations owed to the Asylum Seekers on the MV Tampa' (2002) 14(2/3) International Journal of Refugee Law 290.

28 Lauterpacht and Benthlehem (n 25).

asylum seekers, which would render meaningless the *non-refoulement* obligation. Moreso, as Hathaway maintains, the protection afforded inheres on a provisional basis even before the refugee's status has been assessed by a State party, and it also applies to those who have not expressed their wish to be protected.[29] For this reason, Article 33 of the Refugee Convention presents the primary response of the international community to the need of refugees to enter and remain in an asylum State.

It follows that States will be obligated to determine whether or not a person is a refugee according to the definition of the Refugee Convention.[30] Hathaway, in reflecting on the refugee definition, posits that a 'convention refugee is a person who is outside her country because she reasonably believes that her civil or political status puts her at risk of serious harm in her country, and that her own government cannot or will not protect her'.[31] Following, the duty incumbent on States is a necessary corollary to the right of an individual to seek asylum as laid down in Article 14 of the Universal Declaration of Human Rights (UDHR).[32] However, it needs to be clarified that States are not obligated to grant asylum but that they determine whether or not a person is to be recognized as refugee by reference to the definition.

Relatedly, in the context of refugee protection in the EU, the Charter of the EU establishes in Article 18 that 'the right to asylum shall be guaranteed with due respect for the rules of the Geneva Convention of 28 July 1951 and the Protocol of 31 January 1966'.[33] Further, the Schengen Borders Code (SBC) governing external border control provides that individuals who do not meet the criteria for entry shall be refused admission, albeit 'without prejudice to the application of special provisions concerning the right of asylum',[34] in particular when it comes to *non-refoulement*. By contrast, the ECHR does

29 James C Hathaway, 'Refugees and Asylum' in Brian Opeskin, Richard Perruchoud and Jillyanne Redpath-Cross (eds), *Foundations of International Migration Law* (Cambridge: CUP 2012) 197.

30 Article 1(A)2. Refugee status is granted by a foreign State to a person who has a well-founded fear of persecution in his or her country of origin on the basis of race, religion, nationality, membership of a particular social group or political opinion. In the recent case of *M.A. and Z.R. v Cyprus*, App no 39090/20 (ECtHR, 8 October 2024), the ECtHR unanimously found violations of Articles 3, 4 of Protocol No. 4 and 13 of the ECHR as the Cypriot authorities had performed an illegal push-back, by returning the applicants' to Lebanon and removing them from Cyprus (which the State did not denied) without allowing them to claim for asylum. Jurisdiction was not an issue in this case because the Government accepted that the facts of the case occurred within its jurisdiction. For detailed discussion, see, Aphrodite Papachristdoulou, 'MA and ZR v Cyprus "Pushing Back" on Pushbacks? Debunking Readmission Agreements and Upholding the Rights of Maritime Migrants' (2025) 1 EHRLR 97–105.

31 James Hathaway, *The Law of Refugee Status* (Butterworths 1991) Preface, v.

32 Universal Declaration of Human Rights, UNGA Res 217 A (III) (10 December 1948).

33 EU Charter, Art 18.

34 Article 14(1) Regulation (EU) 2016/399 of the European Parliament and of the Council of 9 March 2016 on a Union Code on the rules governing the movement of persons across borders (Schengen Borders Code or SBC).

not provide for an explicit right to asylum but preserves the right of States to control the entry, residence and expulsion of non-nationals. Notwithstanding, both the ECtHR and the Court of Justice of the European Union (CJEU) have established that for the principle of *non-refoulement* to be effective, a positive obligation exists for States with jurisdiction to grant asylum seekers at their borders access to their territory to lodge their international protection claims and have effective asylum procedures in place.[35] Hence, it is understood that turning away an individual and thus putting them at risk of torture or other forms of inhuman or degrading treatment or punishment is prohibited by the *non-refoulement* principle.[36]

2. A Historical Perspective of Managing Migration in the Mediterranean

Libya under the rule of Muammar Gaddafi was already a country where people were exposed to repression and blatant human rights abuses, with no appropriate mechanisms to hold the government accountable or grant any form of protection to vulnerable groups of people.[37] Most importantly, although Libya holds the status of a 'migration corridor' where thousands of Sub-Saharan Africans are stranded, it has yet no domestic asylum system able to recognize any legal status for refugees and neither is it a party to the Refugee Convention; contrariwise, since the 2000s it has been operating a repressive migration policy.[38] Despite both the EU and Italy being fully aware of the situation in North Africa and the human rights violations under the Gaddafi regime, they chose to make Libya the chief partner in their border externalization policy.

The common interests held between the EU and Libya were grounded in protecting the Mediterranean in relation to 'illegal' migration as it created

35 *Hirsi Jamaa and Others v Italy*, App no 27765/09 (ECtHR, 23 February 2012) paras 198–199, 204; *Sharifi and Others v Italy and Greece*, App no 16643/09 (ECtHR, 21 October 2014) para 169; *Jabari v Turkey*, App no 40035/98 (ECtHR, 11 July 2000) para 39. And, *Commission v Hungary*, Case C-808/18 [2020] 1029, para 87–130.

36 Art 3 of the ECHR. See also, FRA, 'Fundamental Rights of Refugees, Asylum Applicants and Migrants at the European Borders' <https://fra.europa.eu/sites/default/files/fra_uploads/fra-coe-2020-european-law-land-borders_en.pdf>.

37 'Communication to the Office of the Prosecutor of the International Criminal Court Pursuant to the Article 15 of the Rome Statute: EU Migration Policies in the Central Mediterranean and Libya (2014–2019)' 16 (Communication to the ICC) <https://www.statewatch.org/media/documents/news/2019/jun/eu-icc-case-EU-Migration-Policies.pdf>.

38 Sylvie Bredeloup and Olivier Pliez, 'The Libyan Migration Corridor' (European University Institute, Research Report, Case Study, EU-US Immigration Systems 2011/03) <https://cadmus.eui.eu/bitstream/handle/1814/16213/EU-US%20Immigration%20Systems%202011%20-%2003.pdf?sequence=1&isAllowed=y>; See also, George M Bob-Milliar, 'Rescuing Migrants in Libya: The Political Economy of State Responses to Migration Crises – The Case of Ghana' (DIIS Report, 2012:16) <https://pure.diis.dk/ws/files/56074/WP2012_16_Rescuing_migrants_in_Libya_web.pdf>; *Hirsi* (n 1) paras 153–154 and 123–130.

security threats to Europe's southern borders that needed to be moderated.[39] Hence, Libya as a departure point for migrants has always had a crucial role to play in migration between Africa and Europe.[40] It is noteworthy to clarify at this point, that border controls are not carried out by the EU per se but are undertaken by European States and its Border and Coast Guard Agency (Frontex), usually in the form of joint naval operations[41] or under bilateral, multilateral and unilateral forms of cooperation.[42] To this end, conceptualized in this manner, the border becomes a key instrument of migration management, with surveillance technology aggravating the practice of *refoulement* and allowing States to seemingly sidestep any associated obligation of rescue by shifting the responsibility to third countries. In the context of this book's focus, the exercise of border controls happens within the international space of the high seas that does not fall under the sovereignty of any State. Nonetheless the freedom of the high seas does not render this area a space 'devoid of regulation',[43] and human rights must still be respected and realized, though many violations do go unnoticed.[44] For this reason, the limited response facilitated by European States to blatant violations of fundamental rights has raised uncertainties on the applicability of human rights at sea in practice.[45]

Given the increasing number of migrants reaching Italian shores from Libya in 2007, as well as the number of migrants perishing at sea at the same time, the Italian government proceeded by drawing a bilateral anti-immigration cooperation agreement with Libya, 'The Treaty of Friendship', in an attempt to combat 'illegal' migration. The agreement was signed in August 2008 and came into force in May 2009, with the launch of the first joint naval patrols

39 Peter Seeberg, 'EU Strategic Interests in Post-Qadhafi Libya: Perspectives for Cooperation' (2014) XXI(1) Middle East Policy 122.

40 Bredeloup and Pliez (n 38) 7.

41 Pursuant to Art 3(1) of the Frontex Regulation, the Agency may launch joint operations based on the request of a Member State that is having difficulties regarding external border control. Regulation (EU) 656/2014 establishing rules for the surveillance of the external sea borders in the context of operational cooperation coordinated by Frontex also introduced changes to the mandate of the agency, namely in terms of what concerns sea operations coordinated by Frontex. This Regulation was fully integrated and referred to in Regulation (EU) 2016/1624 and now in Regulation (EU) 2019/1896.

42 Thomas Spijkerboer, 'Moving Migrants, States, and Rights: Human Rights and Border Deaths' (2013) 7(2) Law and Ethics of Human Rights 237.

43 Tanja E Aalberts and Thomas Gammeltoft-Hansen, 'Sovereignty at Sea: The Law and Politics of Saving Lives in Mare Liberum' (2014) 17 Journal of International Relations and Development 440; See also, Aphrodite Papachristodoulou, 'The Exercise of State Power Over Migrants at Sea Through Technologies of Remote Control: Reconceptualizing Human Rights Jurisdiction (2024) 73(4) ICLQ 934.

44 Ian Urbina, 'Lawless Ocean: The Link Between Human Rights Abuses and Overfishing' (Yale Environment 360, 20 November 2019) <https://e360.yale.edu/features/lawless-ocean-the-link-between-human-rights-abuses-and-overfishing>.

45 Communication to the ICC (n 37) 37.

in the Central Mediterranean.[46] Essentially, with this agreement, Gaddafi was meant to keep refugees and migrants in Libya, and the Italian authorities were to intercept (by transferring the migrants to a State's navy vessels and delivering them back to their country of origin) – push-back[47] – anyone leaving Libya irregularly, whilst 'migrants would be subjected to mass detention, notably in six detention camps that were built with Italian funds' in Libya.[48] This emblematic agreement marked the start of a direct *refoulement* era, which was later challenged by the ECtHR in the *Hirsi* case.

3. The *Hirsi* Case and Its Aftermath

The seminal case of *Hirsi*, decided on 23 February 2012, is arguably one of the most important ECtHR cases to-date in relation to a State's extraterritorial human rights obligations in maritime rescue operations and in challenging migration policies that have detrimental effects on the human rights of migrants and, in particular, drawn at the expense of the *non-refoulement* principle.

The case concerned an interception of a migrant vessel on the high seas, carried out by Italian authorities under the 2008 Treaty of Friendship agreement with Libya, in which the concerned migrants were transferred to Italian military vessels and returned to the Libyan authorities in Tripoli.[49] The ECtHR condemned Italy for exposing migrants to the risk of being subjected to ill-treatment in Libya and observed – notably in the current context – that 'Italy cannot evade its own responsibility by relying on its obligations arising out of bilateral agreements with Libya'.[50] Ergo, it reasoned that States 'cannot circumvent refugee law and human rights requirements by declaring border control measures . . . to be rescue measures'.[51] Further, the Court confirmed that a State exercises jurisdiction when intercepting vessels on the high seas, as migrants were 'under the continuous and exclusive *de jure* and *de facto* control

46 Treaty on Friendship, Partnership and Cooperation (Italy and Libya) (adopted 30 August 2008); See Natalino Ronzitti, *The Treaty on Friendship, Partnership and Cooperation between Italy and Libya: New Prospects for Cooperation in the Mediterranean?* (Rome: Istituto Aff ari Internazionali, 2009) <http://www.iai.it/pdf/DocIAI/IAI0909.pdf>.

47 Push-back practices include the forced return of migrants, including applicants for international protection, to the country from where they attempted to cross or crossed an international border without allowing them to apply for asylum or submit an appeal, which may lead to a violation of the principle of *non-refoulement*. See, European Commission, 'Migration and Home Affairs 'Glossary' <https://home-affairs.ec.europa.eu/networks/european-migration-network-emn/emn-asylum-and-migration-glossary/glossary/push-back_en#:~:text=Various%20measures%20taken%20by%20states,or%20denied%20of%20any%20individual>.

48 Communication to the ICC (n 37) 17.

49 *Hirsi* (n 1) paras 9–12.

50 Ibid para 129; This was reiterated by the ECtHR in its recent judgment in *M.A. and Z.R. v Cyprus (M.A. and Z.R.)*, App no 39090/20 (ECtHR, 8 October 2024) para 91, in relation to the bilateral agreement Cyprus had with Lebanon for readmissions.

51 Andreas Fischer-Lescano, Tillmann Löhr and T Tohidipur, 'Border Controls at Sea: Requirements under International Human Rights and Refugee Law' (2009) 21 International Journal of Refugee Law 291.

of the Italian authorities'.[52] Consequently, the Court found Italy in violation of Article 3 of the ECHR, the prohibition of torture and inhuman or degrading treatment, Article 4 of Protocol 4 ECHR, covering the prohibition of collective expulsion and Article 13 ECHR, the right to an effective remedy.

Importantly, the case marked a critical milestone in the protection of migrants' rights as it represented a significant departure from previous decisions,[53] insofar as it confirmed that the prohibition of *refoulement* applies extraterritorially. At the outset, the judgment seemed not to afford the opportunity for any future maneuvering of migration policies to stem migration flows by way of cooperation agreements concluded with third countries, which produce effects outside of a State's territory and result in human rights violations. Hence, at that moment, it became clear that the classical *direct* 'push-backs' of migrant vessels, even when interdicted on the high seas, represented a fundamental violation of the principle of *non-refoulement.*

In light of this, it was anticipated that the Court's ruling would be implemented in good faith with a change of attitude on the part of the Italian authorities, at least insofar as to ensure compliance with the country's human rights obligations.[54]

Given the extensively documented deterioration of the human rights situation in Libya and the widely documented abuses suffered by migrants under the control of the LCGN,[55] preventing migrants from departing from Libyan territory or returning individuals to Libya could amount to complicity with arbitrary detention, torture and even violations of the right to life.[56] Ironically, only *a month* after the Court's judgment in *Hirsi*, Italy signed a second Memorandum of Understanding with Libya, which provided once more for the 'exchange of liaison officers, readmission agreement, training activities for Libyan agents and even the recovery of detention centres'.[57] Adding to that, the Council of the EU, in May 2013, established the EU Border Assistance Mission (EUBAM) Libya operation under the Common Security and Defence Policy (CSDP) with a Frontex Officer as part of the mission to *inter alia* support the Libyan authorities in developing border management.[58] However, due to the mounting conflict at the time in Libya, the mission was moved to Tunisia

52 Ibid para 81; See also Annick Pijnenburg, 'From Italian Pushbacks to Libyan Pullbacks: Is Hirsi 2.0 in the Making in Strasbourg?' (2018) 20(4) European Journal of Migration and Law 400.

53 *Sale v Haitian Centers Council*, 113 S. Ct. 2549, 125 L. (92–344), 509 U.S. 155 (1993).

54 Moreno-Lax, '*Hirsi Jamaa and Others v Italy*' (n 6) 595.

55 See Human Rights Council, 'Report of the Independent Fact-Finding Mission on Libya' (2023) A/HRC/52/83; Human Rights Watch, 'No Escape from Hell: EU Policies Contribute to Abuse of Migrants in Libya' (21 January 2019) <https://www.hrw.org/report/2019/01/21/no-escape-hell/eu-policies-contribute-abuse-migrants-libya>.

56 See 'Blaming the Rescuers. Criminalising Solidarity, (Re)enforcing Deterrence' (2017) <http://blamingtherescuers.org/>; Miles Jackson, *Complicity in International Law* (OUP 2015).

57 Communication to the ICC (n 37) 19.

58 Ibid 20; Council Decision 2013/233/CFSP of 22 May 2013 on the European Union Integrated Border Management Assistance Mission in Libya (EUBAM Libya) [2013] OJ L138/15.

in August 2014, albeit this time with limited capacity to advise and train its Libyan personnel. Evidently, these missions attempted to re-establish stringent border measures to control migration movements, yet both have failed because of the political and security situation in Libya in the absence of central power.[59]

The practical effects of the *Hirsi* case were only recognized and upheld later in 2013 by coordinated efforts to systematically address the perceived 'migration crisis', largely through the Italian government's response to public shock at the loss of life at sea occurring beyond its coastline. In particular, the 300 migrants that died in October 2013 outside of Lampedusa precipitated the policy decision to launch the Italian *Mare Nostrum* mission, a humanitarian SAR operation, which had as its core mandate the rescue of migrants travelling on vessels in distress in the Central Mediterranean between Italy and North Africa.[60] Alas, the humanitarian operation lasted only one year, even though it was estimated to have saved at least 130,000 people during its operation. Indeed, the mission has been applauded from many quarters, including the International Organization for Migration (IOM),[61] but at the European level, it remained controversial and, for this reason, was short-lived.

The apparent explanations for the termination of *Mare Nostrum* included: 1) it was intended only as an 'emergency operation' in response to the incident in October 2013 and not a permanent policy initiative; 2) the lack of financial support from neighboring European States led to an unsustainable cost for the Italian government to carry alone; and 3) perhaps most decisively, the widespread criticism that the mission was creating a 'pull-factor' for migrants attempting to cross the Mediterranean in order to reach Europe.[62] However, such assertions appear to be increasingly baseless.[63] Several studies have revealed no actual link between the existence of SAR operations and the number of migratory flows and, in fact, revealed that such operations minimize the risk of border deaths.[64] In contrast, and as I go on to show more fully below, the descriptive statistics do seem to point to the conclusion that the shift in operational emphasis since 2014 has made the humanitarian

59 EUBAM Libya, 'About EU Border Assistance Mission in Libya (EUBAM)' (2016) <https://eeas.europa.eu/csdp-missions-operations/eubam-libya/3859/about-eu-border-assistance-mission-libya-eubam_en>.

60 See Minestero della Difesa, 'Mare Nostrum Operation' <http://www.marina.difesa.it/EN/operations/Pagine/MareNostrum.aspx>.

61 International Organization for Migration, 'IOM Applauds Italy's Life-Saving Mare Nostrum Operation: "Not a Migrant Pull Factor"' (IOM, 31 October 2014) <https://www.iom.int/news/iom-applauds-italys-life-saving-mare-nostrum-operation-not-migrant-pull-factor>.

62 See, e.g., The United Kingdom Parliament (2014) Written Answers. <https://publications.parliament.uk/pa/ld201415/ldhansrd/text/141015w0001.htm>.

63 Eugenio Cusumano, 'Migrant Rescue as Organized Hypocrisy: Eu Maritime Missions Offshore Libya between Humanitarianism and Border Control' (2018) 54(1) Cooperation and Conflict 3.

64 See Charles Heller and Lorenzo Pezzani, 'Death by Rescue. Forensic Architecture Agency' (2016) <https://deathbyrescue.org/report/narrative/>. See for more detailed explanation and empirical analysis, Elias Steinhilper and Rob J Gruijters, 'A Contested Crisis: Policy Narratives and Empirical Evidence on Border Deaths in the Mediterranean' (2018) 52 Sociology 515–533.

plight of migrants far worse. Indeed, it will be demonstrated that despite a dramatic – and foreseeable – drop in the total numbers of crossings in the Mediterranean Sea, the relative mortality rate has increased dramatically. In this vein, Ghezelbash *et al.* attest, 'the clear evidence of spiralling fatality rates in the Mediterranean points, precisely, to the inadequacy of replacing SAR operations with law-enforcement or military missions unfit for purpose'.[65]

4. The EU Institutions and Its Agencies

The concerns over *Mare Nostrum* saw the mission superseded in November 2014 by what was essentially a drastically scaled-back operation in the form of the Frontex-coordinated Joint Operation *Triton*.[66] The operation had as its primary mandate border control and surveillance, though according to Frontex, SAR remained a significant priority. It is clear, however – not least from its significantly reduced budget compared to *Mare Nostrum* – that not only was this not a SAR operation but that saving lives remained a low operational priority overall. It was only a few months after *Triton*'s launch that two large-scale incidents occurred in the Mediterranean in April 2015, where approximately 1,200 people lost their lives.[67] As a result of growing public concern in the face of such loss of life, as well as a broader 'international moral panic' with the number of migrants reaching Europe at over one million in 2015 alone, European leaders' response was to implement even more potent efforts to stem the tide of migrant flows.[68]

A Ten-Point Action Plan was subsequently adopted, itself aimed at implementing the European Agenda on Migration,[69] which resulted in the expan-

65 Daniel Ghezelbash, Violeta Moreno-Lax, Natalie Klein and Brian Opeskin, 'Securitization of Search and Rescue at Sea: The Response to Boat Migration in the Mediterranean and Offshore Australia' (2018) 67(2) ICLQ 334.

66 The main objective of a joint border control operation is border control (detecting, preventing and responding to irregular migration). This consists of border checks and border surveillance as per Schengen Borders Code, Art 2(10). The agency, through the European Border Surveillance System (EUROSUR) established in 2013, uses big data technologies to `predict, control and monitor traffic across European Union borders', Regulation (EU) 1052/2013 of the European Parliament and of the Council of 22 October 2013 establishing the European Border Surveillance System (EUROSUR) L 295/11, 6 November 2013. For in depth discussion on Frontex and accountability , see, Melanie Fink, *Frontex and Human Rights Responsibility in 'Multi-Actor Situations' under the ECHR and EU Public Liability Law* (Meijers Research Institute and Graduate School of the Leiden Law School 2017).

67 See *inter alia* Antonio Denti, 'Hundreds Drown Off Libya, EU Leaders Forced to Reconsider Migrant Crisis' (19 April 2015) <https://www.reuters.com/article/us-europe-migrants/hundreds-drown-off-libya-eu-leaders-forced-to-reconsider-migrant-crisis-idUSKBN0NA07020150419>; BBC News, 'Mediterranean Migrants: Hundreds Feared Dead after Boat Capsizes' (19 April 2015) <https://www.bbc.com/news/world-europe-32371348>.

68 The phrase 'international moral panic' is borrowed from Catherine Dauvergne, 'Sovereignty, Migration and the Rule of Law in Global Times' (2004) 67(4) Modern Law Review 588; See e.g. BBC News, 'Migrant Crisis: Malta Seeks Solutions to Stem the Tide' (21 April 2015) <https://www.bbc.com/news/world-europe-32389754>.

69 European Commission, 'A European Agenda on Migration' (2015) <https://eur-lex.europa.eu/legal-content/EN/TXT/?uri=CELEX%3A52015DC0240>. See also, Council Decision

sion and upscaling of the Operation *Triton* as well as the instigation of the EU's Operation *Sophia*, which was established under the CSDP.[70] This operation marked a clear operational shift in the EU as the aim of the mission was to prevent departures, disrupt smuggling networks and trafficking operations and ultimately, 'to better contain the growing flows of illegal migration'.[71] Its central mandate was 'to undertake systematic efforts to identify, capture and dispose of vessels and enabling assets used or suspected of being used by migrant smugglers or traffickers', which in turn is meant to feed into 'wider EU efforts to disrupt the business model of human smuggling and trafficking networks in the Southern Central Mediterranean and *prevent the further loss of life at sea*'.[72] Whilst both missions, *Triton* and *Sophia*, were thus expected to comply with the legal and moral imperative of saving lives at sea, neither of the two included active SAR activities as part of their mandate.[73]

Of particular concern in this respect were the two supporting tasks adopted by the Council in 2016: the training of the Libyan Coast Guard and Navy (LCGN), and the use of aerial, satellite and maritime assets to contribute to the enforcement of the UN arms embargo on the high seas off the coast of Libya.[74] The long-term goal behind these operational moves was to buttress Libya's capacity to stop migrants leaving its territory – 'for pre-emptive take-backs to ultimately replace SAR, shifting the responsibility for refugee and migrant flows to Libya'.[75] Thus, *Sophia* served political imperatives that fundamentally clashed with humanitarian goals, allowing for interceptions on international waters (migrant pull-backs),[76] summary returns (push-backs) and, as noted above, only incidentally served the

(CFSP) 2015/778 of 18 May 2015 on a European Union military operation in the Southern Central Mediterranean (EUNAVFOR MED), [2015] *OJ* L 122/31.

70 European Council (EC), 'EUNAVFOR MED Operation Sophia: Mandate Extended Until 31 March 2019' (21 December 2018) <https://www.consilium.europa.eu/en/press/press-releases/2018/12/21/eunavfor-med-operation-sophia-mandate-extended-until-31-march-2019/>.

71 See European Council, Council Conclusions (EUCO 22/15) of 26 June 2015, at para 3 <https://data.consilium.europa.eu/doc/document/ST-22-2015-INIT/en/pdf>. See further Ghezelbash *et al* (n 65) 333; Violeta Moreno-Lax, 'The EU Humanitarian Border and The Securitization of Human Rights: The "Rescue- Through-Interdiction/Rescue-Without-Protection" Paradigm' (2017) 56(1) Journal of Common Market Studies 128.

72 European External Action Service (EEAS), 'European Union Naval Force – Mediterranean Operation Sophia' (10 April 2018) <https://www.operationsophia.eu/wp-content/uploads/2018/04/Mission.pdf>.

73 Eugenio Cusumano and James Pattison, 'The Non–Governmental Provision of Search and Rescue in the Mediterranean and the Abdication of State Responsibility' (2018) 31(1) Cambridge Review of International Affairs 53–75.

74 Council Decision (CFSP) 2016/993 of 20 June 2016 amending Decision (CFSP) 2015/778 on a European Union military operation in the Southern Central Mediterranean (EUNAVFOR MED operation SOPHIA).

75 Ghezelbash *et al* (n 65) 335.

76 'Pull-back' or 'take back' practices include departure prevention by third States, see, Nora Markard, 'The Right to Leave by Sea: Legal Limits on EU Migration Control by Third Countries' (2016) 27 EJIL 591.

imperative of saving lives at sea.[77] Such practices raise fundamental concerns, as EU policy has been essentially relying on third States (Libya) to undertake *refoulement*. Along these lines, Kenneth Roth, the former executive director of Human Rights Watch, has also noted that European officials are 'trying to do indirectly what they can't do directly by building up and training the Libyan coastguard so that the Libyans on their own can simply return people back to the traffickers'.[78]

Moreover, another alarming fact is that the deaths occurring in the Central Mediterranean route, for example, in 2018 whilst Operation *Sophia* was in motion represented 57 percent of the fatalities across the whole Mediterranean, despite comprising only 21 percent of the total crossings. As a result, the operation has had an apparent diversionary effect as more than the majority of total crossings (in 2018) occurred in the Western Mediterranean route (57,922 representing 50 percent of the total crossings across the Mediterranean) and Eastern Mediterranean route (33,536 representing 29 percent of the total crossings across the Mediterranean).[79]

Despite these alarming figures, the Council in 2019 adopted the decision to extend its naval Operation *Sophia* up to September 2019, *but* also to suspend all the vessels in the Mediterranean *vis-à-vis* disengaging with SAR activities altogether, relying, in this way, solely on aerial assets.[80] As a consequence, the right of irregular migrants to seek international protection became a fool's hope. With reference to Operation *Sophia*, Amnesty International has expressed the following view:

> The proposal to pull back EU naval operations from search and rescue activities and encourage – and indirectly fund – the Libyan coast guard to plug the gap, is a thinly veiled plan to prevent refugees and migrants reaching Europe. It will trap tens of thousands of people in conflict ravaged country and expose them to the risk of torture and exploitation.[81]

It seems clear that the *modus operandi* has shifted towards border security and is increasingly supported and facilitated by the EU agencies and institutions, both

77 Barbara Miltner, 'The Mediterranean Migration Crisis: A Clash of the Titans' Obligations?' (2015) 22(1) The Brown Journal of World Affairs 215.

78 See AFP, '"Nobody should be forcibly returned to Libya": HRW Chief' (18 January 2018) <https://www.rfi.fr/en/contenu/20180118-nobody-should-be-forcibly-returned-libya-hrw-chief>.

79 These numbers mark a big difference when compared with the figures in 2017 with 30,579 (18%) crossings in the Eastern Mediterranean route, 22,414 (13%) in the Western Mediterranean route, and 119,370 (69%) in the Central Mediterranean route.

80 Council of the European Union, 'EUNAVFOR MED Operation Sophia: Mandate Extended until 30 September 2019' (29 March 2019) <https://www.consilium.europa.eu/en/press/press-releases/2019/03/29/eunavfor-med-operation-sophia-mandate-extended-until-30-september-2019/>.

81 Amnesty International, 'EU: Plans to 'Close' Sea Border Would Lock Refugees and Migrants in Horrendous Conditions in Libya' (2 February 2017) <https://www.amnesty.ie/eu-plans-close-sea-border-lock-refugees-migrants-horrendous-conditions-libya/>.

in terms of the operational priorities of Frontex, but also at the broadest policy level, where the humanitarian imperative of SAR has been subordinated to the security objectives of stemming migrant flows. That has been made clearer by the supersession of *Sophia* in 2020 and the establishment of Operation *Irini* in the Mediterranean, which is very much tasked with a similar operational focus and keeps the controversial element of the training of the LCGN.[82] Moreover, it is primarily tasked with implementing the UN arms embargo on Libya through aerial, satellite and maritime assets, while it makes no reference to some of the more humanitarian aims that *Sophia* had in its mandate, that is, to combat human smuggling and prevent further loss of life at sea.[83] In turn, its remit has an expanded scope that allows for the use of aerial surveillance within Libyan airspace.

Evidently, the attention to saving lives at sea has been compromised by efforts aimed at enhancing the 'management' of irregular migration flows.[84] In this vein, the European Commission in 2020 proposed the 'New Pact on Migration and Asylum' in the form of a simple communication, amidst the failure of its previous 'European Agenda on Migration' [2015][85] to introduce solidarity and address the political divisions between Member States responsibility in examining asylum applications.[86] The EU Pact on Migration and Asylum (EU Pact, or Pact) was adopted on 14 May 2024 by the Council of the EU, a legislative package that will reform the Common European Asylum System.[87]

Among the goals of the proposed Pact is the prevention of irregular departures through 'mutually beneficial partnerships with those [third] countries . . .

82 Council of the European Union, Council Decision (CFSP) 2020/472 of 31 March 2020 on a European Union Military Operation in the Mediterranean (EUNAVFOR MED Irini) <https://eur-lex.europa.eu/eli/dec/2020/472/oj>. Established by the UN Security Council Resolution 1970 (2011).

83 Federico Alagna, 'From Sophia to Irini: EU Mediterranean Policies and the Urgency of "Doing Something"' (2020) <https://www.iai.it/en/pubblicazioni/sophia-irini-eu-mediterranean-policies-and-urgency-doing-something>.

84 Niamh Keady-Tabbal and Itamar Mann, 'Weaponizing Rescue: Law and the Materiality of Migration Management in the Aegean' (2022) 36(1) LJIL 12.

85 European Commission, 'Managing Migration Better in All Aspects: A European Agenda on Migration' (13 May 2015) <https://ec.europa.eu/commission/presscorner/detail/en/IP_15_4956>; Dublin III Regulation.

86 European Commission, 'Communication from the Commission to the European Parliament, the Council, the European Economic and Social Committee and the Committee of the Regions on a New Pact on Migration and Asylum' (European Commission, 23 September 2020) COM (2020) 609 final (Communication 2020) <https://ec.europa.eu/info/sites/default/files/1_en_act_part1_v7_1.pdf>; Philippe De Bruycker, 'The New Pact on Migration and Asylum: What It Is Not and What It Could Have Been' (2020) <https://eumigrationlawblog.eu/the-new-pact-on-migration-and-asylum-what-it-is-not-and-what-it-could-have-been/>; Violeta Moreno-Lax, 'A New Common European Approach to Search and Rescue? Entrenching Proactive Containment' (EU Migration Law Blog, 2021) <https://eumigrationlawblog.eu/a-new-common-european-approach-to-search-and-rescue-entrenching-proactive-containment/>.

87 The Pact is expected to come into effect in 2026 as Member States have two years to implement the laws. Pact on Migration and Asylum <https://home- affairs.ec.europa.eu/policies/migration-and-asylum/pact-migration-and- asylum_en>.

and be based on human rights, rule of law and the respect of the Union's common values'.[88] Despite being couched in language of fundamental rights, it is evident that the Asylum and Migration Management Regulation (AMMR)[89] prioritizes the long-established practice of containment that seeks to fight against irregular migration at *all* costs, preventing movement further into the EU whilst strengthening cooperation with third countries.[90] Yet again, with the unfolding climate crisis affecting many regions in North Africa and Middle East and intersecting with other political and economic crises,[91] the situation and commitment to safeguarding migrants' rights appears even more dire. As other scholars have argued, the Pact seems to be an attempt to further normalize human rights violations that are taking place not only within Europe but also in the countries of origin and transit, where the EU has drawn policies of border externalization as discussed in the previous section.[92]

A further concern relates to the reinforcement and expansion of surveillance technology over migrants in the EU border regime in what seemingly appears to be another attempt to compound border security.[93] Amid repeated criticisms, the Pact 'will normalise the arbitrary use of immigration detention, including for children and families, increase racial profiling, use "crisis" procedures to enable pushbacks, and return individuals to so called "safe third countries" where they are at risk of violence, torture, and arbitrary imprisonment'.[94] Detention in particular is featured in various instruments of the EU Pact

88 Art 5 of the Asylum and Migration Management Regulation (AMMR) 2024.

89 See Art 3–4, 2020/0279 (COD) 26 April 2024; Regulation (EU) 2024/1351 of the European Parliament and of the Council of 14 May 2024 on asylum and migration management, amending Regulations (EU) 2021/1147 and (EU) 2021/1060 and repealing Regulation (EU) No 604/201.

90 For a thorough analysis of the Pact, see Jean-Pierre Cassarino and Luisa Marin, 'The Pact on Migration and Asylum: Turning the European Territory into a Non-Territory?' (2022) 24 EJML 1–26.

91 See for instance, CCPR, *Ioane Teitiota v New Zealand*, CCPR/C/127/D/2728/2016.

92 See for instance, Niamh Keady-Tabbal and Eoghan O Cennabháin, 'Detention, Deportation & Drowning: Ireland's Embrace of Fortress Europe' (Rebel News, 26 June 2024) <https://www.rebelnews.ie/2024/06/26/detention-deportation-and-drowning-irelands-embrace-of-fortress-europe/>.

93 See Regulation (EU) 2024/1358 of the European Parliament and of the Council of 14 May 2024 on the establishment of 'Eurodac' for the comparison of biometric data in order to effectively apply Regulations (EU) 2024/1351 and (EU) 2024/1350 of the European Parliament and of the Council and Council Directive 2001/55/EC and to identify illegally staying third-country nationals and stateless persons and on requests for the comparison with Eurodac data by Member States' law enforcement authorities and Europol for law enforcement purposes, amending Regulations (EU) 2018/1240 and (EU) 2019/818 of the European Parliament and of the Council and repealing Regulation (EU) No 603/2013 of the European Parliament and of the Council (EURODAC).

94 'Over 50 NGOs pen eleventh-hour open letter to EU on human rights risks in Migration Pact' (18 December 2023) <https://picum.org/blog/open-letter-eu-human-rights-risks-migration-pact/>; See also, UNHCR, 'Child Immigration Detention Must Be Prohibited Following Adoption of EU Migration and Asylum Pact, UN Experts Say' (2 May 2024) <https://www.ohchr.org/en/press-releases/2024/05/child-immigration-detention-must-be-prohibited-following-adoption-eu>.

including Articles 44 and 45 of the AMMR, Article 8 (7) of the Screening Regulation, Article 8 of the Reception Conditions Directive and Article 5 of the Return Border Procedure Regulation. At the same time, maritime SAR aspects are addressed in several instruments, reflecting the significance of managing migration flows at sea. In this regard, the Crisis and Force Majeure Regulation (Chapter IV) regulates what will happen in 'exceptional situations of mass influx of third-country nationals or stateless persons'.[95] However, the definition of the term 'mass influx' is absent, leaving ample discretion for maneuvering by States. Arguably, this regulation seems to be an 'exodus' for governments to manage anticipated climate-induced mass migration,[96] worsening the 'border industrial complex' and shrinking human rights protection whilst leading to a fragmented application of the responsibility sharing system.[97] In this way, the Pact appears to strengthen the prioritization of fighting against irregular migration instead of providing the well-anticipated specifications on SAR responsibilities, including in situations of distress, which could have enhanced safety of life at sea and minimized abandonment practices that led to death by drowning.

Moreso, the Pact will allow the mere existence of 'a risk of crisis' to justify derogation from ordinary EU rules that may lead to a fragmented application of the responsibility sharing mechanism set up under the Pact.[98] Particularly, according to its own meaning, *crisis* evokes the formulation of extreme measures to combat an 'alarming' phenomenon. Conceptualizing these movements in this fashion allows not only the regularization of emergencies and a perpetual state of crisis to endure, but also the normalization of stricter measures that neglect the risk of being harmed by rising global temperatures and lived experiences of migrants in the name of exceptional policies to protect State borders from perceived security threats. At its core, however, the current 'crisis' is far from exceptional; the problem is not the plight of migrants attempting to reach Europe but the way their predicament has been negatively perceived. While true problems require solutions, migration is not

95 Art 1 (2) of the Crisis Regulation.

96 Emilio Antonios Hugues, 'Waiting for Godot No More: The Climate Crisis and the New European Asylum Pact' (Oxford Human Rights Hub, 18 April 2024) <https://ohrh.law.ox.ac.uk/waiting-for-godot-no-more-the-climate-crisis-and-the-new-european-asylum-pact/>.

97 United Nations General Assembly, 'Contemporary Forms of Racism, Racial Discrimination, Xenophobia and Related Intolerance' 10 November 2020, A/75/590, <https://digitallibrary.un.org/record/3893019?ln=en>; See also Vicky Kapogianni and Noemi Magugliani, 'When Aerial Surveillance Becomes the Sine Qua Non for Interceptions at Sea: Mapping the EU and Its Member States' Complicity in Border Violence' (2023) EYHR. See also, Patricia Vella de Fremeaux and Felicity G Attard, 'Navigating the Human Rights Trajectory of the EU Migration and Asylum Pact in Search and Rescue Operations (Part Two)' (17 September 2024) <https://opiniojuris.org/2024/09/17/navigating-the-human-rights-trajectory-of-the-eu-migration-and-asylum-pact-in-search-and-rescue-operations-part-two/>.

98 Fremeaux and Attard, ibid.

inherently one of them; rather, migration is a phenomenon that must be addressed constructively. Notwithstanding these concerns, the Pact will arguably allow European States to remain in a state of emergency to assert dominance over vulnerable individuals, victims of trafficking and persons with disabilities, while more people will be forced to leave their homes in the near future.

It follows that the EU's external border policy is geared towards the reinforcement of third countries' capacity to guard their borders and, in this way, distract the attention from the real and complex challenges of migration, forging gaps in refugee and human rights protection.[99] Crucially, in response to the second-largest shipwreck on the Mediterranean since 2015, which occurred outside Greece near the tourist destination and coastal town of Pylos on 14 June 2023, the European Parliament adopted a Resolution on the need for EU action on SAR in the Mediterranean. Specifically, it highlighted that Libya is not a safe place for the disembarkation of rescued persons at sea and that the Commission and its Member States should end cooperation with the Libyan coast guard in the event of serious fundamental rights violations faced by people intercepted at sea.[100] Relatedly, UN experts have often voiced fundamental concerns about the situation of migrants in Libya who allegedly have been held captive and tortured, including acts of enforced disappearance.[101] Adding to this evidence, the latest report of the UN Human Rights Council 'Independent Fact-Finding Mission' on 27 January 2023 concluded that there are grounds to believe that crimes against humanity have been committed by Libyan security forces and armed militia group including the LCGN.[102] In particular, the report highlighted that these entities in Libya are provided *inter alia* with technical, logistical and monetary support from the EU and its Member States for the interception and return of migrants.

Moreover, a 2021 joint report by Human Rights Watch and Border Forensics argues that Frontex and the EU's use of military drones in the Mediterranean increasingly poses a 'threat to migrants and refugees' and that 'Frontex's rhetoric around saving lives remains tragically empty as long as the border

99 Commission Communication, 'The Global Approach to Migration and Mobility' COM (2011) 743 final, 15l. See also, Lilie Chouliaraki and Myria Georgiou, 'Migration – the crisis imaginary' (LSE, 14 July 2023) <https://blogs.lse.ac.uk/europpblog/2023/07/14/migration-the-crisis-imaginary/>. See also Keady-Tabbal and Mann (n 84) 12.

100 European Parliament, 'Resolution on the Need for EU Action on Search and Rescue in the Mediterranean' (13 July 2023) 2023/2787 (RSP) at 10 <https://oeil.secure.europarl.europa.eu/oeil/popups/ficheprocedure.do?lang=en&reference=2023/2787(RSP)>.

101 UNHCR, 'Libya: UN Experts Alarmed at Reports of Trafficking in Persons, Arbitrary Detention, Enforced Disappearances and Torture of Migrants and Refugees' (UNHCR, Special Procedures, 21 July 2023) <https://www.ohchr.org/en/press-releases/2023/07/libya-un-experts-alarmed-reports-trafficking-persons-arbitrary-detention>.

102 UN Human Rights Council, Report of the Independent Fact-Finding Mission on Libya (27 March2023),A/HRC/52/83<https://reliefweb.int/report/libya/report-independent-fact-finding-mission-libya-ahrc5283-advance-edited-version-enar>.

agency doesn't use the technology and information at its disposal to ensure that people are rescued promptly and can disembark at safe ports'.[103] Technology thus plays a leading role in Frontex's capacity to geolocate migrants in proximity of borders and take strategic decisions about whom to alert.[104] Rather than launching a SAR response, Frontex has principally conducted aerial sightings of distress incidents via chartered aircrafts operated by private companies through its Multipurpose Aerial Surveillance (MAS) scheme in the Central Mediterranean. These aircraft transmit video footage and other information to a situation center in Frontex headquarters in Warsaw,[105] which then makes operational decisions about whom to alert, communicating information to various actors, including the LCGN. In so doing, it does not attempt to ensure that pull-backs which would result in increased harm to the lives of migrants will not occur.[106] This is particularly alarming given that Frontex has been repeatedly scrutinized and accused of being complicit in push-back operations by a number of EU bodies, human rights organizations and UN organs, and has faced legal action against its practices and claims that it has overstepped the limits of its powers.[107] The European Ombudsman's decision on the fundamental rights obligations of Frontex with regard to SAR in the context of its maritime surveillance activities has highlighted significant shortcomings in how the agency handles maritime incidents and showed a failure to ensure fundamental rights monitoring in its decisions.[108] Consequently, the increasing reliance on aerial and maritime

103 Human Rights Watch, 'EU: Frontex Complicit in Abuse in Libya: Aerial Surveillance Is Enabling Interceptions Return of Migrants to Harm' (HRW, 12 December 2023) <https://www.hrw.org/news/2022/12/12/eu-frontex-complicit-abuse-libya>.

104 Geolocation refers to the exact geographical location of a person, object or event through the comparison of photographs or videos with satellite imagery.

105 Frontex, 'Frontex Situation Centre: Multipurpose Aerial Surveillance' (2018) <https://op.europa.eu/en/publication-detail/-/publication/b96286e0-1aa8-11e8-ac73-01aa75ed71a1>.

106 Violeta Moreno-Lax, Jennifer Allsopp, Lilian Tsourdi and Philippe De Bruycker, 'The EU Approach on Migration in the Mediterranean' (European Parliament, European Parliament's Committee on Civil Liberties, Justice and Home Affairs 2021) <https://www.europarl.europa.eu/RegData/etudes/STUD/2021/694413/IPOL_STU(2021)694413_EN.pdf> 77.

107 See inter alia, Human Rights Watch, 'EU: Frontex Complicit in Abuse in Libya' (12 December 2022) <https://www.hrw.org/news/2022/12/12/eu-frontex-complicit-abuse-libya>; European Court of Auditors, 'Frontex's Support to External Border Management: Not Sufficiently Effective to Date' (2021) <https://www.eca.europa.eu/Lists/ECADocuments/SR21_08/SR_Frontex_EN.pdf>; OLAF European Anti Fraud Office, Final Report <https://cdn.prod.www.spiegel.de/media/00847a5e-8604-45dc-a0fe-37d920056673/Directorate_A_redacted-2.pdf>; Front-LEX, 'For the First Time, a "Pushback" Victim Sues Frontex for Half a Million Euro' (2024) <https://www.front-lex.eu/alaa-hamoudi>. Case T-600/21, *WS and Others v Frontex*, ECLI:EU:T:2023:492 also demonstrates that Frontex is being challenged over the legality of its actions, albeit in the slightly different context of deportation.

108 European Ombudsman, 'Decision on How the European Border and Coast Guard Agency (Frontex) Complies with Its Fundamental Rights Obligations with Regard to Search and Rescue in the Context of Its Maritime Surveillance Activities, in Particular the Adriana

means of control by Member States operating under Frontex jointly with the LCGN indicates a progressive abstention from SAR activities and a growing disconnect between border technologies, rescue obligations and human rights pertinent in this context.

Even more worrisome appears to be the 'cash for migrants' deal between EU and Tunisia that was signed on 16 July 2023, considering the escalation of racial and xenophobic violence and Tunisia's autocratic shift in 2021.[109] The Memorandum of Understanding (Tunisia MoU) focuses on building a 'strategic and global partnership', where the EU is set to allocate approximately 100 million to Tunisia to implement migration control measures, in addition to a 900 million macro-financial assistance package that encompasses various areas such as trade, investment and energy cooperation.[110] In exchange, Tunisia has committed to cooperating on border security and facilitating the return of its citizens who have irregularly arrived in Europe. The goals behind this strategic deal build on the aforementioned 2014 Mobility Partnership between the EU and the then-democratic government.[111] The policy implications of this newly established cooperation are yet to unfold, though it is crystal clear that the EU perennially professes symbolic politics through informal, soft law policy tools at the expense of accountability and transparency.

Reflecting on the deal, Annick Pijnenburg argued that it is improbable that it will achieve its stated objective of saving lives at sea and fighting against human smuggling and trafficking.[112] This is so because efforts to halt irregular migration flows from one route are likely to push migrants into undertaking even more perilous journeys in the Mediterranean as mentioned earlier. Hence, to avoid the risks associated with Libya, migrants have been driven to take other transit routes in North Africa. Arguably the impetus behind drawing this deal stems from the fact that Tunisia is now widely used as the primary departure point by a significant number of migrants. In fact, between January 2020 and October 2021, irregular migration from Tunisia has risen to the highest point in a decade, with more than 69,000 interceptions conducted

Shipwreck' (26 February 2024) OI/3/2023/MHZ <https://www.ombudsman.europa.eu/fr/decision/en/182665#_ftn24>.

109 Eleonora Vasques, 'EU to Pay Tunisia €785m in 2023 as Part of "Cash for Migrants" deal' (17 July 2023) <https://www.euractiv.com/section/global-europe/news/eu-to-pay-tunisia-e675m-in-2023-as-part-of-cash-for-migrants-deal>.

110 Jones Hayden, 'EU Finalizes Migrant Deal with Tunisia' (16 July 2013, Politico) <https://www.politico.eu/article/eu-migration-deal-tunisia-migrants-africa-european-commission/>.

111 Katharina Natter, 'Reinventing a Broken Wheel: What the EU-Tunisia Deal Reveals Over Europe's Migration Cooperation' (Verfassungsblog, 5 September 2023) <https://verfassungsblog.de/reinventing-a-broken-wheel/>.

112 Annick Pijnenburg, 'Team Europe's Deal: What's Wrong with the EU-Tunisia Migration Agreement?' (Verfassungsblog, 21 August 2023) <https://verfassungsblog.de/team-europes-deal/>.

by the Tunisian and Italian authorities during that time.[113] Evidently, the practice of outsourcing border control has become the linchpin of the European response to managing migration flows, reflecting the Union's concerted efforts to keep out people seeking protection.

5. State Strategies in the Central Mediterranean

The most prominent example of how border control practices have been pushed outwards to third countries – Libya in this case – can be traced in Italy's strategy.[114] Going back to the time just a few months before the launch of Operation *Sophia*, the Italian government established the Operation *Mare Sicuro*, which uses its military vessels and provides communication and technical support to the LCGN.[115] The operation's primary goals are grounded in protecting national interests at sea, 'the overall safety of navigation' and 'controlling and countering illegal immigration'.[116] Moreover, buttressing the above entanglement of the securitization paradigm, the most profound example is the reactivation of the condemned bilateral agreement with Libya signed in 2008, designed to export migration control and deter the arrival of 'irregular' migrants altogether.

Currently, this kind of assistance occurs on the basis of the Memorandum of Understanding (MoU) agreed between Italy and Libya in February 2017, which acts as a continuation of what was already the case ten years ago. However, this time, it goes a step further, as Italy is no longer at the forefront of migrant interceptions and push-backs, since the LCGN has undertaken those tasks.[117] Evidently, the obligation referred to in Articles 1 and 2 echoes the first

113 Matt Herbert, 'Losing Hope: Why Tunisians Are Leading the Surge in Irregular Migration to Europe' (Global Initiative, January 2022) 5 <https://globalinitiative.net/wp-content/uploads/2022/01/GI-TOC-Losing-Hope_Tunisia-Report-2021.pdf>.

114 It is worth noting at this stage that Italy is not the only Member State that adopted such tactics, as others such as Malta, France and Netherlands have provided boats that have been used to deport and detain migrants. See for instance, The National, 'Malta Denounced after Assisting Libyan Coastguard to Intercept Migrant Boat' (2019) <https://www.thenational.ae/world/europe/malta-denounced-after-assisting-libyan-coastguard-to-intercept-migrant-boat-1.856853>; Bénédicte Jeannerod, 'France Gifts Boats to Abusive Libyan Coast Guard' (Human Rights Watch, 13 March 2019) <https://www.hrw.org/news/2019/03/13/france-gifts-boats-abusive-libyan-coast-guard>.

115 Communication to the ICC (n 37) 164; Council of the European Union, *Council Decision (CFSP) 2015/778 on 18 May 2015 on a European Union Military Operation in the Southern Central Mediterranean (EUNVAFOR MED)* <https://eur-lex.europa.eu/legal-content/EN/TXT/?uri=CELEX%3A32015D0778>.

116 Amnesty International, 'A Perfect Storm: The Failure of the European Policies in the Central Mediterranean' (2017) <https://www.amnesty.ie/wp-content/uploads/2017/07/A-Perfect-Storm-EUR0366552017.pdf>.

117 'Memorandum of understanding on cooperation in the fields of development, the fight against illegal immigration, human trafficking and fuel smuggling and on reinforcing the security of borders between the State of Libya and the Italian Republic' (2017) <https://

Treaty on Friendship as it outlines that the purpose is to resume the cooperation between Italy and Libya on irregular migration and security according to their past agreement.[118]

The specified basis of the MoU is the regulation of migration flows – the fight against irregular migration – by providing boats, training and supporting the Libyan personnel, as well as the development of the region through finance and technology programs. As such, the memorandum's salient features manifestly serve to not only control migration by sea in the Central Mediterranean, but ultimately to block exits from Libya to cut back on migratory flows to Italy. The policy itself seems to result in a clear denial of the right to leave a country, including one's own, and to seek and enjoy asylum rights that are enshrined in EU law as much as international law and which European States must respect and protect.[119]

Paradoxically, 'tackling the root causes' translates into assisting undemocratic systems in controlling their borders and preventing their citizens from leaving as well as funding schemes which are used in 'feeding the border industry'.[120] In this regard, the cooperation has received a number of serious criticisms from human rights groups, not least because of the 'considerable concerns about the Libyan coastguard's practices, chain of command, accountability and operational skills and methods'.[121] The United Nations' Human Rights chief Al Hussein has expressed his concern in this respect, that 'the European Union's policy of assisting the Libyan Coast Guard to intercept and return migrants in the Mediterranean (is) inhuman' and that 'the increasing interventions of the EU and its Member States have done nothing so far to reduce the level of abuses suffered by migrants'.[122]

Nonetheless, the above policy was endorsed immediately by the European Council in its Malta declaration in February 2017, supporting Italy's attempts to cooperate once more with Libya and highlighting the importance of the

---

eumigrationlawblog.eu/wp-content/uploads/2017/10/MEMORANDUM_translation_finalversion.doc.pdf>.

118 Anja Palm, 'The Italy–Libya Memorandum of Understanding: The Baseline of a Policy Approach Aimed at Closing All Doors to Europe?' (EU Migration Law Blog, 2017) <http://eumigrationlawblog.eu/the-italy-libya-memorandum-of-understanding-the-baseline-of-a-policy-approach-aimed-at-closing-all-doors-to-europe/>.

119 For a thorough discussion on the right to leave, see, Violeta Moreno-Lax, *Accessing Asylum in Europe: Extraterritorial Border Controls and Refugee Rights under EU Law* (Oxford Studies in European Union Law, OUP 2017); See also, Communication to the HRC, *SDG v Italy*, in particular para 96 <https://c5e65ece-003b-4d73-aa76-854664da4e33.filesusr.com/ugd/14ee1a_e0466b7845f941098730900ede1b51cb.pdf>.

120 Paolo Cuttitta and Tamar Last (eds), *Border Deaths: Causes, Dynamics and Consequences of Migration Related Mortality* (Amsterdam University Press 2020) 15.

121 Amnesty International, 'Europe: A Perfect Storm: The Failure of European Policies in the Central Mediterranean' (6 July 2017) 23 <https://www.amnesty.org/download/Documents/EUR0366552017ENGLISH.PDF>.

122 OHCHR, 'UN Human Rights Chief: Suffering of Migrants in Libya Outrage to Conscience of Humanity' (14 November 2017) <https://www.ohchr.org/en/NewsEvents/Pages/DisplayNews.aspx?NewsID=22393>.

training and support to the LCGN in order to boost operational action to close down the Central Mediterranean corridor.[123] Notably, in 2018 Libya declared its SAR zone, with Italy handing over the responsibility for sea rescue to Libya.[124] These practices, along with the Frontex operations and EU's naval Operation *Sophia,* demonstrate a progressive delegation of border management and the final handing over of SAR activities to the LCGN in 2017 – even if there were other better-equipped vessels, including Italian navy vessels closer to undertake a SAR[125] – making Libya the principal State actor in the Mediterranean apparatus (this issue will be further examined in the last chapter.)

Amidst the tantamount evidence surrounding the situation in Libya and the LCGN's involvement in fundamental rights violations, the Italian government and the Union appear to cynically manipulate the law, insofar as they engage in a cat-and-mouse game of *refoulement* with the loaning of border guards who will pull-back and keep migrants trapped within Libya.[126] In particular, from 2016 to 2022 the EU and Italy acquiesced to the interception and pull-back of more than 82,000 individuals by the LCGN,[127] with 24,684 being intercepted at sea by the LCGN in 2022 alone, whilst that year marked the highest death toll recorded since 2016, with 6,876 documented deaths/missing persons.[128] Even though the situation is well-documented – that is, migrants returned to Libya risk maltreatment, arbitrary arrest and detention and other serious harms – the practices currently witnessed are a metamorphosis of what where Italian *push-backs* into Libyan *pull-backs* and *aerial refoulement.* For instance, coastal State authorities increasingly rely on information gathered from aerial assets, such as unmanned aerial vehicles (UAV, commonly known as drones), to identify the location of a migrant boat; this information is then shared with third-country authorities in order to facilitate their intervention (or, interception) and, ultimately, to deflect boats from reaching the European State's territory. This tactic of outsourcing or 'buck passing'

123 Human Rights Watch, 'EU: Shifting Rescue to Libya Risks Lives' (19 June 2017) <https://www.hrw.org/news/2017/06/19/eu-shifting-rescue-libya-risks-lives>.

124 Bernd Riegert, 'Libya Takes Over from Italy on Rescuing Shipwrecked Migrants' (DW, 5 July 2018) <https://p.dw.com/p/30ue2>.

125 Matteo Villa, 'Outsourcing European Border Control: Recent Trends in Departure, Deaths and Search and Rescue Activities in the Central Mediterranean' (Border Criminologies, 11 September 2018) <https://www.law.ox.ac.uk/research-subject-groups/centre-criminology/centreborder-criminologies/blog/2018/09/outsourcing>.

126 Communication to the ICC (n 37) 18.

127 Ibid 88.

128 Data from IOM, 'Missing Migrants Project Global Data Overview, January 2022-December 2022' (21 June 2023) <https://missingmigrants.iom.int/sites/g/files/tmzbdl601/files/publication/file/MMP%20global%20data%20briefing%202022.pdf>. See also, *inter alia*, Amnesty International, 'Libya/EU: Conditions Remain 'Hellish' as EU Marks 5 Years of Cooperation Agreements' (2022) <https://www.amnesty.org/en/latest/news/2022/01/libya-eu-conditions-remain-hellish-as-eu-marks-5-years-of-cooperation-agreements/>.

of responsibilities[129] has become prevalent as it allows States to avoid direct involvement with the migrants' boats and the associated obligation to rescue together with disembarkation duties that will bring the individuals concerned under the State's *de facto* and *de jure* jurisdiction.

At the time of the writing of this book, a case similar to the *Hirsi* case was brought before the ECtHR by a consortium of public interest lawyers and NGOs, which is specifically aimed at invoking Italy's responsibility for human rights violations due to its indirect support for LCGN pull-backs.[130] This has led some scholars to speculate about the possibility of a '*Hirsi* 2.0' before the Court.[131] The case will be revisited in the closing chapter when contextualizing the extraterritorial reach of human rights obligations and the normative considerations of actors involved in SAR activities. Hence, as the case is still pending, it remains to be seen whether practices of outsourcing border management while effectively hindering the exit of migrants from third countries and facilitating pull-backs will result in a violation of the *non-refoulement* obligation, the right to leave as well as the right to life. The logic behind extending these obligations in such scenario is that 'a state cannot be allowed to perpetrate, on the territory of another state, human rights violations that are not permitted on its own territory'.[132]

6. Private Actors

Lastly, the private sector has a crucial role to play not only in saving lives at sea but also in the dynamics shaping border management. This is especially true insofar as private actors, like NGOs undertaking proactive SAR operations and merchant vessels, come into an apparent direct conflict with the policies of the EU in its attempt to completely shut down the Mediterranean migration corridor. In response to the end of *Mare Nostrum*, many humanitarian organizations started conducting SAR activities – with the first one being the Migrant Offshore Aid Station (MOAS) in 2014 – yet NGO activity has increasingly attracted the hostility of both the Libyan authorities and EU

129 Douglas Guilfoyle, 'Transnational Crime and the Rule of Law at Sea: Responses to Maritime Migration and Piracy Compared' in Violeta Moreno-Lax and Efthymios Papastavridis (eds), *'Boat Refugees' and Migrants at Sea: A Comprehensive Approach: Integrating Maritime Security with Human Rights*, (Vol. 7, International Refugee Law Series, Brill Nijhoff 2016) 174.

130 *S.S. and Others v Italy*, App no 21660/18 (ECtHR, communicated on 26 June 2019) <http://hudoc.echr.coe.int/eng?i=001-194748>.

131 See Pijnenburg (n 52) 396.

132 CCPR, *Lopez Burgos v Uruguay*, Communication No 52/1979, 29 July 1981, UN Doc CCPR/13/D/52/1979, par 12.3; See, also, James Hathaway and Thomas Gammeltoft-Hansen, 'Non-Refoulement in a World of Cooperative Deterrence' (2015) 53 Columbia Journal of Transnational Law 235.

Member States.[133] In particular, the Italian government seeking to be at the forefront of regulating migration movements has waged a war against NGOs; for example, in 2018 alone, approximately 89 people were put under investigation and/or prosecuted for their engagement with SAR as opposed to 20 prosecutions in 2017.[134] After examination by the Italian Senate in 2017, the allegations were dismissed as it found that NGOs are not directly or indirectly involved in migrant smuggling.[135] More recently, on 4 June 2023, the NGO Sea Eye 4 was detained in the Italian port of Ortona after rescuing 32 people because it had carried out a second rescue before disembarking those rescued during the first response, which Italy claims to be in breach of the dubious Italian decree passed on 2 January 2023. In this vein, the decree precludes NGO vessels from carrying out more than one rescue at a time, resulting in a sharp reduction in rescue capacities in the Central Mediterranean *vis-à-vis* contradicting the international framework of SAR which requires that shipmaster's provide immediate assistance to persons in distress at sea.[136]

As was anticipated by these hostile stratagems, the number of NGOs operating in the Mediterranean, particularly the Central Mediterranean at a distance of about 20 to 50 kilometers from Libya's coast, dropped off significantly between 2015–2016 and 2017–2018, with less than three NGOs remaining in the Mediterranean in the first eight months of 2018, and with all having ceased operations by the end of the year. Given the legal vacuum that has been created by the withdrawal and suppression of SAR, the increased risk to the life of migrants crossing the Mediterranean Sea could have been easily forecasted. Indeed, there is a staggering increase in mortality rates in the Central Mediterranean route which suggests a link with the associated decrease in SAR activity, as there were 21 dead/missing per 1000 attempted sea crossings in 2015, whereas in 2019, there were 68 dead/missing per 1000 attempted sea crossings.[137] The stark contrast between the increased risk of dying at sea relative to the lower number of people trying to make such crossing as a result

133 See Paolo Cuttitta, 'Pushing Migrants Back to Libya, Persecuting Rescue NGOs: The End of the Humanitarian Turn (Part I)' (BorderCriminologies, 18 April 2018) <https://www.law.ox.ac.uk/research-subject-groups/centre-criminology/centreborder-criminologies/blog/2018/04/pushing-migrants>.

134 Communication to the ICC (n 37) 56; See also Piper French, 'Rescue a Refugee: Get Charged with Trafficking?' (The New Republic, 5 March 2019) <https://newrepublic.com/article/153216/rescue-refugee-get-charged-trafficking>.

135 FRA, 'Fundamental Rights Considerations: NGO Ships Involved in Search and Rescue in the Mediterranean and Criminal Investigations – Tables and Figures' (1 October 2018) <https://fra.europa.eu/en/publication/2018/ngos-sar-activities>.

136 Freija Jeppesen, 'New Decree Obstructs Lifesaving Rescue Efforts at Sea and Will Cause More Deaths' (5 January 2023) <https://reliefweb.int/report/italy/new-decree-obstructs-lifesaving-rescue-efforts-sea-and-will-cause-more-deaths>.

137 Data was collected from the IOM's Missing Migrant Project. It was then analyzed to get the mortality rates by comparing the number of attempted crossings yearly with the actual number of dead/missing persons.

of the Union's policies is at the very least paradoxical, as one might legitimately expect to see that the fewer people making such crossings will result in fewer fatalities. Nonetheless, these figures represent a five-fold increase in the mortality rates, just five years after significant policy measures and expenditure aimed at 'tackling' the crisis. Ironically, the EU declared the 'migration crisis' as over in 2019 ahead of the European Parliament elections, even though it was the year with the highest probability of dying at sea. At this juncture, Mann, when asked about whether there is a direct link between the 'pull-back' of migrants intercepted in the Mediterranean and the increased number of migrant deaths, has expressed the view that EU policy in this regard can be characterized as 'killing by omission',[138] perhaps itself giving rise to a violation of the right to life.

In this regard, NGOs – which from a human rights perspective could be said to be seeking to uphold human rights rather than being the perpetrators of rights violations – have influenced border management in the sense that the humanitarian assistance provided by way of SAR services to individuals in distress fuelled more robust border measures by State governments. In contrast to Frontex, the operational priority of NGOs has been to provide assistance to migrants in distress at sea and to fill the vacuum of protection created by the scaling back of state-led SAR missions.

With the reduction in NGO activity, it seems that the burden of SAR operations has increasingly fallen on the shipping industry in order to fill the void. Although shipmasters of commercial vessels are well aware of the long-established moral and legal obligation to rescue people in distress at sea, it is likely that commercial pressures and manifestly ill-equipped vessels will undermine their ability and willingness to do so.[139] Worryingly, commercial vessels who have been frequently called to perform rescues in the Mediterranean have recurrently received detrimental instructions and pressures from State authorities that have resulted, at times, in private *refoulement* practice.[140] Conversely, the shipmasters are inevitably caught between

138 Grant (n 15) 52; All Africa, 'Africa: International Law Experts Warn Europe's "Pull-Back" of Migrants is Illegal – Part 2' <https://allafrica.com/stories/201809170625.html>; Grant (n 15) 52.

139 As a matter of fact the implications on merchant vessels in contrast to humanitarian NGOs when conducting SAR activities are far more, as SAR was predominantly an immediate response to an accident and should not be considered a policy solution, for instance: 1) the number of people rescued may exceed the total ship's capacity rendering it unseaworthy; 2) the danger encountered regarding the well-being of the crew and the additional persons taken on board, that may increase the risk of loss of life; 3) possible damage to the vessel during the actual rescue; 4) detrimental commercial costs incurred as a result of deviation from the ship's original route (as just one example here, in the *Tampa* case, the tanker spent eight days on this operation; see, *Ruddock v Vadarlis* [The *Tampa* case] [2001] FCA 1329; 110 RCR 491; 183 ALR 1); and 5) not being properly equipped and fit for large-scale rescues that may in turn result in more tragedies.

140 *SDG v Italy* (n 119).

their law of the sea obligations and an ever-more populist political climate characterized by a moral panic at the prospect of migrant arrivals.[141] Insofar as commercial vessels are concerned, given the hostile reception that they are likely to face in attempting to disembark migrants post-rescue, it is difficult to fathom how shipmasters can be actively incentivized to play not only a more proactive role but also one that complies with international human rights standards. As a result, the fulfilment of this duty has become little more than a fool's hope for the thousands of migrants who choose to face the risk of death or severe injury for the chance to escape their homeland and start a new life overseas. To be clear, part of the difficulties faced by the merchant shipping industry stems from the critical complexities of the legal framework surrounding the duty to rescue at sea, the gaps and deficiencies of its operational framework and the absence of clear standards when conducting rescues.[142] In this vein, the next chapter will examine in detail these complexities surrounding the international law of the sea framework providing for the SAR system.

Another private actor which in the last few years has been increasingly involved in ensuring that States are alerted about possible distress incidents, albeit not executing rescues directly, are NGO activists like 'WatchTheMed Alarm Phone' which created a hotline for people in distress at sea. This marks a notable shift in the actors handling distress calls in the Mediterranean region. This follows from the fact that migrants in distress most often will place a distress call to WatchTheMed Alarm Phone instead of entrusting their emergency status to coastal States who have largely failed to effectively assist them and assess their situation at sea.[143] In turn, the organization informs the relevant coast guard according to the SAR zone of the distress incident, and if such information is not acted upon, they inform NGOs operating in the area and public media to put pressure on the rescue services. In this way, the NGO is also in a critical position to document rights violations, by mapping their location amidst the mounting phenomena of abandonment at sea that resulted in shipwrecks.

141 Amanda Rohloff and Sarah Wright, 'Moral Panic and Social Theory: Beyond the Heuristic' (2020) 58(3) Current Sociology 403 <https://journals.sagepub.com/doi/10.1177/0011392110364039>.

142 For discussion see both Kristof Gombeer, 'Human Rights Adrift? Enabling the Disembarkation of Migrants to a Place of Safety in the Mediterranean' (2017) 10 Irish Yearbook of International Law 23–55; and Ainhoa Campàs Velasco, 'The International Convention on Maritime Search and Rescue: Legal Mechanisms of Responsibility Sharing and Cooperation in the Context of Sea Migration?' (Symposium, 2015) 10 Irish Yearbook of International Law 57.

143 AlarmPhone, 'Continuous Landings, Increasing Violence and Deaths at Sea' (31 July 2023) <https://alarmphone.org/en/2023/07/31/continuous-landings-increasing-violence-and-deaths-at-sea/>.

7. Conclusion

The analysis in this chapter showcased the enduring challenges that lie ahead, the epicenter of which lies between the conflicting arenas of upholding maritime and human rights principles, *videlicet,* protecting human life versus protecting 'European' borders and States' territorial integrity. It was originally hoped that after the *Hirsi* judgment, States would no longer breach the principle of *non-refoulement* on the high seas when they exercise *de jure* and *de facto* control over individuals and accordingly would comply with their human rights obligations. However, as evidenced, European States acting alone or under EU coordination found alternative ways to divest themselves from humanitarian imperatives and achieve the principal aim of disrupting migration flows by 'indirectly' turning migrants back.

The EU and its Member States have progressively redefined their border policies in a manner that not only shows nearly complete disengagement with rescue obligations but also involves delegating SAR activities and border management to third countries in North Africa, where human rights abuses are a concern. In this way, Libya plays a fundamental part in the default European response of controlling migration flows, which lacks any proper evaluation of its humanitarian consequences. However, this shift in operational emphasis since 2014 and the adoption of a more stringent regulation – pre-entry measures – have actually made the humanitarian plight of migrants far worse. This has resulted in a pressing need to revisit the international legal frameworks surrounding the protection of human life at sea. The following two chapters take up this challenge.

2 The Duty to Render Assistance to Persons in Distress at Sea and the Search and Rescue Regime Under International Law of the Sea

The complex character of the phenomenon of irregular migration by sea exposed the fragmentation of international law whereby the imperative of saving lives at sea is undergoing systematic obstruction in the Mediterranean region. This was evidenced by a plethora of alarming reports of deaths and human rights abuses of migrants intercepted by and returned to Libya. The ongoing humanitarian crisis at sea raises difficult questions regarding the normative scope of the duty to render assistance at sea and the obligations that follow. Evidently, in the name of controlling 'illegal' migration and combatting the smuggling business, European States seem to be increasingly sidestepping their international law duties without any legal consequence.

Against this backdrop, the duty to render assistance at sea or, simplified, the duty to rescue,[1] is a well-established moral norm and a core principle of customary international law, now codified in the United Nations Convention on the Law of the Sea (UNCLOS).[2] Certainly, when formulating this duty, the drafters of UNCLOS did not have in mind the massive migration movements we are witnessing today. Instead, this duty was predominantly thought to safeguard the safety of life at sea against the inherent dangers of the sea *in those instances* where something has gone 'wrong'. As such, the duty was meant to be an immediate response to an *accident*, such as the R.M.S. *Titanic*[3] incident. Though this might be an extraordinary example to use, it nonetheless highlights that the duty was not meant to act as a policy response to irregular

1 In this book, I use the terms 'duty to rescue' and 'duty to render assistance at sea' interchangeably as rescue operations always involve the rendering of assistance; these terms arguably carry the same meaning and have been so used in the literature.

2 United Nations Convention on the Law of the Sea (adopted 10 December 1982, entered into force 16 November 1994) 1833 UNTS 397 (UNCLOS). As of September 2023, UNCLOS has 170 State Parties. See Division for Ocean Affairs and the Law of the Sea <https://www.un.org/Depts/los/reference_files/chronological_lists_of_ratifications.htm>.

3 Prior to UNCLOS, the first Convention for the Safety of Life at Sea (SOLAS) was adopted in response to the *Titanic* incident, which resulted in the loss of over 1,500 lives; Convention for the Safety of Life at Sea (adopted 20 January 1914).

DOI: 10.4324/9781003568537-3

migration by sea.[4] Consequently, distress situations have become regularized in the maritime space where, regrettably, thousands of migrants perish each year.

Shipmasters are frequently called upon to respond to distress situations at sea when they are in close proximity to the distress scene and can proceed to undertake a rescue operation.[5] Yet, the duty of the shipmaster does not end upon successfully rescuing people and taking them safely aboard; the shipmaster will still need to disembark those rescued at a 'place of safety'. It is in this light that the complexities in maritime governance arise, as there is an increasingly hostile attitude from European governments towards letting new people in, as expounded in the earlier chapter. Clearly, this also raises serious implications for the shipping industry, as unnecessary time delays due to disembarkation disputes might result, for instance, in the breach of a sea carriage contract or the damage of perishable goods.[6] These logistical challenges might seem inconsequential when compared to the cost of preventing a human tragedy. Nonetheless, in a protracted humanitarian crisis in the Mediterranean Sea, where governments fail to cooperate and adopt a humanitarian response to migration, these are implications that can (and do) disincentivize the shipmasters of commercial vessels from conducting rescues to save people *a priori*.

With this background in mind, this chapter reviews the international law of the sea framework to examine the relevant instruments that afford protection to human life in danger of being lost at sea. The aim in this chapter is to unpack the question as to *why* the duty to render assistance at sea and the international search and rescue (SAR) system suffer from noncompliance and enforcement – and lives imperilled can be lost – especially when facing large-scale migration flows in Mediterranean routes. A closer look at contemporary incidents in the Mediterranean region will prompt questions of international responsibility as well as whether it is time for amendments to the legal framework governing SAR. Such amendments, I argue, could bring greater legal certainty to the normative factors that will activate the duty to render assistance at sea as well as the meaning of the concept of 'distress' amidst States' increasing mismanagement of the duty.

4 See also, Ainhoa Campàs Velasco, 'The International Convention on Maritime Search and Rescue: Legal Mechanisms of Responsibility Sharing and Cooperation in the Context of Sea Migration?' (Symposium, 2015) 10 Irish Yearbook of International Law 64.

5 Felicity G Attard, *The Duty of the Shipmaster to Render Assistance at Sea under International Law* (Queen Mary Studies in International Law, Brill Nijhoff 2020) 6.

6 Rick Button, 'International Law and Search and Rescue' in Jörg Schildknecht, Rebecca Dickey, Martin Fink and Lisa Ferris (eds), *Operational Law in International Straits and Current Maritime Security Challenges* (Springer 2018) 119; For example in 2016 alone, 381 merchant vessels were diverted from their routes and 121 vessels were involved in the rescue of 13; See, for more details, Jean-Pierre Gauci, When Private Vessels Rescue Migrants and Refugees: A Mapping of Legal Considerations' (British Institute of International and Comparative Law, 24 November 2020) <https://www.biicl.org/documents/124_private_vessels_research.pdf>.

1. UNCLOS – Codifying a Cardinal Principle of the Law of the Sea

The law of the sea imposes a long-established duty to rescue persons in distress at sea, which functions as one of the most important tools in ensuring safety of life at sea.[7] Historically speaking, providing assistance to persons in distress at sea was a traditional hallmark of maritime law, arising out of a moral obligation for the purposes of maintaining the safety of life at sea given the inherent dangers of the oceans. Bernard Oxman has argued that 'a universal duty to rescue at sea has existed since time immemorial'.[8] This was first evidenced in the 19th century in the case of *Scaramanga v Stamp*,[9] where the English Court of Appeal held that the purpose of saving life is a justifiable deviation in order to save those aboard a vessel whose lives are in peril.

The customary duty to render assistance to persons in distress at sea, apart from being a long-standing tradition, has been crystalized subsequently in a number of international legal instruments as a practical response to the dangers at sea, including the 1958 Geneva Convention on the High Seas,[10] UNCLOS and the International Maritime Organization's (IMO)[11] Conventions: the International Convention for the Safety of Life at Sea 1974 (SOLAS),[12] the International Convention on Maritime Search and Rescue 1979 (SAR Convention)[13] and the International Convention on Salvage 1989 (Salvage).[14] A number of commentators have confirmed that these five

7 It has been described as 'one of the most ancient and fundamental features of the law of the sea'. See, Emer de Vattel, *The Law of Nations: Or, Principles of the Law of Nature, Applied to the Conduct and Affairs of Nations and Sovereigns, with Three Early Essays on the Origin and Nature of Natural Law and on Luxury* (Richard Whatmore and Béla Kapossy eds, Indianapolis: Liberty Fund 2008) 170.

8 Bernard Oxman, 'Human Rights and the United Nations Convention on the Law of the Sea' (1997) 36 Columbia Journal of Transnational Law 415.

9 *Scaramanga v Stamp* (1880) 5 C.P.D. 295.

10 Convention on the High Seas 1958, in force April 29th, 1968. 450 U.N.T.S., Art 12(1).

11 The IMO was established in 1958 as the 'Specialized Agency of the United Nations' to improve the safety and security of international shipping and to prevent marine pollution from ships. Under UNCLOS, the IMO has a mandate as a global legislative entity to further regulate maritime issues on the basis of many of its provisions. It has a wide acceptance with 170 contracting States representing all regions of the world. See <http://www.imo.org/en/mediacentre/secretarygeneral/speechesbythesecretarygeneral/pages/itlos.aspx>; Explicit reference is also made in UNCLOS, Art 2 of Annex VIII.

12 International Convention for the Safety of Life at Sea, 1974, as amended, 1184 UNTS 278 (adopted 1 November 1974, entered into force 25 May 1980). As of September 2023, SOLAS has 168 Contracting States <https://wwwcdn.imo.org/localresources/en/About/Conventions/StatusOfConventions/Status%202023.pdf>.

13 International Convention on Maritime Search and Rescue, 1979, with annexes, 1405 UNTS 97 (adopted 27 April 1979, entered into force 22 June 1985). As of September 2023, SAR Convention has 114 Contracting States <https://wwwcdn.imo.org/localresources/en/About/Conventions/StatusOfConventions/Status%202023.pdf>.

14 International Convention on Salvage, 1989, UKTS 93 322. As of September 2023, Salvage has 77 Contracting States <https://wwwcdn.imo.org/localresources/en/About/Conventions/StatusOfConventions/Status%202023.pdf>.

Conventions provide an 'expression to the general tradition and practice of all seafarers and of maritime law regarding the rendering of assistance to persons or ships in distress at sea, and the elementary conditions of humanity'.[15]

It must be stressed that UNCLOS is a 'framework convention' that provides, overall, the most fundamental source of international law of the sea that purports to regulate every single action 'on, in, under, and over the sea'.[16] Given its general legal framework, many of the provisions can be implemented, filled in and rounded out only through specific operative regulations in other international agreements and customary international law.[17] The duty to render assistance at sea is one of those provisions. Insofar as UNCLOS is not susceptible to amendments, it is of paramount importance to look at the 'competent international organization' referenced in UNCLOS, which is the IMO.[18] The IMO's role is preeminent in laying down implementation instruments and complementary rules for the fulfilment of rights and duties of States that must be exercised in the different maritime zones. As such, the general basis of the duty to rescue in UNCLOS becomes operational by the support of the international harmonized framework for maritime SAR laid down in the auspices of the IMO instruments.[19]

1.1 The Scope and Application of the Duty

Turning to a close examination of the scope and application of the duty to render assistance at sea, Article 98 of UNCLOS, paragraph 1 provides:

> Every State shall require the master of a ship flying its flag, in so far as he can do so without serious danger to the ship, the crew or the passengers:
>
> (a) to render assistance to any person found at sea in danger of being lost;
> (b) to proceed with all possible speed to the rescue of persons in distress, if informed of their need of assistance, in so far as such action may reasonably be expected of him;

15 Myron H Nordquist (ed), *The United Nations Convention on the Law of the Sea 1982: A Commentary*, Vol VII (The Hague: Martinus Nijhoff 2011) 193. See also Sandford Silverburg, *International Law: Contemporary Issues and Future Developments* (Routledge 2018).

16 Robin R Churchill, 'The 1982 United Nations Convention on the Law of the Sea' in Donald R Rothwell, Alex G Oude Elferink, Karen N Scott and Tim Stephens (eds), *The Oxford Handbook of the Law of the Sea* (OUP 2015) 24.

17 Robert Beckman and Zhen Sun, 'The Relationship between UNCLOS and IMO Instruments' (2017) 2(2) Asia-Pacific Journal of Ocean Law and Policy 201.

18 Secretary-General of the International Maritime Organization, 'The United Nations Convention on the Law of the Sea and the International Maritime Organization Address by Mr. Koji Sekimizu' (18 March 2014) <https://www.imo.org/en/MediaCentre/SecretaryGeneral/Pages/itlos.aspx>.

19 Ilker Basaran, 'The Evolution of the International Maritime Organization's Role in Shipping' (2016) 47(1) Journal of Maritime Law and Commerce 101.

(c) after a collision, to render assistance to the other ship, its crew and its passengers and, where possible, to inform the other ship of the name of his own ship, its port of registry and the nearest port at which it will call.[20]

Whilst the above normative framework clearly establishes the duty to render assistance to persons in distress at sea, there are evident ambiguities in the treaty rules that impinge on its practical implementation. On the face of Article 98(1), an obligation is imposed upon the flag States to ensure that the shipmaster of a vessel flying its flag renders assistance to persons whose life is in danger of being lost at sea.[21] Whilst the provision provides that the duty bearers, *a priori*, are States, it is nonetheless understood that the duty applies to both States and shipmasters alike, including private commercial vessels, military and other state-owned vessels. This is supported by the subsequent international maritime law treaties, such as the Salvage Convention, which makes reference under Article 10 to the duty to render assistance to persons in danger of being lost at sea:

1. Every master is bound, so far as he can do so without serious danger to his vessel and persons thereon, to render assistance to any person in danger of being lost at sea.
2. The States Parties shall adopt the measures necessary to enforce the duty set out in paragraph 1.

Hence, it is supported that the duty-bearers are the masters of a ship,[22] which are bound to abide by this duty by reason of the flag State that must itself comply with the duty to render assistance at sea as part of its international obligations. Evidently, there is a due diligence requirement in the above provision that requires the flag State to take reasonable measures to prevent shipmasters flying its flag from failing to assist persons in distress at sea. In this regard, the flag State duty is generally executed through national legislation, for instance, the imposition of criminal sanctions against shipmasters who fail to provide such assistance.[23]

In taking a closer reading of the above provision with reference to the shipmaster's duty, it appears that there is a subjective element present, in particular where it states 'in so far as he can do so and without serious danger to the

20 UNCLOS, Art 98(1).

21 Irini Papanicolopulu, *International Law and the Protection of People at Sea* (Oxford: OUP 2018) 493.

22 The words 'shipmaster' and 'master of a ship' are used interchangeably herein.

23 Attard (n 5) 44. Flag States should seek to ensure compliance with the relevant rules of rescue. Also, the obligation is often incorporated into the criminal law of flag states. However, Jean-Pierre Gauci has highlighted that in practice, incidents involving failure to rescue persons in distress are unlikely to be prosecuted by flag States or any other State that may exercise some form of jurisdiction. See Gauci (n 6) 10.

ship, crew or passengers'. Arguably, this wording allows shipmasters to decide, based on their subjective judgment, whether to provide assistance or not to persons in distress, according to the circumstances of each incident. While the provision takes on a normative force in imposing such a duty, its enforcement remains elliptical, which is why one can argue that it becomes qualified by the *subjective element* present. Admittedly, the shipmaster's task in guarding human rights in a potential rescue operation is inherently delicate, requiring an evaluation of whether safety concerns of his crew and passengers should take precedence over the saving of lives of persons in distress.

'At Sea' – Maritime Zones

Article 98(1) is spelled out in Part VII of UNCLOS, which refers to the high seas. This is the international area beyond the 200 nautical miles from a State's coastal baseline. In brief, the high seas can be categorized as global commons or as *res communis* and this area is *beyond any national jurisdiction.* It should be noted that the sea covers about 71 percent of the earth's surface and approximately 64 percent is considered as high seas/international waters, which is beyond any State's jurisdiction. Consequently, there is a potential for circumventing international obligations in this space since it is 'too big to police'.[24] Ergo, human rights violations can easily go unnoticed on the high seas, which has been described, quite starkly, as a 'place where anyone can do anything because no one is watching . . . a dystopian place, home to dark inhumanities'.[25] It is in this context that the SAR framework and the duty to render assistance become particularly susceptible to mismanagement.

Whilst situated in this part, it is clear that the duty applies to *all* other maritime zones, notwithstanding the absence of explicit wording to this effect. In particular, Article 58 (2) of UNCLOS, which sets out the rights and duties of other States in the Exclusive Economic Zone (EEZ) (the EEZ extends up to 200 nautical miles from the baseline),[26] confirms that the duty to render

24 Ian Urbina, 'Lawless Ocean: The Link Between Human Rights Abuses and Overfishing' (Yale Environment 360, 20 November 2019) <https://e360.yale.edu/features/lawless-ocean-the-link-between-human-rights-abuses-and-overfishing>.

25 Ian Urbina, 'Stowaways and Crimes Aboard a Scofflaw Ship' *New York Times* (New York, 17 July 2015) <https://www.nytimes.com/2015/07/19/world/stowaway-crime-scofflaw-ship.html>; See also Richard Collins, '"Outlaw Oceans" and "Lawless Sea"? Revisiting the High Seas as a Regulatory Space Under (and After) UNCLOS 1982' in Kristina Siig, Birgit Feldtmann and Fanella MW Billing (eds), *The United Nations Convention on the Law of the Sea: A System of Regulation* (1st edn, Routledge 2023) 26.

26 UNCLOS, Art 57 provides: 'The exclusive economic zone shall not extend beyond 200 nautical miles from the baselines from which the breadth of the territorial sea is measured'; See, Efthymios Papastavridis, 'European Convention of Human Rights and the Law of the Sea: The Strasbourg Court in Unchartered Waters?' in Malgosia Fitzmaurice and Panos Merkouris (eds), *The Interpretation and Application of the European Convention of Human Rights: Legal and Practical Implications* (Queen Mary Studies of International Law 2013).

assistance falls within the rules of international law that apply also to the EEZ. For instance, recalling the events that led to the *Hirsi* case, it can be observed that Italy exercised *de facto* and *de jure* jurisdiction over the migrants' vessel as they intercepted a foreign vessel on the 'high seas' and transferred the persons onto their military ships. It is important to clarify that the interception occurred 35 nautical miles off the Italian coast, which strictly speaking is in the EEZ (and not the high seas), but for the purposes of SAR services and interceptions, the high seas freedoms remain applicable within the EEZ (insofar as they are not incompatible with other provisions on the EEZ regime).[27] Moreover, if we take a look at Article 18(2) of UNCLOS, which refers to the rules applicable to passage in the territorial sea (the area which extends up to 12 nautical miles from a State's baseline),[28] it explicitly provides that passage includes 'stopping and anchoring, but only in so far as the same are incidental to ordinary navigation or are rendered necessary by *force majeure* or distress or for the purpose of rendering assistance to persons, ships or aircraft in danger or distress'.[29] It can therefore be concluded that the text of Article 98 (1) does not place any geographical restrictions to its application and does not explicitly or implicitly limit the scope of the duty, in a way that may jeopardize its effectiveness in rendering assistance to persons in peril.

'Any person'

The obligation found in paragraph 1(a) of Article 98 provides that assistance shall be rendered to 'any person' found at sea. The wording of this provision places no limits or distinctions as to who is to be rescued, regardless of a person's nationality, status or activities performed at sea. This has been illustrated subsequently in SOLAS, as amended, which explicitly spells out the scope of the duty to render assistance. Chapter V, Regulation 33.1 provides:

> The master of a ship at sea which is in a position to be able to provide assistance on receiving information from any source that persons are in distress at sea, is bound to proceed with all speed to their assistance, if possible informing them or the search and rescue service that the ship is doing so. This obligation to provide assistance applies regardless of the nationality or status of such persons or the circumstances in which they are found.[30]

A similar duty is echoed in SAR Convention, Article 2.1.10, and provides, 'Parties shall ensure that assistance be provided to any person in distress at sea. They shall do so regardless of the nationality or status of such a person or the

27 Art 58(2) renders Art 88–115 applicable to the EEZ.
28 UNCLOS, Art 3.
29 UNCLOS, Art 18(2).
30 SOLAS, Ch V, Reg. 33.1.

circumstances in which that person is found'.[31] A conclusion may be inferred from the wording that there is an unqualified application of the duty to assist imperilled individuals, whether these are refugees or migrants or asylum seekers or, even, criminal networks and human smugglers. This is crucial since refugees and migrants trying to reach Europe crossing the Mediterranean Sea, oftentimes referred to as 'boat people',[32] use the same means of travel but for different reasons and are therefore often mixed in the same boat. This phenomenon is widely referred to as *mixed migration by sea* – a hallmark of today's maritime movements. It is irrelevant for this purpose when a person is found at sea whether or not they are entitled to seek protection status upon arrival in Europe or elsewhere.[33]

Consequently, the duty to rescue enjoys an absolute nature in this respect and remains unaffected by a person's nationality. In this light, any subsequent fears, for instance, of a possible presence of criminal networks in such boats shall not hinder the humanitarian objective of saving lives of those in distress at sea. Nonetheless, the right of a coastal State to refuse entry to such boats or rescued individuals distinctly illustrates the clash between protecting State sovereignty and ensuring the protection of human life. This *ipso facto* has given rise to disputes that have yet to be challenged in courts.

'Distress'

One of the most fundamental objects in Article 98(1) which impinges on the scope of the duty, is the term 'distress' found therein. UNCLOS does not itself provide any interpretation, guidance or evaluative criteria as to what the term entails and how to assess an incident. In this respect, interpretative controversies arise when it comes to identifying what constitutes distress and what situations fall under its scope. Yet, the ambiguities that arise can be construed (or not) in a constructive manner. On the one hand, it can be argued that the concept of 'distress' has deliberately been left open to interpretation to facilitate judicial developments and, analogously, to reconcile evolving situations, changing times and attitudes that can be encompassed within the realm of 'distress'. Such flexibility can encompass factual situations and allows shipmasters to evaluate each situation on its own merits, which is still a challenging process of weighing between moral and operational considerations. On the other hand, this flexibility leaves room for insular approaches, which can result

31 SAR Convention, Art 2.1.10.

32 For a thorough discussion, see Efthymios Papastavridis, 'The "Left-to-Die Boat" Incident of March 2011: Questions of International Responsibility Arising from the Failure to Save Refugees at Sea' (2013) Refugee Law Initiative Working Paper No.10 <http://sas-space.sas.ac.uk/4957/1/RLI_Working_Paper_No.10.pdf>.

33 Universal Declaration of Human Rights, UNGA Res 217 A (III) (10 December 1948), Art 14 provides for the right to seek and enjoy asylum.

in rigorous interpretations of the term's scope and, in this way, deviate from the humanitarian imperative of saving lives at sea.

Tracing the duty back to the 19th century, the early judgment of *The Eleanor*[34] provides some useful guidance on the meaning of 'distress'. Attached to the term, there is an implicit need for urgency, but 'there need not be immediate physical necessity'.[35] On this basis, individuals when found in distress at sea do not need to be in a physical state of harm but only in a position that requires urgent assistance. Lord Stowell in his reasoning affirmed that 'real and irresistible distress must be at all times a sufficient passport for human beings under any such application of human laws'.[36] This provides a more nuanced understanding of what the term actually captures, with the protection of life being central in Lord Stowell's judgment. Accordingly, Judge Scott claimed that there needs to be 'an urgent distress; it must be something of grave necessity . . . a moral necessity would justify the act, where, for instance, the ship had sustained previous damage, so as to render it dangerous to the lives of the persons on board to prosecute the voyage'.[37] Although the first part of the reasoning points to a rather stringent interpretation of the term, one that requires grave danger, the latter suggests that a moral necessity, meaning the danger to life, will suffice without requiring danger to occur, that is, actual physical harm.

Later, in the case of *Kate A Hoff*,[38] the US–Mexican General Claims Commission illustrated that a situation of distress may still arise even if the vessel is not 'dashed against the rocks', meaning that the danger to the vessel or person may not be acute but will still qualify as a claim of distress.[39] Notably, this case established a right to access ports by vessels in distress, even though, as aforementioned, international law does not impose an unequivocal duty on States to take rescued persons into their territory.[40] This was also later confirmed by the Irish High Court of Admiralty: 'the right of a foreign vessel

34 *The Eleanor*, 165 English Reports 1058, 1068 (English High Court of Admiralty, 22 November 1809).

35 Ibid 135.

36 Cited after Constantine John Colombos, *The International Law of the Sea* (London: Longmans 1967) 177.

37 *The Eleanor* (n 34).

38 *Kate A. Hoff Administratrix of the Estate of Samuel B Allisson, Decease (USA) v United Mexican States* (2 April 1929) 4 RIAA 444 (*Kate A Hoff* case or also known as the *Rebecca* case).

39 Attard (n 5) 63; Violeta Moreno-Lax, 'Seeking Asylum in the Mediterranean: Against a Fragmentary Reading of EU Member States' Obligations Accruing at Sea' (2011) 23(2) International Journal of Refugee Law 174; See also Rainbow Warrior Affair Case (*New Zealand v France*) (1990) 20 RIAA 217.

40 Patricia Mallia, 'The MV Salamis and the State of Disembarkation at International Law: The Undefinable Goal' (2014) 18(11) American Society of International Law <http://www.asil.org/insights/volume/18/issue/11/mv-salamis-and-state-disembarkation-international-law-undefinable-goal>; see UNCLOS Art 25.

in serious distress to the benefit of a safe haven in the waters of an adjacent coastal state'.[41]

Interestingly, in a 'land-based' tort case about liability for injuries suffered in a rescue operation, Justice Cardozo made the rather bold statement pertinent to the notion of rescues and distress. He said, 'Danger invites rescue. The cry of distress is the summons to relief. The law does not ignore the reactions of the mind in tracing conduct to its consequences. It recognizes them as normal'.[42] Applying the reasoning by analogy in the law of the sea context concerning migrant rescues at sea, it is conceivable to claim that a distress call or information regarding a distress incident will *de facto* suffice to show that people are objectively in danger, thus in a state of distress and in need of assistance. It can be concluded that the jurisprudence in this area encompasses humanitarian considerations and allows for a much more tolerant interpretation of the qualifying principles than the term 'distress' entails, even before one's life is in jeopardy.

Subsequently, the term 'distress phase' has been fleshed out in SAR Convention as a 'situation wherein there is a reasonable certainty that a person, a vessel or other craft is threatened by grave and imminent danger and requires immediate assistance'.[43] The definition provided is in line with the existing judicial guidance. The historical context of overloaded, leaky and unreliable vessels used to transport migrants in the Mediterranean region lends support to the *a priori* inclusion of overcrowded vessels under the distress phase as it indicates unseaworthiness and, hence, a serious threat to human life.[44] Particularly, the vessel's seaworthiness might be at stake only from the fact that the people aboard exceeded its capacity. Moreover, further clarifications have been provided by the Parliamentary Committee of the Council of Europe (PACE), which published a report in 2012 setting out indicators of what the notion of 'distress' entails. Amongst these were: 1) how crowded a boat is; 2) how great the distance from the shore; and 3) how many people aboard presented clear signs of distress.[45] Thus, danger to life qualifies as being imminent from the moment refugees embark on such dangerous journeys. In this way, it can be objectively deduced that they are in a life-threatening situation and within the ambit of the term 'distress' at sea. In this connection, the EU Sea Borders Regulation requires Frontex operations to take into account 'the seaworthiness of the vessel and the likelihood that the vessel will not reach its final distance'

41 *The MV Toledo* [1995] 2 ILRM 30, 48–49.

42 *Wagner v International Ry. Co.*, 232 N.Y. 176, 133 N.E. 437 (1921).

43 SAR Convention, Art 1.3.13 of the Annex.

44 European Commission, 'Communication from the Commission to the European Parliament, the Council, the European Economic and Social Committee and the Committee of the Regions, EU Action Plan Against Migrant Smuggling (2015–2020)' (27 May 2015) <https://eur-lex.europa.eu/legal-content/EN/TXT/?uri=celex:52015DC0285>.

45 Council of Europe: Parliamentary Assembly, 'Lives Lost in the Mediterranean Sea: Who Is Responsible?' (2012) <http://www.unhcr.org/refworld/docid/4f7be86b2.html>.

when determining if there is a distress situation.[46] This is instructive in interpreting the normative content of distress and evaluating information, as opting for a narrow construction might lead to an *irreversible* violation of the right to life. The law accordingly outlines the circumstances under which MAYDAY alerts (distress signals) and other emergency signals – such as uncertainty and alert phrases – should be issued.[47] In addition, even when a situation falls below the threshold of distress, Rescue Coordination Centres (RCCs) (and Frontex) bear legal obligations during the other emergency phases.[48] For instance, during the uncertainty phase, RCCs are obligated to initiate an inquiry to determine the safety of a person, a vessel, or other craft, or to declare the alert phase. Respectively, the alert phase requires RCCs to expand their search efforts for the missing person or vessel, notify the appropriate SAR services and take appropriate actions as needed in light of the circumstances of the particular case. At the moment the distress phase is declared, RCCs are required to follow specific rescue procedures as provided in the plans of operation.[49]

1.2 The Search and Rescue System and Coastal State Obligations

The second paragraph of Article 98 UNCLOS lays down a second duty to be observed for an operative SAR system, shifting the focus to coastal States. It provides the following:

> Every coastal State shall promote the establishment, operation and maintenance of an adequate and effective search and rescue service regarding safety on and over the sea and, where circumstances so require, by way of mutual regional arrangements cooperate with neighbouring States for this purpose.[50]

From the above provision, yet another general duty is imposed individually, this one upon coastal States to promote SAR services and cooperate with States nearby for the purpose of maritime safety in order to strengthen the effectiveness of the duty to render assistance. As Agustín Blanco-Bazan supports, 'no master can properly perform assistance to persons in distress, unless he/she is supported by a robust SAR system under the responsibility of coastal States'.[51]

46 Art 9 (2) (f) EU Sea Borders Regulation.

47 SAR Contention, Annex para 4.4., para 4.2.4.

48 Nassim Madjidian, 'In Search of (Ir)Responsibility: The Crotone Shipwreck and the Quest for the Legally Responsible' (12 June 2023) <https://verfassungsblog.de/in-search-of-irresponsibility/>.

49 SAR Convention, Annex para 4.5.3 and para 4.1.3.

50 UNCLOS, Art 98 (2).

51 Agustín Blanco-Bazan, 'The IMO: Working within the UNCLOS Framework and Global Ocean Governance' in David Joseph Attard (ed), *The IMLI Treatise on Ocean Global Governance Volume III: IMO and Global Ocean Governance* (OUP 2018) 48.

Relatedly, SOLAS requires Contracting governments to set up SAR facilities to effectively render assistance to those in distress and around their coasts. Moreover, the provision stresses that upon the communication of distress, governments should ensure that the necessary arrangements are made to locate the persons in distress and assist them, either by state-owned vessels (e.g., coast guards) or by other vessels (e.g., merchant vessels) that navigate in the area.[52]

With regards to the obligation laid down in UNCLOS, it can translate in the following way: the coastal State has authority over its SAR zone and holds an obligation of due diligence to provide adequate and effective SAR services in its SAR zone.[53] As Guy-Goodwin notes, this is *not* a counsel of perfection, but rather 'an obligation to deploy adequate means, to exercise best possible efforts, to do the utmost, to obtain this result'.[54] In fact, this is a critical duty, which can give rise to the accountability and responsibility of a State, if proven that they failed or delayed in offering or cooperating in the provision of such assistance. It is evident that the framing of this provision leaves much discretion and choice in the hands of coastal States with regard to SAR activities. Arguably, it is because of this widely conferred discretion that problems of noncompliance subsequently arise. In this vein, it has been argued that SOLAS obliges coastal States to 'undertake' to ensure that necessary arrangements for SAR services are made, such as, the establishment of maritime safety facilities for the purpose of locating persons in distress but does not require an obligation of international cooperation to provide such services. Further, the obligation laid down in paragraph 2 of Article 98 does not require a coastal State to directly undertake a SAR operation. The wording suggests that it is not a mere obligation to provide the means, 'but an obligation to reach a certain level of service'.

Additionally, just as a definition of the term 'distress' is absent from UNCLOS, the fundamental terms 'search' and 'rescue', which *prima facie* shape the *ratione materiae* scope of the duty imposed upon coastal States, also remain undefined. Once more, UNCLOS does not stipulate any specific prerequisites or impose technical obligations on States *vis-à-vis* execution of SAR activities. Relatedly, upon the adoption of the SAR Convention, the IMO's Maritime Safety Committee has divided the world's oceans into 13 national SAR

52 SOLAS, Ch V, Reg 7.1; See also further discussion by Papanicolopulu (n 21) 499.

53 Seline Trevisanut, 'Is There a Right to Be Rescued at Sea? A Constructive View' (Questions of International Law, Zoom-In, 23 June 2014) <http://www.qil-qdi.org/is-there-a-right-to-be-rescued-at-sea-a-constructive-view/>.

54 Guy Goodwin-Gill, 'Drowning in the Mediterranean: Time to Think and Act Regionally' (EJIL: Talk!, 12 April 2021) <https://www.ejiltalk.org/drowning-in-the-mediterranean-time-to-think-and-act-regionally/>; International Tribunal for the Law of the Sea, Seabed Disputes Chamber, *Responsibilities and Obligations of States with Respect to Activities in the Area*, Advisory Opinion, 1 February 2011, ITLOS *Reports* 2011, 10, para 110).

regions.[55] For this reason, the IMO guidance suggests which State will be primarily *responsible* for ensuring that distress calls are received and responded to according to the different SAR regions delimited to them. For instance, if a boat in distress finds itself within a State's search and rescue region (SRR) (e.g., Italy), it is the *responsibility* of that State (Italy) to coordinate the operation and ensure that assistance is rendered. Crucially, the IMO has stressed that the limits of SAR areas should not be perceived by coastal or SAR States as barriers to rendering assistance to persons in distress.[56] Ergo, the SAR Convention becomes a critical instrument in supporting the operational fulfilment of the duty to rescue at sea, as it provides *the* international system underpinning SAR operations.[57] Arguably, this 'territorialisation of mare liberum' through the SAR regime can be perceived as a way to govern the high seas by uniting the freedom of this area with responsibility.[58]

Moreover, the SAR Convention requires States to satisfy certain criteria for the establishment of an effective SAR system, including to: 1) establish a national framework for the overall coordination of SAR services; 2) assign rescue coordination centers and rescue subcenters; 3) organize available State resources for SAR operations; and 4) develop communication facilities and equipment for each rescue unit.[59] Following, an RCC is a unit responsible for promoting the efficient organization of SAR activities within its SRR and must be capable of objectively assessing a situation and acting on the basis of relevant information. Crucially, RCCs are the cornerstones of the operability of the SAR system, as they provide *instructions* to shipmasters upon the receipt of distress communication. In addition to this, RCCs are required to take immediate action to assist and to inform the responsible RCC if they receive information about an emergency situation that is beyond its SAR zone.[60]

Turning to the meaning of the terms 'search' and 'rescue', these have been for the first time fleshed out in Chapter 1 of the SAR Convention, following

55 Following the adoption of the 1979 SAR Convention <https://www.imo.org/en/About/Conventions/Pages/International-Convention-on-Maritime-Search-and-Rescue-(SAR).aspx>.

56 Attard (n 5) 57.

57 IMO, 'International Convention on Maritime Search and Rescue' <https://www.imo.org/en/About/Conventions/Pages/International-Convention-on-Maritime-Search-and-Rescue-(SAR).aspx>.

58 Tanja E Aalberts and Thomas Gammeltoft-Hansen, 'Sovereignty at Sea: The Law and Politics of Saving Lives in Mare Liberum' (2014) 17 Journal of International Relations and Development 458.

59 Annex to the SAR Convention, paras 2.2, 2.2.1, 2.2.2, 2.1.2, 2.5.

60 Art 4.3 of the Annex SAR Convention; See also Lisa-Marie Komp, 'The Duty to Assist Persons in Distress: An Alternative Source of Protection against the Return of Migrants and Asylum Seekers to the High Seas?' in Violeta Moreno-Lax and Efthymios Papastavridis (eds), *'Boat Refugees' and Migrants at Sea: A Comprehensive Approach: Integrating Maritime Security with Human Rights* (Vol. 7, International Refugee Law Series, Brill Nijhoff 2016) 229–230.

the 1998 amendments,[61] which offered to some extent useful guidance as to the operational components therein: 'search' is 'an operation, normally coordinated by rescue co-ordination centre or rescue sub-centre, using available personnel and facilities to locate persons in distress'; and 'rescue' is 'an operation to retrieve persons in distress, provide for their initial medical or other needs, and deliver them to a place of safety'.[62]

The amendments adopted in 1998 were an attempt to provide guidance to the rather ***pathological*** concept of the 'place of safety' – the last component to be fulfiled for the rescue to be ***concluded*** – insofar as it proves to be the key aspect of the operational dysfunctionality surrounding the SAR system. Besides the fact that the amendments did result in an expansion of the scope of the duty, in terms of the additional protection made available to 'vulnerable' individuals, the concept entailed no concomitant obligation on States to accept the rescued persons in their territory, but only to ensure that such a place is afforded. Conversely, the obligation falls upon shipmasters to provide assistance and to deliver them to a place of safety and for coastal States to coordinate and cooperate. Hence, even though international law establishes a clear legal obligation for coastal States to maintain SAR services, this obligation is undermined by post-rescue uncertainties concerning the State responsible for accepting the rescued persons on its territory.

Debates have since long surrounded the meaning of the word 'safety' and what it essentially connotes for disembarkation to take place, as it plays a decisive role in the functionality of the SAR system, one that can put its effectiveness at stake insofar as it protects human life at sea. Most importantly, in complying with this duty, States should refrain from returning migrants to a place where their life or liberty could be at risk.[63] Accordingly, the prohibition of *refoulement* under international refugee law ties into the disembarkation of persons to a 'place of safety' in order for a rescue operation to be marked as completed.[64] This alone stands to be among the underlying reasons why

61 IMO Maritime Safety Committee (MSC) Resolution MSC.70(69) 18 May 1998, adopting the amendments to the SAR Convention.

62 Annex to the SAR Convention, paras 1.3.3 and 1.3.4; see also Violeta Moreno-Lax and Efthymios Papastavridis, 'Introduction: Tracing the Bases of an Integrated Paradigm for Maritime Security and Human Rights at Sea' in Violeta Moreno-Lax and Efthymios Papastavridis (eds), *'Boat Refugees' and Migrants at Sea: A Comprehensive Approach: Integrating Maritime Security with Human Rights* (Vol. 7, International Refugee Law Series, Brill Nijhoff 2016) 196.

63 Refugee Convention, Art 33; The interpretation of the term 'place of safety' has channelled through the debates on disembarkation and received much scholarly attention, see *inter alia* Violeta Moreno-Lax, Daniel Ghezelbash and Natalie Klein, 'Between Life, Security and Rights: Framing the Interdiction of "Boat Migrants" in the Central Mediterranean and Australia' (2019) 32(4) LJIL 715; Killian S O'Brien, 'Refugees on the High Seas: International Refugee Law Solutions to a Law of the Sea Problem' (2001) 3(2) Goettingen Journal of International Law 715.

64 Kees Wouters and Maarten Den Heijer, 'The *Marine I* Case: A Comment' (2009) 22(1) International Journal of Refugee Law 6.

governments have increasingly limited SAR capacity in the Mediterranean and have adopted a 'closed-ports' approach even before the outbreak of Covid-19 as expounded in the preceding chapter.[65] The tangential question that remains in respect of the duty to render assistance at sea relates to *which State* bears the responsibility to accept the rescued persons. It was for the first time in 2001 that a case was brought before an international court addressing the challenges of disembarkation that arise subsequent to the rescue of migrants. This is the well-known *Ruddock v Vadarlis* (*Tampa*) case,[66] which has successfully shaken up the legal certainty surrounding the international SAR system.

2. The *Tampa* Case

2.1 Background of the Case

On 26 August 2001, the MV *Tampa*, a Norwegian tanker *en route* from Australia to Singapore, responded to an Australian-coordinated SAR operation of an overcrowded fishing vessel with 433 Afghan asylum seekers heading from Indonesia to Australia. Subsequent to a successful rescue of the distressed individuals – and even though the *Tampa*'s explicit capacity allowance was no more than 50 people aboard – the Australian authorities ordered the tanker to divert to Indonesia and return the migrants to the country of embarkation. Strikingly, prior to this command, the shipmaster of the *Tampa* first asked the Australian Coast Guard where to disembark the rescued persons, and the guard member responded that *he did not know*.[67] When the rescued persons became aware that the boat was returning them back to their origin, a riot broke out, whereby a number of individuals threatened to commit suicide if they were not taken to Australia. Whilst the master of *Tampa* was facing a huge dilemma, having felt duress, he complied with their demands and continued towards the Australian port of Christmas Island but outside its territorial sea.

The Australian authorities once more threatened to fine the shipowners if they proceeded with an illegal entry into their territorial waters, holding that the rescued passengers should be taken back to where they embarked – Indonesia – and that the State responsible for the asylum seekers aboard was the flag State (Norway, in this instance). At the same time, insufficient food and water supplies posed a further risk to the lives of those aboard. As a result, three days later the shipmaster of the *Tampa* decided to enter Australian territorial waters, where

65 The closure of ports to vessels transporting migrants was first introduced on 24.09.2018 by the then Minister of the Interior, Matteo Salvini <https://www.gazzettaufficiale.it/eli/id/2018/10/04/18G00140/s>.

66 *Ruddock v Vadarlis* [2001] FCA 1329; 110 RCR 491; 183 ALR 1 (The *Tampa* case). The *Tampa* case is a seminal one in this field, even though dating back to 2001, given that very few cases concerning SAR activities and sea migration have been brought before a court.

67 Cecilia Bailliet, 'The Tampa Case and Its Impact on Burden Sharing at Sea' (2003) 25(3) Human Rights Quarterly 742.

the Australian armed forces proceeded to transfer the rescued passengers to their warship. As Australia refused to allow the migrants to enter its territory and make subsequent asylum claims, it proposed sending them to the neighboring countries with which it had an agreement, Nauru and New Zealand, for their claims to be processed there. By this time, action was taken to the Australian courts to assess the legality of such measures, where the Full Federal Court decided that the executive government was right to exclude aliens.

The *Tampa* incident epitomized the critical complexities of the legal framework surrounding the duty to rescue at sea, highlighting the gaps and deficiencies of its operational framework that risk hindering the principle of safety of life at sea *pari passu* the right to life.[68] Grounded in uncertainty, the above situation raises fundamental questions pertinent to the law of the sea, human rights and refugee law. The various legal implications of the *Tampa* case will be now dissected below.

2.2 *Commercial Implications*

The first crucial issue that one might overlook mainly by reason of its non-humanitarian value – but nonetheless significant in the operational functionality of the SAR regime – is the commercial implications that fall on the shipping industry. As noted above, States can either perform directly the SAR operation, through the maintenance and availability of SAR services, or they can ask a vessel which is located in close proximity to the distressed persons to proceed and perform the rescue; this can be, for example, a private (merchant) vessel or a State vessel of another country. In this instance, the *Tampa* was close to the distressed boat and thus, Australia – the SAR region responsible – acted accordingly by ordering the merchant vessel to perform the rescue.[69] At the same time, the fact that the *Tampa* took more people aboard than it was permitted, exceeding the vessel's permitted allowance by *nine times*, raises serious safety concerns.

The vexing question surrounding a commercial vessel's fitness to perform such massive rescues, endangering not only the vessel's seaworthiness due to overcapacity, but also the safety of the people aboard, is one that begs for a revision of the safety standards of commercial vessels. As a consequence, it can be submitted that commercial vessels are often poorly equipped to accommodate the necessary needs of, as well as medical supplies for, the hundreds of additional people rescued, as was observed above in light of the *Tampa*'s

68 For discussion see, Kristof Gombeer, 'Human Rights Adrift? Enabling the Disembarkation of Migrants to a Place of Safety in the Mediterranean' (2017) 10 Irish Yearbook of International Law 23–55; Velasco (n 4).

69 According to SAR Convention Annex 1.3.4, a SAR region is 'An area of defined dimensions associated with a rescue coordination centre within which search and rescue services are provided'.

insufficient supplies of food and water. Hence, a vessel's access to the nearest port of call for disembarkation purposes is essential.

Notwithstanding the clear customary and moral obligation to assist any person found in distress at sea and in line with Article 98 UNCLOS, it is perhaps appropriate to support that commercial vessels were never meant to serve or respond to such massive migration movements, as SAR was predominantly manifested as an immediate response to an accident. To view the shipping community as a policy solution to an ongoing cardinal humanitarian crisis at sea is clearly undesirable.

As illustrated in this instance, the Australian government was threatening the shipmaster with trafficking offences under the Australian Migration Act 1958, and this amplified the heavy onus that fell upon him and complicated the rescue operation to a huge degree.[70] In this manner, State reluctance to allow disembarkation and asylum processing amply increases the strain on private actors (the shipping industry in this case) and primarily discourages those vessels that might otherwise be ready to intervene. Obviously, the shipping industry is forced to bear high risks when conducting a large-scale rescue operation, which are exacerbated by the political standoffs regarding the identification of a disembarkation port.[71] Hence, compliance with this humanitarian duty comes with great costs to commercial businesses.

2.3 Disembarkation and Place of Safety

The critical question remains: where are the rescued persons to be disembarked? The answer entails a threefold approach drawing upon international human rights, refugee law and law of the sea considerations. The general principles that regulate disembarkation derive, first, from the sovereign right of States to grant or refuse access to their territory to vessels and, second, from the *non-refoulement* principle. Looking first at sovereignty, international law does not impose an unequivocal duty on any State to take rescued persons into its territory. The rule that is evidenced in the *Nicaragua* line of cases, where the International Court of Justice (ICJ) viewed the principle of sovereignty as bound to the notion of legal 'personality', is simply one that allows to a great extent the coastal State to regulate access to its ports by virtue of its sovereignty.[72]

The Australian authorities in *Tampa* continuously refused to allow for the vessel to disembark the rescued persons at its port. As such, the incidents

70 Michael C Pugh, 'Drowning not Waving: Boat People and Humanitarianism at Sea' (2004) 17 Journal of Refugee Studies 59.

71 For instance, see Guglielmo Mangiapane, 'Italian Political Standoff Keeps Rescued Migrants Stranded at Sea' (Reuters, 19 December 2019) <https://www.euronews.com/2019/08/16/italian-political-standoff-keeps-rescued-migrants-stranded-at-sea>.

72 Military and Paramilitary Activities in and against Nicaragua (*Nicaragua v United States of America*)1986 I.C.J. 14.

illustrated the ambiguity that surrounds the duty to save lives at sea, as 'an absolute refusal to accept disembarkation limits the possibility or likelihood of a rescue taking place and thus it could be seen as undermining the execution of rescue in the first place'.[73] It suffices to briefly state that if rescues are then not taking place according to the law, then the right to life of the imperilled individuals is arguably put at risk. As traditionally understood, the law of the sea framework itself does not confer a claimable ***right to be rescued at sea*** upon individuals, hence their life is entirely dependent upon the execution of rescue missions. Despite this, Bernard Oxman recognized decades ago that a Hohfeldian might argue that international law establishes a ***right to be rescued at sea*** by reason of the duty to render assistance. This can be, in turn, extrapolated from the existing right to life as it presents an umbrella or a more generic parent right, which courts have consistently interpreted as encompassing other, more specific rights or even as giving rise to newly proclaimed rights. In this way, the right to life, as found in international human rights instruments, is most pertinent to the duty to rescue and can foster positive obligations upon States to protect life at risk of being lost.[74] It is fair thus to assume that human rights concerns come into play in the SAR system, as noncompliance with such a critical duty might also be a violation of the positive obligations arising from right to life. The right to life is explored in detail in the following chapter.

Lastly, it may be further inferred that the performance of rescue operations is dependent on right of entry and disembarkation guarantees by coastal States.[75] In the *Tampa*, even though the vessel itself was not in distress, the people aboard the vessel were; the majority required medical attention, the sanitary conditions faltered and 15 of the rescued passengers were reported to have lost consciousness. Clearly, the situation on the vessel started to deteriorate in respect to the rescued persons' well-being to such an extent that it not only put their lives in jeopardy but also arguably constituted a breach of the freedom from torture and other cruel, inhuman or degrading treatment and punishment.

2.4 *The Principle of Non-Refoulement*

The principle of ***non-refoulement*** is the second general principle manifestly regulating disembarkation. As explored in Chapter 1, the obligation provides that States should refrain from returning refugees to a place where their life or

73 O'Brien (n 63) 723.

74 Establishing a direct link between rescue at sea and the right to life, see for example, HRC, *CCPR General Comment No 36 (2018) on Article 6 of the International Covenant on Civil and Political Rights, on the Right to Life*, adopted 30 October 2018, CCPR/C/GC/36, para 63.

75 Bailliet (n 67) 750.

liberty would likely be at risk,[76] and this includes practices of direct, indirect or chain *refoulement*.[77]

The *Tampa* is clearly not an isolated example of a situation where a State purports to prevent access to its territory, though, it must be acknowledged that, at the outset, Australia complied with the requirements of the SAR Convention, insofar as it coordinated the SAR operation. Yet, when considering the legal duty to assist persons in distress at sea, Australia closed its territorial waters to a vessel in distress for reasons of national security and sovereignty, which it justified by utilizing the dehumanizing phrase 'illegal migrants'. The Australian government further appeared to comply with Article 33 of the Refugee Convention by not returning the rescued passengers and by arranging for the persons aboard the vessel to be disembarked at Nauru and New Zealand. Yet, this does not erase the fact that they had (insistently) requested from the start the return of the rescued persons. In simple terms, Australia had a legal duty to assist the *Tampa* and not turn it away in the first place. The question that comes to mind is this: had the master of the *Tampa* complied with the orders and returned the Afghan asylum seekers to Indonesia, would this have been a violation of the *non-refoulement* principle? The answer would most likely be affirmative, as the Australian government would have been in breach of its obligation under customary international law and the Refugee Convention.

3. The 2004 Amendments to the SAR and SOLAS Conventions

The seminal case of *Tampa* was a crucial stepping stone in realizing that the time was ripe to deal with the then deficiencies of the SAR legal framework that rendered the practice of saving lives at sea a perplexing mission. The wider ramifications of the case, in the wake of similar incidents of non-rescue and disagreement disputes in disembarkation of those rescued, paved the way for discussions at the global level that led to the well-anticipated amendments adopted by the IMO in 2004 in its SAR and SOLAS Conventions.[78] At the same time, the IMO with a view to provide coherence in the SAR system and clarify the imperfect *status quo* of the international duty to render assistance at sea, issued the *Guidelines on the Treatment of Persons Rescued at Sea* 2004 (IMO Guidelines)[79]

76 Richard Barnes, 'Refugee Law at Sea' (2008) 53(1) International and Comparative Law Quarterly 62.

77 Douglas Guilfoyle, *Shipping Interdiction and the Law of the Sea* (CUP 2009) 223.

78 IMO Maritime Safety Committee Resolution MSC.155 (78), of 20 May 2004, adopting the amendments to the SAR Convention; IMO Maritime Safety Committee Resolution MSC.153 (78), 20 May 2004, adopting the amendments to SOLAS. Both of the amendments became operative in 2006.

79 The purpose of the IMO Guidelines is set out in paragraph 1.1. as a means to provide guidance to both 'Governments' and 'shipmasters'; IMO Maritime Safety Committee Resolution

At the outset, the amendments sought to clarify the States' (and masters') duty in respect to providing assistance to those in distress at sea, setting out that:

> Parties *shall* co-ordinate and co-operate to ensure that masters of ships providing assistance by embarking persons in distress at sea are released from their obligations with minimum further deviation from the ships' intended voyage, provided that releasing the master of the ship from these obligations does not further endanger the safety of life at sea. The Party responsible for the *search and rescue region* in which such assistance is rendered *shall* exercise *primary responsibility* for ensuring such co-ordination and cooperation occurs, so that survivors assisted are disembarked from the assisting ship and delivered to a place of safety, taking into account the particular circumstances of the case and *guidelines* developed by the Organization. In these cases, the relevant Parties shall arrange for such disembarkation to be effected *as soon as reasonably practicable.*[80]

From the above, it can be observed that the amendments sought to employ mandatory language – the use of 'shall' – in elucidating the States' duties. As Severance has supported, 'the duty to provide search and rescue services [in the SAR Convention] thereby went from being a suggestion to a binding duty'.[81] Moreover, it can be argued that the amendments do not seek to demystify the primary area of confusion as no criteria are entailed in any manner that will provide an answer to the recurring question: where should the rescued persons be disembarked? As such, it is fundamental to fully comprehend the inherent limitations of the adopted amendments. At a close reading, what the text does is lay down – for the first time – a clear obligation that the State in whose SAR region the assistance takes place *shall* have the primary responsibility to coordinate and cooperate so that the rescued persons are delivered to a 'place of safety'. However, the precise meaning of 'primary responsibility' is unclear and States might fear that disembarkation responsibilities now align with SAR areas. As Gammeltoft-Hansen – convincingly I contend –argues, this might lead to 'jurisdiction shopping'[82] as it arguably creates a legal basis for destination States to shift both procedural and substantive asylum and refugee protection obligations to a neighboring coastal state. At this point it is crucial

MSC.167(78), 20 May 2004, adopting the Guidelines on the Treatment of Persons Rescued at Sea (IMO Guidelines).

80 SAR Convention, Chapter 3.1.9, (emphasis added); A similar text was adopted in the revised SOLAS Convention in Regulation 4.1.1.

81 Arthur A Severance, 'The Duty to Render Assistance in the Satellite Age' (2006) 26(2) California Western International Law Journal 391.

82 Thomas Gammeltoft-Hansen, *Access to Asylum – International Refugee Law and the Globalisation of Migration Control* (CUP 2011) 142f.

to highlight that Malta has not ratified the 2004 Amendments to the SOLAS and SAR Convention, neither has Malta accepted the corresponding IMO Guidelines. This implies that Malta is only bound by the pre-amendment legislation, that is, to only adhere to the practice that all rescued persons within the Maltese SAR zone should be disembarked in the nearest place of safety, without assuming any additional associated responsibility. Of critical relevance is to note that Malta's SAR zone covers a wide part of the Mediterranean Sea and, in particular, its SAR zone is equivalent to 750 times its territory and partly overlaps with the Italian SAR zone.[83] Hence, Malta's objection to the amendments is particularly unfortunate in this context, especially considering its location on the frontlines of the Central Mediterranean migration route. Still, this should not negate its international law of the sea obligations towards persons in distress at sea.

It can be argued that the responsibility mentioned in the amendments is only one of 'co-ordination and cooperation' and does not in any way suggest that the disembarkation in question shall occur within the territory of the State which is primarily responsible for the SAR region in question. Second, even though the text adds that such disembarkation shall take place 'as soon as reasonably practicable', there is nothing in the provision that prevents State parties from denying disembarkation at their ports. As such, a State's discretion and sovereignty that are *prima facie* the reason for employing avoidance measures and sidestepping in this way SAR obligations remain unaffected by the amendments. In fact, they are empowering the executive branch of States with more discretion to make decisions rather than identifying or defining or entailing any obligation to accept the rescued persons.

What the IMO sought to do is illustrate that disembarkation should occur with minimal disruption to the ship's planned itinerary and to a place of safety, which seeks to prevent the situation in the *Tampa* from recurring where persons faced an operative threat to their lives both aboard the vessel and also if returned.[84] With reference to disembarkation, the IMO Guidelines put forth in paragraph 5.1.6 that masters of ships should 'seek to ensure that survivors are not disembarked to a place where their safety would be further jeopardized'.[85] This is a welcomed feature as it gives emphasis to people's safety *pari passu* life, especially when considering the current humanitarian crisis at sea, where thousands of migrants are fleeing from North African countries to escape blatant human right abuses. This paragraph can be in fact translated to be in line

83 Selive Trevisanut, 'Search and Rescue Operations in the Mediterranean: Factor of Cooperation or Conflict?' (2010) 25 The International Journal of Marine and Coastal Law 524.

84 Efthymios Papastavridis, 'Rescuing Migrants at Sea: The Responsibility of States under International Law' in Guy S Goodwin-Gill and Ph Weckel (eds), *Migration and Refugee Protection in the 21st Century. International Aspects, Hague Academy of International Law* (Leiden: Martinus Nijhoff 2015) 269.

85 Kathleen S Goddard, 'Rescuing Refugees and Migrants at Sea: Some Commercial Shipping Implications' (2015) 21(5) The Journal of International Maritime Law 360.

with, or else reflecting traits of, the principle of *non-refoulement*. This is more concretely defined further in the IMO Guidelines in which explicit reference to the needs of migrants rescued at sea is made, providing 'the need to avoid disembarkation in territories where the lives and freedoms of those alleging a well-founded fear of persecution would be threatened is a consideration in the case of asylum-seekers and refugees recovered at sea'.[86] Having done so, the IMO Guidelines do not in any way purport to place a duty on the master of a ship to determine the legal status of the persons rescued; the obligation is one that provides for maintaining their safety and for cooperating in their disembarkation. It can be submitted that all migrants should be able to avail themselves of the opportunity to claim asylum, without them being returned back to their country of origin.[87]

As regards the amorphous term 'place of safety', the IMO hoped that with the issuing of its IMO Guidelines, despite their soft law status, it would be able to explicate the meaning of the term and the confusions that center around the contested matter of disembarkation. Yet, its attempt proved to be rather oblique as it did not eliminate the mystifying features of identifying a location for the rescue to come to an end. This is reflected in paragraph 6.12 of the IMO Guidelines that lay down:

> A place of safety . . . is a location where rescue operations are considered to terminate. It is also a place where the survivors' safety of life is no longer threatened and where their basic human needs (such as food, shelter and medical needs) can be met. Further, it is a place from which transportation arrangements can be made for the survivors' next or final destination.[88]

For Moreno-Lax, the first line of the provision is described as creating 'an obligation of result'; for the operation to be considered completed the persons need to be effectively disembarked.[89] It aims to provide guidance to the master of a ship by setting down normative criteria that should inform their decisions when effecting rescues at all times. Yet, this obligation stands on its own and does not purport to point to which State will be responsible each time, nor does it identify a default place for disembarkation to occur.

As a result, the question of disembarkation to a 'place of safety' has always been perceived as a grey area, whereby controversial tactics by governments determine the fate of seaborne migrants. Some authors and, suffice to

86 IMO Guidelines (n 79) para 6.17.

87 Silja Klepp, 'A Double Bind: Malta and the Rescue of Unwanted Migrants at Sea, a Legal Anthropological Perspective on the Humanitarian Law of the Sea' (2011) 23 International Journal of Refugee Law 548.

88 IMO Guidelines (n 79) para 6.12.

89 Moreno-Lax, 'Seeking Asylum in the Mediterranean' (n 39) 196.

say, detractors have expressed that the amendments brought to the IMO's Conventions address the issue of disembarkation 'somewhat, elliptically'.[90] The amendments refrain from elaborating any normative criteria for a place of safety, allowing for such interpretation to be varying in practice and allowing for *ad hoc* arrangements every time. In this regard, the European Commission has recognized that this is an important gap that still exists in the international law of the sea framework regulating SAR operations.[91] To conclude, while these changes are welcomed, they have nonetheless failed to bring the much-needed legal clarity to important issues surrounding the 'place of safety' that preceded the *Tampa* incident.

It is also important to stress that the IMO Guidelines are of a nonbinding character. While this might question their functionality, they may be indirectly persuasive in fleshing out the hard-law obligations. As expounded above, they contain more detailed and precise provisions for States and shipmasters 'in interpreting, understanding and implementing their international obligations when rendering assistance and undertaking SAR operations'.[92] This view is in line with the IMO amendments, which specifically require – 'shall' – States to take into account the *Guidelines*; hence, it can be concluded that they acquire an 'elevated' status. It follows that the lack of legally binding status 'does not necessarily mean some kind of "diminished function"; these norms may well be as valuable as legal norms'.[93] As Richard Barnes goes on to support, 'it is arguable that they [the IMO Guidelines] may contribute to the formation of new customary rules on the treatment of persons rescued at sea'.[94]

4. Contemporary Practices in the Mediterranean Post-2004 IMO Amendments

The calls to end the practice of non-assistance at sea, which undermines well-established obligations of international law, are countless. This section exhibits several incidents that occurred in the Mediterranean Sea following the 2004 IMO amendments, particularly in the lead-up to Europe's 'migration' crisis, which serve to illustrate the present-day fragmented nature of the duty

90 Daniel Ghezelbash, Violeta Moreno-Lax, Natalie Klein and Brian Opeskin, 'Securitization of Search and Rescue at Sea: The Response to Boat Migration in the Mediterranean and Offshore Australia' (2018) 67(2) International and Comparative Law Quarterly 315.

91 Crucial to note is that the IMO instruments cannot be enforced by the IMO as it has no enforcement powers; therefore, it is the duty of States to enforce those roles by incorporating them into domestic law.

92 Attard (n 5) 110, 113; IMO Guidelines (n 79) para 1.1; Papastavridis, 'Rescuing Migrants at Sea' (n 84) 12.

93 László Blutman, 'In the Trap of a Legal Metaphor: International Soft Law' (2010) 59(3) ICLQ 612.

94 Richard Barnes, 'The International Law of the Sea and Migration Control' in Vassilis Mitsilegas and Bernard Ryan (eds), *Extraterritorial Immigration Control* (The Hague: Brill 2010) 142.

to rescue at sea. The practical application of this duty, especially in recent years, has attracted controversial tactics in which governments, for example, refuse to allow private actors to disembark rescued people in their ports. This was first witnessed with commercial vessels performing rescues in order to curb migration and has now escalated to hostile practices against NGOs who undertake proactive operations and border surveillance that facilitates interdiction by third actors, as mentioned in Chapter 1. Below, I turn to examine these practices in a twofold manner: 1) privatized *refoulement* and aerial *refoulement*; and 2) abandonment at sea.

4.1 Privatized Refoulement and Aerial Refoulement

The MV Salamis and the Adakent, 2013: Unpacking the diplomatic (and legal) quarrels which increasingly unfold between State governments can be first evidenced in the MV *Salamis* and the *Adakent* incidents – two rescue tales that involved *de facto* push-backs of rescued migrants. The events occurred in the summer of 2013 when hundreds of people lost their lives in the Mediterranean Sea whilst attempting to reach Europe's shores. In these two cases, the shipmaster took a different approach when interpreting the 'place of safety' to disembark rescued persons.

On 4 August 2013, the MV *Salamis*, a Liberian tanker, rescued 102 African migrants from a boat in distress off the Libyan coast, operating under the instructions of the Italian Maritime Rescue Coordination Centre (MRCC).[95] Despite the MRCC's order to return the rescued persons to Libya, which it considered to be the nearest port of safety for disembarkation to occur, the shipmaster continued on his planned voyage to Malta (to disembark migrants there). Subsequently, Malta refused to allow access to the MV *Salamis* to disembark rescued migrants, leading to a deadlock. Eventually, three days later, Italy decided to accept the rescued migrants to be disembarked in Syracuse. This incident reveals the legal loopholes that govern SAR at sea with disembarkation and place of safety being the principal reasons for creating such definitional uncertainties and disagreements between States. One may venture so far as to ponder whether, had the shipmaster abided by the MRCC's instructions, this would have triggered *refoulement* by Italy who gave the instructions that would have led to foreseeable *refoulement*. On this view, the European Court of Human Rights (ECtHR or Strasbourg Court or Court) one year earlier in its *Hirsi* judgment[96] had stressed that Libya does not constitute a place of safety and that the return of rescued people to Libya would likely breach international law.

95 Mallia (n 40).
96 *Hirsi Jamaa and Others v Italy*, App no 27765/09 (ECtHR, 23 February 2012) paras 126–137.

The charged atmosphere can be observed in a similar incident involving the *Adakent* (Turkish cargo ship), which took place the same week as the MV *Salamis* case. The ship was again directed by the Italian authorities to perform the rescue. However this time, the master having rescued 96 migrants complied with the Italian orders and returned the migrants to Libyan authorities in Tripoli which was its planned destination from the start and the nearest port of call. Subsequent to that, both the IMO and UNHCR issued guidelines based on the SAR and the Refugee Convention to shipmasters addressing these two aforesaid situations. The guidelines put forward the idea that if there is some reason to believe that a rescued person is an asylum seeker, then the shipmaster must take this into account with regards to the disembarkation place of the rescued persons. Bearing in mind the situation that is unfolding in the Mediterranean, Malta and Italy (and other European States) are well aware that most (if not all) migrants departing from Libya by boats are asylum seekers. Notoriously, States seemingly find other avenues to circumvent their international obligations through private actors operating push-backs. For this reason, States acting individually in the Mediterranean have a major role to play in the SAR system and one that can put its effectiveness at risk.

The Lady Sham, 2019: On 20 January 2019, a cargo ship flying a Sierra Leone flag (the *Lady Sham*) upon rescuing 140 migrants in the Mediterranean, took them back to the port of Misrata, Libya, where they were taken to a detention center.[97] Upon their rescue, the crew (misleadingly) told the migrants that they would be disembarked in Germany. This is believed to have been done because of fears of protests by migrants should they have realized they were being taken back.[98] Consequently, the Italian MRCC, acting as the *de facto* coordinator of the SAR operation, *directed* a private actor, *Lady Sham*, in performing an act that violates the principle of *non-refoulement* as well as protection of human life and personal security. This incident, in principle, amounted to yet another privatized push-back. Yet, like the *Adakent* and many other cases, it was never judicially challenged.

The Nivin case, 2018: On 7 November 2018, a Spanish surveillance aircraft (part of the then EU's anti-smuggling mission Operation *Sophia*) spotted a

97 Marion MacGregor, 'Migrants Rescued by "Lady Sham" Detained in Libya' (23 January 2019) <https://www.infomigrants.net/en/post/14678/migrants-rescued-by-lady-sham-detained-in-libya>.

98 In particular, domestic courts have found that actions by rescued persons amidst fear of being return back to their countries (e.g. Libya) e.g. pressuring shipmasters, were justified under the principles of self-defense. For more, see Jean-Pierre Gauci, 'When Private Vessels Rescue Migrants and Refugees: A mapping of Legal Considerations' (British Institute of International and Comparative Law, 24 November 2020) 13 <https://www.biicl.org/documents/124_private_vessels_research.pdf>. Moreover, for similar incidents, see, Aphrodite Papachristodoulou, 'The Principle of Saving Lives at Sea: Just a Fool's Hope' (International Law Blog, 27 June 2019) <https://internationallaw.blog/2019/06/27/the-principle-of-saving-lives-at-sea-just-a-fools-hope/>.

migrants' boat in the Libya SAR zone and passed this information to both the Italian and Libyan Coast Guards, who then instructed the *Nivin,* a Panama-flagged merchant vessel that was nearby, to take all rescued passengers back to Libya, in violation of their rights. The incident resulted in an individual complaint currently before the Committee, the *SDG v Italy.*[99] The complaint argues that the Italian authorities, through their coordination with and on behalf of the LYGN of the *Nivin*, had impacted the right to life of the individuals involved in a direct and reasonably foreseeable manner.

Firstly, it is imperative to note, that the Italian authorities acquired knowledge about the migrants' boat by virtue of the data transmitted by the Operation *Sophia*. Secondly, as the Libyan Coast Guard and Navy (LCGN) could not deploy its own vessels to perform the 'rescue' of migrants at that time, the *Nivin* was instructed on their behalf to undertake the task.[100] In what followed, migrants realized that they were taken back to Libya and locked themselves in the hold of the ship, resulting in a standoff in the port of Misrata which lasted ten days. The Libyan security forces then intervened and forcefully removed the captured passengers from the vessel and subjected them to various forms of ill-treatment, including torture. This case illuminates the systematic pattern of EU aerial surveillance strategies that facilitate the privatized push-backs of migrants to Libya, impede access to asylum and expose migrants to abuse and threats to life.[101] It further epitomizes the practice of 'remote control' that is exercised the moment an individual attempts to leave her country. Thirdly, it amplifies commercial implications that fall on the shipping industry, as there could be enormous (financial, legal and logistical) consequences of having a merchant vessel detained for ten days. Hence, these practices seemingly disincentivize private actors like the shipping industry from engaging in SAR operations and encourage derelict compliance with this humanitarian duty.

At this stage, one might ponder: what, then, are the responsibilities of the flag State? To answer this question, it is imperative to first recall the International Law Commission's (ILC) Articles on State Responsibility, particularly Article 3 which puts forth: 'the characterisation of an act of a State as an international wrongful act is governed by international law. Such characterisation is not affected by the characterisation of the same act as lawful by internal law'. Consequently, the fact that, in the above illustrations, States instruct private shipmasters to return persons to a place in violation of the *non-refoulement*, does not negate their responsibility for such action. Arguably, the instruction

99 'Communication to the United Nations Human Rights Committee In the Case of SDG against Italy (Anonymized Version) Submitted for Consideration under the Optional Protocol to the International Covenant on Civil and Political Rights to The United Nations Human Rights Committee' (GLAN 2019).

100 Forensic Architecture, 'Privatized Push-Back of the Nivin' (18 December 2019) <https://forensic-architecture.org/investigation/nivin>.

101 GLAN, 'Privatised Migrant Abuse by Italy and Libya' <https://www.glanlaw.org/nivincase>.

itself which leads to the foreseeable violation of the principle of *non-refoulement* is a wrongful act and attributable to the State by virtue of being provided by the RCC which is a State organ.[102] It remains yet to be seen what the outcome will be of the *Nivin* incident as it raises concerns regarding the State's responsibility for giving detrimental instructions to private actors, in addition to the consequences of being returned to a place in violation of the *non-refoulement*, including the detention and the risk of trafficking and slavery-like conditions.

4.2 *Abandonment at Sea*

The Left-to-Die Boat, 2011: The 'left-to-die boat' was one of the most tragic incidents that manifested *inter alia* the existence of a dysfunctional international legal framework surrounding rescues at sea even before the proliferation of migrants crossing the sea. On 27 March 2011, a small rubber boat, in a desperate attempt to cross the Central Mediterranean route, had left Tripoli with 72 African migrants aboard destined for European shores. The boat was washed up on Libya's shores 15 days later, with only nine survivors. Notwithstanding the launching of distress calls by the Italian and Maltese Maritime Rescue Coordination Centres, and despite a helicopter's presence at the location of the boat while it was in distress, in addition to two merchant vessels and a large military vessel passing closely by, 63 individuals died at sea – arguably a clear-cut result of the above actors' *choice* to turn a blind eye to their legal obligations to render assistance to people in distress at sea.[103]

As Itamar Mann has argued, the history of migration at sea exposes the very fact that because some people are protected by no government, they are able to challenge State governments with an existential dilemma: 'either save a stranger's life, or let the stranger die'.[104] Despite evidence gathered by several investigations, including those of the Parliamentary Assembly of the Council of Europe (PACE)[105] and the expert documentation by the Forensic Oceanography project, the national courts where the complaints were filed failed to give justice to the survivors, allowing for the crime of non-assistance to prevail. This might be the result of the lack of a competent judicial authority given that national judges may not be competent to consider cases of breach of a duty

102 Gauci (n 98) 26.

103 Charles Heller, Lorenzo Pezzani and SITU Research, 'Case: "Left-to-die Boat"' (2014) <https://www.forensic-architecture.org/case/left-die-boat/>.

104 Itamar Mann, *Humanity at Sea: Maritime Migration and the Foundations of International Law* (CUP 2016) 11.

105 Tineke Strik, Lives Lost in the Mediterranean Sea: Who Is Responsible?, report prepared for the Parliamentary Assembly of the Council of Europe (PACE), 29 March 2013 <https://assembly.coe.int/CommitteeDocs/2012/20120329_mig_RPT.EN.pdf>; Charles Heller, Lorenzo Pezzani and Situ Studio, Report on the "Left-To-Die Boat", Forensic Architecture, May 2014 <www.forensic-architecture.org/wp-content/uploads/2014/05/FO-report.pdf>.

under the law of the sea framework.[106] Considering, however, Hohfeld's model that was presented in the Introduction of this book, the logical correlative of this duty is a human right to be rescued at sea. Therefore, by acknowledging this right, the courts will be able to delve into an ***actual process*** of specification and definition that helps give the right ***a new legal shape*** or ***fill important gaps*** in the protection of human rights for irregular migrants. At the same time, it will provide victims of such violations or their relatives with a procedural right to an effective remedy. This is exemplified in more detail in the subsequent chapters.

The Cutro shipwreck, 2023: The factual context of this incident significantly differs from the above illustrations, yet it reflects the practice of abandonment at sea.[107] On 22 February 2023, a Turkish wooden vessel carrying more than 150 migrants navigated along the Calabria route towards Italy. During its journey, the vessel encountered adverse weather conditions and became in distress as large quantities of water entered the boat. A Frontex aircraft, part of the Operation *Themis* surveilling the area, detected the boat 40 nautical miles from Italy and communicated this information to the Italian law enforcement authorities and those of maritime rescue. Thermal imaging provided information to the authorities that not only was the boat overcrowded but also that there 'might be people below the deck'.[108] However, no rescue operation was ever launched. Instead, Italy mobilized two patrol boats of Guardia di Finanza (GDF) initiating a police operation to investigate the situation, who had to then return to the port due to bad weather and sea conditions. It is important to note that the GDF is ill-equipped to conduct a SAR operation; had the Italian coast guard been deployed though, they would have been able to navigate and undertake a SAR, even under worse weather conditions, as they are professionally equipped to undertake such rescue missions.

While no distress call was placed from the migrants' boat to alert the Italian authorities, the use of technology by Frontex in this case alerted the relevant authorities (Italy) of a strong likelihood of an emergency that arguably should have been marked as a SAR event. It seems that the primary cause of this human tragedy stems from Italy's negligent acts *vis-à-vis* failure to launch a SAR mission within its SAR zone, resulting in fatal consequences. What appears from the case is that there is an apparent confusion surrounding the meaning of 'distress' that will trigger a State's knowledge and duty thereof to

106 Irini Papanicolopulu, 'The Duty to Rescue at Sea, in Peacetime and in War: A General Overview' (2016) 98(2) International Review of the Red Cross 502.

107 I have analyzed this incident earlier in a blogpost, see Aphrodite Papachristodoulou, 'The Crotone Migrant Shipwreck: A Cat-and-Mouse Blame Game and the Role of Technologies at External Borders' (EJIL:Talk!, 12 April 2023) <https://www.ejiltalk.org/the-crotone-migrant-shipwreck-a-cat-and-mouse-blame-game-and-the-role-of-technologies-at-external-borders/>.

108 EU Observer, 'Crotone Shipwreck Triggers Police vs Coastguard Blame Game' (2 March 2023) <https://euobserver.com/migration/156776>.

assist persons. Whilst in the case Frontex submitted that there appeared to be 'no signs of distress', the evidence from the surveillance technology indicated strong evidence that the vessel was in distress as it showed a high number of people on board under adverse sea conditions, meaning that the situation at sea was extremely perilous. Adding to this, given the history of casualties along Mediterranean migration routes, States are reasonably expected to apprehend that such information manifested a certain risk to the life of individuals that was foreseeable. As argued above, the fact that the vessel was overcrowded meant that it was unseaworthy and in need of help. Hence, it is posited that the duty to render assistance to those in distress at sea should be activated the moment State authorities receive knowledge that reasonably indicates an impending distress situation.

The Pylos shipwreck, 2023: This incident stands today as the second deadliest shipwreck on record in the Mediterranean since 18 April 2015, when 1,100 migrants lost their lives off the coast of Libya. From what we know so far, the shipwreck on 14 June 2023 resulted in approximately 600 deaths and 104 confirmed survivors outside the tourist island of Pylos in Greece. On 13 June, the Hellenic Coast Guard received information from Frontex and the WatchTheMed Alarm Phone that there were people in distress asking for help within Greece's SAR zone. Despite this information about a potential distress situation raised with the Hellenic Coast Guard and the fact that later that evening the boat in distress (the *Adriana*) made contact with a Hellenic merchant vessel (the *Faithful Warrior*) that was in close proximity as well as with a coast guard vessel from Crete, no rescue attempt was initiated. It was also reported that migrants were given food and water, yet this is unlikely to satisfy the duty to render assistance given the object and purpose of the provision, which is to prevent the loss of life at sea. As Bríd Ní Ghráinne argues, assistance that would only marginally prolong one's life would not suffice to fulfil the obligation in good faith.[109]

It follows that the Hellenic Coast Guard had a due diligence obligation to exercise best efforts to activate the available SAR services in that geographical area and to employ all adequate measures to provide rescue services to preserve the safety of life at sea. Yet again, the uncertainty encompassing the interpretation of the term 'distress' was exploited by the authorities as an attempt to justify their failure to comply with the duty to rescue. In this vein, the EU Sea Borders Regulation provides a definition for 'distress', which includes situations in which positive information is available regarding the fact that a vessel or the persons aboard are in need of immediate assistance.[110] Interestingly in this case, shipping activity documented in an animated map showed that the migrants' boat

109 For a similar analysis on a comparable situation, see Bríd Ní Ghráinne, 'Left to Die at Sea: State Responsibility for the May 2015 Thai, Indonesian and Malaysian Pushback Operations' (2017) 10 Irish Yearbook of International Law 18.

110 Article 9(2)(a) EU Sea Borders Regulation.

had barely moved from its location in the previous seven hours, casting doubts on the Hellenic Coast Guard's claim that the boat experienced no problems. On top of this, the maritime area was closely monitored. In particular, a coast guard boat from Crete 'discreetly observed' the migrants' boat from a distance hours before it sank. In addition, according to the available information, the boat in distress had been initially assisted by a Maltese-flagged tanker (the *Lucky Sailor*) following instructions from the Greek authorities, who provided them with food and water. Thereafter, the Greek authorities asked a Greek-flagged merchant vessel to deliver water to the boat.

This is not another case of migrants ending up missing; as unpalatable as this may seem. This is a case where migrants called for help, several actors witnessed and came in close contact with the boat in question and yet all parties involved chose to remain inactive. In light of this, the issue of shared responsibility may arise in the event of a wrongful act given the multiplicity of actors involved,[111] State and non-State actors, in the observance of the duty to render assistance at sea. A plethora of questions remain unanswered in the Pylos shipwreck: what steps did Frontex take after its first sighting of the *Adriana* boat the morning of 13 June 2023? Why did the merchant vessels that were in close proximity to the migrants' boat fail to intervene? Will this failure engage flag State responsibility? How did the other authorities, Italy and Malta, who received the information, respond? These issues, along with the above illustrations, bring to the forefront the question of international legal responsibility – who is responsible, what is the scope of their responsibilities and what are their actual obligations under the realms of international law of the sea, refugee law and human rights law.

With reference to the question of flag State responsibility for failure to ensure SAR services, *in casu*, while a Maltese private vessel, the *Lucky Sailor*, was in close proximity and the shipmaster had provided supplies (food and water) to the concerned people in distress, the Articles on State Responsibility (ASR) Commentary provide:

> If it is to be regarded as an act of the State for purposes of international responsibility, the conduct of an entity must accordingly concern governmental activity and another other private or commercial activity in which the entity may engage.[112]

It follows that it will be difficult for such an omission (or misbehavior) in the context of SAR operations to be attributed to the respective State (Malta), as

111 See Andre Nollkaemper and Dov Jacobs, 'Shared Responsibility in International Law: A Conceptual Framework' (2013) 34 MIJIL 360–361.

112 See International Law Commission, Articles on the Responsibility of States for Internationally Wrongful Acts with Commentaries, Yearbook of the International Law Commission, 2001, vol. II (ASR) commentary at 43.

the shipmaster of the private vessel is neither a *de jure* organ nor a *de facto* organ of the State.[113] This applies also to the abovementioned incidents. However, pursuant to Article 98(1) of UNCLOS, all States are required to take all necessary steps to ensure that shipmasters flying their flags assist persons in distress and adopt measures that are necessary to enforce the duty. Following, a flag State may not be held responsible insofar as the shipmaster's misconduct is concerned but for failing to enforce the duty to save life on masters that have not complied.[114] Exceptionally, in the case that the flag State in question is informed about the boat in distress and instructs their shipmasters not to render assistances, then the persons would fall under the jurisdiction of this State(s). In accordance with Article 8 of ASR, the State will be responsible if the internationally wrongful act is conducted by a private vessel upon instruction or direction of the State as the shipmaster will then be a '*de facto* organ' of the State. However, it needs to be noted that it is not standard practice for commercial shipping to notify flag State authorities regarding such incidents of distress.

With reference to coastal States responsibilities, in this case Greece, it is imperative to highlight that people within a SAR zone do not *ipso facto* fall within the jurisdiction of the respective coastal State, as there must be some additional factual element that will link the persons and the coastal State concerned, such as receiving information about people in danger at sea.[115] The coastal State in whose SAR zone the mismanagement of the duty to render assistance at sea occurs is thus under a due diligence obligation to ensure the adequacy and effectiveness of the SAR services. Further, in the hypothetical scenario where the State (its rescue and coordination center) receiving the distress information is not the coastal State where the mismanagement occurs, it would still be under the obligation to exercise due diligence by notifying the competent authorities, and if those refuse to intervene, then that State would remain responsible for the coordination and management of the SAR services.

Lastly, the European Ombudsman issued a decision on 26 February 2024 on the fundamental rights obligations of Frontex with regard to SAR in the context of its maritime surveillance activities.[116] The decision concerns the Py-

113 Efthymios Papastavridis, 'The "Left-to-Die Boat" Incident of March 2011: Questions of International Responsibility arising from the Failure to Save Refugees at Sea' (2013) Refugee Law Initiative Working Paper No.10, 14 <http://sas-space.sas.ac.uk/4957/1/RLI_Working_Paper_No.10.pdf>; Art 4 and Art 8 of the ILC Articles on Responsibility of States for Internationally Wrongful Acts.

114 Papanicolopulu (n 106) 503.

115 Patricia Vella de Fremeaux (Mallia) and Felicity G Attard, 'Rescue at Sea and the Establishment of Jurisdiction: New Direction from the Human Rights Committee? Part I' (OpinioJuris, 3 March 2021) <http://opiniojuris.org/2021/03/03/rescue-at-sea-and-the-establishment-of-jurisdiction-new-direction-from-the-human-rights-committee-part-i/>.

116 I have written a blogpost reflecting on the Ombudsman decision, see Aphrodite Papachristodoulou, 'Shipwreck after Shipwreck: Frontex Emergency Signals and the Integration of AI systems' (Verfassungsblog, 11 March 2024) <https://verfassungsblog.de/shipwreck-after-shipwreck/>.

los shipwreck and exposed significant shortcomings in how the agency handles maritime incidents, including the issuance of emergency signals, both in the context of joint operations and its separate multipurpose aerial surveillance activities. In particular, the European Ombudsman highlighted the need for Frontex to explicitly lay down guidance for its staff as to when emergency signals of distress should be issued so that the appropriate authorities are notified in a timely manner.[117] Undoubtedly, the Pylos shipwreck is an appalling illustration of the ongoing failure of the EU and its Member States both to address the structural causes of the burgeoning number of border deaths[118] and to provide a humanitarian response to migration. Ergo, the ongoing incidents of preventable migrant shipwrecks provide further substance for proclaiming the existence of the right to be rescued at sea.

5. Final Remarks

Undoubtedly, the above examples reveal a breakdown of State cooperation in contravention of maritime conventions leading to a weakened international SAR system, which is inadequate in preserving the principle of saving lives at sea. It follows that the mismanagement of SAR services or the failure to adequately observe the duty to render assistance at sea might attract the shared responsibility of the various actors involved. Hence, the analysis revealed that SAR operations have been a source of conflict among neighboring States, rather than of cooperation as envisaged by the UNCLOS.[119] Certainly, current efforts to address the particular challenges faced by migrants at sea are not effective, as the attention is deflected to security measures for deterring people

117 European Ombudsman, 'Decision on How the European Border and Coast Guard Agency (Frontex) Complies with Its Fundamental Rights Obligations with Regard to Search and Rescue in the Context of Its Maritime Surveillance Activities, in Particular the Adriana Shipwreck' (26 February 2024) OI/3/2023/MHZ, at 64 <https://www.ombudsman.europa.eu/fr/decision/en/182665#_ftn24>.

118 These migrant drownings have been described in the literature as 'border deaths' even though there is no fixed definition. In the broadest sense, they 'describe the premature deaths of persons whose movement or presence has been unauthorized and irregularized as they navigate or interact with State-made boundaries'. Paolo Cuttitta and Tamara Last (eds), *Border Deaths: Causes, Dynamics and Consequences of Migration Related Mortality* (Amsterdam University Press 2020) 21. See also Maurizio Albahari, *Crimes of Peace: Mediterranean Migrations at the World's Deadliest Border* (Philadelphia: University of Pennsylvania Press 2015) 21, where Albahari argues 'Thousands of deaths in the Mediterranean, over two decades, are not misfortunate accidents, inevitable fatalities, acts of God or of nature. They are crimes of peace'.

119 The need to enhance cooperation among European States has been reaffirmed by the European Commission in its Action Plan for the Central Mediterranean and endorsed by the extraordinary Justice and Home Affairs Council on 25 November 2022 and in the meeting of the European Council 9–10 February 2023. See <https://www.consilium.europa.eu/media/60347/fin-pres-summary-migration.pdf>and<https://data.consilium.europa.eu/doc/document/ST-1-2023-INIT/en/pdf>.

from leaving their countries in the first place, rather than efforts to provide for an adequate SAR system which will preserve their rights and *lives*.

Given the uncertainty that surrounds not only the concept of 'place of safety' for disembarkation purposes but also the meaning of 'distress', the study puts forth the argument that the time might be ripe for new amendments to the relevant IMO Conventions safeguarding life at sea in order to effectively address these ambiguities that lead to the death of thousands every year. Evidently, there is no common interpretation of distress and hence, its normative content casts doubt as to when exactly States will have to provide SAR services. As argued by Lisa-Marie Komp, who embraces a teleological approach to the meaning of distress, a wide construction of the term needs to be adopted in order to comply with the object and purpose of the provisions within which it is inscribed.[120] For these reasons, there is a need for a more accurate and common consensus of situations of distress at the operational level, based on commonly approved criteria on the basis of existing rules and practices.[121]

In conclusion, it is submitted that the duty to render assistance at sea is the operational obligation deriving from the application of the right to life at sea. Against this understanding, the issue of protecting human life at sea begs serious consideration of how human rights obligations can filter down to the relevant actors involved to operationalize protection of the right to life at sea. Ultimately, then, any such developments will come from positive development of the law in a way that strengthens State compliance with the duty to save lives at sea. Undoubtedly, the time is ripe for recognizing an individual right to be rescued at sea given the increasing expansion of sovereign power that has allowed for remote control techniques to be extended beyond the physical frontiers of States, arbitrarily creating gaps and vacuums of protection. Adopting, therefore, a human-rights-based approach to the reconceptualization of distress incidents at sea that threaten the enjoyment of the right to life justifies a progressive interpretation of treaty law in a manner that is responsive to the protection needs of migrants and allows for the recognition of the right to be rescued at sea in international law.

120 Komp (n 60) 232–234.
121 See 'Working paper for a discussion on a Draft Roadmap towards a "European Framework for Operational Cooperation on Search and Rescue in the Mediterranean Sea"' <https://www.statewatch.org/media/3904/eu-com-sar-roadmap-plan.pdf>.

3 The Right to Life Under International Human Rights Law

Undoubtedly, the inextricable link between the duty to render assistance at sea as enshrined in the law of the sea instruments and the right to life as enshrined in human rights instruments cannot be dismissed for the apparent reason that both serve the same purpose: the protection of human life. This is notably evident in the detailed obligations to preserve the safety of life against specific risks of sea travel as demonstrated in the previous chapter through the general framework of the United Nations Convention on the Law of the Sea (UNCLOS)[1] and the detailed obligations in the International Convention for the Safety of Life at Sea (SOLAS) and the International Convention on Maritime Search and Rescue (SAR Convention). In addition to these legal instruments, the 2000 Protocol Against the Smuggling of Migrants by Land, Sea and Air makes clear in Article 16 (1) that States are required to take:

> All appropriate measures, including legislation if necessary, to preserve and protect the rights of persons who have been the object of conduct set forth in article 6 of this Protocol [smuggling] as accorded under applicable international law, in particular the right to life and the right not to be subjected to torture or other cruel, inhuman or degrading treatment or punishment.[2]

In this framework, it is assumed that the majority of irregular migrants use the services of smuggling networks at some point in their journey in order to cross borders.[3] Nonetheless, the thousands of lives that perish each year in the Mediterranean region have become a humanitarian concern that is grow-

1 United Nations Convention on the Law of the Sea (adopted 10 December 1982, entered into force 16 November 1994) 1833 UNTS 397 (UNCLOS).

2 Resolution adopted by UN General Assembly on 15 November 2020, by resolution 55/25, United Nations Convention against Transnational Organized Crime <https://www.unodc.org/pdf/crime/a_res_55/res5525e.pdf>.

3 UNDOC, 'Issue Paper: Smuggling of Migrants by Sea' (2011) 11 <https://www.unodc.org/documents/human-trafficking/Migrant-Smuggling/Issue-Papers/Issue_Paper_-_Smuggling_of_Migrants_by_Sea.pdf>.

DOI: 10.4324/9781003568537-4

ing in scale and demanding significant attention. In particular, the former UN Special Rapporteur on the Human Rights of Migrants, François Crépeau, stressed that 'allowing people to die at Europe's borders just because of their administrative status is a complete disregard for the value of human life'.[4] This statement was, however, made back in 2014, predating both the proliferation of migrant crossings in the Mediterranean and the intensified externalization measures currently observed between the EU, its Member States and third countries of origin and transit.

In light of this, the ongoing situation in the Mediterranean underscores the importance of solidifying extraterritorial human rights obligations during maritime crossings, as the risk to life is particularly heightened during migration by sea. The situational and structural vulnerability of migrants at sea not only relates to navigational hazards and migrant smuggling or human trafficking but also extends to exclusionary border control practices[5] or 'non-entrée' policies,[6] applied from the moment an individual attempts to leave their country as seen in Chapters 1 and 2.

For this reason, switching the attention to the realm of human rights becomes paramount in operationalizing human rights protection that an individual formally has by virtue of their humanity and not by being citizens of a particular State. Equally, beyond the positive obligations of assistance found in the international law of the sea framework, individual rights are protected under international human rights law, which States should guarantee for everyone under their jurisdiction through exercising best efforts. On the one hand, international institutions have sought to interpret positive obligations arising under the right to life in a manner that broadens the scope of application of the right. On the other hand, States appear to adopt a differential treatment in securing the right to life according to the *group* of people they are called upon to save. For instance, Thomas Spijkerboer has rightly observed that 'states have assumed far-reaching positive obligations to protect the right to life for regular travellers, but recognize only limited obligations vis-à-vis irregularized travellers'.[7]

Much of what has been discussed thus far raised questions as to the nature and scope of the right to life as well as its capability of being secured in an area – the high seas – that is often considered to be a *de facto lawless* space,

4 OHCHR, 'Europe/Migrants: "Let Them Die, This Is a Good Deterrence" – UN Human Rights Expert' (30 October 2014) <https://www.ohchr.org/EN/NewsEvents/Pages/DisplayNews.aspx?NewsID=15239&LangID=E>.

5 On tactics of 'remote control', see David Scott FitzGerald, 'Remote Control of Migration: Theorising Territoriality, Shared Coercion and Deterrence' (2020) 46(1) Journal of Ethnic and Migration Studies 4–22.

6 Thomas Gammeltoft-Hansen and James C Hathaway, '*Non-Refoulement* in a World of Cooperative Deterrence' (2015) 53 Columbia Journal of Transnational Law 235.

7 Thomas Spijkerboer, 'Wasted Lives: Borders and the Right to Life of People Crossing Them' (2017) 20 Nordic Journal of International Law.

where individuals are perceived as rightless.[8] This chapter sheds light on the former by evaluating the obligations endowed on States to safeguard the right to life as they have been developed by judicial and quasi-judicial bodies, while the latter will be examined in Chapters 5 and 6 of this book. Hence, the grounds of extraterritorial jurisdiction will not be considered in this chapter; it is assumed that jurisdiction is established in all the cases to be observed, as my primary concern is to examine the scope and extent of positive obligations arising from the right to life. This is an analytically critical step to then clearly delineate the duties incumbent on States (and other actors) that safeguard human life at sea.

1. The Importance and Legal Status of the Right to Life

It is undeniable that the right to life is of unparalleled value and significance, especially given its irreversible nature as the exercise of all other subsequent rights depend on the very preexistence of life itself.[9] In the literature it is depicted as 'the most fundamental of all rights' and 'the supreme right . . . whose effective protection is the prerequisite for the enjoyment of all other human rights'.[10] Against this backdrop, the right to life gained cardinal importance in response to the atrocities which preceded its proclamation; as Count Carton de Wiart has argued, 'it was more than ever necessary to affirm the right to life, as the right had been so gravely violated by the Nazis'.[11]

In the wake of World War II, the UN set out the right to life in the Universal Declaration of Human Rights (UDHR or Declaration)[12] as a response to the atrocities and barbarous acts of the war which shocked the conscience of humankind. The Declaration puts forth in Article 3 that 'everyone has the right to life, liberty and security of person'. In this regard, taking a closer look at the Declaration, *stricto sensu*, this is the first substantive right ascribed to individuals – highlighting its canonical and hierarchical value – as Article 1 affirms the principle of equality and subsequently Article 2 provides for the principle of nondiscrimination.

At this juncture, the Special Rapporteur of the UN Commission on Human Rights, in highlighting the fundamental nature of the right to life, affirmed

8 Itamar Mann, 'Maritime Legal Black Holes: Migration and Rightlessness in International Law' (2018) 29(2) EJIL 357.

9 Giorgia Bevilacqua, 'The Right to Life at Sea Seventy Years after the Proclamation of the Universal Declaration of Human Rights' (2019) 76(3–4) Europa Ethnica 149–154.

10 HRC, *CCPR General Comment No 36 (2018) on Article 6 of the International Covenant on Civil and Political Rights, on the Right to Life*, adopted 30 October 2018, CCPR/C/GC/36, para 2.

11 Johannes Morsink, *The Universal Declaration of Human Rights: Origins, Drafting and Intent* (University of Pennsylvania Press 1999) 40 quoting therein: Committee Records, U.N. GAOR, 3rd Session, United Nations Doc. A/C.3/3 (1958) 84th-180 Meetings, 173.

12 Universal Declaration of Human Rights, UNGA Res 217 A (III) (10 December 1948).

that 'the right to life is . . . a fundamental right in any society, irrespective of its degree of development or the type of culture which characterizes it since this right forms part of *jus cogens* in international human rights law'.[13] Its non-derogable nature under *jus cogens* essentially means that no government may deny its existence, and a superior duty, as well as a heightened level of protection, is imposed on States.[14] Though many scholars have sought to attach to the right to life the status of *jus cogens,* highlighting the prominence placed on the preservation of human life,[15] this remains much contested. Unlike the right to be free from torture, the right to life, as most rights, does not enjoy an absolute scope; instead, there are some limited controlled exceptions that are permitted, including limitations provided in treaty provisions and in times of emergency, which will justify exceptional measures, for instance, in effecting a lawful arrest or in defense of others as prescribed by law.[16] In fact, its non-absolute nature makes it a more complex concept, as considerations where life might be deprived or what will trigger a State's positive obligations to act in order to prevent a violation is a daunting task left for the courts to develop.[17]

It needs be noted that while the UDHR provides a declaratory list of all the norms that our actions ought to conform to as the basis of international human rights law, this 'list' is non-exhaustive. For this reason, not all universal rights we acquire today are enshrined therein but are often the subject of progressive development and interpretation of international human rights law by judicial bodies. This is so as constant societal and structural changes in the international legal order can create protection gaps at times unless specific norms are developed to better safeguard the human rights at stake. In this context, the right to life presents an umbrella or a more generic, parent right, which courts have consistently interpreted as encompassing other, more specific rights or even as giving rise to newly proclaimed rights, like the right to water. This understanding is based on the intrinsic and unarguable value that life has to all persons, which justifies the imposition of duties to secure that interest.[18] Ergo, adopting a human-rights-based approach to the reconceptualization of distress incidents at sea that threaten the enjoyment of the right to life justifies a progressive interpretation of treaty law in a manner that is responsive to the protection needs of migrants.

13 See Bertrand G Ramcharan (ed), *The Right to Life in International Law* (Martinus Nijhoff 1983) 14.

14 Ibid 15.

15 Ibid.

16 See, e.g., ECHR, Art 2; See also Fionnuala Ní Aoláin, 'The Evolving Jurisprudence of the European Convention Concerning the Right to Life' (2001) 19(1) Netherlands Quarterly Human Rights 23.

17 Nigel S Rodley, 'Integrity of the Person' in Daniel Moeckli, Sangeeta Shah and Sandesh Sivakumaran (eds), *International Human Rights Law* (3rd edn, OUP 2017) 175.

18 Joseph Raz, 'Legal Rights' (1984) 4(1) Oxford Journal of Legal Studies 14.

While the UDHR is a nonbinding instrument, the right to life has been subsequently stipulated in a plethora of international human rights treaties and regional instruments, and there is a consensus that it acquires international customary law status.[19] Clearly, the importance of the right to life in the entire international community is undisputed. Pertinently, the thousands of migrants that are recurrently abandoned at sea might additionally be brought within the context of crimes against humanity. In fact, a Communication filed to the International Criminal Court (ICC) in 2019 against the EU and some of its Member States, including Italy, for mismanaging Mediterranean migrations, makes this compelling case:

> A systematic targeting of the most vulnerable civilian populations, at their most helpless moment: crossing the Mediterranean in overcrowded boats, facing real risk of death by drowning. Persecution in this context includes refraining from rescuing, causing either death or deportation coupled with detention . . . exposing the migrant population to other forms of crimes against humanity.[20]

Such discussion centers on examining the attribution of legal responsibility for rights violations, which is beyond the scope of this chapter to engage with these issues. It suffices to add that such factual references remain vital for contextualizing the current crisis in order to justify thicker human rights protection standards and a reconsideration of States' extraterritorial obligations. Hence, the State 'responsibility' aspect I am most concerned with is not the attribution of legal responsibility (after a breach has taken place), but the need to ensure compliance with human rights *beforehand*. Admittedly though, comprehensive delineations of human rights obligations and clarifications regarding the scope of protection always result from alleged violations brought before institutional organs responsible for overseeing and implementing of international human rights.

2. The Right to Life Under International Human Rights Instruments

The architecture of international human rights regimes is designed to provide a bulwark safeguarding the individual against human rights abuses.[21] In contrast

19 See Irini Papanicolopulu, 'Human Rights and the Law of the Sea' in David J Attard, Malgosia Fizmaurice and Norman A Martínez Gutiérrez (eds), *The IMLI Manual on International Maritime Law: Volume I: The Law of the Sea* (OUP 20214).

20 Communication to the Office of the Prosecutor of the International Criminal Court Pursuant to the Article 15 of the Rome Statute: EU Migration Policies in the Central Mediterranean and Libya (2014–2019)' (Communication to the ICC) 163 <https://www.statewatch.org/media/documents/news/2019/jun/eu-icc-case-EU-Migration-Policies.pdf>.

21 Rene Provost and Colleen Sheppard, *Dialogues on Human Rights and Legal Pluralism* (Springer 2013) 63.

to the nature of the vast number of international law treaties that are more State-centric, international human rights law places attention on the rights of the *individual* in relation to the State. For example, in the previous chapter, where the international law of the sea framework was presented, we could observe that the focus was retained *inter alia* on ascribing rights and duties to States and any disputes will result in inter-State proceedings. In essence, then, individuals that are affected by State activities taking place in the maritime space are duty-recipients but are not perceived as right-holders, as UNCLOS does not grant, *explicitly* at least, individual rights that can be claimed or 'received'. Hence, it is posited that the law of the sea offers the *means* which make it possible to realize the ends of international human rights law and, in this case, the protection of human life at sea.[22] For this reason, shifting the emphasis to the realm of international human rights plays a pivotal role in enhancing the protection of migrants during cross-border maritime crossings.

Subsequent to the adoption of the UDHR, the European Convention on Human Rights (ECHR) set forth the right to life in its text, providing in Article 2:

> Everyone's right to life shall be protected by law. No one shall be deprived of his life intentionally save in the execution of a sentence of a court following his conviction of a crime for which this penalty is provided by law.[23]

Also, the International Covenant on Civil and Political Rights (ICCPR) sets out in Article 6, paragraph 1: 'Every human being has the inherent right to life. This right shall be protected by law. No one shall be arbitrarily deprived of his life'.[24] Notice here that the wording of the provision in the ICCPR fundamentally differs from that of the ECHR. In particular, the use of the word 'inherent' underscores its hierarchy, as well as confirming its customary nature. In a similar way, Article 4, paragraph 1 of the American Convention on Human Rights (ACHR) reads: 'Every person has the right to have his life respected. This right shall be protected by law and, in general, from the moment of conception. No one shall be arbitrarily deprived of his life'.[25] Additionally, the African Charter on Human and People's Rights (ACHPR), grants the right to life in a slightly different format and puts forth in Article 4: 'Human beings are inviolable. Every human being shall be entitled to respect for his

22 Vassilis P Tzevelekos and Elena Katselli Proukaki, 'Migrants at Sea: A Duty of Plural States to Protect (Extraterritorially)?' (2017) 86 Nordic Journal of International Law 437.

23 Convention for the Protection of Human Rights and Fundamental Freedoms (adopted 4 November 1950, entered into force 3 September 1953) 213 UNTS 222, Art 2.

24 International Covenant on Civil and Political Rights (adopted 16 December 1966, entered into force 23 March 1976) 999 UNTS 171, Art 6.

25 American Convention on Human Rights (adopted 22 November 1969, entered into force 18 July 1978) 1144 UNTS 123 (ACHR), Art 4.

life and the integrity of his person. No one may be arbitrarily deprived of this right'.[26] The right to life is also protected in EU law under its own Charter of Fundamental Rights of the European Union 2000 (EU Charter) and provides in Article 2, paragraph 1: 'Everyone has the right to life'.[27]

Notwithstanding minor differences in terminology in the way the right to life is prescribed in the above sources, it can be submitted that all the instruments are sufficiently broad, enshrining positive as well as negative obligations binding upon States to secure the right to life.

3. The Types of Human Rights Obligations

In the terrain of human rights law, there are different types of positive obligations imposed on States in order to secure the rights of those under their jurisdiction. The triptych typology of how human rights obligations should be secured is enshrined in three well-known obligations that are closely intertwined to identify the different ways in which States need to discharge their obligations.[28] This section will briefly address those obligations endowed on States, namely, to 'respect', 'protect' and 'fulfil' human rights.

3.1 *Respect*

The duty to respect human rights carries a fundamentally negative aspect. As Frédéric Mégret has observed, the duty is characterized by securing those rights.[29] One theory that can be argued is that a State fulfils its obligation to respect a right by not violating it. In this regard, States, through their agents, have a negative obligation to refrain from interfering with any particular human right, unless there is some reasoned basis for such interference.

3.2 *Protect*

In contrast, the duty to protect in international human rights law carries a positive obligation, requiring States to prevent human rights violations. The positive effect of human rights rules is associated with and stems from a due diligence obligation.[30] In this vein, the principle of due diligence which can be described as ancillary to human rights obligations, establishes obligations of means/conduct (and not of result), requiring States to take

26 ACHPR, Art 4.

27 EU Charter, Art 2.

28 Frédéric Mégret, 'Nature of Obligations' in Daniel Moeckli, Sangeeta Shah and Sandesh Sivakumaran (eds), *International Human Rights Law* (3rd edn, OUP 2017) 99.

29 Ibid 97. Article 1 of the ECHR 'Obligation to respect Hunan Rights' provides: 'The High Contracting Parties shall secure to everyone within their jurisdiction the rights and freedoms defined in Section I of this Convention'.

30 Tzevelekos and Katselli Prukaki (n 22) 432.

all reasonable measures and efforts within their capacity to ensure that these rights are protected.[31] The notion of protection perhaps has become more-than-ever imperative today, as there is the need to protect individuals from human rights violations, especially, vulnerable groups, as is the case with migrants in peril at sea whenever States acquire ***knowledge vis-à-vis*** a certain risk to life that is foreseeable. In this respect, a State's obligation to protect human rights from violations is not unlimited; a State will only be held responsible for those failures that it could have prevented – the criteria of ***reasonableness*** and the ***capacities*** criterion.[32] As it will become apparent below from case law, the types of actions that will constitute a violation or inactions thereof varies and sometimes competing policy considerations might outweigh protection of individual rights.

3.3 Fulfil

The third typology of how human rights should be secured is the fulfilment obligation, which essentially translates into a duty endowed upon States to take positives steps to secure the greater enjoyment of rights.[33] This obligation necessitates a remedy, whether judicial or administrative, to all victims of human rights violations. As follows, it can be understood that States are required to take affirmative, proactive action in order to ensure compliance with the rights under the Convention. As with the obligation to protect, the obligation to fulfil carries elements of the due diligence standard in its execution.

4. The Scope of the Right to Life

The jurisprudence of international judicial and quasi-judicial bodies provides a significant degree of assistance in constructing State duties for safeguarding human life. Over time, these institutions have clarified the scope of positive obligations and have specified what type of conduct is required to comply with a State's human rights obligations and/or to ensure better realization of rights. The exploration below unpacks the evolving nature of obligations arising from the right to life as they have been construed primarily by the European Court of Human Rights (ECtHR or Strasbourg Court or Court) in interpreting Article 2 of the ECHR, and also by the UN Human Rights Committee (HRC or Committee) in interpreting Article 6 of the ICCPR. These two institutions form the leading organs (at least in the European context) entrusted to authoritatively interpret the right to life and have, to date, established far-reaching positive obligations for the protection of an individual's right to life. It needs be noted that the ECtHR as a judicial body issues binding judgments whereas

31 Sarah Joseph and Sam Dipnall, 'Scope of Application' in Daniel Moeckli, Sangeeta Shah and Sandesh Sivakumaran (eds), *International Human Rights Law* (3rd edn, OUP 2017) 115.

32 Ibid; *X and Y v The Netherlands* (1986) 8 EHRR 235.

33 Mégret (n 28) 98.

the HRC's decisions or the so-called 'Views of the Committee' in dealing with individual 'communications' under the Optional Control are not binding in nature. Yet, it is understood that States should take them into account and perform them in good faith.[34] Hence, a decision by a UN human rights body holds no lesser significance or 'legal' value as these bodies play an important role in interpreting the normative content of the corresponding instruments while also giving concrete meaning to individual rights and state obligations.[35]

4.1 *The Osman Test*

The ECtHR initially developed the positive duties arising from the right to life in the context of threats against the lives of identified individuals by non-State actors. In the leading case of *Osman v the United Kingdom*,[36] the Court laid down the necessary criteria for imposing positive obligations on States to safeguard the right to life by formulating the '*Osman* test'. The Court notably clarified that the duty would arise when authorities *knew, or ought* to have known at the time, of the existence of a *real and immediate* risk to an identified individual's life from the criminal acts of another individual.[37] In a nutshell, the tailored criteria that will trigger the protection of human life are as follows: 1) knowledge; 2) a real and immediate risk to an identifiable individual; and 3) failure to take reasonable measures. With reference to knowledge, the Court explained that the standard of knowledge of a possible threat cannot be placed too high.[38] In this light, if there are elements that a person might be in danger and there are measures that the authorities could take to mitigate the risk, they must do so. However, the Court was extremely cautious not to overexpand the duty to take 'reasonable measures' in a way that would impose an impossible or disproportionate burden on the authorities.[39] Henceforth, unreasonable expectations will not be fashioned against a State in relation to its *capacity* to protect life. In this understanding, *knowledge* (actual or putative) about a particular individual at risk *triggers a State's positive obligations.*

34 VLCT, Art 26.

35 Fay Pazartizs and Panos Merkouris, 'Preliminary Report on the Interpretative Practice of the Human Rights Committee and Other UN Human Rights Treaty Bodies' (2018) <https://papers.ssrn.com/sol3/papers.cfm?abstract_id=3797716>; For further discussion see OHCHR, 'Statement by Mr. Zeid Ra'ad Al Hussein, United Nations High Commissioner for Human Rights, at the International Law Commission' (OHCHR, 21 July 2015) <https://www.ohchr.org/EN/NewsEvents/Pages/DisplayNews.aspx?NewsID=16254&LangID=E>.

36 *Osman v the United Kingdom*, App no 23452/94 (ECtHR, 28 October 1998).

37 Ibid para 115.

38 Lisa-Marie Komp, 'The Duty to Assist Persons in Distress: An Alternative Source of Protection against the Return of Migrants and Asylum Seekers to the High Seas?' in Violeta Moreno-Lax and Efthymios Papastavridis (eds), *'Boat Refugees' and Migrants at Sea: A Comprehensive Approach: Integrating Maritime Security with Human Rights* (Vol. 7, International Refugee Law Series, Brill Nijhoff 2016) 239.

39 Ibid para 116.

4.2 Knowledge and Foreseeability

Another critical case is *Opuz v Turkey*,[40] where the Court, by applying the *Osman* test, reiterated that positive obligations arising under the right to life require States to take preventive operational measures to protect life at risk from criminal acts of another individual. On the facts of the case, the Court concluded that Turkey could have foreseen a lethal attack against the victim and should have exercised due diligence to prevent the murder of the individual in question.[41] It is as such understood that the right to life prescribes a duty to prevent a violation from occurring, introducing a due diligence standard in international human rights law, in circumstances where it is foreseeable or known that life is at risk. Hence, the due diligence verge of positive obligations can be perceived as a risk-management tool developed by courts in order to adjust protection levels in the various factual circumstances that may arise within a case. Evidently, there is an early consensus that merely abstaining from the arbitrary deprivation of life will not suffice under the Convention. In addition, the duty to prevent loss of life according to a due diligence standard was also evidenced in the *Osman* case, where the Court identified a 'reasonable knowledge' condition which provided that the preventive positive obligation arises if the State's authorities knew or should have known of a real and immediate risk to the life of an identified individual(s).[42]

In this vein, the knowledge criterion rests on a factual assessment of the circumstances which will be triggered by a certain risk that is foreseeable for States. This component is used by the Court to explain the doctrine of positive obligations emanating from the right to life. In the context of maritime migration and border management, it can be analogously argued that the knowledge criterion will be satisfied when a State (its rescue and coordination center) receives information about a distress incident that alerts them of a probable result – the foreseeable risk to the life of migrants who are in distress – and requires immediate action.

Actual or putative knowledge will of course rest on the factual circumstances. Yet given the history of casualties taking place across the Mediterranean Sea (especially over the last decade), coupled with preexisting knowledge of the Mediterranean migration routes, coastal States are reasonably expected to apprehend that when they receive information about a possible distress incident at sea, whether in the form of a direct distress call from the migrants in distress or from another source – there is a certain risk to the life of migrants that is foreseeable. This will translate into a positive obligation to exercise due diligence in preventing drowning by rescue in a State's search and rescue (SAR) zone more generally, but more relevantly when the

40 *Opuz v Turkey*, App no 33401/02 (ECtHR, 9 June 2009) para 144.
41 Ibid paras 137 and 149.
42 *Osman* (n 36) paras 116–117.

authorities are informed of a possible distress incident at sea. However, as Stoyanova highlights, the standard of 'ought to have known' of the existence of a risk of harm to life remains unclear in the Court's jurisprudence.[43] The suggestion put forth, that States authorities should have known of the risk, 'based on the information that was *in fact* before them at the particular point in time' stands to be the most reasonable and least 'onerous' in this context.[44] This is so as the appreciation of knowledge is made with regard to the information that was *actually* before the State authorities. For this reason, the ECtHR in its jurisprudence has tied the examination of knowledge with reasonableness, in order to avoid adding an excessive burden on States.

Pursuant to the above, it is clear that a State's positive obligations to protect the right to life encompass a duty to 'prevent' loss of life according to a due diligence standard. To be sure, this is not an absolute duty as there are boundaries in delimiting the preventive measures a State would need to take, even though these are not clear-cut in the Court's jurisprudence. In this vein, the Strasbourg Court frequently refers to judgments from other judicial bodies, and in the context of interpreting the due diligence standard has referred to the Inter-American Court's decisions,[45] in particular to the case of *Velásquez Rodríguez v Honduras*, where the court illustrated in a similar manner the substance of the due diligence standard: 'The State has a legal duty to take reasonable steps to prevent human rights violations and to use the means at its disposal to carry out a serious investigation of violations committed within its jurisdiction'.[46]

In fact, the Inter-American Court's case law affirms the principle of due diligence by repeatedly holding States responsible on account of their lack of due diligence to prevent human rights violations as well as to investigate and sanction perpetrators.[47] The due diligence verge of the positive obligation to protect life was also explicitly confirmed by the HRC in its *General Comment No 31* on the right to life under the ICCPR. In particular, paragraph 8 provides:

> There may be circumstances in which a failure to ensure Covenant rights as required by article 2 would give rise to violations by States Parties of those rights, as a result of States Parties' permitting or failing to take appropriate measures or to exercise due diligence to prevent, punish,

43 Vladislava Stoyanova, *Positive Obligations under the European Convention on Human Rights: Within and Beyond Boundaries* (Oxford: OUP 2023) 26.

44 Ibid 28.

45 Yoon Jim Shin, *A Transnational Human Rights Approach to Human Trafficking: Empowering the Powerless* (Brill 2017) 225.

46 See for instance the reasoning by the IACHR in *Velásquez-Rodríguez v Honduras*, Series C No. 4 (29 July 1988) para 174.

47 *Opuz v Turkey* (n 40) para 84.

investigate or redress the harm caused by such acts by private persons or entities.[48]

From the above illustrations, it is useful to mark the existence of a transnational judicial dialogue. This has a significant force in the development of international human rights law, as it shows that judges share a consensus, but not always,[49] when developing obligations under human rights law and frequently refer to other courts' jurisprudence as a guide to their own decisions. This will become central to my analysis in the last two chapters of this book when examining the latest developments in the HRC's jurisprudence and the analogous expectations from the ECtHR to follow.

4.3 Harm from Activities of Public Authorities/Dangerous Activities

Continuing, the ECtHR reformulated once more its *Osman* test in the case of *Öneryildiz v Turkey*.[50] It emphasized *inter alia* that the positive obligation to take all appropriate steps to safeguard life requires 'above all' a primary duty on States to put in place a legislative and administrative framework to prevent loss of life. *In casu*, the Court treated the operation of waste-collection sites as a dangerous activity, which activated the State's duty to protect the right to life. Accordingly, it stretched the obligation to protect beyond the scope of private individuals, encompassing 'any activity, whether public or not' in which the right to life may be at stake.[51] Hence, the positive obligation to protect life will apply to all possible circumstances and even extends to general structural risks against the population at large, where the State is aware or should have been aware that these risks might lead to the loss of life.[52] It is important to note here that the Court did not require that the individuals at risk were identifiable, but that a *group of people* who lived in the area was exposed to the risk.

Analogously, the *Osman* criterion of risk to an *identifiable* individual has been explicitly abandoned in the case of *Mastromatteo v Italy*,[53] where the

48 HRC, *CCPR General Comment No 31: The Nature of the General Legal Obligation Imposed on States Parties to the Covenant*, adopted 29 March 2004, CCPR/C/21/Rev.1/Add.13, para 80.

49 Compare for instance the findings of the Committee on the Rights of the Child in *L.H. et al v France* (30 September 2020) and *F.B. et al v France* (CRC/C/86/D/R.77/2019)(4 February 2021) and the ECtHR's reasoning a year later in *H.F. and Others v France, Applications* Nos 24384/19 and 44234/20 (ECtHR, 14 September 2022), in the context of France's failure to repatriate French children and their mothers that have been held in Syrian detention camps.

50 *Öneryildiz v Turkey*, App no 48939/99 (ECtHR, 30 November 2004) para 89.

51 Ibid para 71.

52 Vladislava Stoyanova, 'The Right to Life Under the EU Charter and Cooperation with Third States to Combat Human Smuggling' (2020) 21(3) German Law Journal 447.

53 *Mastromatteo v Italy*, App no 37703/97 (ECtHR, 24 October 2002).

Court emphasized that the elements of 'real and immediate risk' as set out in *Osman* are not a requirement for an identifiable individual or identifiable group of individuals.[54] In this way, the Court altered the *Osman* test criterion, allowing a positive obligation to be triggered if there is a risk to life for members of the public at large.[55] It appears that the Court is taking an active role in expanding the concept of what protecting the right to life means by altering the criteria applied, not only when actions or omissions affect an identified individual(s) but also in cases where they impact the general protection of society.[56]

Of particular relevance is the case of *Budayeva v Russia*,[57] where the Court found a positive duty to protect life in a case concerning a village in an area known to be affected by mudslides.[58] Expressly, the Court affirmed that the State's duty is activated when the natural hazard is imminent and clearly identifiable, especially 'where it concern[s] a recurring calamity affecting a distinct area developed for human habitation or use'.[59] The Court also stressed that the right to life under the Convention imposes a 'duty to do everything within the authorities' power' to protect human life.[60] This reasoning can be arguably applied to the situation in the Mediterranean, finding a positive duty to protect life at sea on the grounds that States carry a substantial degree of knowledge of the imminent existence of the threat to life. Arguably, only by requiring action at a time when it can still have an effect can the positive dimension of the right to life be effectively interpreted. To be sure though, the Court will never fashion an obligation that places a disproportionate burden on States. In this vein, Maria Monnheimer has argued that the due diligence obligation can be an attractive tool for the Court to utilize as it is flexible enough to address new challenges and can be adjusted relatively quickly.[61] It is evident that human rights bodies increasingly complement existing positive obligations with due diligence ones as witnessed in the Strasbourg Court's case law.[62]

4.4 *Procedural Requirements*

The ECtHR further established another set of obligations on States in the context of procedural requirements under the right to life, that is, a duty to provide arrangements to secure legal accountability for those responsible for

54 Ibid para 68.
55 Ibid para 74.
56 Ibid para 69.
57 *Budayeva and others v Russia*, App nos 15339/02, 21166/02, 20058/02, 11673/02 and 15343/02 (ECtHR, 20 March 2008) 27.
58 Martin Ratkovich, 'International Law and the Rescue of Refugees at Sea' (PhD thesis, Sweden: Stockholm University 2019) 154.
59 *Budayeva* (n 57) para 137.
60 Ibid 175.
61 Maria Monnheimer, *Due Diligence Obligations in International Human Rights Law* (CUP 2021).
62 Ibid.

a violation of the right to life. This was exemplified in *Kaya v Turkey*,[63] where the Court found a violation of Article 2 on the basis of an ineffective investigation into the death of the applicant's brother following the exercise of lethal force. In holding so, it highlighted the positive nature of the obligations arising under the provision by prescribing that States need to ensure the accountability for deaths occurring under the responsibility of a State's agents for acts they did or did not do. Simplified, a lack of accountability into the circumstances of the death will constitute a violation of Article 2 under the Convention.[64] Connecting the lack of effective investigation with a violation of the right to life is consistent with the legal prohibition on arbitrary killing, as the latter will be rendered vain if there is no procedure for reviewing the lawfulness of the use of force by the State and its agents.[65]

In addition, the Court illustrated in *Cyprus v Turkey*[66] that there is also another positive obligation to investigate suspicious deaths. Specifically, the Court found a violation on the grounds of the Turkish authorities' failure to conduct an effective investigation into the fate of nine men who disappeared in life-threatening circumstances.[67] Moreover, another significant development that emphasizes the scope of the obligation to undertake an effective investigation is the *Xhavara and Others v Italy and Albania* case[68] brought in the context of migrant interceptions. *In casu*, 58 migrants drowned due to their vessel being struck by an Italian navy vessel. The Court held in this instance that the Italian authorities were under an obligation pursuant to Article 2 of the Convention to instigate an effective investigation into the deaths of the victims. The same obligation will hold for the deaths/disappearances of migrants in the Mediterranean; for instance, if a flag State becomes aware that its shipmaster failed to render assistance, then it is under a due diligence obligation to investigate the deaths that occurred in breach of the right to life.

4.5 *Vulnerable Group of Individuals*

Pertinently, the Court continues to expand the scope of obligations arising under Article 2 by taking into account normative considerations which emanate from the nature of the applicant's complaint. In particular, in assessing the general protection of the right to life required by States, the court will consider the

63 *Kaya v Turkey*, App no 22729/93 (ECtHR, 19 February 1998).

64 See, also, Christof Heyns and Thomas Probert, 'Securing the Right to Life: A Cornerstone of the Human Rights System' (*EJIL:Talk!*, 11 May 2016) <https://www.ejiltalk.org/securing-the-right-to-life-a-cornerstone-of-the-human-rights-system/>.

65 Ní Aoláin (n 16) 33; The HRC confirmed this as well in *Amirov v Russian Federation*, Communication No 1447/2006, 2 April 2009, UN Doc CCPR/C/95/D/1447/2006.

66 *Cyprus v Turkey*, App no 25781/94 (ECtHR, 10 May 2001).

67 The positive obligation was later also confirmed in *Eshenov v Uzbekistan*, HRC, Comm. No. 1225/2003 (2010).

68 *Xhavara and Others v Italy and Albania*, App no 39473/98 (ECtHR, 11 January 2001).

specific and unique needs of the individual in question with regards to protecting her right to life.[69] In *Kemaloglu v Turkey*,[70] the Court was ready to find a violation of Article 2 in circumstances where the authorities failed to take measures which might have otherwise been expected to avoid that risk to life. The case concerned the failure of the school authorities to fulfil their duties by neglecting to inform the bus of the school's early closure, which led to a 7-year-old's death after the school let him walk home alone in heavy snow. The judgment is instructive as the Court found a positive obligation to protect the right to life by reason of the individual's young age, which signified an inherent vulnerability. In its line of reasoning, the Court referred to the *Öneryildiz* judgment to emphasize once more that a State's positive obligation under Article 2 applied in the context of *any activity*, whether public or not, in which the right to life is at stake. Still, the Court reiterated that not every risk to life would oblige the authorities to take operational measures to prevent the risk from materializing. Notwithstanding the circumstances of the case, the Court adopted a vulnerability-based approach and found that it was within the school's exclusive power to avoid exposing students' life to risk. In coming to this decision, the duty to prevent violations of the right to life received a wide-ranging conceptual underpinning.[71]

The same holds true for the precarious state of migrants at sea. It can be anticipated that rubber, inflatable, leaky and overloaded vessels signify that the vehicles used to migrate suffer *a priori* from unseaworthiness and, for this reason, present a serious threat to human life from the start of their journey. Therefore, migrants embarking on sea journeys can be identified as vulnerable, in need of protection, from the outset as danger to life qualifies as being imminent from the moment migrants embark on such dangerous journeys. In conjunction with this, the controversial cooperation agreements frequently drawn between European States and third countries make it even more dangerous for migrants to travel by diverting them to more perilous sea routes and exposing them to heightened life risks, and should not be overlooked.[72] In fact, the continuing large-scale loss of life at sea should prompt States to review the applicable regulatory system, as Lisa-Marie Komp convincingly posits, 'with an eye to the question whether it actually prevents the loss of life in practice'.[73]

69 Ní Aoláin (n 16) 25.

70 *Kemaloglu v Turkey*, App no 19986/06 (ECtHR, 10 April 2012).

71 Franz Christian Ebert and Romina I Sijniensky, 'Preventing Violations of the Right to Life in the European and the Inter-American Human Rights Systems: From the Osman Test to a Coherent Doctrine on Risk Prevention?' (2015) 15(2) Human Rights Law Review 346.

72 Communication to the ICC (n 20) para 491; Paolo Cuttitta and Tamar Last (eds), *Border Deaths: Causes, Dynamics and Consequences of Migration Related Mortality* (Amsterdam University Press 2020) 15; Van Liempt, 'Tunisia Deal Unlikely to Reduce Illegal Migration, Say Experts' (Dutch News, 20 July 2023) <https://www.dutchnews.nl/2023/07/tunisia-deal-unlikely-to-reduce-illegal-migration-say-experts/>.

73 Lisa-Marie Komp, *Border Deaths at Sea under the Right to Life in the European Convention on Human Rights* (Routledge: Taylor & Francis 2022) 157.

In this context, the ECtHR has, at times, ascribed migrants as a 'vulnerable' group due to the distressful circumstances they had experienced before entering a State. Accordingly, the *Principles and Guidelines* elaborated by the Global Migration Group and the UN High Commissioner for Human Rights in 2018 defines that protection must be even broader when extended to migrants in particular conditions of *vulnerability* and cannot be restricted due to the demands of border control and management.[74] Moreover, the Court in *M.S.S. v Belgium and Greece* signified asylum seekers' status as 'particularly underprivileged and vulnerable' and in need of 'special protection'.[75] However, this stance in migration-related cases has not been frequently employed by the Court.[76]

In this context, the above case of *Kemaloglu* is of particular relevance as it highlights that the Court was willing to extend the scope of the right to life and find a violation in order to protect vulnerable individuals – a 7-year-old boy, showcasing that in light of the 'vulnerability' of the person, the Court might require a different degree of specific protective duties to secure the right to life. Indeed, the vulnerability paradigm is an authoritative analytical scheme the Court uses to decide cases and bring about enhanced and tailored protection to a specific group of persons.[77] This case can be contrasted with the Court's decision one year earlier in *Berü v Turkey*,[78] where the child's vulnerability due to their young age was not a decisive factor or even a factor for imposing a positive obligation upon State authorities.

Turning to the *Berü case*, the Court here was not ready to stretch the positive obligations to protect the right to life of a young girl who was attacked and killed

74 Global Migration Group, Office of the UN High Commissioner for Human Rights, Principles and Guidelines, Supported by Practical Guidance, on the Human Rights Protection of Migrants in Vulnerable Situations, 2018. On the concept of vulnerability, see Ben Hudson, 'Migration in the Mediterranean: Exposing the Limits of Vulnerability at the European Court of Human Rights' (2018) 4 Maritime Safety and Security Law Journal 26–27.

75 *M.S.S. v Belgium and Greece*, App no 30696/09 (ECtHR, 21 January 2011) para 251; Siobhán Mullally, 'A Crisis of Protection in Europe: Migrants at Sea' (2016) 110 Proceedings of the ASIL Annual Meeting 175 <https://www.cambridge.org/core/journals/proceedings-of-the-asil-annual-meeting/article/abs/crisis-of-protection-in-europe-migrants-at-sea/A664A0B464DEA0EDF45EFC595BBC5A00>.

76 For instance, in the *Khlaifia* case, the Court did not accord any significance to the trauma of the shipwreck and its after-effects in deciding whether the applicants were vulnerable. See *Khlaifia and Others v Italy*, App no 16483/12 (ECtHR, 15 December 2016). Still, the ECtHR has recently ruled in an illegal maritime push-back case that the group of applicants as would-be asylum seekers was a determining factor to finding a violation of Article 4 Protocol No. 4 of the Convention; this poses a risk for future cases of collective expulsions, as there should be a universal application, regardless of a person's status or behavior when crossing borders. See *M.A. and Z.R. v Cyprus*, App no 39090/20 (ECtHR, 8 October 2024) para 118.

77 Ingrid Nifosi-Sutton, *The Protection of Vulnerable Groups under International Human Rights Law* (Routledge: Taylor & Francis 2017) 243.

78 *Berü v Turkey*, App no 47304/07 (ECtHR, 11 January 2011).

by stray dogs; even though the dogs were already known to be dangerous in the context of a series of attacks on other people in that area. In the instant case, the Court reasoned that there was no evidence suggesting that authorities knew or ought to have known of the *immediate risk* to the child's life in order to take the required preventive measures. The rationale behind the Court's reasoning was not to overstretch the State's responsibility in an excessive manner, which would, in turn, add an excessive burden on the authorities and is justified by the need to manage limited scarce resources.[79] On the other hand, in his dissenting opinion, Judge Popovic questioned the proportionality principle that was applied by the majority in setting out the positive obligations of a State and relied on the rule laid down in *Öneryildiz v Turkey*.[80] He was of the view that it was the failure of the public authorities to fulfil the positive obligation to protect life which formed the basis of the State's responsibility, as the protection against stray dogs is not an 'unachievable task' for the State, as the public authorities had to ensure the safety of its citizens. As with the judgment provided in *Öneryildiz*, the view was that the authorities had not done everything that could reasonably be expected of them within the scope of their powers to prevent the risks materializing.[81] *In casu*, while the threats might not have been expressly directed against the victim, I share the same view as Judge Popovic that the authorities violated their respective obligations. The case presents a clear-cut example of a real and known risk in an area to which everyone could have been exposed; hence, it should have activated the authorities' obligations to take reasonable measures to prevent the particular risk from materializing. Still, it is worth distinguishing the facts of *Berü* from those of *Kemaloglou*, particularly regarding the young age of the children involved. In *Bëru*, the entire population living in that area could have been exposed to the danger, whereas, in the latter case, the danger was exclusively towards children in the school. In a subsequent case, *Cervioğlu v Turkey*,[82] involving a child that drowned in a water pit at a construction site, the Court reiterated that the accident could not have been foreseeable since the construction had only recently started. Nonetheless, it concluded that the State knew about it as a construction permit had been issued and necessary safety precautions were necessary as any construction site has the potential for life-endangering accidents, not only for professional construction workers but vulnerable groups such as children.[83]

Insofar as the 'realness' criterion is concerned as to the nature of the risk that the State knew or ought to have known about, there is a nonuniform standard adopted. In the case of *Keenan v the United Kingdom*,[84] the Court held that immediacy of the risk varied *during* and *prior* to the suicide in the

79 Ibid para 47.

80 Mentioning explicitly para 71 of *Öneryildiz* (n 50).

81 *Öneryildiz* (n 50) para 87.

82 *Cervioğlu v Turkey*, App no 69546/12 (ECtHR, 4 October 2016) para 68.

83 Ibid para 67.

84 *Keenan v United Kingdom*, App no 27229/95 (ECtHR, 3 April 2001).

case. The upshot of this case is that the Court, when interpreting the criteria laid down in the *Osman* test, treats the 'realness' of the risk to be a 'significant likelihood that the risk will materialise unless preventative measures are taken'.[85] In contrast, the term 'immediacy' has been treated with more ambiguity as to the time frame within which a risk can be considered imminent.[86] For example, in the *Öneryildiz* case, the Court expanded the meaning of 'immediacy' to include a very long time frame as it considered the risk of explosion to have been imminent years before the incident actually occurred. All these examples prove that the Court uses a case-by-case approach when interpreting the factors which will trigger a State's positive obligations to protect the right to life. At the same time, most recent developments in UN's human rights case law show that a significant amount of time before the risk materializes will not trigger the positive obligations under the ICCPR. In particular, the HRC ruling in *Ioane Teitiota v New Zealand*[87] is instructive. This case involved a Kiribati citizen who claimed New Zealand violated his right to life by denying him asylum, arguing that climate change rendered Kiribati uninhabitable. The HRC ruled that the State's decision was not arbitrary and did not amount to a manifest error or a denial of justice. The Committee highlighted that 'given that the risk of an entire country becoming submerged under water is such an extreme risk, the conditions of life in such a country may become incompatible with the right to life with dignity before the risk is realized'.[88] Insofar as the Committee accepted the claim that Kiribati might become uninhabitable due to sea level rise, it reasoned that a 10- to 15-year time frame is sufficient time for affirmative actions by the government to protects its citizens from climate change.[89] Yet in his powerful dissenting opinion, Muhumza illustrated that it would be 'counterintuitive to the protection of life, to wait for deaths to be very frequent and considerable' and questioned at what point the situation would be considered sufficiently grave to recognize a threat to life. This recent case underscores the evolving understanding of the positive obligations under the right life that require both proactive and preventive measures to address risks posed by climate change and environmental degradation, prioritizing early intervention to ensure adequate protection.

4.6 *Potential Victims of a Violation of the Right to Life*

Turning to a different set of positive obligations, the Court's judgment in *Makaratzis v Greece*[90] is particularly instructive, as it highlighted that on several occasions, Article 2 of the Convention might apply even if a person whose right to life

85 Ibid para 96; Ebert and Sijniensky (n 71) 359.
86 See Stoyanova (n 43) 34–36.
87 UN Human Rights Committee (HRC), *Ioane Teitiota v New Zealand* (advance unedited version now available: 23 September 2020) UN Doc CCPR/C/127/D/2728/2016 (7 January 2020).
88 Ibid para 9.11.
89 Ibid para 9.12.
90 *Makaratzis v Greece*, App no 50385/99 (ECtHR, 20 December 2004).

was allegedly breached has not lost her life.[91] *In casu*, a complaint was brought against Greece for the police officers' excessive firepower against him, putting his life at risk as well as the absence of an adequate and effective investigation into the incident from the authorities. Importantly, in this case, the Court contemplated a merely 'potential' or 'virtual' victim of a violation of the right to life is allowed to take action under the ECHR in certain circumstances.[92] By finding a virtual violation of the right to life, the Court went further, and in so doing, broadened the scope of State protection, preventing the moment of death alone from becoming the defining factor for a violation to be found. The line of reasoning fundamentally extended the scope of the right to life beyond a presumption of death, which allows for situations that endanger one's life to be taken into account. Notably, the Court stressed that 'there should be no waiting for an irreversible violation of the right to life'.[93] Hence, States should take appropriate measures to protect human life against risks, regardless of whether or not the risk materializes.[94]

The *Marakatzis* case can be distinguished from the above examples, as the Court applied this reasoning to a case of lethal force by police forces and considered this to be an *exceptional* circumstance.[95] Nevertheless, the Court continuously proves its readiness to be innovative in assessing the obligations necessary to protect the right to life. In fact, the *McCann* reasoning could be employed in this context to accentuate this outcome, insofar as the Strasbourg Court was willing to extend the protection before the death *to the planning of an operation which may capture a suspect.*[96] Hence, the Court has not only recognized that protection of life is not isolated to the moment of fatality, but also if it did result in an individual's death, it would be then immaterial whether the outcome was intended or not.

Insofar as a breach of positive obligations is found, the ECtHR however does not, in principle, specifically identify what would have been best or most optimal measure to fulfil these obligations. The Court has noted:

> The choice of means for ensuring the positive obligations under Article 2 [the right to life] is in principle a matter that falls within the Contracting State's margin of appreciation. There are a number of avenues for ensuring Convention rights, and even if the State has failed to apply one particular measure provided for by domestic law, it may still fulfill its positive duty by other means.[97]

91 Ibid para 55.
92 Ibid paras 43 and 45.
93 Ibid para 43.
94 Ibid; Elizabeth Wisks, 'The Meaning of "Life": Dignity and the Right to Life in International Human Rights Treaties' (2012) 12(2) Human Rights Law Review 202.
95 *Makaratzis* (n 90) para 56.
96 *McCann and Others v the United Kingdom*, App no 18984/91 (ECtHR, 27 September 1995).
97 E.g. see *Cevrioglu v Turkey* App no 69546/12 (ECtHR, 4 October 2016) para 55; *Fadeyeva v Russia* App no 55723/00 (ECtHR, 9 June 2005) para 96; *Budayeva and Others v Russia* App no 15339/02

Hence, States have increasing discretion to decide how to comply with a Court's final judgment and to perform its 'execution'.[98] As Stoyanova argues, proposals of some specific potential measures need to be proposed as alternatives to the omissions in order for the reasoning to be performed.[99]

4.7 Reckless Persons

Lastly, the Court has emphasized several times that the right to life 'cannot be interpreted as guaranteeing to every individual an absolute level of security in any activity in which the right to life may be at stake, in particular when the person concerned bears a degree of responsibility for the accident having exposed himself or herself to unjustified danger'.[100] The victim might have assumed risks by willingly exposing herself to a known and appreciated risk. In this regard, the Court illustrated in *Molie v Romania* that the State does not have a positive obligation to protect reckless persons.[101] Essentially, here the Court was trying to limit the scope of obligations arising under the right to life by prescribing some qualifications on the 'any activity' part of the test, namely, if the risk is to some extent created by the individual(s) in question.

To an extent, the analysis with regard to reckless persons may hold for migrants since it can be argued that migrants are making an autonomous decision to expose themselves to an obvious danger. This is so, as migrants habitually choose to embark on risky sea journeys with the foreknowledge that they will need to be rescued at some point and therefore should be at least aware of the dangers of travelling irregularly by sea. Hence, given the agency of migrants, it could be considered unreasonable to place a disproportionate burden on States to avoid these risks from materializing. Nonetheless, other rules of international law come into play, such as the law of the sea along with other international obligations that should be read together before adopting such a narrow approach.[102] The law of the sea imposes a duty to assist persons

(ECtHR, 20 March 2008) para 134–135; *Öneryildiz v Turkey*, App no 48939/99 (ECtHR, 30 November 2004) para 107.

98 Execution is supervised by the Committee of Ministers. Başak Çali and Anne Koch, 'Foxes Guarding the Foxes? The Peer Review of Human Rights Judgments by the Committee of Ministers of the Council of Europe' (2014) 14(2) Human Rights Law Review 301.

99 Vladislava Stoyanova, 'Correlativity Between Human Rights and Positive Obligations and Its Role for the Execution of Judgments Delivered by the European Court of Human Rights' (2024) European Convention on Human Rights Law Review 15.

100 ECtHR, 'Guide on Article 2 of the European Convention on Human Rights' (2018) 8 <https://fln.dk/-/media/FLN/Publikationer-og-notater/EMRK/Guide-on-Article-2-of-the-European-Convention-on-Human-Rights.pdf?la=da&hash=90AF97C1CA74479FFED7012EBC0C91479D0686CF>.

101 *Molie v Romania*, App no 13754/02 (ECtHR, 1 September 2009) para 44; Also relevant is *Gökdemir v Turkey*, App no 66309/09 (ECtHR, 19 May 2015) para 17, whereby a person has 'exposed himself to unjustified danger' by falling into the sea.

102 VCLT, Art 33.

in distress at sea, and this duty does not become qualified in situations where people have exposed themselves to danger; it is *absolute* in this regard. Besides, what other legal avenues are there to avoid this odyssey in order to seek international protection? As already exemplified, migration by sea is one of the (non-legal) channels that refugees have to seek protection *vis-à-vis* asylum in another country, as there is not one country in the world that allows refugees to arrive legally to seek asylum.[103] The ECtHR further stressed that the duty to prevent the loss of life should not be interpreted in an overly 'paternalistic' manner, leaving room for the choices of individuals even if those choices may expose them to certain risks.[104]

In fact, the *Öneryildiz* judgment can be applied in the context of migration controls. This is so because the various European migration policies and cooperation agreements established with third countries (as evidenced in Chapter 1) not only intensify the underlying risks to life but arguably drive migrants to take riskier routes in order to avoid border control authorities. As Spijkerboer has argued, States should incorporate in their policies a 'serious effort to minimize unintended side-effects', and this duty is even more critical given that these side effects include the foreseeable death of migrants.[105] Therefore, there is a requirement to discontinue a measure that turns out to be a threat to the right to life.[106] Certainly, as foreseen, the EU and its Member States have adopted policies which, to a certain *foreseeable* extent, negatively affect the lives of individuals who are trying to cross borders. It is in this context that positive obligations to protect the right to life might be triggered, as States will still be required to take all reasonable measures to prevent the loss of life.

Outside the maritime space but in a similar context concerning migrant land crossings, the recent judgment of the Court in *N.D. and N.T. v Spain*[107] can prove problematic towards adopting a more lenient understanding pertaining to reckless behavior. *In casu,* the Court found no breach if the deportees have caused the collective expulsion by their own 'culpable conduct' as they did not go through regular border procedures.[108] As Markard argues, this approach seems to consider that push-backs of persons crossing the border in an irregular manner will never breach the prohibition of collective expulsions as long as there is the possibility to cross the border in a regular manner.

103 This is arguably the result of the Refugee Convention that requires refugees to be outside their country of origin in order to claim protection.

104 *Prilutskiy v Ukraine*, App no 40429/08 (ECtHR, 2005) 32; Komp (n 73) 155.

105 See also Thomas Spijkerboer, 'Moving Migrants, States, and Rights: Human Rights and Border Deaths' (2013) 7(2) Law and Ethics of Human Rights 232.

106 Komp (n 73) 131.

107 *N.D. and N.T. v Spain*, App nos 8675/15 and 8697/15 (ECtHR, 13 February 2020).

108 Nora Markard, 'A Hole of Unclear Dimensions: Reading ND and NT v. Spain' (EU Migration Law Blog, 1 April 2020) <https://eumigrationlawblog.eu/a-hole-of-unclear-dimensions-reading-nd-and-nt-v-spain/>.

Following, it is assumed that if in theory an application for protection can be made at a checkpoint, even if a third country effectively prevents such access, States are 'now free to use pushbacks everywhere else'.[109] The individual is thus displaced 'from the heart towards the periphery of the ECHR system'.[110] As a result, despite the widespread adoption of a universal human rights language by various actors, including States, 'there remains a gap between the promise of human rights for all, and the reality of discrimination and abjection routinely faced by many migrants'.[111]

In comparing this situation to migrant sea crossings, it might as well be the case in the future that judges will apply the 'own culpable conduct' test on the part of irregular migrants who cross the sea in large numbers. But will the Court do so, in the context of Article 2, the right to life, under the Convention? In any respect, the Court's reasoning falls short of rendering Convention' rights practical and effective and further accentuates the distinction between citizens and non-citizens as right bearers. A year before this judgment, Judge Pinto de Albuquerque of the ECtHR voiced his view that 'to allow people to be rejected at land borders and returned without assessing the individual claims amounts to treating them like animals. Migrants are not cattle than can be driven away like this'.[112]

5. Recent Developments and Concluding Remarks

An equally important development in this terrain was the adoption of *General Comment No 36* on the right to life (Article 6, ICCPR) in 2018 by the HRC.[113] Specifically, in paragraph 63, the HRC specified that States have an obligation to protect and ensure the right to life for all persons under their authority and control and 'this includes persons *located outside any territory* effectively controlled by the State, whose right to life is nonetheless impacted *by its military or other activities* in a *direct* and *reasonably foreseeable* manner'.[114] Moreover, it authoritatively confirmed that international law of the sea correlates with a State's duty to protect the right to life at sea, by adding that 'States parties are also required to respect and protect the lives of all individuals located on marine vessels . . . and of those individuals who find themselves in a situation of distress at sea, in accordance with their international obligations

109 Ibid.

110 Sergio Carrerra, 'The Strasbourg Court Judgement *N.D. and N.T. v Spain*. A Carte Blanche to Push Backs at EU External Borders?' (2020) Robert Schuman Centre for Advanced Studies, EUI Working Paper RSCAS 2020/21, 2.

111 Marie-Bénédicte Dembour and Tobias Kelly (eds), *Are Human Rights for Migrants? Critical Reflections on the Status of Irregular in Europe and the United States* (Routledge 2011) 3.

112 *M.A. and Others v Lithuania*, App no 59793/17 (ECtHR, 11 December 2018) Concurring Opinion of Judge Pinto de Albuquerque para 54.

113 *General Comment No 36* (n 10).

114 Ibid para 63 (emphasis added).

on rescue at sea'.[115] These positive obligations to protect have been applied in the most recent decision of the HRC, the *A.S.*,[116] offering a beacon of hope for migrants that they will no longer be kept outside the reach of human rights protection. The decision will be presented in Chapter 5 along with the extra-territorial application of human rights obligations.

A recent, critical development is to be found in the Court's historic judgment in *Safi and Others v Greece*[117] which tackled for the first time the right to life in maritime rescue operations in the Aegean Sea. Also known as the *Farmakonisi* shipwreck of 2014, the ECtHR unanimously found a violation of both the procedural and the substantive parts of Article 2 by virtue of the Hellenic Coast Guard's bungled rescue operation. The former part was violated by the failure of the Greek authorities to carry out an exhaustive and effective investigation into the sinking of the vessel whilst the latter was violated on account of the failure of Greece to take all reasonably expected measures to adequately respond to the risk to the applicants' lives.[118] The sinking in question occurred as a result of two high-speed towing attempts (to push-back the migrants' boat), which led to water entering the vessel, causing it to capsize and resulting in the deaths of 11 out of the 27 migrants aboard. Several consequences of the judgment are important to understand from this case. The Court's reasoning primarily focused on whether the authorities acted in a manner which sought to ensure the protection of life in a sufficient and adequate manner.[119] Hence, the Court placed importance on the considerable delays of rescue assistance – a practice that has become the norm in the Mediterranean – in particular, over an hour after the boat had completely sunk.[120] It therefore made clear that *time is of essence* in cases where drowning can be reasonably apprehended.[121] The judgment, even though it came seven years after the application was brought before the ECtHR, is crucial in upholding the humanitarian imperative of saving lives at sea over the protection of borders and echoes some of the current practices in the Mediterranean, particularly as seen in the Pylos shipwreck in June 2023. It therefore manifests a positive development in this area and provides hope for the future trajectory of the ECtHR's jurisprudence,[122] but most importantly, for condemning State practices that are an affront to human rights.

115 Ibid.
116 CCPR, *A.S. and Others v Italy*, 27 January 2021, UN Doc CCPR/C/130/D/3042/2017, 23.
117 App no 5418/15 (ECtHR, 7 July 2022).
118 For analysis see also Mariana Gkliati, Danai Angeli, Elizabeth Mabropoulou and Niovi Vavoula, 'Greece Boat Disaster: Questions of International Law' (OpinioJuris, 5 August 2023) <http://opiniojuris.org/2023/08/05/greece-boat-disaster-questions-of-international-law/>.
119 Para 148.
120 Hannah Katz and Itamar Mann, 'From Farmakonisi to Pylos at the ECtHR' (*EJIL:Talk!*, 12 July 2023) <https://www.ejiltalk.org/from-farmakonisi-to-pylos-at-the-ecthr/>.
121 McCann (n 96) para 162.
122 E.g., *S.S. and Others v Italy*, App no 21660/18 (ECtHR, communicated on 26 June 2019).

As evidenced, the right to life has been developing systematically by the courts and quasi-judicial bodies and continues to inspire the development of the law in order to afford the protection it deserves.[123] Thus, the Strasbourg Court has clarified a broad interpretation of human rights obligations imposed on States to protect, respect and fulfil the right to life, encompassing a due diligence standard as a threshold for assessing risk. It is submitted that narrow or restrictive approaches to the interpretation of the right to life should not be fashioned as they risk undermining the principal value of the object and purpose of the legal provision. Hence, it is posited that judicial bodies should always be guided by normative considerations and push beyond the traditional approach, which tends to apply an insular interpretation of human rights provisions in order to extend necessary protections to situations that are difficult to govern.[124] In summarizing, the threshold question applied to establish a positive obligation to protect human life can be reformulated from the above jurisprudence in the following way: did the authorities do all that could be reasonably expected of them to avoid a real and immediate risk to life of which they knew or ought to have knowledge about?[125]

Instead, the positive duties under the normative frameworks of the law of the sea and international human rights law seem to merge in an effort to best protect human life at sea.[126] Hence, it is my argument that the duty to protect the right to life together with the duty to render assistance at sea and the specific provisions of the SOLAS and SAR Conventions, which focus on ensuring the protection of life at sea, offer a solid legal basis for proclaiming *a right to be rescued at sea*. As mentioned at the beginning, the right to life as a parent right has long been understood as capable of encompassing other rights under it, like the right to food, sanitation and water, as well as protection for indigenous populations from forced expulsions. Given the poignant flaws of the legal system governing rescue at sea, which are exacerbated by national security and sovereignty concerns, the time is ripe to explore alternative avenues that can minimize the vacuum of human rights protection at sea and address systemic violations against migrants.

123 Fionnuala Ní Aoláin, 'The Evolving Jurisprudence of the European Convention Concerning the Right to Life' (2001) 19(1) Netherlands Quarterly Human Rights 31.

124 Bertrand G Ramcharan (ed), *The Right to Life in International Law* (Martinus Nijhoff 1983) 6.

125 ECtHR, 'Guide on Article 2' (n 100) 9.

126 Irini Papanicolopulu, *International Law and the Protection of People at Sea* (Oxford: OUP 2018) 192.

4 Recognizing a Right to Be Rescued at Sea

Migrants, particularly those designated as irregular, undocumented or otherwise classified as 'illegal', frequently encounter significant challenges in securing recognition and enforcement of their human rights.[1] Having explored specific instances of this reality, along with the international legal framework governing the protection of human life at sea, which is supposed to ensure the safety and rights of all individuals, this chapter aims to demonstrate *how* a human-rights-based approach can enhance compliance with the dysfunctional search and rescue (SAR) framework. It will undertake this task in an innovative manner, primarily by drawing upon the Hohfeldian theory of rights that was first presented in the Introduction.[2] Apropos the earlier analysis, it is posited that the recognition of the right to be rescued at sea emanates from the normative contours of the law of the sea and the international human rights law framework taken together, finding voice in the duty to render assistance at sea and the right to life, respectively. Hence, the legal basis for recognizing the existence of this claim-right is well-founded; what is therefore essential is to expound on the formal framework of this right and elucidate how the Hohfeldian legal theory propels a rights-based account to irregular migration by sea.

Within the terrain of legal practice, courts that have employed Hohfeld's correlativity scheme (either explicitly or implicitly) and have recognized the existence of correlative rights from duties (and *vice versa*) have arguably reached more comprehensive outcomes. I therefore contend that the utilization of Hohfeld's theory in a legal case allows judges to develop the law in a progressive yet logical and coherent manner without the fear of this approach being labelled as 'judicial activism', arbitrary or ill-informed. Hohfeld's correlativity scheme acts as a means of realizing the *pro-homine* teleological approach

1 Marie-Bénédicte Dembour and Tobias Kelly (eds), *Are Human Rights for Migrants? Critical Reflections on the Status of Irregular in Europe and the United States* (Routledge 2011).

2 Wesley Newcomb Hohfeld, 'Some Fundamental Legal Conceptions as Applied in Judicial Reasoning' (1913) 23 Yale Law Journal (YLJ) 16 (Hohfeld 1913). Then, the second article is Wesley Newcomb Hohfeld, 'Fundamental Legal Conceptions as Applied in Judicial Reasoning' (1917) 26 YLJ 710 (Hohfeld 1917).

DOI: 10.4324/9781003568537-5

of this book in the pursuit of more potent protection of the rights of migrants. Certainly, human rights are a work-in-progress, particularly in light of the need to systematically confront new challenges and emerging issues in the international community, while also adapting to evolving patterns, migration being a prominent example in that regard.

The analysis seeks to build on Hohfeld's correlativity scheme in order to demonstrate the logical existence of a right to be rescued at sea by way of its correlative duty to render assistance at sea. In doing so, it considers the theoretical underpinnings of how rights and duties correlate, because assuming that rights imply duties is often tacit, but this also begs the question of whether duties (the duty to rescue in this case) can equally confer rights.[3] Certainly, such a discussion moves away from Hohfeld's definitional framework to an empirical analysis which examines the conceptual parameters of duties in specific circumstances; Hohfeld's philosophy was not about identifying the duty-bearers or the right-holders, but on delineating their relational character. In this way, the subject matter shifts to the specification of a duty-bearer, which on its own can act as the determining factor for the establishment of rights. In fact, this inquiry presents one of the most vital objections to the existence of correlative rights, the so-called 'claimability objection', articulated most notably by Onora O'Neill. Simplified, the objection is concerned with the identification of specific duty-bearers, maintaining that if the duty-bearers are unidentified, then rights are unclaimable *vis-à-vis* being ***not rights at all***.[4]

In this connection, Chapter 2 of this book has observed the operational difficulties in identifying a duty-bearer which will be tasked to undertake a rescue in case of distress information, as there is a diverse mixture of State and non-State actors involved each time in search and rescue (SAR) operations and each with different degree of responsibilities. In O'Neill's theory this will translate as an objection to the existence of an individual right to be rescued at sea. The analysis will strive to show that claimability is an ***unnecessary*** condition for the existence of rights, while not downplaying its practical significance for their *subsequent* realization.[5] Against this premise, it contemplates the following, rather perplexing questions: can the right to be rescued at sea be claimable? Or does it need to be claimable (in the same sense that O'Neill ascribes) in order to recognize its existence as a right? In particular, diverse accounts from contemporary rights theorists like John Tasioulas, Kathryn Sikkink, Amartya Sen, Seyla Benhabib and Jeremy Waldron provide distinctive and detailed philosophical responses to these recurrent questions by employing a more robust account of human rights attentive to the underlying interests and values they protect.

3 See David Lyons, 'The Correlativity of Rights and Duties' (1970) 4(1) Noûs 45.

4 Onora O'Neill, *Towards Justice and Virtue* (CUP 1996).

5 John Tasioulas, 'The Moral Reality of Human Rights' in Thomas Pogge (ed), *Freedom from Poverty as a Human Right: Who Owes What to the Very Poor?* (Oxford: Unesco 2007) 75, 101.

This chapter has a threefold ambition. The first is to build upon Hohfeld's correlativity scheme, which provides courts with an analytical tool to support a normative argument that structures a right to be rescued at sea within the existing right to life. The second considers alternative avenues, which will justify its recognition, in contrast to adopting a framework which arguably misses the intrinsic nature of rights, in which human rights exist prior to and independently of their ability to be claimed. In this way, it shows that the existence of a right to be rescued at sea is verified as a mere matter of a Hohfeldian analysis and escapes any empirical denunciations at the stage of its identification as a norm. The third is to move beyond the philosophical debates to showcase the ways in which this right can become fully recognized (legally binding) by employing interpretative techniques (in particular, advancing from a teleological perspective) for achieving this end.[6] Ergo, it will show that Hohfeld's correlativity scheme acts as a means of realizing the human-rights-based approach of this book in the pursuit to advance norms in situations where the status of an individual is under threat.

1. Hohfeld's Scheme of Relations and Correlativity in Judicial Reasoning

As comprehensively presented in the Introduction of this book, the American jurist expounded a matrix of normative positions that can be used to analyze any rights' relationship. His theory of legal relations was mainly set out over the course of two seminal articles published in 1913 and 1917: *Fundamental Legal Relations as Applied in Judicial Reasoning*.[7] An important element to grasp from the phrase 'as Applied in Judicial Reasoning' is that it captures the true character of his scheme, that is, fundamental legal concepts not in the abstract, but utilized especially in the solving of 'practical, every-day problems of the law'.[8] By observing the vexing meaning of the word 'right' and likewise, its wide-ranging inclusiveness covering all legal relations, Hohfeld wished to limit its 'chameleon-hued' character to a definite and appropriate meaning, as the word rested on uncertainty, often causing ambiguities and misuse when applied in judicial reasoning.[9]

Andrew Halpin, a proponent of Hohfeld's theory, claims that the actual state of any normative system, moral or legal, can best be represented by

6 1969 Vienna Convention on the Law of Treaties 1155 UNTS 331, at Art. 31. See also Suzanne Egan, 'The Doctrinal Approach in International Human Rights Scholarship' at 12, SSRN, 5 December 2017 <papers.ssrn.com/sol3/papers.cfm?abstract_id=3082194>.

7 Hohfeld 1913 (n 2) 4.

8 Walter Wheeler Cook, 'Hohfeld's Contributions to the Science of Law' (1919) 28(8) YLJ 723.

9 Hohfeld 1913 (n 2) 31, 35; See for instance *Lonas v State* (1871) 3 Heisk. (Tenn.) 306–307, in the words of Mr. Justice Sneed 'It is said that the words rights, privileges and immunities, are abusively used, as if they were synonymous. The word right is generic, common, embracing whatever may be lawfully claimed'.

an analysis of correlativity found within Hohfeld's analytical scheme.[10] The Hohfeldian table is included below for the purpose of recollecting its legal relations:

Jural Correlatives

Right	Privilege	Power	Immunity
Duty	No-right	Liability	Disability

Jural Opposites

Right	Privilege	Power	Immunity
No-Right	Duty	Disability	Liability

Focusing on the first pair of his jural correlatives, right–duty, Hohfeld sought to articulate a narrow and proper meaning for the word 'right' with reference to its correlative relation, duty, and he used the term 'claim-right', which signifies that a right is an affirmative claim against another.[11] Put simply, Hohfeld's jural correlative right–duty assumes that if X has a claim, then Y has a correlating duty. The reverse is also true according to this correlative axiom: if X has a duty, then Y has a claim.[12] Based on the Hohfeldian model, it is submitted that the right to life and the duty to render assistance at sea fall under the right–duty pair of jural correlatives. Through the remainder of this chapter, the word 'right' shall be employed with the Hohfeldian parlance – claim – according to which it correlates with a duty of equivalent content that is owed to a right-bearer.[13]

1.1 Detour – Rights v Privileges

It is worthwhile here to undertake a short detour before considering how the correlativity theory has been utilized in judicial reasoning, in order to explain a little further why it is of enduring significance to precisely use and correctly understand the Hohfeldian positions when elucidating their meaning.

In the Hohfeldian table above, each of the eight concepts is distinct, that is, a *duty* for example, cannot also be a *privilege* of any of the other concepts. A similar conclusion is reached by Morss. 'If X has a duty to perform Y (thus

10 Andrew Halpin, 'Choosing Axioms of Correlativity' (2019) 64(2) The American Journal of Jurisprudence 225.

11 Hohfeld 1913 (n 2) 33; See, also Allan D Cullison, 'A Review of Hohfeld's Fundamental Legal Concepts' (1967) 16(3) Marshall Law Review 559.

12 Marcus Agnafors, 'On Disjunctive Rights' (2017) 55(2) The Southern Journal of Philosophy 147.

13 Hohfeld in his Article chooses the word 'claim 'as what seems to be the most appropriate synonym for the word right, see Hohfeld 1913 (n 2) 32, 36; See, also, Robert Mullins, 'Moral Conflict and the Logic of Rights' (2018) 177(3) Philosophical Studies 633.

honouring a claim-right held by Z), X cannot at the same time have a *privilege* to perform Y'.[14] Taking Hohfeld's taxonomy into account, a privilege is the opposite of a duty, and the correlative of a no-right. To fathom their distinctive form, it is helpful to examine the duty to render assistance at sea, which is the subject of analysis in this book. A shipmaster who has a duty to render assistance to persons in distress at sea cannot also be said to acquire a privilege to do so. Whilst, as argued, there are elements in the way the provision is drafted in Article 98 of the United Nations Convention on the Law of the Sea (UNCLOS),[15] which allow a shipmaster to exercise subjective judgment as to his/her capacity to undertake a rescue – references such as 'in so far as he can do so' and 'without danger to the ship, the crew or the passengers' – these qualifications nonetheless do not change the nature of the duty. Purportedly, its scope is limited by the way the provision prescribes the duty, but this will not give a *privilege* to the shipmaster or the State to *choose* if they would adhere to their obligations.[16]

In this vein, Hohfeld's analysis mirrors that of Thomas Hobbes, who was equally careful to distinguish between duty and privilege in the context of rights; the latter conveys *optionality* or *choice* as in the waiving of an entitlement. Most importantly the term privilege denotes *absence* of duty on the part of one having the privilege. Consequently, if shipmasters have a privilege to rescue migrants, that means they certainly do not have a duty to do so, which contradicts the provision laid down in Article 98 and the customary duty to save life. If that is the case, then this is fundamentally an incorrect interpretation of the paramount *duty* to save life at sea. In the words of Peter Schlag, the confusion of privileges with rights is a conceptual error, but above all, it is an error with consequences.[17] In fact, one of Hohfeld's objectives was to elucidate this error of reasoning that often arose from the confusion of rights and privileges and the abusive derivation of one from the other.[18]

Consequently, the two concepts together are incompatible; the reason simply being that one cannot get *a must* from *a may* and *vice versa*. This analytical detour follows earlier scholarship by Itamar Mann in which he explicitly employs Hohfeld's theory to argue that the *duty* to rescue gives also a *privilege* to perform rescue in such a way that civil society rescuers acquire

14 John R Morss, 'Power and International Law: Hohfeld to the Rescue?' (2011) 3(2) The Western Australian Jurist 103.

15 United Nations Convention on the Law of the Sea (adopted 10 December 1982, entered into force 16 November 1994) 1833 UNTS 397 (UNCLOS).

16 Curtis Nyquist, 'Teaching Wesley Hohfeld's Theory of Legal Relations' (2002) 52(1/2) Journal of Legal Education 240.

17 Peter Schlag, 'How to Do Things with Hohfeld' (2015) 78(1&2) Law and Contemporary Problems 211.

18 Ibid 204; Hohfeld used the case *Quinn v Leathem* [1901] AC 495, to showcase the erroneous distinction between rights and privileges, shadowed in Lord Lindley's reasoning.

a *right* to rescue at sea.[19] In particular, he argues (in the context of migrants at sea): 'come closer to the person at risk, and your privilege to rescue them will transform, due to the rules of the law of the sea, into a duty to do so'.[20] The interchangeability of the two terms seems, perhaps, erroneous given his preceding statement which draws the focus to the location of the persons in distress: 'X may have a "privilege" to decide whether to "render assistance" to person A or not'.[21] The confusion seems to lie in two focal assumptions: whether Mann treats the duty under Article 98 (UNCLOS provides explicitly that this is 'a *duty* to render assistance') as a privilege, or whether that is of a transforming nature, which can attract different legal relations depending on various factors shifting from a privilege to a duty and forth to creating a right. For this reason, it seems unclear if the argument supports a right to rescue (as explicit in the title of the article) or a privilege to rescue as per the analysis contained therein. Either of these will make little sense as the analysis employs loose language – and it will be a complete misnomer to morph a privilege into a right and abuse Hohfeld's scheme. Evidently, the idea falls within the ambit of clarifying the meaning of the words, which will characterize best the legal relation in question – persons in distress at sea (the party receiving the service) and rescuers (the party providing the service).

In sum, the above account seems to be flawed based on Hohfeld's model, mainly in two respects: 1) a duty to do A cannot also be a privilege to do A; and 2) a Hohfeldian privilege is correlative with a no-right, which means that the migrants in this case (the recipients of the act) will have no claim against nonperformance or noncompliance with such a fundamental duty.

Nevertheless, I am sympathetic to the reasons Mann tries to advocate for a right to rescue at sea vested in civil society rescue organizations, and in no way do I wish to undermine the paramount role these actors play in rescue operations. Yet, I submit that it would be more useful to look at the claim-rights migrants can posit, such that States cannot interfere with the shipmasters' operations or in effecting the duty. As such, the operational question needs to focus on the right of the individual which correlates with the duty to rescue. Connecting the dots of this 'detoured' analysis with Hohfeld's scheme, this illustration shows how Hohfeld's scheme can be used in analyzing complex legal problems by putting emphasis, preliminarily, on the correct usage of language in delineating the legal relationship in question. Otherwise, different definitions would yield different and arguably erroneous outcomes having considerable effects on one's rights. On the other hand, Mann's engagement, for one, demonstrates that the academic community will employ the

19 Itamar Mann, 'The Right to Perform Rescue at Sea: Jurisprudence and Drowning' (2020) 21(3) German Law Journal 601.
20 Ibid 602.
21 Ibid.

Hohfeldian analytical tool when advocating for the proclamation of new rights and providing the structure of rights and duties.[22]

2. Case Law Utilizing Correlativity

The below analysis transposes the theoretical framework onto the specifics of courts' case law across various legal systems. It is useful to mention, to avoid any misunderstandings, that the Hohfeldian schema applies to all interests the law might seek to protect. As such, the four normative positions elaborated above (claim-right, privilege, power, immunity) are all legal interests. In delineating the courts' reasoning, the word 'interest' (of the individual) is often employed, meaning that it can carry any of the four incidents Hohfeld laid down in expounding the meaning of 'right' – depending on what kind of *interest* a person has in a particular legal action.

Before proceeding, a caveat is in order. Whilst Hohfeld's theory has been widely employed in literature on rights discourse, there are hardly any explicit utilizations of his scheme, for instance, by the ECtHR and the European Court of Justice (ECJ). In fact, by undertaking a thorough review of the courts' databases, I was able to trace just one such reference made by the ECtHR in the context of interpreting the Convention rights, and it was briefly dealt with and was part of a dissenting opinion.[23] Similarly the ECJ in a recent case has referred to the scheme of Hohfeld but, again, such reference was only in passing in a footnote. Nonetheless, it illustrated that a Hohfeldian analysis provides an *important tool in conceptualizing the legal issues* at the stage of *applying theory to the facts* at hand in order to reach a conclusion.[24] It referred to Hohfeld in order to explain that the 'existence of a right to claim compensation based on Article 101 TFEU presupposes that there is a legal obligation that has been infringed'.[25] In particular, it stressed the idea of correlativity between rights and legal obligations by tracing it back to Hohfeld. Nonetheless, the majority of cases utilizing a correlativity theory have not appreciated the relevance of Hohfeld's scheme, as will be shown below. Despite the absence of explicit references to Hohfeld, correlativity on its own gains wider acceptance and has been greatly employed by judges. For this reason, I submit that the fact that direct references to Hohfeld

22 Recent scholarship by Stoyanova also robustly applies Hohfeld's correlativity scheme to examine the enforcement of judgments and the obligations on States imposed in cases of human rights violations, see Vladislava Stoyanova, 'Correlativity Between Human Rights and Positive Obligations and Its Role for the Execution of Judgments Delivered by the European Court of Human Rights' (2024) 5(4) European Convention on Human Rights Law Review 455–486.

23 *Szanyi v Hungary*, App no 35493/13 (ECtHR, 8 November 2016) dissenting opinion of Judge Wojtyczek, para 6.

24 Vanitha Sundra-Karean, 'In Defense of Soft Law and Public-Private Initiatives: A Means to an End? – The Malaysian Case' (2011) 12(2) Theoretical Inquiries in Law 479.

25 Case C-724/17, *Vantaan kaupunki v Skanska Industrial Solutions Oy and Others*, 6 February 2019, Opinion of Advocate General Wahl, para 61 and fn 28.

might appear to some extent neglected in courts' jurisprudence does not underrate his theory nor the value it can have in providing a framework for conceptualizing rights. Besides, the crucial point to recognize is not the frequency or specific courts that have employed Hohfeld's jurisprudential analysis, but rather that those that have done so have provided a more lucid and more transparent methodological framework.

Perhaps the most powerful example confirming the irrefutable correlation between rights and duties is the ECJ's (as the CJEU was then known) ruling in the famous founding case of *Van Gend en Loos* from 1963. The judgment is substantive in its (implicit) advances of the Hohfeldian methodology, establishing a reshaped legal order, or even a statement of a new legal order, which the Court was setting out to develop based on correlativity of rights (in the area of trade agreements in this instance).[26] The ECJ tackled the issue of individual, enforceable rights in the EU in a delicate yet sophisticated manner, incorporating jural correlativity; however, the Court was not making any direct reference to Hohfeld. Nonetheless, the scheme of jural correlatives, and particularly the right-duty pair, has been employed by the court in a way which one can characterize as expanding the horizon of rights. In line with a Hohfeldian approach, the ECJ reasoned that 'Community law therefore not only imposes obligations on individuals but is also intended to confer upon them rights which become part of their legal heritage'.[27] It continued by stressing that individual rights 'arise not only where they are expressly granted by the Treaty', but they can also be derived from precise obligations which are imposed by EU law on individuals, Member States or EU institutions.[28]

Consequently, the Court was able to recognize that individual rights are enforceable by very large and ill-defined groups of individuals, given that a provision of the Treaty is found to impose an obligation capable of giving rise to correlative rights.[29] The judgment, evidently, adopts a purposive construction to mold the meaning of Article 12 so as to allow for the correlative of an existing obligation – right – to be recognized and individuals to benefit. It is important to stress that the Court treated this correlation based on the degree of discretion allowed by the given provision and singled out those conditions – whether the obligation imposed is sufficiently precise, clear and unconditional – which are then proportional to the possibility of recognizing

26 Joseph HH Weiler, 'Van Gend en Loos: The Individual as Subject and Object and the Dilemma of European Legitimacy' (2014) 12(1) International Journal of Constitutional Law 94.

27 Case 26/62, N.V. Algemeine Transport- en Expeditie Onderneming van Gend & Loos v. Netherlands Inland Revenue Administration, 1963 E.C.R. 1 (*Van Gend en Loos*).

28 Ibid para 3.

29 See for instance discussion by Catherine Warin, 'Individual Rights in EU Migration and Asylum Law' (EU Migration Blog 2020) <http://eumigrationlawblog.eu/individual-rights-in-eu-migration-and-asylum-law/>.

a right in concrete situations.[30] The semantics of this ruling are of considerable importance insofar as it not only affirmed that the correlative axiom 'right–duty' can withstand both directions (rebutting the debates on priority of rights) – a right can give rise to a correlative duty, the same way as a duty can give rise to a correlative right – but also reinforced that the correlation between rights and duties is key in structuring 'new' rights. As far as this judgment might be perceived as revolutionary, it nonetheless shows that the court was able to *support a normative position* through constructing a claim-right in a way which was *logical* and *coherent*; the reason being to protect the sanctity of the legal order.[31]

Hohfeld's correlativity scheme began to be traced in later cases in different jurisdictions, sometimes explicitly and other times implicitly. The dynamic correlativity of Hohfeld's legal concepts can be traced for instance in an English revenue case in 1969, *Bromilow & Edwards Ltd. v Inland Revenue Commissioners*.[32] Therein, Judge Megarry referred to the 'celebrated classification' in Hohfeld's legal concepts with appreciation to its value, whilst exploring the meaning of the word 'liability' and its correlative axiom.[33] Later on, the dynamic correlativity of Hohfeld's legal concepts can be traced in *Kelly Pipelines Ltd v British Gas plc*,[34] where judge John Davies QC proceeded on a Hohfeldian line of analysis. The learned judge applied the jural correlative pair right–duty and provided that 'if Kelly has a *duty* to supply a minimum number of gangs, that duty had as a correlative a right to have a minimum number of gangs employed'. However, his lordship pointed out that to have concluded in this way will 'misunderstand' the purpose of Hohfeld's work, that is, to assume 'that every duty carries with it a correlative right' as it will assume that 'a particular duty is also a Hohfeldian duty'. Insofar as the judge affirmed the correlation between a right and duty in this passage, his lordship explained that this error may arise because the word 'duty' might be, for example, a Hohfeldian *liability*, the correlative of which is a *power*. In doing so, his lordship believed that this case was more closely related to the correlative pair power-liability, rather than the traditional pair right–duty. The line of reasoning pursued is substantive as it proves that the use of precise and

30 Ibid; this was also confirmed by the CJEU in Case C–413/99 *Baumbast and R v Secretary of State for the Home Department*, 17 September 2002.

31 See also Case C-724/17, *Vantaan Kaupunki v Skanska Industrial Solutions Oy and Others*, 6 February 2019, Opinion of Advocate General Wahl, para 61 and fn 28, referred to Hohfeld that explain the 'existence of a right to claim compensation based on Article 101 TFEU presupposes that there is a legal obligation that has been infringed'. Ergo, the reasoning illustrates that a Hohfeldian analysis provides an *important tool in conceptualizing the legal issues* at the stage of *applying theory to the facts* at hand in order to reach a conclusion.

32 *Bromilow & Edwards Ltd. v. Inland Revenue Commissioners* [1969] 1 WLR 1180.

33 Another example is provided in the case of *City Inn Ltd v Shepherd Construction Ltd* [2006] ScotCS CSOH_94, where Lord Drummond Young based his analysis on Hohfeld's scheme of jural relations, and limited the doctrine of waiver in this instance, to the claim-right pair, which accordingly corresponds with an obligation.

34 *Kelly Pipelines Ltd v British Gas plc* (1990) 48 BLR 126.

clear language can act as a powerful source of resolving uncertainties in legal relationships and can sufficiently protect parties' interests.

One final example of the Hohfeldian engagement in judicial reasoning is the Australian immigration case of *Minister for Immigration and Multicultural and Indigenous Affairs v Al Khafaji*.[35] The line of reasoning pursued by Judge Gummow made explicit reference to Hohfeld's scheme in arguing that 'even those who use the word and the conception "right" in the broadest possible way are accustomed to thinking of "duty" as the invariable correlative'.[36] By reinvigorating the Hohfeldian logic, the judge was able to find a correlative duty owed to the respondent by Syria with regards to the protection of his visa application. As such, it proves that the acknowledgment of the correlation between rights and duties is vital in establishing claimable rights in law. Judge Gummow also, importantly, illustrated that this duty may arise not only in municipal law, but 'it may also be that there is a duty owed to him, or to Australia, as an international obligation'.[37] Even though the judge did not go a step further to explore the intersection between municipal and international law, it can be arguably submitted that this did in part entice the application of the correlative axiom, right–duty, to the international context of obligations placed upon States.

3. A Hohfeldian Right to Be Rescued at Sea

The above cases have utilized Hohfeld's theory on legal rights (directly and indirectly) and, particularly, acknowledged the notion of correlativity in legal incidents as central for identifying rights and duties. Additionally, the cases upheld the relationship between rights and duties, which can manifestly withstand both directions, without the one incident taking priority over the other. Apart from this, this analysis served to illustrate that the use of the Hohfeldian theory advances judicial reasoning and allows the law to be developed in a progressive yet coherent and logical way to achieve effective protection of individual interests. In this way, applying Hohfeld's model to the present study of irregular migration by sea, it can be logically concluded that the correlative of the existing duty to render assistance at sea is a legal right to be rescued at sea, vested in individuals, which will transpose as follows: ***shipmasters are under a duty to rescue at sea subject to an individual's right to be rescued at sea.*** Even though I am purportedly arguing that this right acquires *legal* status by way of employing Hohfeld's theory, this is so only in theory; in practice, it will require *inter alia* a court to proclaim its legal existence. I turn back to this in the section below.

35 *Minister for Immigration and Multicultural and Indigenous Affairs v Al Khafaji* [2004] HCA 38; (2004) 219 CLR 664; (2004) 208 ALR 201; (2004) 78 ALJR 1156 (6 August 2004).
36 Ibid para 19.
37 Ibid para 20.

In this regard, it is worth re-emphasizing that Article 12 in *Van Gend en Loos* did not explicitly confer rights to individuals in the same way as Article 98 of UNCLOS falls short of prescribing any rights to individuals to be rescued at sea. As evidenced in the previous chapters, UNCLOS attributes rights and duties to States within their own and different maritime zones and makes no direct reference to persons;[38] as such, any examination of persons as right-holders will result implicitly from the rights and duties of States in the form of correlative obligations and rights. In order to tie this basic disconnect between a State's duty and an individual's right, the examination needs to move beyond the conceptual considerations of UNCLOS and international human rights law to the reconceptualization of jurisdiction. This will be expounded in Chapter 5.

In this juncture, there are some provisions in UNCLOS which *de facto* reflect the rights and interests of individuals at sea, one of them being the duty to render assistance at sea. Another illustration that holds true is Article 94(3), which provides:

> Every State shall take such measures for ships flying its flag as are necessary to ensure safety at sea with regard, inter alia, to:
>
> (a) the construction, equipment and seaworthiness of ships;
> (b) the manning of ships, labour conditions and the training of crews, taking into account the applicable international instruments;
> (c) the use of signals, the maintenance of communications and the prevention of collisions.

The above is an example of a duty imposed upon flag States to ensure that there is a safe environment at work (aboard the ship). Yet, this is a duty which does not attribute a right directly to individuals. In that respect its correlative right should be that individuals/employees have a right to safety at work. In this scenario, the existing legal relationship subsists in international law, as an equivalent right can be found in the International Covenant on Economic, Social and Cultural Rights (ICESCR) 1966, Article 7 (b), which provides:

> The States Parties to the present Covenant recognize the right of everyone to the enjoyment of just and favourable conditions of work which ensure, in particular:
>
> (a) . . .
> (b) Safe and healthy working conditions.[39]

38 Irini Papanicolopulu, 'The Law of the Sea Convention: No Place for Persons?' (2012) 27(4) International Journal of Marine and Coastal Law 871.

39 International Covenant on Economic, Social and Cultural Rights (ICESCR) (adopted 16 December 1966, entered into force 3 January 1976) 993 UNTS 3, Art 7(b).

From the above, a subjective connection can be identified between UNCLOS and the ICESCR, a human rights treaty, because intra-systematically there is no provision in UNCLOS that precludes the applicability of human rights treaties. Building on this interpretation, the normative relationship governing individuals in distress at sea and States/shipmasters who are under a duty to perform rescues, it can be inferred that a *right to be rescued at sea* ought to be recognized as the ultimate correlative of the duty. The claim maintained herein is that the obligations emanating from UNCLOS cannot be looked at in isolation from broader human rights and other international legal obligations. Likewise, in order for human rights to be comprehensively protected and developed to rectify egregious human rights violations, courts need to interpret human rights provisions with the assistance of other international law rules in developing existing norms.

Against this background, jurisprudential developments in UNCLOS have tended to show that relevant tribunals, including the International Tribunal of the Law of the Sea (ITLOS), frequently utilize human rights provisions in fleshing out obligations under a law of the sea dispute by reference to 'considerations of humanity'.[40] Similarly, international human rights courts and bodies are increasingly relied upon by individuals for disputes taking place at sea, especially migration-related cases. For example, ITLOS has employed human rights in the context of a law of the sea dispute, by reiterating the concept of 'considerations of humanity', first used in the *Corfu Channel* judgment by the ICJ, in its *M/V Saiga (No. 2)* case concerning enforcement activities at sea.[41] The case concerned the use of excessive force in stopping and arresting the ship as well as its crew. Undoubtedly, actions such as the arrest of victims affect in a direct manner the human rights of the individuals concerned and, particularly, the right to liberty of the crew and the right to property of the shipowner.[42] The rather bold statement was made that acknowledged protection of human rights in the law of the sea framework 'the obligation of prompt release of vessel and crews includes elementary consideration of humanity and due process of law'.[43] In this vein, Judge Treves correctly stated 'the Law of the Sea and the law of human rights are not separate planets rotating in different

40 *Corfu Channel (United Kingdom of Great Britain and Northern Ireland v Albania) (Merits)* [1949] ICJ Rep 4.

41 *The M/V 'Saiga' (No 2) (Saint Vincent and the Grenadines v Guinea)* (Judgment of 1 July 1999) ITLOS Reports 1999, 10.

42 Anna Petrig and Marta Bo, 'The International Tribunal for the Law of the Sea and Human Rights' in Martin Scheinin (ed), *Human Rights Norms in 'Other' International Courts* (CUP 2019) 356.

43 *The M/V 'Saiga' (No 2)* (n 41) para 77; *Arctic Sunrise' (Kingdom of the Netherlands v Russian Federation)*, Provisional Measures, Request for Provisional Measures Submitted by the Netherlands, 21 October 2013; *The M/V 'Louisa' (Saint Vincent and the Grenadines v Kingdom of Spain)*, 28 May 2013, ITLOS Reports (2013) 4; *The 'Enrica Lexie' Incident* (*Italy v India*), PCA Case No. 2015–28.

orbits. Instead, they meet in many situations'.[44] These intra-systemic relations are indeed feasible in UNCLOS adjudication, even if jurisdictionally a relevant tribunal could not hear a case that was primarily about human rights or about environmental law.[45]

Accordingly, UNCLOS does not provide the availability of mechanisms to address violations of duties by States, but rather, as an inter-State dispute settlement mechanism, it only allows States to bring complaints against another State. Hence, persons are in a precarious state as they cannot be parties to a proceeding, having no *locus standi.* This is primarily why I am advocating that the formal recognition of the right to be rescued at sea should take place under the existing corpus of international human rights law, as implicit in the right to life, because only there can it attain and gain meaning. Therefore, it is essential to focus the study on human rights as it allows one to address the individual's interests, rights and remedies. As Tzevelekos and Katselli Proukaki argue, the law of the sea offers the means that make it possible to achieve the end marks of human rights law.[46] In fact, this amalgamation of different conventions serves to offer a more generalized principle of international law to protect people at sea, as Papanicolopulu asserts 'to take all reasonable measures necessary to ensure that this objective is achieved'.[47]

What Hohfeld's theory adds to these discourses is a resourceful tool to buttress the theorization of a right to be rescued at sea in law, by virtue of its normative correlation, which is – I claim – logically and philosophically straightforward. In this way, it provides a tool for judges for developing the law in a consistently justified manner that puts emphasis on the rights of individuals and provides a remedy for violations. Using the method of logical correlativity, the courts have managed in numerous occasions to vindicate rights which would otherwise have not been entertained. Before moving away from the theoretical discourse on rights, it is vital to lastly consider one major critique to the proclamation of a right to be rescued at sea. This inquiry will focus on whether this right needs to be *claimable* in order to recognize its existence both in theory and in practice.

4. The Claimability Condition to the Recognition of Rights

Delving into an examination of the 'claimability' of rights, the study shifts focus to the character of duties which, as will be shown, presents a major

44 Tullio Treves, 'Human Rights and the Law of the Sea' (2010) 28(1) Berkeley Journal of International Law 1.

45 See *The Republic of Philippines v. The People's Republic of China, PCA case No. 2013–19;* See also *Artic Sunrise* case; Petrig and Bo (n 42) 386.

46 Vassilis P Tzevelekos and Elena Katselli Proukaki, 'Migrants at Sea: A Duty of Plural States to Protect (Extraterritorially)?' (2017) 86 Nordic Journal of International Law 432.

47 Irini Papanicolopulu, *International Law and the Protection of People at Sea* (Oxford: OUP 2018) 17, 160.

objection to the existence of new rights. As earlier expounded, a right to be rescued at sea falls in the category of claim-rights; a *claim* against others. The synonym Hohfeld espoused, *claim,* to describe the word 'right' in the strictest sense carries with it an important sense of this type of right; it concerns actions or omissions by someone else. Applying the Hohfeldian theory will mean that an individual's claim-right to be rescued is directed against some duty-bearer(s) to perform this act. The confusion that then arises is the identification of *someone* responsible to perform the duty or in the case of non-performance, identifying the violator. In this way, the subject matter shifts to the specification of a duty-bearer, which on its own can act as the determining factor for the establishment of rights.

O'Neill developed her philosophy of rights based on the character of duties, which functions as a criterion to the recognition of rights. Specifically, she argues that on a normative basis, rights cannot exist unless there are specified duty-bearers who are under an obligation to ensure compliance with the right.[48] Consequently, the theorist presents a concept of rights which should be *prima facie* something actually claimable; in order for rights to be recognized as rights, specific duty-bearers need to be identified or rights cannot be *claimed, waived* or *enforced.*[49] This is so, as the absence of a treaty (for instance) will suggest that there is no State compliance *vis-à-vis* ensuring that the rights in question will be protected or provided. Notwithstanding the apparent soundness of this logic, there are a number of shortcomings with the argument of trying to promote or implement human rights in this, arguably insular, way: 1) the level of control it will require over duty-bearers; and 2) the amount of blame which might in fact attach to them.[50]

Proponents of O'Neill's theory will maintain that a codified legitimate formal structure is a necessary element to achieve successful compliance with rights, hence making them claimable.[51] In fact, O'Neill's school of thought centers upon the Kantian tradition of ethics and morals, focusing on individual duties. Notably, as highlighted in the preceding chapter, the Kantian philosophy places emphasis on identifying a specific duty-bearer that owes the performance to the right-holder in question, who can in turn, *claim* for it. On the other hand, leading theorists of human rights, like Sen, argue that it would be a mistake to presume in general that if a human right is important, then it must be legislated (or, enshrined in a treaty) into an enforceable legal right.[52]

48 Onora O'Neill, 'The Dark Side of Human Rights' (2005) 81(2) International Affairs 427.

49 Rowan Cruft, 'Rights: Beyond Interest Theory and Will Theory?' (2003) 23(4) Law and Philosophy 359.

50 Jesse Tomalty, 'The Force of the Claimability Objection to the Human Right to Subsistence' (2014) 44(1) Canadian Journal of Philosophy 1, 2.

51 Eric Brandstedt and Anna-Karin Bergman, 'Climate Rights: Feasible or Not?' (2013) 22(3) Environmental Politics 400.

52 Amartya Sen, 'Elements of a Theory of Human Rights' (2004) 32(4) Philosophy and Public Affairs 345.

On this kind of approach, the effectiveness of human rights does not rest on seeing them systematically as putative proposals for legal enactment. In fact, Tasioulas argues that the mere fact that a right might achieve legal enactment in a treaty or legislation does not automatically grant the legal authority to enforce it; hence, it might be effectively unenforceable due to deficiencies in the capabilities of duty-bearers.[53] Consequently, a human right will exist independently of enforcement mechanisms or an associated remedy; for example, it can just be declaratory. This approach is in harmony with Hohfeld's theory.

Interestingly, O'Neill's article *On the Dark Side of Human Rights* starts with the bold question posed by Edmund Burke: *what is the point of having a right?* In particular, '*what is the point of having an abstract right, unless you also have a way of securing whatever it is that you have a right to*?' The question posed by Burke is one that tests if the right is being actually enjoyed by the right-holder *vis-à-vis* whether it is enforceable.[54] As such, it probes the point behind having natural or abstract rights if it is not possible to ensure that someone will protect them. In this regard, O'Neill further supports that if we are to consider rights seriously and view them as normative rather than aspirational, we must take duties seriously too. If we are to take human rights as aspirational, then the costs are high because this would mean that if the human right is unmet then there will be no breach of obligation and thus no one to be held accountable.[55] At first reading, there is nothing wrong with anticipating that obligations should be taken seriously in order for rights to be recognized, after all this is a *bona fide* concern; yet, such theory misrepresents the whole idea of human rights and places an unrealistic condition on the existence of human rights. The claimability condition to the existence of human rights, to put it bluntly, does not result in anything more than allocating duties to specifiable agents, which might not even bring the anticipated enforceability or compliance with such rights.

4.1 The Existing Duty to Render Assistance at Sea

In a nutshell, claimability for O'Neill rests on the premise that a right needs to have a justified claim that has two axes: 1) a claim must have an object – it must be a claim to something; 2) a claim must have a direction – it must be a claim against some duty-bearer. In order for a right to be claimable both the object and the direction must be justified – if not, then it is not claimable. In this realm, a right to be rescued at sea is a *claim of assistance*, in other words, a claim to be rescued when found in distress at sea; hence, it has an object. The confusion arises when considering the second axis, the *direction*

53 Tasioulas (n 5) 84.

54 Maurice Cranston, 'Human Rights, Real and Supposed' in DD Raphael (ed), *Political Theory and the Rights of Man* (Bloomington: Indiana University Press 1967) 44.

55 O'Neill (n 48) 430.

of a (potential) claim to be rescued at sea, that rests upon identifying the duty-bearer that shall carry out this duty. In this vein, O'Neill supports that if the duties are undirected (also referred to, as 'imperfect'),[56] then correlative rights cannot exist because no one will be in a position to lawfully claim that its performance is directed to her.[57] Although I am advocating for abandoning the claimability condition to the existence of rights, it is still vital to shed light on the complexities arising from the duty to render assistance at sea, to demonstrate how, in particular, its correlative right can escape this critique. For the purposes of avoiding repetition with Chapter 2, this section will be concise.

As has been observed so far, the duty to render assistance to those in distress at sea applies to both States and shipmasters flying a State's flag, including private vessels, military and other state-owned vessels. Yet, what does it really mean to say that a shipmaster of a vessel has a duty *to* another person?[58] We can identify that this duty is *prima facie* positive, since it requires positive action to provide assistance. Indeed, this is a case where positive duties are owed towards distant strangers; hence, the acknowledgment of duties occurs across borders. The difficulty arises in considering the subjective elements within the provision which has the potential of allowing duty-bearers to opt not to carry out the rescue operation. In this way, one can argue that the duty fails to meet the claimability condition as we cannot identify *a priori* the duty-bearer(s) because each situation will be treated on ad-hoc arrangements. Nonetheless, this unrealistic requirement can be defeated by the fact that all shipmasters are potentially duty-bearers and therefore all are under a duty to make the assessment as to the capability to carry out the rescue – and if capable, are thereafter under the duty to undertake the rescue.

Relatedly, the International Convention for the Safety of Life at Sea (SOLAS) provides that, upon the launch of a distress signal, governments should ensure that the necessary arrangements are made to locate the persons in distress and assist them.[59] Accordingly, the right to be rescued at sea will be triggered by the *knowledge* of the State of the apprehended risk to the life of persons, which is determined by the 'knew or should have known' standard in relation to the events in question.[60] Conversely, the argument is not that a right to be rescued at sea is absolute or unlimited in scope; the positive obligations emanating from its application will be obligations to exercise due diligence to prevent

56 See Henry Shue, 'Mediating Duties' (1988) 98(4) Ethics 687.

57 Ibid at 688; See also Zofia Stemplowska, 'On the Real World Duties Imposed on Us by Human Rights' (2009) 40(4) Journal of Social Philosophy 466.

58 See, for similar questions posed, Tom Hayward, 'On Prepositional Duties' (2013) 123(2) Ethics 264.

59 SOLAS, Ch V, Reg 7.1; See, also, further discussion by Irini Papanicolopulu, 'The Duty to Rescue at Sea, in Peacetime and in War: A General Overview' (2016) 98(2) International Review of the Red Cross 499.

60 *Corfu Channel (United Kingdom of Great Britain and Northern Ireland v Albania)* (Merits) [1949] ICJ Rep 4, 18.

foreseeable loss of life – requiring a State to make *best efforts* toward a certain result within the means available.[61]

5. Philosophical Justifications of a Right to Be Rescued at Sea

The above analysis has shown that the so-called claimability requirement presents an obstacle to the effective realization of a right to be rescued at sea, but not to its existence as a human right. In this section, I resume elucidating the most dynamic responses to O'Neill's work, which will allow the justification of a right to be rescued at sea, while rejecting the claimability requirement to the existence of rights. The premise is based on the understanding that human rights are (primarily) moral claims, that all humans have and should enjoy rights by virtue of their humanity, so their existence and justification is not dependent upon institutions and subsequent interpretation of their content.[62] However, O'Neill's theory is in contradiction with this view; in her account, the justification of rights will always rest on the existence of coordinating institutions that allocate the relevant duties and delineate the contours of those rights.

Tasioulas presents a powerful response to this view, as his theory challenges the notion of claimability, which he sees as not a necessary condition for the existence of rights.[63] He supports an account of rights according to which 'a right exists if an individual's interest, taken by itself, has the requisite kind of importance to justify the imposition of duties on others variously to respect, protect and promote that interest'.[64] In this context, the interest will serve to ground a claim to a right to be rescued at sea by virtue of the fundamental value that *life* has to all persons, the inherent dignity of a person and the long-standing maritime tradition of rendering assistance to those in distress. It follows then, that if this right is (once) violated then the interest being protected will be irreversibly extinguished.[65] Primarily, the doctrinal basis is grounded on the values underlying human rights, 'or,

61 CCPR, *A.S. and Others v Italy*, 27 January 2021, UN Doc CCPR/C/130/D/3042/2017, Annex 4, para 3; On due diligence obligations see, Alice Ollino, *Due Diligence Obligations in International Law* (CUP 2022) 134.

62 Tasioulas (n 5) 77.

63 Ibid 81.

64 Ibid 77; Tasioulas in his Article refers interchangeably to 'duties to respect, protect, promote' and 'duties to respect, protect, and further it, etc.' – in international law, the tripartite set of duties that States have are to 'respect, protect, fulfil' human rights. The duty to fulfil comprises the State's obligations to take positive actions to facilitate, promote and provide the enjoyment of basic human rights; I take it that Tasioulas by 'promote' and 'further it' arguably refers to the duty to 'fulfil' which subsumes those terms; For similar analysis see, Takele Soboka Bulto, *The Extraterritorial Application of the Human Right to Water in Africa* (CUP 2003) 90.

65 Lawrence C Becker and Charlotte B Becker (eds), *Encyclopedia of Ethics* (Routledge 2001) 855.

put differently, the considerations to which we need to appeal in order to justify belief in the existence of human rights'.[66] Consequently, I concur with Tasioulas that institutions are essential for the allocation of duties to duty-bearers, yet we are still justified in affirming rights prior to their institutionalization, hence, prior to the identification of the duty-bearer. This approach escapes the unnaturally demanding theory of O'Neill, which imposes unnecessary limits on the proclamation of rights and reinforces the Hohfeldian logic to the existence of rights. Alternatively, allocation can be seen as a *separate, supplementary* question, which it is unnecessary to answer in order to *recognize* a right.

Sen presents an alternative philosophical account in his conceptual justification for rights, which centers on the standing of human rights. Sen argues that human rights generate reasons for action and consequently both perfect and imperfect obligations are correlative with human rights (whereas O'Neill maintains that only perfect obligations can create correlative rights).[67] In this regard, Sen claims:

> The implementation of human rights can go well beyond legislation, and a theory of human rights cannot be sensibly confined within the juridical model in which it is frequently incarcerated. For example, public recognition and agitation (including the monitoring of violations) can be part of the obligations – often imperfect – generated by the acknowledgment of human rights.[68]

Public recognition and agitation are in fact important processes in the recognition stages of a human right. In this regard, recognition can take multiple forms, the simplest and initial one being a resolution passed by the UN General Assembly (UNGA) formalizing the norm in soft law and stipulating further steps in the process of turning it into a formal binding rule.[69] This kind of recognition follows the traditional route of rights recognition in international law, the strongest example being the Universal Declaration of Human Rights (UDHR). While the UDHR does not enjoy legally binding status, nor does it entail mechanisms of international enforcement, it has nonetheless received universal acceptance as a basis for the recognition of rights in international

66 Effy Vayena and John Tasioulas, 'The Dynamics of Big Data and Human Rights: The Case of Scientific Research' (2016) 374(2083) Philosophical Transactions of The Royal Society A Mathematical Physical and Engineering Sciences 5.

67 Sen (n 52) 319.

68 Ibid.

69 Kerstin von der Decken and Nikolaus Koch, 'Recognition of New Human Rights: Phases, Techniques and the Approach of "Differentiated Traditionalism"' in Andreas von Arnauld, Kerstin von der Decken and Mart Susi (eds), *The Cambridge Handbook of New Human Rights: Recognition, Novelty and Rhetoric* (CUP 2020) 12.

human rights law.[70] Undoubtedly, the list of internationally recognized human rights has not remained constant; we are steadily witnessing the emergence of treaties and documents that further advance some of the basic concepts laid down in the UDHR. As with the drafters of the UDHR, the hope remains that the recognition route is a primary step that can help illuminate the journey towards the full realization of the right to be rescued at sea.

Pertinently, Waldron points out that positive law does not 'simply spring into existence', but it slowly emerges and its existence 'as law can be a matter of degree'.[71] I appeal to Waldron's philosophy, which persistently argues that norms coming into being begin from a soft law, declaratory status and gradually crystallize in positive law. Ergo, there is no decisive moment in which human rights emerge. As Sikkink perceives, the world is not working according to 'iron laws', but instead we construct the world of the political and the social at certain moments and certain times according to changing realities.[72] Interestingly, Sikkink claims that human rights 'provide[s] a morally defensible starting place for talking about progressive change in the world'.[73]

In the area of migration, both MSF Sea and Amnesty International, to name a few relevant humanitarian organizations, have an extremely active role in advancing the interests of migrants and promoting such claims as well as the overall respect and mobilization for the protection of human rights; for example, they take part in legal action against governments and/or try to promote rights and enhance public awareness through their activities.[74] In particular, MSF Sea has been voluntarily active in SAR in the Mediterranean, in an effort to uphold the duty to render assistance at sea.[75] Therefore, we can see how NGOs are critical players, not only in the advancement and protection of human rights of vulnerable people but also in promoting recognition in the absence of legislation and/or enforcement.

Adding to the above, effective synergies, for example, between civil society organizations and academics can also play a salient role in human rights movements. One dynamic synergy is the Global Legal Action Network (GLAN), which brings together distinguished academics, legal practitioners as well as

70 Universal Declaration of Human Rights, UNGA Res 217 A (III) (10 December 1948) (UDHR); Seyla Benhabib, 'Claiming Rights Across Borders: International Human Rights and Democratic Sovereignty' (2009) 103(4) American Political Science Review 699.

71 Jeremy Waldron, 'Cosmopolitan Norms' in Seyla Benhabib (ed), *Another Cosmopolitanism* (OUP 2006) 95.

72 Kathryn Sikkink, *Evidence for Hope: Making Human Rights Work in the 21st Century* (Princeton University Press 2017); Patrick William Kelly, 'What Is Hope for?' (7 July 2018) <https://lareviewofbooks.org/article/what-is-hope-for/>.

73 Ibid 15.

74 Communication to the Office of the Prosecutor of the International Criminal Court Pursuant to the Article 15 of the Rome Statute: EU Migration Policies in the Central Mediterranean and Libya (2014–2019)' (Communication to the ICC) 163 <https://www.statewatch.org/media/documents/news/2019/jun/eu-icc-case-EU-Migration-Policies.pdf>.

75 Medecins Sans Frontieres, 'Saving Lives at Sea' <http://searchandrescue.msf.org>.

investigative journalists to mobilize law in preventing and responding to human rights violations through international legal strategies.[76] These kind of channels allow for expansion of the actors involved in the human rights community beyond the sovereign State that can be more compelling and effective in promoting the recognition of human rights and norms movement.[77] This is further bolstered by the recent establishment of the International Law Association Committee on the 'Protection of People at Sea',[78] which aims to address *inter alia* how different notions of 'jurisdiction' under the law of the sea and human rights law can be combined to maximize protection for people at sea. In this way, public argument, deliberation and exchange in legal scholarship present effective means, which universalist claim-rights can be contested and contextualized, pointing towards their legalization and juridification everywhere.[79]

6. Recognizing the Existence of 'New' Rights

This section sketches some of the practical recognition avenues in which the right to be rescued at sea can be seen to emerge as a legal concept. First, it will consider potential soft law emanations, which can recognize the existence of this right, and then it will progress to show how interpretative techniques by courts can harvest its full recognition (become binding law).[80]

The analysis will center solely on the ability of judges to positively construct the right to life in a manner that is not considered as 'judicial activism' but instead as *interpreting* the law in light of present-day conditions, 'and in accordance with developments in international law, so as to reflect the increasingly high standard being required in the area of the protection of human rights'.[81] As Alan Boyle and Christine Chinkin have argued, judges present a vital source of contemporary international law-making.[82] Relatedly, Ingo Venzke

76 The pending case before the ECtHR, *S.S. and Others v Italy*, App no 21660/18 (ECtHR, communicated on 26 June 2019), is a powerful example of their work, see GLAN <https://www.glanlaw.org/migrationandborders>.

77 John Tasioulas, 'Saving Human Rights from Human Rights Law' (2019) 52 Vanderbilt Journal of Transnational Law 1169.

78 International Law Association, 'Protection of People at Sea' <https://www.ila-hq.org/en_GB/committees/protection-of-people-at-sea>.

79 Benhabib (n 70) 698.

80 By full recognition, I mean, when a right becomes legally binding.

81 *Demir and Baykara v Turkey*, App no 34503/97 (ECtHR, 12 November 2008) para 146. The 'living instrument' doctrine which upholds this interpretative task was first articulated in *Tyrer v United Kingdom*, App no 5856/72 (ECtHR, 25 April 1978) para 31. The doctrine has been vastly applied in the ECtHR's case law, see *inter alia Loizidou v Turkey*, App no 15318/89 (ECtHR, 18 December 1996) para 43 'the Convention must be interpreted in light of the rules of interpretation'; *Öcalan v Turkey*, App no 46221/99 (ECtHR, 12 May 2005) para 163, quoting the Chamber's conclusions, para 190, 'the Convention cannot be interpreted in a vacuum'.

82 Alan Boyle and Christine Chinkin, *The Making of International Law* (New York: OUP 2007); See also, Anne Peters, *Beyond Human Rights: The Legal Status of Individuals in International Law* (CUP 2016) 437–448.

has stressed that in international law, 'we make up the rules "as we go along"'.[83] Ideally then, the exercise of interpretation is to carve out the real meaning of a legal provision 'in the totality of what surrounds the words, their *context*' to provide certainty about a provision's meaning.[84] Following, legal reasoning, as Hohfeld's analytical scheme exemplified, is an activity of finding the law that already exists. Hence, there is 'no agency, no politics, and no problem' in the interpretative practice.[85] Instead, as Venzke has argued, the development of international norms through interpretation is a legitimate practice in international law, one that is valid and binding upon States. Yet, some will remain skeptical if the interpretative way of approaching existing doctrine is the best choice to solve this structural problem on the high seas; indeed, the practice of judicial institutions is not free from defects.[86] The argument will be that the court's role as the authoritative voice of human rights, in the case of the ECtHR for Europe, has been previously subjected to high levels of criticism in relation to specific judgments, although it has been developing positive obligations under the European Convention on Human Rights. Vitally then, Hohfeld's theory advances judicial reasoning and allows the law to be developed in a progressive yet coherent and logical way.

Before proceeding a caveat is in order. The analysis below will not consider other traditional paths of making international law – through a treaty and/or customary international law.[87] This is a deliberate shortcut, as I maintain that Hohfeld's analytical scheme together with the teleological *pro-homine* treaty interpretation is a more tempting avenue in determining international law as it allows judges to derive a right to be rescued at sea from the existing right to life and so become part of *lex lata* instantly.[88] In contrast, participation in a treaty is at the discretion of States and, in a hotly contested area like irregular migration by sea, will hardly bear fruit.

83 Ingo Venzke, 'Is Interpretation in International Law a Game?' in Andrea Bianchi, Daniel Peat and Matthew Windsor (eds), *Interpretation in International Law* (OUP 2015) 354; Quoting therein, Ludwig Wittgenstein, *Philosophical Investigations* (Basil Blackwell 1958) 83.

84 Ingo Venzke, *How Interpretation Makes International Law: On Semantic Change and Normative Twists* (OUP 2012) 3.

85 Ibid.

86 On the democratic legitimacy of courts see, Andreas von Staden, 'The Democratic Legitimacy of Judicial Review Beyond the State: Normative Subsidiarity and Judicial Standards of Review' (2012) 10(4) International Journal of Constitutional Law 1024–1026.

87 Statute of the International Court of Justice(ICJ) (26 June 1945) 33 UNTS 993, Art 38(1) provides the sources of international law: '1. International conventions, whether general or particular, establishing rules expressly recognized by the consenting states; 2. International custom, as evidence of general practice accepted as law; 3. The general principles of law recognized by civilized nations; 4. Subject to the provisions of Article 59, judicial decisions and the teaching of the most highly qualified publicists of the various nations, as subsidiary mean for the determination of rules of law'.

88 For a thorough analysis on the practice of interpretation as a significant source of making international law, see Ingo Venzke, *How Interpretation Makes International Law: On Semantic Change and Normative Twists* (OUP 2012).

It was for the first time in 2018, with the development of the Global Compact on Migration (Compact), that the UNGA recognized the connection between the two regimes of international law, human rights and the law of the sea.[89] Particularly, it explicitly affirmed in Objective *8*, the need of States to 'save lives and established coordinated efforts on missing migrants'. Additionally, it stressed the need for States to 'commit to cooperate internationally to save lives and prevent migrant deaths and injuries through individual or joint search and rescue operations,. . . assuming collective responsibility to preserve the lives of all migrants, in accordance with international law'. In particular, in order to realize this objective, it called upon States to 'develop procedures and agreements on search and rescue of migrants, with the *primary* objective to protect migrants' right to life'. Importantly, the Compact, by making a strong reference to realizing the need to protect migrants' right to life *at sea*, arguably accommodated a right to be rescued at sea within the existing corpus of human rights. As such, the need to address and prevent *foreseeable* deaths on maritime migrant routes buttresses this premise and accordingly translates as: *if States must save lives, then correlatively, migrants have the right to be saved.*

In this connection, a key endeavor to bridge the law of the sea and international human rights law was evidenced by the launch of the Geneva Declaration on Human Rights at Sea[90] in 2022, developed under the auspices of the NGO Human Rights at Sea.[91] The Declaration, though a soft-law mechanism, holds particular importance in complementing international lawmaking efforts by highlighting the scale of human rights violations occurring at sea. It strongly aligns with other initiatives of civil society actors to allocate responsibilities to States to uphold human rights in the different maritime zones and remedying their violation. By affirming the universality of human rights, namely, that they apply at sea as they do on land, it reinforces the doctrinal foundations supporting the right to be rescued at sea. Therefore, the recognition of this right goes beyond solely being a matter of legal coherence; it is a critical step towards ensuring that individuals in distress receive the protection they are entitled to under international law.

Another important actor in the process of recognizing rights, as evidenced above, are international bodies, which often undertake a considerable amount of interpretation. Whilst these treaty interpretations are not binding on States,

89 General Assembly, 'Global Compact for Safe, Orderly and Regular Migration' (19 December 2018) Res.73/195.

90 The Geneva Declaration was drafted by David Hammond, Professor Steven Haines, Professor Anna Petrig, Professor Irini Papanicolopulu, Dr Sofia Galani and Dr Elizabeth Mavropoulou. It was also reviewed by practitioners in several British law firms. See, Human Rights at Sea, *Geneva Declaration on Human Rights at Sea* (launched 1 March 2022) <https://www.humanrightsatsea.org/GDHRAS>.

91 Natalie Klein, 'Geneva Declaration on Human Rights at Sea: An Endeavor to Connect Law of the Sea and International Human Rights Law' (2022) 53(2–3) Ocean Development & International Law 233–235.

they form a fundamental part of the actions required towards achieving the development of a legal norm. In this terrain, an equally remarkable development that followed on the same year with the Compact is the adoption of *General Comment No 36* on the right to life (Article 6, ICCPR) by the UN Human Rights Committee (HRC or Committee), as was expounded in Chapter 3.[92] Through this avenue, the HRC radically broadened the applicability of the right to life extraterritorially in a manner that sustains a right to be rescued at sea.[93]

Moreover, the ECtHR has given a wide margin of appreciation to States on the issue of 'reasonable steps' – positive intervention – to be taken to prevent loss of life, risk to life and/or to reduce this risk.[94] For example, in *Leray v France*,[95] the ECtHR held that SAR operations are susceptible to judicial review in light of the right to life.[96] This is an important step for present purposes as the Strasbourg Court is showing a willingness to step up to the difficulties that the protection of the right to life faces at sea. Accordingly, the Court has appreciated that SAR operations are intertwined with the safety of life at sea principle and should thus endow positive obligations on States to prevent the deaths of those within its jurisdiction. Such discussions provide doctrinal clarity for expanding the traditional 'territorial' notion of jurisdiction as will be observed in the following chapter.

Recognizing a right to be rescued at sea is not a utopian or rhetorical gesture; it requires a full exploration of the conceptual relationship between the two areas of international law, the law of the sea and human rights, in order to define its substance and delineate its contours. In fact, the HRC in adopting a more expansive approach to the application of the ICCPR, in contrast to the ECtHR's jurisprudence, has effectively situated the right to life in the maritime

92 HRC, *CCPR General Comment No 36 (2018) on Article 6 of the International Covenant on Civil and Political Rights, on the Right to Life*, adopted 30 October 2018, CCPR/C/GC/36; International Covenant on Civil and Political Rights (adopted 16 December 1966, entered into force 23 March 1976) 999 UNTS 171.

93 In a different terrain, the process of declaring new human rights can be shadowed by the Human Rights Council that proclaimed a new human right to clear, healthy and sustainable environment in 2021. This declaration was endorsed a year later by the UN General Assembly. UNGA Res. 76/300, The human right to clean, healthy and sustainable environment, adopted on 28 July 2022, UN Doc. A/76/L.75 (2022). On the case of new human rights see analysis by Yuval Shany, 'The Case of a New Right to a Human Decision Under International Human Rights Law' (2023) SSRN Working Draft <http://doi.org/10.2139/ssrn.4592244>.

94 Vladislava Stoyanova, 'The Right to Life Under the EU Charter and Cooperation with Third States to Combat Human Smuggling' (2020) 21(3) German Law Journal 446.

95 *Leray v France*, App no 44617/98 (ECtHR, 16 January 2001).

96 For an elaborated discussion see Lisa-Marie Komp, 'The Duty to Assist Persons in Distress: An Alternative Source of Protection against the Return of Migrants and Asylum Seekers to the High Seas?' in Violeta Moreno-Lax and Efthymios Papastavridis (eds), *'Boat Refugees' and Migrants at Sea: A Comprehensive Approach: Integrating Maritime Security with Human Rights* (Vol. 7, International Refugee Law Series, Brill Nijhoff 2016) 236.

context. To be sure, the HRC could have stretched the meaning of the right to life by employing the Hohfeldian analytical tool to have proclaimed the existence of a right to be rescued at sea as implicit in the right to life. Such exposition would have allowed the subsequent utilization of the teleological approach to shape its contours and define its scope of application. Nonetheless, both the HRC's *General Comment No 36* and its recent ruling in the *A.S.* case (which will be looked at next), constitute paramount, initial steps towards the full recognition of a right to be rescued at sea. Its realization will accordingly depend on the activity of courts to make its philosophical 'universality' part of the *lex lata*.

It is my belief that international judges are powerful players in the process of international lawmaking that can exercise their authority to *juris dicere* and recognize the existence of rights. Acknowledging though that a right to be rescued at sea has not (yet) progressed to the juridification process, the chapter sought to lay down the normative foundations and highlight the steps that will lead to its full recognition.

7. Final Remarks

This chapter's aim was to prove through the Hohfeldian correlativity theory that a right to be rescued at sea exists as a norm and is a stable assumption. Crucially, the operative reality of human rights is neither their claimability, nor their enforceability, but rather their gradual recognition, which manifests normative standards to which our choices and actions ought to conform. The imperative role of claimability and enforcement through institutionalization mechanisms for the realization of rights is beyond doubt. But rights need to be recognized first in some way, as normative ideals through advocacy and scholarly works, progressing to acquiring soft law recognition and universally applicable human right status, paving the way for explicit recognition in international law. To downgrade the importance of rights according to their legal status would be a clear mischaracterization of the premise underlying human rights as normative standards.

Consequently, I have consistently upheld the view that courts are best positioned to expand the scope of human rights obligations and sanction the existence of (a nonexistent) right within the right to life. This will allow an examination of functional questions, concerning procedural and substantive obligations to be borne by States. Hence, conferring a right upon individuals to be rescued at sea could act as a way to remedy mismanagement of the duty to render assistance at sea and strengthen compliance by States, in this way enhancing the enjoyment of the right to life and minimizing its hindrances. Foremost, such an attempt will challenge the boundaries of rights and is well overdue. On this account, the following chapter will delve into the concept of extraterritorial human rights jurisdiction, which is a fundamental prerequisite for the practical realization of a right to be rescued at sea.

5 A Functional Understanding of Human Rights Jurisdiction

On 27 January 2021, the UN Human Rights Committee (HRC or Committee) delivered two novel decisions in *A.S. and Others v Italy*[1] and *A.S. and Others v Malta*,[2] confirming that the right to life, under Article 6 of the International Covenant on Civil and Political Rights (ICCPR),[3] applies in the conduct of maritime search and rescue (SAR) operations and extends beyond a strict interpretation of territorial jurisdiction. Striking a groundbreaking moment for the history of human rights and analogously for the rights of migrants, the Committee found a jurisdictional nexus between the persons in distress (right-holders) and the States who coordinated the rescue incident (duty-bearers). Remarkably Hélène Tigroudja, in her individual opinion, admitted that the majority's views are an attempt to address 'maritime legal black holes' which give substance to an emerging 'right to be rescued at sea'. Manifestly, such explicit reference is a first step towards the formal recognition of the existence of a right to be rescued at sea in international law. The outcome manifests an encouraging development for the applicability of human rights beyond sovereign territory, not only because it utilized for the first time a functional concept of jurisdiction that expanded the normative contours of human rights, placing principal value on the object and purpose of the right to life, but also for striving to combat notions of migrant 'rightlessness' at sea.

At this stage, one might reasonably ponder: what will a functional understanding of jurisdiction bring to the current *corpus juris* of international human rights for the protection of migrants' rights in *mare liberum*? As expounded in the Introduction, the use of the term *functional* is premised on a State's capacity (or potential) to impact the human rights of individuals, who are outside its national territory, but for whom it is nonetheless in a position

1 CCPR, *A.S. and Others v Italy*, 27 January 2021, UN Doc CCPR/C/130/D/3042/2017 (*A.S.* case (against Italy) or *A.S.* case).

2 CCPR, *A.S. and Others v Malta*, 27 January 2021, UN Doc CCPR/C/128/D/30423/2017 (*A.S.* case (against Malta)).

3 International Covenant on Civil and Political Rights (adopted 16 December 1966, entered into force 23 March 1976) 999 UNTS 171.

DOI: 10.4324/9781003568537-6

to respect, protect and fulfil, given that it has the means to do so. In this way, this functional capacity will connect the State to the individual in a specific situation. Consequently, the extraterritorial application of human rights treaties is premised on the exercise of jurisdiction by the State. In turn, the notion of jurisdiction raises a series of bewildering questions for human rights theory and practice.

Certainly, jurisdiction has not always been perceived as functional; it is understood as principally territorial (but not necessarily), as judicial institutions have sought to apply jurisdiction beyond a State's national territory only in 'exceptional' circumstances. Arguably, the various interpretations and 'versions' of extraterritorial jurisdiction have opened the Pandora's box we are dealing with today, where all meanings and interpretations of jurisdiction are possible, yet none provides predictability as to when human rights obligations will arise beyond sovereign territory.

In the literature, the concept of jurisdiction has been used with different and sometimes contradictory meanings, apparently without reaching any consensus on its scope and when it will trigger States' human rights obligations beyond their national sovereignty. Following, the absence of human rights jurisdiction *ipso facto* means that individuals cannot claim protection against a State to secure their human rights.[4] For this reason, jurisdiction presents the *Achilles heel of human rights applicability beyond sovereign territory.* Ergo, a right to be rescued at sea has inherently an extraterritorial reach, or simpliciter, it is a right that by the very nature of where it needs to be secured – at sea – requires the establishment of a jurisdictional link between the duty-bearing State and the potential right-holding individual. In this respect, the need for developing a functional concept of jurisdiction is centered on the fact that for this right to be secured and realized, jurisdiction ought to be expanded to circumstances where a State has the *capacity* to protect life that is under risk.[5]

As expounded in the previous chapters, the case made in this book supports the theorization of a right to be rescued at sea that is based not only on Hohfeld's analytical scheme of relations but is also underpinned by a Kantian respect for the inherent dignity of a person. Together they provide a robust justification for the courts to start the jurisprudential inquiry by identifying a right to be rescued as correlative to the duty to render assistance at sea. Thereafter, the emphasis shifts to establishing the facts of each case, including the risk to life of the migrants adrift at sea and what the state *knew* or *ought* to have known in the circumstances. In other words, the first issue is the identification of the right, before then determining whether it has been violated on the facts. Against this Hohfeldian backdrop, the courts will be able to delve into an

4 See, *inter alia*, Sigrun I Skogly, *Beyond National Borders: States' Human Rights Obligations in International Cooperation* (1st edn, Intersentia 2006) 45.

5 Vassilis P Tzevelekos and Elena Katselli Proukaki, 'Migrants at Sea: A Duty of Plural States to Protect (Extraterritorially)?' (2017) 86 Nordic Journal of International Law 460.

analysis of jurisdiction (extraterritoriality) and shape the normative contours of this right by engaging with the methods of treaty interpretation.

On this account, the apropos question that needs to be answered in the applications concerning seaborne migration is whether the applicants were within the jurisdiction of the respondent State. It follows that jurisdiction can no longer be perceived in its traditional, territorial sense as external border control practices and migration policies constantly challenge existing concepts of how States exercise jurisdiction beyond their territory – extraterritorially. This chapter seeks to unpack the normative premise unifying the types of extraterritorial jurisdiction. On this foundation, it aims to conceptualize jurisdiction in such a way that it can be reconciled with human personhood (instead of citizenship). Apart from the above HRC's decisions, which will be dissected below, personhood could be easily undermined by State authorities and border control practices in the context of migration at sea, justified on the grounds of territorial sovereignty.

Through advocating for the recognition of a right to be rescued at sea, the aim is to establish the normative considerations (and factors) which will trigger a State's human rights obligations towards persons in distress in a number of different factual scenarios that could arise during irregular sea crossings. As Eleni Kannis – rightly, I contend – posits 'the current law triggering human rights protection extraterritorially is inadequate and requires considerable reform'.[6]

1. The Concept of Jurisdiction

As is apparent by now, a State is clearly not responsible for every act or omission which violates human rights, regardless of the perpetrator or location where it occurs. Importantly, States have presumed human rights obligations towards only those individuals that find themselves within their jurisdiction. In this section, I shall evaluate the jurisdictional clauses in the relevant human rights treaties in order to observe the notion of jurisdiction. By doing so, I will examine how the meaning of jurisdiction has been obscured with other types of jurisdiction and, sometimes, has even been equated with the concept of jurisdiction as found in international law. I posit that such misconstructions blur the lines of interpretation, creating confusion as to when States will have to secure human rights obligations beyond their territory, something that risks undermining the effectiveness of human rights.

When looking at the territorial scope of a State's jurisdiction for the purposes of human rights law, Article 29 of the Vienna Convention on the Law of the Treaties 1969 (VCLT) provides that 'unless a different intention appears from the treaty or is otherwise established, a treaty is binding upon each party in

6 Eleni Kannis, 'Pulling (Apart) the Triggers of Extraterritorial Jurisdiction' (2015) 40 The University of Western Australia Law Review 243.

respect of its entire territory'. As earlier explained in Chapter 2, the territorial sea, which extends up to 12 nautical miles from a State's baseline, comes as well within a State's territory. Interestingly in this context, border control practices, interception measures and distress incidents at sea most often pertain beyond the territorial sea, and in particular, take place in the Exclusive Economic Zone (EEZ), which for SAR purposes, is treated as if it is the high seas. In this regard, the VCLT fails to deal with the application of treaties beyond the territory of a State party, as it does not provide any general or specific information to direct us beyond a *verbatim* consideration of territorial boundaries.

In turn, the International Law Commission's (ILC) statement in its commentaries to the draft articles on the VCLT illustrates that 'certain types of treaty, by reason of their subject matter, are hardly susceptible of territorial application in the ordinary sense. Most treaties, however, have application to territory and a question may arise as to what is their precise scope territorially'.[7] Human rights treaties fall within the latter category. The ILC demonstrated that by looking at the subject matter of a treaty – the content of the rights and obligations it creates. We can ascertain whether and how these rights and obligations should apply.

Consequently, one might ponder whether individuals have rights that could be feasibly secured in practice outside a State's territory should a violation takes place. The answer to this question must be simple – yes (at least, in theory). If human rights are universal and inherent in every human being by virtue of their humanity, then why should it matter whether one is located within a State's territory or outside? In this regard, the Universal Declaration of Human Rights (UDHR) unequivocally provides in Article 2:

> Everyone is entitled to all the rights and freedoms set forth in this Declaration, without distinction of any kind, such as race, colour, sex, language, religion, political or other opinion, national or social origin, property, birth or other status. Furthermore, no distinction shall be made on the basis of the political, *jurisdictional* or international status of the country or territory to which a person belongs.[8]

Apropos the philosophical encounters of the preceding chapter, boundaries should not reduce a person's human rights *vis-à-vis* their legal personhood. This understanding is also supported in the Preamble of the ICCPR, which provides that human rights 'derive from the inherent dignity of the human person'. Frankly, if a person is to be perceived as rightless by virtue of their location, how might accountability for human rights violations be sought?

7 ILC, 'Draft Articles on the Law of Treaties with Commentaries 1966' (1966) 2 Yearbook of the ILC 213.

8 Art 2, Universal Declaration of Human Rights, UNGA Res 217 A (III) (10 December 1948) (UDHR) (emphasis added).

Thus, it would be impossible to redress or denounce any violations beyond the geographical limits of a State's territory.[9] The legal answer to this question is much more complex and deserves further attention.

1.1 Jurisdictional Clauses in International Human Rights Treaties

The main international human rights treaties on civil and political rights, the ICCPR, the American Convention on Human Rights (ACHR) and the European Convention on Human Rights (ECHR) and their Protocols,[10] conceive State responsibility for securing the rights they contain only in terms of the State's 'jurisdiction'. Looking at the ICCPR, Article 2 (1) provides that a State party 'undertakes to respect and to ensure to all individuals *within its territory* and *subject to its* jurisdiction' the rights recognized in the Covenant.[11] Accordingly, albeit with a significantly different formulation than the ICCPR, the ECHR provides in Article 1 that its State parties 'shall secure to everyone *within their jurisdiction*' the rights and freedoms provided in the Convention. Other human rights treaties contain similar jurisdictional clauses.[12] The ICCPR clearly places emphasis on individuals 'within' a State's territory, whereas the ECHR uses only the term 'within their jurisdiction'. This might point to the conclusion that the notion of jurisdiction should be strictly understood to be limited to a State's territorial boundaries, thereby any extraterritorial scope of the Convention is ruled out. However, such readings were not apparent from the HRC's interpretations of the Covenant provisions nor from the ICJ's reading which affirmed the extraterritoriality of the ICCPR.[13]

Human rights jurisdiction can be both territorial and extraterritorial. As Samantha Besson asserts, the notion of extraterritoriality implies that the territorial application of human rights treaties is the norm; however, there can be exceptions.[14] Thus, jurisdiction requires that a right-holder falls under

9 For instance, see the approach by the US Supreme Court in *Boumediene v Bush*, 128 Supreme Court 2229 (2008), where the court rejected a state-centric approach that would rely on nationality or location of individuals and maintained a functional approach to jurisdiction. See Gerald L Neuman, 'The Extraterritorial Constitution after *Boumediene v. Bush*' (2009) 82 Southern California Law Review 261.

10 Convention for the Protection of Human Rights and Fundamental Freedoms (adopted 4 November 1950, entered into force 3 September 1953) 213 UNTS 222.

11 ICCPR, Art 2(1) (emphasis added).

12 ACHR Art 1, CAT Art 2, Convention on the Rights of the Child 1989 (CRC) Art 2 (1).

13 E.g., HRC, *CCPR General Comment No 31:* The nature of the general legal obligation imposed on States Parties to the Covenant, adopted 29 March 2004, CCPR/C/21/Rev.1/Add.13, para 2 and 10; *Legal Consequences of the Construction of a Wall in the Occupied Palestinian Territory (Advisory Opinion)* [2004] ICJ Rep 136 para 109, 112 (*The Wall* case) 106; See also, Skogly (n 4) 153.

14 Samantha Besson, 'The Extraterritoriality of the European Convention on Human Rights: Why Human Rights Depend on Jurisdiction and What Jurisdiction Amounts to' (2012) 25(4) LJIL 862.

the control of the State in order for human rights obligations to arise in the first place.[15] For this reason, the jurisprudence in this area is manifestly situation-specific. Hence, judicial intervention becomes paramount in construing what jurisdiction entails to secure one's rights and freedoms beyond a State's sovereign territory.

At this juncture, it needs be underscored that Frontex's operations at sea are, in principle, required to abide by EU law, including the Charter of Fundamental Rights of the European Union (EU Charter) and relevant international law, including the provisions of UNCLOS.[16] The EU Charter, in particular, pertains to all actions taken by the EU institutions, bodies and agencies as well as its Member States whenever EU law is being implemented, whether territorially or extraterritorially.[17] There is thus no jurisdictional threshold requirement for the applicability of EU human rights law, as unlike the ECHR, the EU Charter does not contain a jurisdictional clause, and it can offer more extensive protection than the ECHR under Article 52(3).[18] Therefore, both the EU institutions and its Member States are bound by the EU Charter irrespective of the potential impact of their decisions[19] or the location of the affected individuals in question. As Ryngaert notes, when the EU exercises its powers, 'it owes human rights obligations to persons affected by such exercise of power, irrespective of the location of those persons'.[20] However, it is important to stress the challenge of providing definitive answers regarding the

15 See also Marko Milanovic, 'From Compromise to Principle: Clarifying the Concept of State Jurisdiction in Human Rights Treaties' (2008) 8(3) Human Rights Law Review 416. The ECtHR admits that 'the exercise of jurisdiction is a necessary condition for a Contracting State to be able to be held responsible for acts or omissions imputable to it which give rise to an allegation of the infringement of rights and freedoms set forth in the Convention' in *Catan and Others v Moldova and Russia*, App nos 43370/04, 8252/05, and 18454/06 (ECtHR, 19 October 2012) para 103.

16 EU Regulation No 2019/1896, Art 9 (1); United Nations Convention on the Law of the Sea (adopted 10 December 1982, entered into force 16 November 1994) 1833 UNTS 397 (UNCLOS); See also Efthymios Papastavridis, 'Rescuing Migrants at Sea and the Law of International Responsibility' in Thomas Gammeltoft-Hansen and J Vedsted-Hansen (eds), *Human Rights and the Dark Side of Globalisation: Transnational Law Enforcement and Migration Control* (Taylor & Francis Group 2016) 170.

17 Border control measures fall under the scope of EU law (Consolidated versions of the Treaty on European Union and the Treaty on the Functioning of the European Union (TFEU) 2012/C 326/01, art 9), yet SAR operations are regulated by the international law of the sea framework.

18 'EU fundamental rights obligations simply track EU activities, whether they take place within or without territorial boundaries', Violetta Moreno-Lax and Cathryn Costello, 'The Extraterritorial Application of the EU Charter of Fundamental Rights: From Territoriality to Facticity–the Effectiveness Model' in Steve Peers et al. (eds), *The EU Charter of Fundamental Rights: A Commentary* (Hart Publishing 2014) 1662.

19 Vladislava Stoyanova, 'The Right to Life Under the EU Charter and Cooperation with Third States to Combat Human Smuggling' (2020) 21(3) GLJ 448.

20 Cedric Ryngaert, 'EU Trade Agreements and Human Rights: From Extraterritorial to Territorial Obligations' (2018) 20 International Law Community Review 380.

extraterritorial reach of the EU Charter, which remains an area surrounded by ambiguity.

1.2 *The Meaning of Human Rights Jurisdiction*

The meaning of jurisdiction has been so far obscured with other types of jurisdiction and, sometimes, has even been equated with the concept of jurisdiction as found in international law. Such misconstructions, however, blur the lines of interpretation, creating confusion as to when States will have to secure human rights obligations beyond their territory, something that risks undermining the effectiveness of human rights.

It is well established that jurisdiction in international human rights law is fundamentally different from jurisdiction as it is primarily understood in public international law.[21] Jurisdiction in international human rights law is understood as responsibility giving rise to specific human rights obligations.[22] Accordingly, if a State is to observe their human rights obligations towards particular individuals, that State needs to have jurisdiction over them.[23] Hence, jurisdiction in international human rights treaties acts as a threshold criterion for human rights obligations. On the other hand, as Milanovic puts it, jurisdiction in public international law concerns a State's *right* to regulate its own public order;[24] hence, it is concerned with whether or not a State's activity constitutes a lawful exercise of jurisdiction. Raible further distinguishes jurisdiction in international human rights as a question of *duty*, whereas jurisdiction in international law is a question of *right*.[25] Thence, jurisdiction in international human rights law exists *de facto*, meaning, even when the exercise of power by the State falls outside its legal competence.

Accordingly, the two terms should not be interchangeably used by courts, both for clarity purposes and for understanding the normative considerations that will trigger extraterritorial human rights obligations.[26] For instance, if a State exercises jurisdiction under international law, it is presumed to have jurisdiction under international human rights law, at least on its sovereign territory,

21 Jurisdiction under international law refers to the competence of a State to make, apply and enforce its laws. The State can exercise this competence by way of prescription, adjudication or enforcement. Thereby jurisdiction under international law can fall into one of the following five headings– territoriality, nationality, passive personality principle, protective principle and universality principle. In this way, jurisdiction in international law attracts many meanings.

22 Tilmann Altwicker, 'Transnationalizing Rights: International Human Rights Law in Cross-Border Contexts' (2018) 29(2) EJIL 582.

23 Lea Raible, *Human Rights Unbound: A Theory of Extraterritoriality* (OUP 2020) 320.

24 Milanovic, 'From Compromise to Principle' (n 15) 420.

25 Raible (n 23) 320; Alex Mills, 'Rethinking Jurisdiction in International Law' (2014) 84(1) British Yearbook of International Law 187.

26 The main differences that distinguish jurisdiction in international human rights law and in general international law are summarized by Besson (n 14). For detailed account on this topic, see also Milanovic, 'From Compromise to Principle' (n 15).

and this could also be established where there is evidence of effective control in the case of extraterritorial jurisdiction within the limits of international law. Papastavridis further posits that the notion of jurisdiction relates to a question of fact and simply means actual power, whether exercised lawfully or not.[27] Therefore, 'factivity' will create 'normativity' or in the language of Strasbourg Court, '*de facto* control gives rise to *de jure* responsibilities'.[28]

Banković v Belgium, one of the most controversial cases in the ECtHR's history, offers an excellent illustration of the above confusions.[29] The events of the case occurred during the Kosovo conflict, whereby a bombing attack directed by NATO pilots against a TV station building in Belgrade resulted in the death of 16 civilians.[30] The Court, in interpreting the meaning of jurisdiction under Article 1 of the ECHR, preferred to utilize the meaning of jurisdiction in international law by assuming that it is the same concept.[31] Why is such a reading then problematic for the purposes of interpreting jurisdiction under international human rights law? Taking a step back to look at the ECtHR's pre-*Banković* case law, the first landmark case decided on the extraterritorial application of the Convention is *Loizidou v Turkey*.[32] The Court emphasized that a State's responsibility might arise 'when as a consequence of military action – *whether lawful or unlawful* – it exercised *effective control of an area* outside its national territory'.[33] The Court in laying down the first test for triggering applicability of the Convention's rights – effective overall control over an area – found that the control exercised by Turkey, through the presence of its own military and the occupation of the northern part of Cyprus, was of such *scope and intensity*, that there was no reason why Turkey should not guarantee the human rights of the people in that territory just as it does for the people on its sovereign territory. Accordingly, the ECtHR did not make any reference to the meaning of jurisdiction under international law.

Turning to the *Banković* ruling, it is understood that a State needs to have a legal basis in order to exercise its power extraterritorially. Analogously, if the same reasoning had been applied in *Loizidou*, it would have meant that Turkey was exercising its jurisdiction, assuming that the Turkish law applies to

27 Efthymios Papastavridis, 'The "Left-to-Die Boat" Incident of March 2011: Questions of International Responsibility Arising from the Failure to Save Refugees at Sea' (2013) Refugee Law Initiative Working Paper No.10, 8 <http://sas-space.sas.ac.uk/4957/1/RLI_Working_Paper_No.10.pdf>; See, also, Martin Sheinin, 'Extraterritorial Effect of the International Covenant on Civil and Political Rights' in F Coomans et al. (eds), *Extraterritorial Application of Human Rights* (Antwerp: Intersentia 2004) 81.

28 Papastavridis ibid; ECtHR, *Al-Saadoon and Mufdhi v the United Kingdom*, App no 61498/08 (ECtHR, 2 March 2010) para 88.

29 *Banković v Belgium*, App no 52207/99 (ECtHR, 12 December 2001).

30 Yuval Shany, 'Taking Universality Seriously: A Functional Approach to Extraterritoriality in International Human Rights Law' (2013) 7(1) Law & Ethics of Human Rights 54.

31 *Banković* case (n 29) para 59–61.

32 *Loizidou v Turkey*, App no 15318/89 (ECtHR, 18 December 1996).

33 Ibid para 62 (emphasis added).

Cyprus and that the Cypriot inhabitants were *de jure* bound by it. Quite to the contrary, Turkey created a separate regime in the northern part of Cyprus, the Turkish Republic of Northern Cyprus, which is recognized only by Turkey. This illustration shows that the notion of jurisdiction in international law is distinguishable from and serves an entirely different purpose from that developed by the ECtHR in *Loizidou*: 'it sets out limits on the domestic legal orders of states, so that they do not infringe upon the sovereignty of other states'.[34]

Certainly, any confusion between these two concepts of jurisdiction results when jurisdiction is applied beyond a State's territory – extraterritorially – which necessitates a factual assessment of the circumstances. Additionally, jurisdiction in human rights law should also be demarcated from the law on State responsibility, especially the principles surrounding attribution of conduct. Jurisdiction in this book centers on the meaning elaborated in international human rights law. This is understood as jurisdiction tied to the emergence of the State's obligations so that a State secures – *takes responsibility for* – the rights of individuals it has jurisdiction over. Conversely, with regards to the law of State responsibility, Besson argues that 'attribution of certain acts to a public institution and State agents, and, more generally, responsibility, only come later once the State's duties have arisen in the first place and have been violated'.[35] As such, without State jurisdiction (in international human rights law) there can be no assessment of violations of human rights and accordingly no acts or omissions that would violate the State's duties given their *prima facie* absence. Ergo, there can be no attribution to a State and no potential responsibility of the State for violating those duties thereafter.

2. Jurisdiction Beyond the Territory of the State

The ECtHR has decided a vast number of cases arising in different contexts where jurisdiction of the State was extended beyond the territorial scope of the Convention, providing grounds for extraterritorial jurisdiction in situations, including: 1) a State's acts occurring on territory outside of the ECHR space;[36] 2) military intervention;[37] 3) military presence;[38] 4) a State's acts on its own territory producing effects in another State;[39] and 5) acts on high

34 Ibid 425. The International Community considers that it is only the Cypriot Government which is recognized internationally as the Government of the Republic of Cyprus, see para 42 in *Loizidou*.

35 Besson (n 14) 867.

36 *Öcalan v Turkey*, App no 46221/99 (ECtHR, 12 May 2005).

37 *Banković* case (n 29); *Pad and Others v. Turkey*, App no 60167/00 (ECtHR, 28 June 2007).

38 *Loizidou* case (n 32); *Al-Skeini and Others v the United Kingdom*, App no 55721/07 (ECtHR, 7 July 2011); *Al-Jedda v United Kingdom*, App no 27021/08 (ECtHR, 7 July 2011).

39 *Soering v United Kingdom* (1989) 11 EHRR 439; *Isaak and others v Turkey*, App no 44587/98 (ECtHR, 28 September 2006); *Andreou v Turkey*, App no 45653/99 (ECtHR, 3 June 2008).

seas.[40] In all these instances, the key question before the Court could even examine any human rights violations was whether jurisdiction could be said to extend beyond a State's sovereign territory. The ECtHR in its jurisprudence on extraterritoriality has so far employed two types of jurisdiction in order to determine the applicability of the ECHR outside a State's own territory: 1) jurisdiction defined spatially, the 'spatial model', also known as 'control over an area'; and 2) jurisdiction defined personally, the 'personal model', also known as 'state-agent authority or control' or 'power over an individual'.

As expounded in the previous section, the first landmark case of the ECtHR examining the extraterritorial application of human rights treaties is *Loizidou*, in which the Court developed the famous spatial type of jurisdiction.[41] Yet, this concept of jurisdiction might be too restrictive as it cannot cover the many different ways and situations in which States might violate human rights abroad without exercising effective control over an *area*. Consequently, the *Banković* case, decided later, effectively brought the spatial type of jurisdiction to a breaking point. In interpreting jurisdiction in the *Banković* case, the ECtHR ruled that the people killed in the airstrike were not within the jurisdiction of the NATO States, explaining that airstrikes over a territory do not establish control over the actual area. Disappointingly, it held that jurisdiction is primarily territorial and did not agree with the applicants' submission that 'anyone adversely affected by an act imputable to a Contracting State, wherever in the world that act may have been committed or its consequences felt, is thereby brought within the jurisdiction of that State', finding that the text of Article 1 did not support such an approach to jurisdiction.[42] Had the Court interpreted the jurisdictional clause in Article 1 of the Convention 'as a principle that should protect individuals, rather than a principle that can be used as a tool for states to avoid responsibility for their actions, this case would have upheld the *fundamentality* and *universality* of human rights'.[43]

Since then, there have been several remarkable developments attempting to alleviate the stringency of the *Banković* rule. In *Ilaşcu and Others v Moldova and Russia* decided a few years later, the ECtHR held that jurisdiction may persist even in parts of the State's own territory that are not under its effective control.[44] The State still has a positive obligation under Article 1 of the ECHR to take all appropriate measures within its power, in accordance with international law, to secure to the applicants the rights guaranteed by the

40 *Medvedyev and others v France*, App no 3394/03 (ECtHR, 29 March 2010).

41 *Loizidou* case (n 32) para 62; Following, the spatial model received overwhelming support from the major international courts, including The International Court of Justice in *Armed Activities on the Territory of the Congo (Congo v Uganda)*, Judgment 19 December 2005.

42 *Banković* case (n 29) para 75.

43 Skogly (n 4) 180 (emphasis added).

44 *Ilasçu and Others v Moldova and Russia*, App no 48787/99 (ECHR, 8 July 2004) paras 312–319.

Convention, even in the absence of effective control.[45] Moreover, the ECtHR in *Issa v Turkey*[46] recalled that the concept of jurisdiction under the Convention was not limited to the national territory of States and affirmed that in *exceptional* circumstances, the acts of contracting States performed outside their territory, or which *produced effects* there, might amount to exercise by them of their jurisdiction. This case concerned the alleged unlawful arrest, detention, ill-treatment and subsequent killing of a group of Iraqi nationals in the course of a Turkish military operation in northern Iraq. Yet, in the absence of sufficient factual evidence to find that the victims were arrested by Turkish security forces, the Court declared the case inadmissible. What is essential, then, to grasp from this case is that the Court took the opportunity to reiterate that Article 1 of the Convention could not be interpreted so as to allow a contracting State to perpetrate violations of the Convention on the territory of another State, which it could not perpetrate on its own territory.[47] Evidently, the reasoning manifests a move away from the perception that jurisdiction is primarily territorial; a premise that essentially overturns the Court's previous conclusions in *Banković* with regard to the geographical scope of the Convention.[48] Importantly, the reasoning echoes the HRC's earlier decision in *Lopez Burgos v Uruguay*,[49] which utilized the concept of the personal type of jurisdiction, whereby 'jurisdiction' implies authority and control exercised by States over individuals. *In casu,* the Committee had to decide whether the individual was subject to Uruguay's jurisdiction, despite the fact that his arrest and detention had (allegedly) taken place outside of Uruguayan territory and jurisdiction. Accordingly, the Committee gave emphasis to the relationship between the State and the individual in relation to a violation of his rights, instead of allowing the location where the violation occurred to act as the determining factor for the applicability of the ICCPR.

In this light, the HRC has reiterated the above approach in its *General Comment No 31*, which attempts to shed light on the extraterritorial impact of the ICCPR. Particularly, paragraph 10 provides:

> States Parties are required by article 2, paragraph 1, to respect and to ensure the Covenant rights to all persons who may be within their territory and to all persons subject to their jurisdiction. This means that a State party must respect and ensure the rights laid down in the Covenant

45 Ibid 331.

46 *Issa v Turkey*, App no 31821/96 (ECtHR, 16 November 2004).

47 Ibid para 71; CCPR, *Lopez Burgos v Uruguay*, Communication No 52/1979, 29 July 1981, UN Doc CCPR/13/D/52/1979, para 12.3.

48 *Banković* case (n 29) para 80; See, also, Sarah Miller, 'Revisiting Extraterritorial Jurisdiction: A Territorial Justification for Extraterritorial Jurisdiction under the European Convention' (2009) 20(4) European Journal of International Law 1228.

49 CCPR, *Lopez Burgos v Uruguay*, Communication No 52/1979, 29 July 1981, UN Doc CCPR/13/D/52/1979.

> to anyone *within the power or effective control* of that State Party, even if not situated within the territory of the State Party. As indicated in Comment 15 adopted at the twenty-seventh session (1986), the enjoyment of Covenant rights is *not limited to citizens of States Parties* but must also be available to all individuals, *regardless of nationality or statelessness, such as asylum seekers, refugees, migrant workers and other persons,* who may find themselves in the territory or subject to the jurisdiction of the State Party. This principle also applies to those with the *power* or *effective control* of the forces of a State Party *acting outside its territory.*[50]

Arguably, the focus of the Committee in demystifying the concept of jurisdiction seems to be on the State's relationship with the relevant impugned act and the person affected by it, rather than its relationship with the territory where a relevant act takes place. Evidently, the HRC embraces a personal concept of jurisdiction which requires the State (or its agents) to exercise 'power or effective control' over a victim, in this way appealing to the universality of human rights. At this point, it shall be noted that even though the HRC decisions or the so-called 'Views of the Committee' are advisory in character (in contrast to the ECtHR, for example, which has a binding authority) they do carry a normative and institutional legitimacy that carries with it a justifiable expectation of compliance.[51] In fact, in the area of extraterritorial jurisdiction, the HRC appears to be more willing to broaden the scope of human rights treaties, whereas the ECtHR's approach is, at times, hopelessly narrow.[52] Such a stance, Marie-Bénédicte Dembour has argued, can be particularly seen in Strasbourg's migration-related cases,

50 *General Comment No 31* (n 13) (emphasis added).

51 The impact of the decisions and on treaty's interpretations by the Committee remains disputed. See also Malcolm D Evans, 'Adjudicating Human Rights' in James A Green and Christopher PM Waters (eds), *Adjudicating International Human Rights: Essays in Honour of Sandy Ghandhi* (Brill Nijhoff 2015) 214. Evans posits that the 'views' of the Committee are not judicial and compliance with its 'views' is quite poor. See, Thomas Buergenthal, 'The U.N. Human Rights Committee' (2001) 5 Max Planck Yearbook of United Nations Law 397; See also, Nikolaos Sitaropoulos, 'States are Bound to Consider the UN Human Rights Committee's Views in Good Faith' (Oxford Human Rights Hub, 11 March 2015) <https://ohrh.law.ox.ac.uk/states-are-bound-to-consider-the-un-human-rights-committees-views-in-good-faith/>; HRC, CCPR *General Comment No 33: Obligations of State Parties under the Optional Protocol to the International Covenant on Civil and Political Rights*, adopted 25 June 2019, CCPR/C/GC/33, para 11.

52 Lea Raible, 'Extraterritoriality between a Rock and Hard Place' (Question of International Law, Zoom-in, 30 June 2021) <http://www.qil-qdi.org/extraterritoriality-between-a-rock-and-hard-place/#_ftn1>. In particular the ECtHR is now seen to be returning back to upholding its infamous *Banković* insular stance in interpreting the scope of the ECHR, see in particular *Georgia v Russia (No 2)*, App no 38263/08 (ECtHR, 21 January 2021); see also, Marko Milanovic, 'Georgia v. Russia No. 2: The European Court's Resurrection of Bankovic in the Contexts of Chaos' (*EJIL:Talk!*, 25 January 2021) <www.ejiltalk.org/georgia-v-russia-no-2-the-european-courts-resurrection-of-bankovic-in-the-contexts-of-chaos/>.

as will be observed below, where the Court has conceived migrants as threatening 'others'.[53]

Turning back to the ECtHR's jurisprudence on extraterritoriality, the groundbreaking case which is still the precedent followed today in the Strasbourg Court is the famous *Al-Skeini and Others v the United Kingdom* ruling (decided ten years after *Banković*). The case of *Al-Skeini* concerned the killing of six Iraqi nationals by British soldiers in Al-Basrah at the time the UK was the occupying power in southern Iraq. In interpreting jurisdiction, the Court took the opportunity to affirm the personal type of jurisdiction. With regards to the latter, it stressed that:

> It is clear that, whenever the State through its *agents exercises control and authority* over an individual, and thus jurisdiction, the State is under an obligation under Article 1 to secure to that individual the rights and freedoms under Section 1 of the Convention that are relevant to the situation of that individual.[54]

In casu, the Court laid down three instances which will trigger a State's extraterritorial jurisdiction: 1) where the alleged violations arose from the acts or omissions of diplomatic or consular agents operating abroad in accordance with international law; 2) where a person was in *physical* power and control of a State, or on a ship controlled by the relevant State, or aircraft for example; and 3) where a State was carrying out public functions such as executive or jurisdictional functions on the territory of another State.

Following, the Court found jurisdiction over the killing of all six applicants by utilizing the personal concept of jurisdiction. Arguably the Court opened the doors towards a more expansive approach to the extraterritorial application of the Convention, essentially overturning some of the stringent *Banković* conclusions and providing a sounder footing to the notion of extraterritorial jurisdiction. In this respect, the Court rejected the *espace juridique* theory embraced in *Banković*, that is, the application of the ECHR to the borders of the Council of Europe, as legally flawed. Moreover, the Court affirmed that the Convention '*can* be "divided and tailored"' insofar as cases concerning control over individuals are concerned, in this way reversing the *Banković* holding of an 'all-or-nothing' approach. Although these are welcome advances, the Court nonetheless was not ready to abandon the 'exceptionalist' approach adopted in *Banković* nor affirm the spatial concept of jurisdiction. Indeed, the Court had the opportunity to decide the applicability

53 Marie-Bénédicte Dembour, *When Humans Become Migrants: Study of the European Court of Human Rights with an Inter-American Counterpoint* (OUP 2015) 504. For how the 'other' has been used see, for instance, thorough analysis by Judith Butler, Judith Butler, *Precarious Life: The Powers of Mourning and Violence* (Verso 2004).

54 *Al-Skeini* case (n 38) para 137 (emphasis added).

of Article 1 of the Convention by providing that the UK had effective control over Al-Basrah, therefore jurisdiction. Instead, the Court in its effort to clarify the threshold criterion of jurisdiction added that:

> The Court does not consider that jurisdiction in the above cases arose solely from the control exercised by the Contracting State over the buildings, aircraft or ship in which the individuals were held. What is decisive in such cases is the exercise of *physical power and control* over the person in question.[55]

Hence, the Court's reasoning embraced the personal concept of jurisdiction, leaving '*Bankovic*-type killings' off the table.[56] As a result, it was a missed opportunity to provide an answer in general terms as to when the Convention's rights will be triggered and offered only guidance on the specific incident. It is for this reason, then, that Judge Bonello – convincingly, I contend – maintains that the absence of a coherent and axiomatic regime of jurisdiction signifies the failure of judicial institutions to recognize the universal status of personhood which is the essence of human rights.[57]

3. Jurisdiction in the Maritime Space

Following the above discussion on extraterritoriality, human rights bodies – alongside specialized bodies and tribunals governing the law of the sea– have recognized that human rights extend and apply at sea in an analogous manner so long as jurisdiction of the State can be established. Accordingly, many scholars have provided detailed scholarship on the application of human rights treaties at sea,[58] pointing out that the law of the sea pursues the protection of human rights indirectly. Although saving lives in *mare liberum* comes with inevitable regulatory gaps, Collins argues that we should not treat this space as 'lawless' in the literal sense of the term, where people arguably are not afforded any protection.[59] Certainly, the freedom of the high seas is of paramount significance to the formation of international law of the sea, but

55 *Al-Skeini* case (n 38) para 136 (emphasis added).

56 Marko Milanovic, 'European Court Decides Al-Skeini and Al-Jeeda' (*EJIL:Talk!*, 7 July 2011) <https://www.ejiltalk.org/european-court-decides-al-skeini-and-al-jedda/>.

57 Concurring Opinion of Judge Bonello in *Al-Skeini* case (n 38) para 4.

58 See, *inter alia*, Sophie Cacciaguidi-Fahy, 'The Law of the Sea and Human Rights' (2007) 2(9) Panóptica, Vitória 1; Bernard Oxman, 'Human Rights and the United Nations Convention on the Law of the Sea' (1997) 36 Columbia Journal of Transnational Law 399; Tullio Treves, 'Human Rights and the Law of the Sea' (2010) 28(1) Berkeley Journal of International Law 1.

59 Richard Collins, '"Outlaw Oceans" and "Lawless Sea"? Revisiting the High Seas as a Regulatory Space Under (and After) UNCLOS 1982' in Kristina Siig, Birgit Feldtmann and Fanella MW Billing (eds), *The United Nations Convention on the Law of the Sea: A System of Regulation* (1st edn, Routledge 2023) 29.

this does not render this area as a space 'devoid of regulation'.[60] For this reason, it is important to be able to secure and maintain that human rights are respected and realized on the high seas, since many human rights violations can go unnoticed.

The case of *Xhavara* was the sole case heard by the ECtHR invoking a violation of the right to life under Article 2 of the ECHR in the context of extraterritorial migration policies, as the incident resulted in the drowning of 58 migrants.[61] The case concerned Albanian nationals who had attempted to enter Italy in an irregular manner aboard an Albanian vessel and who had been intercepted by an Italian military vessel approximately 35 nautical miles off the Italian coast.[62] The attempt of the Italian authorities to prevent the migrants from entering Italy resulted from the existing bilateral agreement between Italy and Albania. Importantly, the Court found that the incident was in fact caused by the Italian military vessel in the course of the agreement they had with Albania, and hence the victims had been within Italy's jurisdiction on the basis of the factual circumstances of the collision.[63] While the case was inadmissible because the applicants did not exhaust all domestic remedies, there are important insights to gain from the Court's reasoning in deciding to rule that there was jurisdiction. It seems that the Court implicitly confirmed that migration controls through the construction of bilateral agreements can give rise to the exercise of jurisdiction as they confer enforcement powers on a State. Accordingly, this will bring the persons concerned within the ambit of the ECHR. In turn, States will have a negative obligation to abstain from causing the voluntary death of a person and, also, a positive duty to take all necessary and precautionary measures to protect the life of a person under its jurisdiction and investigate the cause of deaths.

Following *Xhavara*, the case of *Medvedyev and others v France* arose out of the use of lethal force during an interception on the high seas by a French warship boarding another ship and placing the crew under arrest on the suspicion of drug trafficking. Oddly, the issue of a violation of the right to life was not raised in this case. Nonetheless, the Court reached the conclusion that jurisdiction had been established, as the persons were under the *full* and *exclusive control* of the French authorities, notwithstanding the fact that the incident happened on the high seas. Hence, the outcome of the case makes

60 Tanja E Aalberts and Thomas Gammeltoft-Hansen, 'Sovereignty at Sea: The Law and Politics of Saving Lives in Mare Liberum' (2014) 17 Journal of International Relations and Development 440.

61 For an analysis of this case see earlier, Chapter 3, 11; *Xhavara and Others v Italy and Albania*, App no 39473/98 (ECtHR, 11 January 2001).

62 Annick Pijnenburg, 'From Italian Pushbacks to Libyan Pullbacks: Is Hirsi 2.0 in the Making in Strasbourg?' (2018) 20(4) European Journal of Migration and Law 410.

63 Seline Trevisanut, 'Is There a Right to Be Rescued at Sea? A Constructive View' (Questions of International Law, Zoom-In, 23 June 2014) <http://www.qil-qdi.org/is-there-a-right-to-be-rescued-at-sea-a-constructive-view/>.

clear that the interdiction of vessels on the high seas will be subjected to human rights law insofar as a State exercises *full* and *exclusive* control over individuals.

Perhaps the most important ECtHR case to date in relation to extraterritorial human rights obligations in rescue operations in the maritime space is *Hirsi*, analyzed earlier in this book,[64] where the Court emphasized that 'the special nature of the maritime environment cannot justify an area outside the law where individuals are covered by no legal system capable of affording them enjoyment of the rights and guarantees protected by the Convention'.[65] To briefly recap, the case concerned the contested push-back action of the migrants' boat on the high seas by the Italian authorities. In its reasoning, the Court confirmed that a State exercises jurisdiction when intercepting vessels on the high seas, as migrants are 'under the continuous and exclusive *de jure* and *de facto* control' of the State.[66] Accordingly, the Court clarified the extraterritorial reach of human rights obligations under the Convention, confirming that jurisdiction extends across borders and applies on the high seas where a State's *border control operations* threaten the rights of migrants.[67] In particular, the applicants have been under the *physical* control of the coast guard who intercepted their migrant vessel and returned them to Libya by transferring them to a state-owned vessel.

The events of the *Hirsi* case can be distinguished from the current practices in the Mediterranean because, following the *Hirsi* decision, European States have opted for alternative avenues to circumvent their human rights and law of the sea obligations. In this way, the requirement of direct physical control over individuals adds a limiting tenet to the notion of jurisdiction, as the instances where States exercise, to use Moreno-Lax's terminology, 'contactless control' over individuals have become the norm. For example, this leaves outside of the scope several factual scenarios where migrants place a distress call and a rescue mission is unduly delayed or, more generally, instances where there is no direct physical contact between the State authorities and the individuals in distress, yet the State still exerts a sufficient degree of effective control over the enjoyment of their rights in a contactless/remote manner. What then becomes paramount in deconstructing the notion of jurisdiction is the *knowledge* of a reasonably foreseeable outcome, whereas the location of the action

64 For the facts of the case see, Chapter 1, 8–9.

65 *Hirsi Jamaa and Others v Italy*, App no 27765/09 (ECtHR, 23 February 2012) para 178.

66 Ibid paras 74–75, 81; See also *Kebe and Others v Ukraine*, App no 12552/12 (ECtHR, 12 January 2017) para 74.

67 The Court quoted *inter alia* in its reasoning the Parliamentary Assembly of the Council of Europe, *The interception and rescue at sea of asylum seekers, refugees and irregular migrants* (2011) Resolution 1821, para 8 '[t]he high seas are not an area where States are exempt from their legal obligations, including those emerging from international human rights law and international refugee law'.

(or omission) is immaterial.[68] Consider one practice, now well documented, whereby a State, let us say Italy, acquires knowledge of a migrants' boat in distress by virtue of continuous data transmitted from aerial surveillance deployed in the Central Mediterranean and subsequently communicates this information to the Libyan Coast Guard and Navy (LCGN), who, following instructions from the Italian Maritime Rescue Coordination Centre (MRCC), pulls-back the concerned migrants' boat. Clearly, this scenario illuminates the practice of aerial *refoulement* embedded in the Union's strategy which results not only in the (indirect) push-backs of migrants to Libya but also impedes access to asylum and exposes migrants to abuse and threats to life, *all achieved remotely*. Consequently, it appears that the creation of a technological infrastructure of surveillance ultimately serves as an accountability avoidance tool that allows coastal States to exploit their interpretative discretion as to what information they perceive as 'distress' that will oblige them to ensure that assistance is provided to persons in distress. At this juncture, the ECtHR has made clear that direct physical contact is not *always* required as long as the control exercised is effective.[69] Arguably, the logic behind extending these obligations in such scenarios is that 'a state cannot be allowed to perpetrate, on the territory of another state, human rights violations that it could not perpetrate on its own territory'.[70]

Importantly, the Court, in concluding *Hirsi*, retained the basic *Banković* position that recognition of extraterritorial jurisdiction must remain *exceptional*. As such, the Court appears to be cautious about overexpanding the notion of jurisdiction and prefers to construe a limited understanding of extraterritorial jurisdiction. Judge Pinto de Albuquerque, in his powerful concurring opinion, made various important remarks with regards to the protection of human rights at sea, stressing *inter alia*:

> The Hirsi Jamaa case is about the international protection of refugees, on the one hand, and the compatibility of immigration and border-control policies with international law, on the other hand. The ultimate question in this case is how Europe should recognise that refugees have "the right to have rights", to quote Hannah Arendt.[71]

68 Violeta Moreno-Lax, 'The Architecture of Functional Jurisdiction: Unpacking Contactless Control – On Public Powers, *S.S. and Others v Italy*, and the "Operational Model"' (2020) 21(3) German Law Journal 406.

69 Yet, when considering the application of the personal model, the Court tends to treat the exercise of physical power as a decisive element to a finding of jurisdiction. See Moreno-Lax (n 68) 401; *Women on Waves and Others v Portugal*, App no 31276/05 (ECtHR, 3 February 2009).

70 James Hathaway and Thomas Gammeltoft-Hansen, '*Non- Refoulement* in a World of Cooperative Deterrence' (2015) 53 Columbia Journal of Transnational Law 235.

71 Judge Pinto de Albuquerque in *Hirsi* case (n 64), introductory paragraph at 62.

This part of the reasoning merits further comment, not only for contesting the condition of 'rightlessness' created by border control policies but for identifying the plight of migrants at sea for what it really is – in need of protection. It can be inferred from the above statement that Europe is arguably circumventing migrants' 'right to have rights' by reason of the place they are found, that is, the high seas.[72] The fact that governments have long attached to migrants the condition of rightlessness and, for this very reason, still shape their policies with dishonest humanitarianism, is a clear affront to human rights and dignity of the person. Hence, it is posited that what is required is to try to identify clear normative structures of jurisdiction in order to achieve effective realization of human rights and, in particular, for States to no longer eschew their obligations and responsibilities at sea. As Seyla Benhabib elucidates in her forceful account, the 'right to have rights' in Arendt's words, should be contemporarily understood to mean 'the recognition of the universal status of personhood of each and every human being independently of their national sovereignty'.[73] Hence, the burden shifts to judicial bodies to build an international regime of jurisdiction which 'decouple[s] the right to have rights from one's nationality status' by espousing a *pro-homine* approach to migrants in irregular situations.

In the context of cases arising in the maritime space, it could be argued that a human rights court may not have expert knowledge to rule on disputes that take place at sea and hence attract different jurisdictional rules. However, given the absence of a specialized refugee treaty body or a migration court or other supranational supervisory mechanism dealing with these matters as well as the apparent implausibility of mounting a legal challenge for a violation of the duty to render assistance at sea under the dispute settlement provisions of the United Nations Convention on the Law of the Sea (UNCLOS) (given the unlikelihood of an inter-State legal challenge), adjudication rests primarily on national avenues and then, international human rights bodies. Hence, the responsibility for administrating justice in situations where gross human rights violations can easily go unnoticed or unpunished at sea falls on human rights bodies. Considering this, the ECtHR as a court of last resort has an instrumental role to play in condemning extraterritorial practices that hinder human rights protection but also in guiding the EU and its Member States with regard to migration policies and, above all, ensuring that an 'a la carte' respect for human rights is no longer entertained.

4. A Case Study: *A.S. and Others v Italy, A.S. and Others v Malta*

The following discussion centers on the landmark findings of the HRC, which was briefly introduced at the beginning of this chapter. The outcome

72 See also Adel-Naim Reyhani, 'Absolute Rightlessness Sur Place Through Excessive Externalisation – The Case of Libya' (2019) European Yearbook on Human Rights 133–156.

73 Seyla Benhabib, *The Rights of Others* (CUP 2004) 68.

of the case against Italy represents a sea change in extraterritorial human rights scholarship. It was brought about after at least a decade of human rights activism, advocacy and scholarly debates trying to challenge the so-far contested notion of jurisdiction with regards to the State's obligations to protect human rights extraterritorially. Here it need only be noted that this is the only case that applied the right to life at sea and established an alternative meaning to State jurisdiction. Hence, there are important lessons to be learned from this decision with regards to the future of extraterritorial human rights jurisdiction given similar pending cases before the ECtHR.

Before proceeding, a caveat is in order. Most of the analysis will be based on the case against Italy, the reason being that the parallel case against Malta was deemed inadmissible because of non-exhaustion of domestic remedies. Nonetheless, the decision is still important to reflect upon as the Committee grasped the opportunity to rule on Malta's jurisdiction.

4.1 The Events, Legal Issues and Majority Reasoning

On 11 October 2013, a fishing vessel bound for Europe with more than 400 migrants aboard departed from Libya in order to reach a 'safer' haven. In the course of this voyage on the Central Mediterranean, the vessel was shot at by a passing boat causing large quantities of water to enter the vessel. Around 11:00 AM, the first distress call was placed to the Italian number for emergencies at sea, explaining the situation, highlighting that there were children aboard the vessel and forwarding the geographical coordinates to the operator.[74] The first call was followed by many others. Despite the passing hours, when another distress call was received, the Italian operator advised the migrants that their vessel was in the Maltese SAR zone and directed them to call the rescue coordination center (RCC) of Malta. The situation continued to escalate, with several distress calls now placed to the RCC Malta with the vessel finally receiving reassurance that it had been identified and that a rescue operation would be conducted within 45 minutes by the Armed Forces of Malta (AFM). Unfortunately, rescuers did not arrive until many more hours had passed – specifically at 5:50 PM – and after the vessel had capsized, leading to an estimated 200 deaths. It is important to stress that the Italian navy ship, which in the end had conducted the rescue, had been in the vicinity of the migrants' vessel the entire time (one hour sailing time away). Yet the Italian and Maltese authorities did not cooperate effectively in agreeing who should undertake the rescue, and as a result, help arrived seven hours after the first distress call to Italy's MRCC. The case arose out of a joint complaint lodged by three Syrians and a Palestinian national who survived the wreck of their vessel but lost their relatives in the shipwreck.

74 *A.S.* case (against Italy) (n 1) 5.2.

Obviously, the principal reason for the human tragedy was the inability of *both* States to reach an agreement and coordinate the rescue in a competent manner, which could have minimized the risk to the individuals' lives. The issue before the Committee was not whether the shipwreck occurred within the State party's territory, as it clearly did not, but rather whether the alleged violations of the right to life could be considered to have been within the power or effective control of the State, despite taking place outside its territory. Here it is imperative to note Italy's observations which reveal an apparent confusion as to when jurisdiction will arise according to the current power and control test. Accordingly, Italy claimed that the State responsible should be the RCC for that SAR area – which the Committee ruled it also was (joint responsibility) – and that its 'interventions' do not fall within the power and control meaning so as to establish jurisdiction. Surprisingly, Italy's argument implicitly accepts that should a distress incident arise within a State's SAR area and, accordingly, the RCC makes a formal undertaking of coordinating the rescue operation, this will *de facto* establish the 'intention' of the State to exercise jurisdiction over the rescue operation. The presence of a person in a State's SAR zone alone will not bring that person within the jurisdiction of the State, as these areas do not equate to jurisdictional zones.[75] Instead, and as Malta argued, these are regions where State parties must ensure cooperation and coordination of SAR activities.[76]

The Committee found that the existence of certain factual elements in this case established 'a special relationship of dependency' between the individuals in distress and Italy from the moment the MRCC answered the distress call and onwards.[77] Accordingly, this brought the individuals within the effective control of the State. In essence, this can be conceptualized as a functional understanding of jurisdiction, as the decisive elements forming this relationship were the *functions the State exercised* and *its capacity to directly affect the lives of individuals,*[78] consisting of the following normative considerations: 1) the initial conduct made by the persons in distress with the MRCC; 2) the close proximity of the Italian navy vessel to the distress incident; and 3) its ongoing involvement in the rescue coordination even after the RCC of Malta accepted responsibility to coordinate rescue. In this light, the functional approach adopted by the Committee can also be regarded as a *capability approach*.

75 Patricia Vella de Fremeaux (Mallia) and Felicity G Attard, 'Rescue at Sea and the Establishment of Jurisdiction: New Direction from the Human Rights Committee? Part I' (OpinioJuris, 3 March 2021) <http://opiniojuris.org/2021/03/03/rescue-at-sea-and-the-establishment-of-jurisdiction-new-direction-from-the-human-rights-committee-part-i/>.

76 SAR Convention, Annex Cap 2.1.1; See *A.S.* case (against Malta) (n 2) para 4.3.

77 See, also, Human Rights at Sea, 'The Right to Life: Italy Found by UN in Violation of the Right to Life of Migrants at Sea' (28 January 2021) <https://www.humanrightsatsea.org/2021/01/28/the-right-to-life-italy-found-by-un-in-violation-of-the-right-to-life-of-migrants-at-sea/>.

78 *A.S.* case (against Italy) (n 1) 7.5; See also Annex 6 Individual opinion of Vasilka Sancin (Concurring), para 3.

Importantly, the Committee also took into account the relevant legal obligations under the law of the sea that Italy should have adhered to, 'including a duty to *respond in a reasonable manner to calls of distress* pursuant to the International Convention for Safety of Life at Sea (SOLAS) regulations and a duty to *appropriately cooperate with other States* undertaking rescue operations' pursuant to the International Convention on Maritime Search and Rescue (SAR Convention).[79]

Consequently, the Committee reasoned that 'the individuals on the vessel in distress were *directly affected* by the decisions taken by the Italian authorities in a manner that was reasonably foreseeable' notwithstanding the fact that they were concurrently subject to the jurisdiction of Malta, who had assumed formally primary responsibility to coordinate the rescue operation as the migrants' vessel was in its SAR zone.[80] Hence, the fact that there can be multiple duty-bearers does not preclude a finding of more than one State exercising concurrent jurisdiction (shared responsibility) over the same individuals and the same situation,[81] if their acts or omissions impact the lives of individuals in a direct and reasonably foreseeable manner. Accordingly, by treating both States as duty-bearers, the Committee confirms the argument posited in the preceding chapter, that is, for rights to be claimable (and in order to *exist* as rights) it is not necessary to identify the duty-bearer(s) *a priori* because each situation will be treated on the basis of the factual circumstances in which it arose. Ergo, the findings of the Committee confirm that a right to be rescued at sea could be drawn from the right to life without having to identify the duty-bearers beforehand. Instead, what is needed in order to realize this right are clear guidelines to appreciate the normative considerations that will trigger the jurisdictional link and, hence, extraterritorial human rights obligations.

Ultimately, the HRC found a violation of the right to life by Italy as it failed to carry out its positive obligations to protect the lives of persons in distress at sea from foreseeable threats by virtue of its negligent acts and omissions in the rescue operations, which had fatal consequences.[82] In reaching this decision, the Committee grasped the opportunity to adopt its views enshrined in its latest *General Comment No 36* on the right to life, where it interpreted jurisdiction in functional terms, discussing the ability of a State to affect the

79 SOLAS Reg. 33; SAR Convention Art 4.6 (emphasis added).

80 *A.S.* case (against Italy) (n 1) 8.5; *A.S.* case (against Malta) (n 2) 6.7.

81 This follows the ECtHR's jurisprudence in the context of asylum e.g. in the *M.S.S. v Belgium and Greece*, App no 30696/09 (ECtHR, 21 January 2011), where both respondent States were found internationally responsible for the treatment of the applicant, an asylum-seeker returned from Belgium to Greece.

82 See Marko Milanovic, 'Drowning Migrants, the Human Rights Committee, and Extraterritorial Human Rights Obligations' (*EJIL:Talk!*, 16 March 2021) <https://www.ejiltalk.org/drowning-migrants-the-human-rights-committee-and-extraterritorial-human-rights-obligations/>.

enjoyment of the right to life of a person outside its territory.[83] Particularly, it quoted paragraph 63, where it observed that a State has an obligation to protect and ensure the right to life for all persons over whom it exercises power or effective control and 'this includes persons *located outside any territory* effectively controlled by the State, whose right to life is nonetheless *impacted by its military or other activities* in a *direct* and *reasonably foreseeable manner*'.[84] In this provision, the HRC sought to use 'impact' as a ground for applying the Covenant when a State exercises power in extraterritorial settings. Accordingly, the 'impact model' that the Committee embraced shifts the focus to an assessment based on the requirements of causality and knowledge. Consequently, the Committee effectively broadened the concept of control, since it was not required to be over the person, but rather over the *enjoyment of* (the relevant) *human rights*. This facilitates attribution of certain types of rights violations where the physical element is not present.

Continuing, while the Committee reaffirmed that the right to life imposes positive obligations on States to protect life from all reasonably foreseeable threats, such due diligence requirement involves taking 'reasonable, positive measures that do not impose disproportionate burdens on State parties in response to reasonably foreseeable threats to life'.[85] The same rationale can be traced in the ECtHR's jurisprudence, providing that the right to life prescribes a duty to prevent a violation from occurring, encompassing a due diligence standard in international human rights law, in circumstances where it is foreseeable or known that life is exposed to danger.[86] This was reiterated by the ECtHR in its recent migration ruling, *Safi and Others v Greece* (also known, as the *Farmakonisi shipwreck*) explored in Chapter 3, by reasoning that States must do all that can be reasonably expected of them to provide people in distress with the level of protection required by the right to life under the Convention.[87] Stoyanova in this regard posits that the more foreseeable the risk to life, the more reasonable it is to anticipate the State to take measures to prevent the loss of life.[88] In this case, Italy failed to meet its due diligence obligations arising under the right to life and to minimize the risk

83 HRC, *CCPR General Comment No 36 (2018) on Article 6 of the International Covenant on Civil and Political Rights, on the Right to Life*, adopted 30 October 2018, CCPR/C/GC/36.

84 Ibid para 63 (emphasis added); See also Paolo Busco, 'Not All That Glitters Is Gold: The Human Rights Committee's Test for the Extraterritorial Application of the ICCPR in the Context of Search and Rescue Operations' (*OpinioJuris*, 2 March 2021) <https://opiniojuris.org/2021/03/02/not-all-that-glitters-is-gold-the-human-rights-committees-test-for-the-extraterritorial-application-of-the-iccpr-in-the-context-of-search-and-rescue-operations/>.

85 *A.S.* case (against Italy) (n 1) 8.3.

86 For example, see *Opuz v Turkey*, App no 33401/02 (ECtHR, 9 June 2009) para 144. For further discussion see Maria Monnheimer, *Due Diligence Obligations in International Human Rights Law* (CUP 2021).

87 *Safi and Others v Greece*, App no 5418/15 (ECtHR, 7 July 2022) para 166.

88 Vladislava Stoyanova, 'The Right to Life Under the EU Charter and Cooperation with Third States to Combat Human Smuggling' (2020) 21(3) German Law Journal 448.

from materializing while it was within its *capacity* and power to do so. Hence, it becomes a normative issue regarding the State's responsibility for an omission *vis-à-vis* failing to comply with positive obligations. As Milanovic puts it, 'the fundamental functional question on the merits – did Italy do everything it feasibly or practically could have done to save those in distress – is equally and easily answerable'.[89]

The due diligence standard of obligations *also* follows (in addition to human rights law) from the SAR regime; though it does not oblige coastal States to conduct a SAR operation *per se*, it nonetheless requires States to appropriately cooperate with other States and ensure the existence of adequate services. *In casu*, clearly, both States effectively exercised jurisdiction over the distressed individuals as it was within their power whether a breach of the right to life would be committed. As a result, the concurrent responsibility of Italy in the matter was held by 9 votes to 6; the dissenting opinions mainly concerned the fear of going too far in what might appear as an expansive outcome.

An interesting, worthwhile analogy can be made with the ECtHR's decision in *Banković*, though in that case, the majority's overwhelming concern of going too far prevailed, with the result of adopting a restrictive approach to jurisdiction affording no protection to victims of violations. Yet, the exegesis provided by Milanovic sheds light on the then majority decision and the now minority decision. The *Banković* case was decided in 2001, only a few months after the 9/11 attack. Hence, from that standpoint, the Court was concerned with opening the floodgates to cases alleging violations for all uses of force by European States abroad, a task it was institutionally unsuited for, and for which it lacked the necessary evidence and competence. However, *Banković* was a different scenario to the present context of external border and migration management, albeit also featuring competing policy considerations.

4.2 Dissenting Opinions

The decisive elements for the dissenting members of the Committee – Shany, Heyns and Pazartzis – in finding that Italy had no jurisdiction over the individuals in distress, were the fact that Malta assumed primary responsibility for the SAR operations in that zone, and that Italy had a 'mere supportive role'.[90] Notably, they have characterized the outcome as the majority's 'failure' to distinguish between situations in which a State has the *potential* to place under their effective control individuals who are outside its territory and situations involving the *actual* placement of individuals under effective control – arguing that only the latter will establish jurisdiction. It is posited that this part of the reasoning might be misplaced; having the *potential* to exercise effective control in a situation carries the same degree of power

89 Milanovic, 'Drowning Migrants' (n 82).

90 *A.S.* case (against Italy) (n 1) para 7 of the dissenting opinions.

as *actual* placement. The justification for supporting this conclusion finds its origins, to a considerable degree, at the height of Aristotle's thought in demystifying the relationship between *potentiality* and *actuality* of positive obligations.[91] The former translates into power (δύναμη), while the latter translates into activity (ενέργεια). On the one hand, potentiality is power to affect a certain outcome; on the other hand, actuality is the realm of events and facts. Ontologically then, the two are not to be equated but carry the same degree of power, that is, a State has the capacity (whether it acts on it or not) to impact the situation of imperilled migrants by its acts or omissions. At this nexus, Raible among other authors maintains that power to do something is potential, and if and when it is exercised, results in control.[92] Intriguingly, the above reasoning comes as a surprise from Shany's part, who has long advocated in favor of a functional approach and has previously highlighted elsewhere that the key aspect of jurisdiction is not about the actual act or omission, but 'about states having the *potential* (or *functional capacity*) to comply with or violate IHRL [international human rights law] obligations'.[93] A genuinely functional approach to jurisdiction must apply in all circumstances in which the duty of protection can feasibly be complied with. Consequently, the functional model embraced in this book focuses on the *power over the migrants' situation abroad* as the important factor, whether or not that power be physically manifest.[94]

Continuing, Zimmermann has warned in his individual opinion (dissenting) that the Committee's outcome will be perceived 'as providing for a general applicability of the Convention as far as persons are concerned that find themselves in distress at sea either *in the SAR zone of a State party* or *close to a ship flying the flag of a State party*'.[95] For Zimmermann, this is problematic as it can deflect compliance with the duty to render assistance because States will be disincentivized and 'even try to avoid coming close to boats in distress so as to avoid any impressions of a "special relationship of dependency" having been created'.[96] To an extent, one could sympathize with this legitimate concern. However, this is not satisfactory enough to provide grounds to outweigh judicial oversight over clear violations of the paramount right to life, especially when compared to the cost of preventing a human tragedy. After all,

91 Joe Sachs (trans.), *Aristotle's Metaphysics* (Santa Fe: Green Lion Press, 1999).

92 Raible (n 23) 102–105; See also Samatha Besson, 'The Extraterritoriality of the European Convention on Human Rights: Why Human Rights Depend on Jurisdiction and What Jurisdiction Amounts to' (2012) 25 LJIL 863; For an in-depth analysis on capacity, see also Alice Ollino, *Due Diligence Obligations in International Law* (CUP 2022) 134–136.

93 Shany (n 30) 66.

94 See also Jesper Lindholm, 'Remote Migration Control at Sea: Jurisdiction Relating to Joint or Proxy Interception in Foreign Waters or Foreign Search and Rescue Regions' in Siig, Feldtmann and Billing (n 59) 157.

95 *A.S.* case (against Italy) (n 1) para 4 of the dissenting opinions (emphasis added).

96 Ibid para 3.

a disincentivized practice and a shifting attitude of States within the context of contemporary migration controls have been witnessed for a long time now.

For these reasons, I posit that reaching the opposite outcome would have been absolute neglect from the Committee to uphold migrants' 'right to have rights', in a situation where it was clear that the Italian authorities could have minimized the risk to the persons' lives. Given the multiplication of practices and a consistent failure by European governments and the EU to adopt a humanitarian migration response in the Mediterranean, constantly alibi-hunting, the courts as salient guardians of human rights need to accentuate their efforts and condemn those violations like the Committee did in this case, and as the ECtHR did in *Hirsi*.[97]

5. The Emergence of a Right to Be Rescued at Sea

As mentioned at the beginning of this chapter, Tigroudja's individual opinion clearly presents a manifestation of the affirmation that the right to life in international human rights law encompasses a right to be rescued at sea. Overall, the Committee appears to have taken the first, yet foundational steps towards the recognition of this right in order to bolster State compliance with rescue obligations. In a similar vein, academic literature has interpreted the Committee's decision as an attempt to *effectively* crystallize this right and extend the application of extraterritorial jurisdiction.[98] In this connection, the Hohfeldian theory adds a solid basis to structure a right to be rescued at sea in international law by virtue of its normative correlative, which is logically and philosophically straightforward. Having established the plausibility of this right exhaustively in Chapter 4, the recognition of this right provides the functional logic necessary to reconceptualize jurisdiction.

In this context, the ECtHR has the authority to identify a right to be rescued at sea in its case law and use it as the basis to adjudicate disputes before it. Subsequently, progressive interpretation will allow for its realization and to shape its scope. Ergo, introducing this human right conveys a clear message: the right is *important*, it should be *seen*, and it should be *respected* and *protected* by those in power.[99] It would (positively) impact the most vulnerable people (stateless and displaced) who find themselves in distress at sea, in the absence of legal means to leave from their countries. For this right to be fully realized, the ECtHR will need to step up to current jurisdictional challenges and specify the requirements incumbent upon States in a straightforward manner.

97 Concurring Opinion of Judge Bonello in the *Al-Skeini* case (n 38) 15.

98 Silvia Dimitrova, 'Rethinking "Jurisdiction" in International Human Rights Law in Rescue Operations at Sea in the Light of AS and Others v Italy and AS and Others v Malta: A New Right to be Rescued at Sea?' (2023) 56 Israel Law Review 120–121.

99 Janneke Gerards, 'A Right of Access to Law – or Rather a Right of Legality and Legal Aid?' in Andreas von Arnauld, Kerstin von der Decken and Mart Susi (eds), *The Cambridge Handbook of New Human Rights: Recognition, Novelty and Rhetoric* (CUP 2020) 556.

The Committee's decision has the potential to completely reset the limits of human rights applicability beyond a State's borders and, in particular, on the high seas. Still, it is posited that it would have strengthened the Committee's conclusions if they had adopted a clearer and more coherent test for interpreting the notion of jurisdiction. While the majority's reasoning placed the doctrine of extraterritorial jurisdiction on a firmer footing than ever before, it seems to introduce even more ambiguity into an already confused field, especially with regards to the likely implications it can have on future cases. For example, the Committee's finding of a 'special relationship of dependency' seems to be limiting its functional perception down to 'special' circumstances. Certain troubling questions arise with regards to the positive obligations that will emanate in the case where jurisdiction is established: how will dependency be judged in cases where distress calls are ignored or where authorities receive information about a distress incident from another source (i.e., in the absence of a direct distress call by migrants)? Is dependency really a necessary element to extraterritorial human rights obligations? And finally, what is 'special' about the relationship in this instance?

In view of what has been discussed so far, the moment the Italian MRCC received the distress call, and therefore acquired *knowledge* of a distress situation, triggered its law of the sea obligations under Article 98 of UNCLOS and the subsequent SOLAS and SAR Conventions. For this reason, Italy had to require a shipmaster, whether a State's vessel or a commercial ship flying its flag, to proceed *with all possible speed* to the rescue of persons in distress if it was possible to do so. Whilst the necessary elements were present to activate the duty to render assistance at sea, it was then up to the RCC who first received the call to coordinate the rescue and hand it over to the responsible center according to the SAR zone in which the persons in distress were located; and if the latter was unable, the first center still had the obligation to ensure that they coordinated the rescue in order to uphold the safety of life at sea. Consequently, from that moment onwards, Italy had human rights jurisdiction as it was within its *capacity* to *impact* the concerned individuals' rights in a direct and reasonably foreseeable manner by its decisions.

It is also pivotal to comprehend that the law of the sea duty to rescue does not rest on *de jure* or *de facto* control of the State over the individual; hence, it is not necessary to establish jurisdiction under the law of the sea alone – unlike the duties that flow from the right to life. That is *why* reconciling the duties that emanate from human rights law with the law of the sea obligations has the *potential to maximize* protection of people in distress at sea. For this reason, this is a clear-cut case that created due diligence positive obligations on Italy to coordinate the rescue in a diligent manner and, if it had the means to do so, to carry out the rescue operation.

It is difficult to find anything 'special' in the case's circumstances or even a dependency link – it was within Italy's power to render assistance to the persons in distress, and Italy was therefore bound to observe its law of the sea duties, as any State would have been. Perhaps the reason behind the Committee's terminology, the use of the term 'special' in order to define the relationship, is to reinvigorate or to keep alive the 'exceptionalist' notion of extraterritorial jurisdiction developed in *Banković*. By referring to 'a special relationship of dependency', the Committee appears to limit its holding as to when extraterritorial human rights obligations will arise arguably in order to deflect criticism of overt judicial activism in its interpretation of jurisdiction. In this regard, Milanovic argues that 'it's not that migrants were dependent on Italy' because Italy made no explicit promise to save them that they had relied upon – thus, the notion of a special relationship of dependency is incoherent.[100] This is pivotal to be clarified amidst the notable shift in the actors handling distress calls that have been witnessed in the past years in the Mediterranean. As exemplified in Chapter 1, it has been increasingly noticed that migrants will most often place a distress call to activists like the WatchTheMed Alarm Phone instead of entrusting their emergency status to State authorities who have largely failed to effectively assist them and assess their situation at sea.

6. A Functional Approach to Human Rights Jurisdiction

The Committee's decision in the *A.S.* case indicates that the scope of human rights jurisdiction may extend to situations where a yet-to-be identified duty-bearing State exerts *effective (remote) control*, rather than merely *de facto* control over individuals, by virtue of its power to protect or violate human rights. On this note, Kristof Gombeer and Stefaan Smis have observed that the exercise of power over the migrants' situation abroad has not been consistently recognized as a trigger for human rights jurisdiction.[101] Despite such anticipated reluctance, I contend that effective control is, in the same way, capable of being exercised from a 'long-distance',[102] that is, remotely, and that jurisdiction in those circumstances is triggered from the moment a State becomes aware of a distress incident. That moment activates a State's capacity to secure human rights extraterritorially and, accordingly, will give rise to positive due diligence obligations under human rights law. Still, the Committee in this case based its findings on three factors as mentioned above (initial contact/launch of distress call, continuous involvement and the presence of a flag State vessel in close proximity). As much as the majority's approach is motivated by the best of intentions, the Committee members failed to dwell on whether *all* these elements need to be present in order to manifest jurisdiction and to give rise to *de jure* responsibilities outside of a State's SAR zone. Accordingly, several troubling scenarios remain unanswered from the Committee's finding

100 See also for further analysis and insights, Milanovic, 'Drowning Migrants' (n 82).

101 Kristof Gombeer and Stefaan Smis, 'The Establishment of ETOs in the Context of Externalized Migration Control' (2021) in Mark Gibney Gamze Erdem Türkelli, Markus Krajewski and Wouter Vandenhole (eds), *The Routledge Handbook on Extraterritorial Human Rights Obligations* (1st edn, Routledge, Routledge International Handbooks Series 2021) 175.

102 This terminology is employed by Trevisanut (n 63).

of jurisdiction, which can exacerbate the uncertainty surrounding a State's human rights obligations in the conduct of rescue operations.

One question that might arise is whether the launch of a distress call *alone* will suffice to trigger a coastal State's extraterritorial human rights obligations and hence reach the jurisdictional threshold. In line with the above understanding of jurisdiction, it is reasonable to conclude that the moment the State authority receives a distress call (or relevant information), a causal link is created between the notified State and the persons in distress, which should suffice to establish jurisdiction. Analogously, this view is maintained by Trevisanut who further posits that States could be perceived as exercising 'exclusive long distance *de facto* control' in SAR operations.[103] Of course, strictly speaking, the coastal State who receives the information of a distress incident within its SAR zone does not *have* to intervene and perform the SAR operation *per se*, but rather it has a due diligence obligation to exercise best efforts so that it activates the available SAR services in that geographical area and employs all adequate measures to provide rescue services.[104] Otherwise the SAR zone would lack its *raison d'être*. Accordingly, the *de facto* control gives *de jure* responsibilities in those cases where the distress boat is located within the SAR zone of the coastal State.

Distress calls are now increasingly placed to different actors who will then communicate this information to the relevant coastal State according to the SAR region where the distressed boat is located – as in the Pylos shipwreck of June 2023 or cases where the use of surveillance technology is capable of alerting the authorities of a potential distress situation, as in the *Cutro* shipwreck of February 2023. Despite this fact, it is imperative to address these scenarios as well as adopt a broad interpretation of the meaning of 'distress'. The SAR Convention sheds light in these burning issues by providing in Article 2.1.9 of the Annex that 'on *receiving information* that a person is in distress at sea in an area within which a Party provides for the overall co-ordination of search and rescue operations, the responsible authorities of that Party shall take urgent steps to provide the most appropriate assistance available' (emphasis added). This is also reflected in Regulation 33 Chapter V of the 1974 International Convention for the Safety of Life at Sea (SOLAS) with reference to shipmasters who are in a position to be able to provide assistance 'on receiving information *from any source*' (emphasis added). It needs to be stressed that the word 'signal' was originally included in the aforementioned provision and was later replaced by 'information' in the 2004 IMO amendments.

103 Trevisanut (n 63).

104 'State Responsibility: Second Report on State Responsibility, by Mr. James Crawford, Special Rapporteur' UN Doc. A/CN.4/498 (19 July 1999) para 67 <https://legal.un.org/ilc/documentation/english/a_cn4_498.pdf>.

In light of the foregoing, this amendment is important to comprehend as it arguably expands the scope of protection to cases where, for example, individuals might not have the means or are unable to make a distress call themselves to alert the authorities. In such cases, the authorities are alerted about an emergency situation by other means (and actors like WatchTheMed Alarm Phone) – for example, through satellite imagery and thermal signs. Hence, the existence of positive information about a vessel in danger signifies a reasonably certain distress incident, which should be the threshold of the application of the duty to render assistance at sea. For this reason, it is posited, that the lack of a direct distress call alone will not *relieve* coastal States of their international obligations on rescue at sea because 'if a state is [becomes] aware of a distress situation, it must act'.[105] After all, an RCC is a unit responsible for promoting the efficient organization of SAR activities within its SRR and must be capable of objectively assessing a situation and act based on relevant information. To support otherwise would undermine the very purpose of the duty to render assistance, which is to protect human life at sea, and the entire SAR system. Thus, both the duty to respond to distress calls and the duty to promptly handle such information through coordination needs to be operationalized, and this could be best achieved by incorporating them as concrete measures demanded by the positive obligation to secure the right to be rescued at sea.

It can be in turn posited that the right to be rescued at sea is activated at the same moment as the duty of the State to provide SAR services and positive obligations to protect human life at sea arise. Therefore, unduly delaying or negligently handling a SAR service, handing it knowingly to an incompetent authority to execute or not responding to information indicating a distress situation at sea will arguably amount to an exercise of jurisdiction as the State will be acting in the knowledge (exercising its discretion) that the life of persons is at risk. This is perhaps a radical submission to make compared to Papastavridis who supports idea that acknowledgment of a distress call is important to trigger a State's knowledge of an immediate risk to a person's life.[106] This view derives support from a land-rescue case, *Furdík v Slovakia*,[107] in which the Court took the opportunity to clarify that the obligations of States to protect the right to life under the ECHR extends to emergency services 'where it has been brought to the notice of the authorities' that life or health of an individual is at risk. Whilst there is certainly merit in this argument and

105 Lisa M Komp, 'The Duty to Assist Persons in Distress: An Alternative Source of Protection against the Return of Migrants and Asylum Seekers to the High Seas?' in Violeta Moreno-Lax and Efthymios Papastavridis (eds), *'Boat Refugees' and Migrants at Sea: A Comprehensive Approach: Integrating Maritime Security with Human Rights* (Vol. 7, International Refugee Law Series, Brill Nijhoff 2016) 244.

106 Efthymios Papastavridis, 'Is There a Right to Be Rescued at Sea? A Skeptical View' (QIL, Zoom-In, 23 June 2014) <https://www.qil-qdi.org/is-there-a-right-to-be-rescued-at-sea-a-skeptical-view/>.

107 *Furdík v Slovakia*, App no 42994/05 (ECtHR, 2 December 2008).

could, in fact, rebut the establishment of a jurisdictional link, a closer reading of the SAR Convention suggests there is no such 'acknowledgment' requirement. In the case of a coastal State, whose rescue coordination center receives the distress information and, therefore, becomes aware of the incident in its SAR zone, it must ensure that assistance is provided. For this reason, in reconceptualizing human rights jurisdiction in these types of cases, it is imperative for the Court to take into account the relevant law of the sea considerations. It is telling that a recent judgment of the Court concerning maritime border operations reiterated the obligations of States to respect the lives of migrants at sea, when it found Greece to be in violation of a Syrian's refugee right to life when its coast guard shot at a vessel carrying migrants.[108]

At a high level of generality, all the questions posed above can be disentangled by answering the following principal question: from which moment onwards will migrants in distress at sea be considered subject to a State's jurisdiction? It is submitted that the jurisdictional link will be activated whenever it falls within the notified-State's functional capacity (power) to impact through its decisions (acts and/or omissions, including [detrimental] instructions to a third party) the relevant rights of individuals.[109] In this way, what makes control over the rights of individuals at sea 'effective' is the State's 'capacity to determine the material course of events' and compliance with the duty of protection.[110] A causal link is created at that instance, such that a State's positive human rights obligations to exercise due diligence in coordinating rescue efforts is triggered, and at the same time, a right to be rescued at sea starts to be realized. In this way, the right to be rescued at sea operates *ex ante*, before rescue efforts are initiated, in order to stimulate conduct that will be in line with the SAR system and international human rights law. The justification of this interpretation is clear: it is only by requiring action at a stage when it can still have effect that the right to life is adequately safeguarded. Thereafter it is indubitable that both flag and coastal States are obliged to adhere by the principle of *non-refoulement* and ensure that those rescued are taken to a place that qualifies as safe.

108 *Alkhatib and Others v. Greece*, App no 3566/16 (ECtHR, 16 January 2024).

109 This position builds also from Shany's formulation of a functional jurisdiction see (n 30) 65, albeit without the element of 'significant' potential impact. In this vein, the climate change cases are a pivotal example of the attempt to reconceptualize a functional conception of jurisdiction based on the impact of state activities. For the most recent case, see the application submitted in 'The Portuguese Youth Case', (particularly, 6–12) before the ECtHR <https://youth4climatejustice.org/wp-content/uploads/2020/12/Application-form-annex.pdf>, the case was recently declared inadmissible by the Strasbourg Court, *Case of Duarte Agostinho and Others v Portugal and 32 Others*, App no 39371/20 (ECtHR, 9 April 2024).

110 Moreno-Lax (n 68) 385, 414.

7. Concluding Remarks

In this chapter, I have maintained that for human rights law to adhere to its universalist ethos, State jurisdiction ought to be expanded to circumstances where human life is in danger, even if that risk occurs outside a State's territory. Reconceptualizing jurisdiction as functional in the manner I have presented in this book has the potential to remedy the structural challenges of international law and help minimize the normative gap that State authorities constantly exploit. Notwithstanding my skepticism towards various aspects of the HRC's reasoning, the *A.S.* is a groundbreaking decision insofar as it operationalizes protection of human life at sea and sends a clear message: we need to rethink about the scope of human rights applicability *vis-à-vis* jurisdiction in an entirely different fashion. Achieving the latter can help not only to confront the humanitarian crisis in the Mediterranean Sea, but also ensure that the protection against egregious human rights violations is prioritized.

It is only hoped that international human rights bodies will follow in the Committee's footsteps and will eventually expand the notion of jurisdiction in analogous cases concerning migrants in distress by proclaiming a right to be rescued at sea, thereby expanding the mantle of the protection of life. The concluding remark of this chapter is that international courts as an auxiliary source of international law can operate as an 'escape window' to the systemic deadlocks of international law and as a source of legitimate, authoritative change against dissolution in its order. Much remains blurred, however, and hence, the following chapter summarizes the reasons for the importance of recognizing a right to be rescued at sea and reflects on the future trajectory of human rights jurisprudence in the context of maritime migration.

6 The Place Where We Stand

The previous chapters in this book have thoroughly documented the phenomenon of irregular migration by sea from the events pertaining in the Mediterranean in what has been perceived as a 'European migration/refugee crisis'. The issues arising from migration movements have been approached from a human rights angle, guided by the premise that rights inhere in all human beings *qua* being human. Yet, in practice, irregular migrants appear to be excluded from protection in a plethora of situations. The analysis has shown the poignant flaws of the legal system governing the protection of human life at sea, which are exacerbated by nationalistic sensitivities and sovereignty concerns. To this end, the European governments' minimal response to blatant violations of fundamental rights in the maritime context has raised theoretical uncertainties on the dogmatic applicability of human rights at sea, leading to an urgent need to reconcile the challenges that migrants encounter during sea crossings.

An overarching question guided the discussion of these issues: how can a human-rights-based approach buttress the protection of human life in the context of irregular migration by sea? To unravel the normative premises of protection, Chapter 1 scrutinized the rather unintended lethal effect of European migration policies, which have been adopted to tackle migration movements and, at the same time, to protect European borders. The purpose of this inquiry was to closely depict how the externalization and securitization of the EU's stronghold, in conjunction with Member States activities beyond their *terra firma*, have not only muddied the already grey waters of jurisdiction but also exacerbated the vulnerability of migrants.

Following, Chapter 2 unraveled the beleaguered international search and rescue (SAR) system along with the cornerstone duty to render assistance to persons in distress as provided in the international law of the sea framework. By exposing the difficulties in policing the high seas and having effective enforcement mechanisms in an area perceived free from State sovereignty, the 'maritime legal black holes' highlighted the precarious state that migrants find themselves in when attempting to cross the sea. This analysis further revealed that compliance with international obligations has become fraught. The thesis advanced in this analysis is that the duty to render assistance at sea is the

DOI: 10.4324/9781003568537-7

operational obligation deriving from the application of the right to life *at sea*. Against this premise, Chapter 3 examined the obligations emanating from the application of the right to life as found in international human rights law. In particular, this exploration has shown that courts and human rights bodies have increasingly rooted a due diligence standard in the positive obligations emanating from the right to life in situations where a State has actual or putative knowledge that life is at risk. In this way, the due diligence standard of positive obligations is frequently conceptualized as a critical risk-management tool, which the courts will often employ in order to adjust protection levels in the various factual circumstances that may arise within a case.

Before entering into the discussion of the scope of human rights treaties and extraterritorial human rights obligations, Chapter 4 sought to conceptualize in a novel way the right to life in a manner that sustains a right to be rescued at sea. The philosophical front for arguing this thesis was Hohfeld's analytical framework, which provides a solid, logical basis for recognizing correlative rights and obligations. Conversely, the argument posited was shaped on the likelihood of international judges employing the Hohfeldian theory to expand the scope of human rights obligations and recognize the existence of (a nonexistent) right within the existing right to life. By constructing a right grounded on the Hohfeldian doctrine of correlativity, the analysis provided a justification as to why it would not be 'controversial' for a court to legitimately expand the scope of protection afforded by the right to life and ensure that responsibility moves along with the exercise of powers with transnational effects. For this reason, in exploring the recognition of the right to be rescued at sea in international law, the book sought to provide a fresh jurisprudential reading to the duty to render assistance at sea in a manner that seeks to operationalize protection of human life beyond national borders.

The following view guided the spirit of this book: 'the prevention of human rights abuses is what the "idea" of human rights is, ultimately, all about'.[1] Notwithstanding the current unsettling reality that human rights violations, pertinently in the context of migration at sea, are so far without any legal consequence, should not stop our efforts to promote and protect human rights for all individuals. In advocating for the recognition of a right to be rescued at sea, which arguably exists independently of interpretation or any subsequent institutionalization, the analysis has revealed that the right has slowly started to gain soft-law status. It was for the first time articulated by the Human Rights Committee's (HRC or the Committee) decision in the *A.S* case as a matter of addressing the jurisdictional controversies on the high seas that have undermined human rights protection.

1 Malcolm D Evans, 'Adjudicating Human Rights' in James A Green and Christopher PM Waters (eds), *Adjudicating International Human Rights: Essays in Honour of Sandy Ghandhi* (Brill Nijhoff 2015) 212.

What ensues from the preceding chapter is what I believe to be a more convincing theory of jurisdiction that has the potential to remedy the current systemic deficiencies of the SAR system. I have advocated that the adoption of a functional concept of jurisdiction, which is in line with a teleological interpretation, becomes pertinent in light of the changing patterns of migration controls, borders and the consolidating geopolitics of mobility. The aim of this analysis was to demystify the moment that the normative relationship between a (potential) right-bearer, persons in distress at sea, and a duty-bearer(s), State(s), will be triggered for extraterritorial human rights obligations to arise *prior* to any potential violations. Hence, the question was framed functionally as being one of jurisdiction as State power (and its exercise) over an individual's (or a group of individuals') rights. It was maintained that the exercise of power results in control, linking power to human rights obligations. Nonetheless, compliance with human rights obligations should not be seen as a burden to the State and, therefore, the due diligence standard of positive obligations mitigates any potential inflexibilities in this argument, as the obligations imposed on State governments are of *conduct* and not of result.

Against this backdrop, States have a margin of appreciation as to what measures to take to fulfil their primary positive obligations and execute the European Court of Human Rights' (ECtHR or the Strasbourg Court or the Court) judgments, as the Court will not explicitly identify those measures in its finding of a breach of the Convention right(s). This is problematic, because for the right to be rescued at sea to be properly articulated, the Court will be required to set out and concretize the measures required to be taken by the States so that 1) the reasoning can be performed; and 2) the conclusion can be justified that, due to an omission, a right has been violated.[2] Hohfeld's correlativity theory becomes pertinent again here, in supporting this conclusion, as rights are understood as conclusions that specifically regulate the conduct of the duty-bearer(s). Hence, if the ECtHR is truly motivated in changing the conduct of obligation-holders, it needs to incorporate certain considerations in the reasoning of its judgments, as these ultimately provide the justification for reaching a particular conclusion. By recognizing a right to be rescued at sea and identifying the primary obligations that will correspond to this right, the Court will not only help guide future State conduct beyond territory and enhance compliance with its judgments, but also operationalize protection of human life at sea.

2 Vladislava Stoyanova, 'Correlativity Between Human Rights and Positive Obligations and Its Role for the Execution of Judgments Delivered by the European Court of Human Rights' (2024) 5(4) European Convention on Human Rights Law Review 32.

1. The Need to Recognize a Right to Be Rescued at Sea

As demonstrated by the analysis conducted thus far, I have consistently argued that a right to be rescued at sea exists by virtue of its correlative duty, the duty to render assistance at sea, and that it is viable to be recognized in human rights law. This book has endeavored to answer potential denunciations of the usefulness of recognizing a *new* right, when the right to life already exists and has been recognized as of paramount significance. Why, then, recognize such a right explicitly, if extending the right to life extraterritorially will technically capture those rescue scenarios? And finally, what will it *add* to the human rights field that is not already there?

The answer to this is far simpler than the questions it evokes. To put it simply, proclaiming the existence of a right to be rescued at sea will operationalize rescue as an international legal concept. Its recognition will be of *symbolic and normative value*; it will mean that its significance is at the forefront and it will promote the rule of law by strengthening State accountability in complying with international obligations in the context of maritime operations. Accordingly, most 'new' human rights are indeed refinements of existing rights, which somehow have come to be regarded as deserving protection in their own right.[3]

From a legal perspective, this new human right is already protected if it is an extension of an existing human right.[4] As such, recognition of such an aspect would have legal value if it does not simply highlight the new right, but there is an *actual process* of specification and definition that helps give the right *a new legal shape* or *fill important gaps* in the protection of human rights.[5] It will try to remedy international law's systemic deficiencies beyond the sovereign State, and it will aim to fill the gap in migrant protection that neither the Refugee Convention nor human rights law could have foreseen.[6]

Its realization will come from shaping the normative contours of the existence of extraterritorial jurisdiction in the human rights context and will do so by imposing obligations that strengthen compliance so that States no longer barter off their responsibilities. As Collins argues the high seas are undoubtedly 'not lawless in any literal sense of the term. These waters are, however,

3 Janneke Gerards, 'A Right of Access to Law – or Rather a Right of Legality and Legal Aid?' in Andreas von Arnauld, Kerstin von der Decken and Mart Susi (eds), *The Cambridge Handbook of New Human Rights: Recognition, Novelty and Rhetoric* (CUP 2020) 555.

4 Ibid 556.

5 Ibid.

6 For instance, Venzke argues that the work of the UNHCR serves as an example of how an international institution has tackled the changing needs and circumstances of refugees amidst no forthcoming amendments to the Refugee Convention or a new treaty law to tackle emerging issues. See Ingo Venzke, *How Interpretation Makes International Law: On Semantic Change and Normative Twists* (OUP 2012) 8.

notoriously difficult to police'.[7] As such, its invocation, its recognition and its proclamation will demand that its content be fleshed out, clarified and adapted to the specific circumstances of *mare liberum*. Accordingly, formal recognition of a right to be rescued at sea would seem to provide a highly useful addition to the existing body of human rights. Of course, such change will not happen overnight, nor will it become automatically realizable, but it will transpire gradually as with the crafting of all new rights. It is telling that a recent judgment of the Strasbourg Court in this domain reiterated the obligations of States to respect the lives of migrants at sea in the context of maritime operations, when it found Greece to be in violation of a Syrian's refugee right to life when its coast guard shot at a vessel carrying migrants.[8]

It must be remembered that human rights came along when humanity was dying. Likewise, a right to be rescued at sea needs to 'be born' because humanity at sea is dying. By recognizing the individual's right to be rescued at sea, the courts determined that individuals under certain grounds qualify for such protection, and if the right is not observed, it would provide individuals with a procedural right to an effective remedy to challenge the situation before a national authority. Hence, persons at sea need to acquire the chance to gain standing in order to secure action against human rights violations at the international level.

While this book did not significantly touch upon *non-refoulement* issues that arise from (direct and indirect) push-back practices during SAR activities as witnessed in Chapters 1 and 2,[9] my analysis supports the idea that the recognition of a right to be rescued at sea can also serve as a bulwark against *refoulement* practices. This is so because the obligations stemming from the United Nations Convention on the Law of the Sea (UNCLOS) to provide SAR service and to deliver rescued persons to a 'place of safety' should be exercised in line with obligations from international refugee law, that is, protection against maltreatment, including return to a country where their life would be at stake.[10] As such, the prohibition of *refoulement* under international refugee law ties into the disembarkation of persons to a 'place of safety' in order for

7 Richard Collins, '"Outlaw Oceans" and "Lawless Sea"? Revisiting the High Seas as a Regulatory Space Under (and After) UNCLOS 1982' in Kristina Siig, Birgit Feldtmann and Fanella MW Billing (eds), *The United Nations Convention on the Law of the Sea: A System of Regulation* (1st edn, Routledge 2023) 43.

8 *Alkhatib and Others v. Greece*, App no 3566/16 (ECtHR, 16 January 2024).

9 As there is a significant body of literature on *non-refoulement* and irregular migration in the Mediterranean, for example, see, James Hathaway and Thomas Gammeltoft-Hansen, 'Non-Refoulement in a World of Cooperative Deterrence' (2015) 53 Columbia Journal of Transnational Law 235.

10 United Nations Convention on the Law of the Sea (adopted 10 December 1982, entered into force 16 November 1994) 1833 UNTS 397 (UNCLOS); Kees Wouters and Maarten Den Heijer, 'The *Marine I* Case: A Comment' (2009) 22(1) International Journal of Refugee Law 6.

a rescue operation to be marked as completed.[11] The United Nations High Commissioner for Refugees (UNCHR) has frequently remarked that human rights and refugee law principles are a pivotal point of reference in the provision of maritime SAR.[12] Consequently, States should be required to consider the right to be rescued at sea when designing policies aimed at tackling migrant flows and, accordingly, incorporate into their border control policies an effort to minimize side effects (including foreseeable deaths of people and *refoulement* practices). By recognizing and upholding this right, international law imposes an obligation on States to adopt proactive measures – beyond merely responding to emergencies – that actively safeguard life at sea. In particular, this could include allocation of resources for proactive monitoring and the development of cooperative frameworks among States to ensure effective collaboration between (capable) emergency response units.

Following, this book has sought to highlight the myriad ways a State can exercise effective control over the rights of migrants at sea, including policy and operational arrangements, outsourcing border control as well as detrimental rescue instructions that have created a vacuum in human rights protection at sea. Having examined the latter through the events that unfolded in the *A.S.* case in the preceding chapter, the remainder of this concluding chapter will explore the former through the promising, pending *S.S. and Others v Italy* case (the *S.S.*)[13] before the ECtHR. In this regard, *S.S.* is in many ways similar to the incidents manifested in *A.S.* and *Hirsi* and depicts the changing pattern(s) of external border management analyzed thus far – from direct *refoulement* to 'contactless' interceptions. In considering this case, the ECtHR has a real opportunity to consolidate its jurisprudence on the extraterritorial application of human rights at sea and, in particular, when a State issues instructions to a third actor which have an extraterritorial effect. Moreover, it also offers the Court the chance to address this matter by espousing Hohfeld's scheme, thereby recognizing a right to be rescued at sea by virtue of its correlative duty to rescue. Ergo, the Court will be in a position to explore the content and scope of such a right by delineating the substantive protections that will flow from it, including extraterritorial human rights obligations to take strong preemptive and precautionary measures when formulating border control policies and cooperation agreements with third countries.

11 See also Martin Ratkovich, 'International Law and the Rescue of Refugees at Sea' (PhD thesis, Sweden: Stockholm University 2019) 260–265.

12 Wouters and Heijer (n 10) 7; See also UNHCR, *The Treatment of Persons Rescued at Sea: Conclusions and Recommendations from Recent Meetings and Expert Round Tables Convened by the Office of the United Nations High Commissioner for Refugees: Report of the Office of the United Nations High Commissioner for Refugees* (11 April 2008) A/AC.259/17, para 8 <www.unhcr.org/refworld/docid/49997aeb27.html>.

13 *S.S. and Others v Italy*, App no 21660/18 (Communicated, 26 June 2019).

2. *S.S. and Others v Italy*: A Real Chance to Serve Justice by the Strasbourg Court

Following on from the above, the discussion of this case was left on purpose for the concluding chapter as it presents an opportunity to reflect on how the arguments put forth in this book could prove helpful for future litigation efforts and have real and practical implications in the courtroom and in the outside world. This section sketches out the *S.S.* events by applying both the HRC's alternative reading of jurisdiction and the functional test of jurisdiction I have developed in the preceding chapter. For most, attempts to reconceptualize jurisdiction as functional have a common goal; to use Moreno-Lax's words, it is an attempt to 'reconcile[s] the universal ethos of human rights with the existence of national borders in an interdependent, globalized world'.[14]

2.1 Background and Legal Issues

In brief, the incident unfolded in 2017 and concerned an interception of a migrants' vessel carrying around 150 migrants on the high seas by the Libyan Coast Guard and Navy (LCGN); the migrants' vessel had begun to capsize soon after its embarkment from Tripoli.[15] Very much like in *A.S.*, the first distress call was received by the Italian Maritime Rescue Coordination Centre (MRCC), which thereafter communicated to all ships 'transiting in the area' to assist the vessel.[16] Various actors were in close proximity to the vessel (Operation *Sophia*, Operation *Mare Sicuro*, a French warship, and an Italian navy helicopter) at the time of the distress call, and an hour later, the NGO Sea Watch 3 (SW3) and the LCGN arrived at the scene.[17] The NGO assumed on-scene coordination as the LCGN initially objected to taking that role (and did not have the necessary equipment to carry out the rescue).

The applicants maintained that before the NGO had arrived at the scene, the LCGN authorities 'beat people with ropes who were in the water', threw objects at them and tried to keep the SW3 as far away as possible, suggesting that they had orders from the Italian MRCC to assist the vessel in distress.[18] Without going into extensive detail of the contested orders, it appears to be the case that a communication was made by the Italian authorities to the LCGN to take charge of the rescue, which the LCGN later accepted. In

14 Violeta Moreno-Lax, 'The Architecture of Functional Jurisdiction: Unpacking Contactless Control – On Public Powers, *S.S. and Others v Italy*, and the "Operational Model"' (2020) 21(3) *German Law Journal* 386.
15 Ibid 388.
16 Efthymios Papastavridis, 'European Convention of Human Rights and the Law of the Sea: The Strasbourg Court in Unchartered Waters?' in Malgosia Fitzmaurice and Panos Merkouris (eds), *The Interpretation and Application of the European Convention of Human Rights: Legal and Practical Implications* (Queen Mary Studies of International Law 2013) 417.
17 Moreno-Lax, 'The Architecture of Functional Jurisdiction' (n 14) 389.
18 Ibid.

the end, some of the individuals managed to get rescued by the SW3; some, including a child, drowned amidst the unraveling of this chaotic situation, and some were taken by the LCGN back to a camp in Libya where they were reportedly abused for a month.[19]

2.2 *Strategic Human Rights Litigation Against European Migration Policies: The Counsel's Arguments*

The case was brought before the ECtHR in 2018 by an application made by the Global Legal Action Network (GLAN) against Italy alleging violations of Article 2 (right to life), Article 3 (prohibition of torture and inhuman or degrading treatment) and Article 4 of Protocol 4 (prohibition of collective expulsions) of the European Convention on Human Rights (ECHR or the Convention).[20] As expounded in Chapter 1, the incidents are countless in which Italy assigns rescue to the LCGN to try to avoid any direct physical contact that would bring the persons in distress under its jurisdiction. Remarkably, the application claims:

> In light of the rescue obligation and of the Court's and other international human rights bodies' jurisprudence, the interveners submit that, under article 1 ECHR, States establish jurisdiction on the high seas when their agents exercise authority in a manner that has *proximate and foreseeable effects* on Convention rights. Such authority is particularly manifest when the authorities' power to issue the decisions and take action with extraterritorial effect is based on international legal obligations. Finally, a jurisdictional link is established whenever a State's authority, due to its *powers* under international law – and, on the high seas, under the international law of the sea – issues *instructions to a third actor with extraterritorial effect.*[21]

The approach adopted by the victims' counsels is undoubtedly functional and mirrors in many aspects the *A.S.* ruling. While the application does not abandon the use of 'effective control or authority', such control or authority is argued to be exercised *over the actors* involved in a SAR operation. This is a distinct reading, as the term 'actors' does not necessarily mean '*individuals*' (hence personal type of jurisdiction). Instead, it differs from the conventional

19 Ibid 390.
20 Convention for the Protection of Human Rights and Fundamental Freedoms (adopted 4 November 1950, entered into force 3 September 1953) 213 UNTS 222.
21 See, Written Submission on behalf of the AIRE CENTRE (Advise on Individual Rights in Europe), The Dutch Refugee Council (DCR), the European Council on Refugees and Exiles (ECRE) and the International Commission of Jurists (ICJ) *S.S. and Others v. Italy* (11 November 2019) 4 <https://www.icj.org/wp-content/uploads/2019/11/ECtHR-SS_v_Italy_final-JointTPI-ICJECREAIREDCR-English-2019.pdf>.

view and implies that control might be exercised over *all* possible parties involved in a rescue operation; the LCGN (different State agents), the SW3 (probably carrying the flag of a different State than the one who received first the call or from the coastal State in which the incident unfolded) and the individuals in distress.

Reflecting on the case, Papastavridis has expressed the view that the knowledge of the distress incident alongside control over the persons in the case are decisive for the ECtHR to establish its jurisdiction.[22] Accordingly as I have supported earlier in this chapter, the State(s) who receives knowledge of distress information at sea has power to exercise control, whether *de facto* or remote, as to how the situation will unfold. Importantly, by taking into account human rights law, law of the sea and refugee law, the counsels argued that Italy by way of exercising its jurisdiction – operating through the MRCC – has the obligation *not* to transfer coordination of the rescue to the authority of another State 'unless they are satisfied that the other State will ensure rescue, treatment and disembarkation in full respect of the obligation not to expose a person to a risk of serious violation of human rights'.[23] It is difficult to disagree with this assertion.

Marking a positive evolution in this arena, the European Parliament on 11 July 2023 has adopted a Resolution on the need for EU action on SAR in the Mediterranean, which emphasized *inter alia* that States should end the cooperation with Libyan coast guard and that Libya is not a safe place for the disembarkation of rescued persons at sea.[24] Consequently, although States are entitled to control their borders, they are also under a duty to appreciate when human lives and human rights will be exposed to danger and, accordingly, adopt preventive measures that, in a reasonable manner, aim to avoid risks from materializing. It is proposed that such an obligation should be refined as one flowing from the application of a right to be rescued at sea.

Survivors of such incidents might be even considered *virtual* victims of the violation of a right to life arising from the failure to properly coordinate a rescue operation and avoid preventable deaths. As discussed, the ECtHR has emphasized before that, in certain circumstances, a merely 'potential' or 'virtual' victim of a violation of the right to life may be enough to take action under the ECHR.[25] Respectively, if a rescue operation is knowingly handed to an authority incapable of carrying it out in a safe manner or will disembark people to a place that is considered unsafe, then arguably the State coordinating this operation will have failed in its positive obligation to prevent a violation of the right to life and the principle of *non-refoulement*.

22 Efthymios Papastavridis, 'The European Convention of Human Rights and Migration at Sea: Reading the "Jurisdictional Threshold" of the Convention under the Law of the Sea Paradigm' (2020) 21 German Law Journal 3.

23 Ibid 8.

24 Resolution 2023/2787 (RSP).

25 *Makaratzis v Greece*, App no 50385/99 (ECtHR, 20 December 2004) paras 43, 45.

As Moreno-Lax argues:

> When jurisdiction is understood in a functional sense, as an expression of public powers that may combine elements of legislative, executive, and/or judicial action, there is no longer a need for unjustified distinctions between territorial and extraterritorial, or between personal and spatial manifestations. Ultimately, what underpins the various jurisdictional models . . . is the sovereign-authority nexus established between the state and the individual in an exercise of 'public powers'.[26]

In this way, in extraterritorial settings, the jurisdictional threshold will be reached not only through the exercise of *de facto* control over persons in distress, but also through remote management techniques. Hence, what makes jurisdiction in this kind of scenario 'effective' under the functional understanding of jurisdiction is the State's *capacity* to affect a 'change in the real and/or legal position of those concerned with human rights-relevant implications'.[27] Thence, capacity to affect creates the potential for the State to act. From this perspective, State jurisdiction ought to be expanded and applied to circumstances where a State might have the *capacity* to directly affect the rights of migrants that are relevant in the circumstances. For this reason, it is maintained that an interaction with the vessel in question or the migrants in distress aboard – *de facto* control – should not be perceived as the primary normative consideration when assessing the effectiveness required for establishing extraterritorial jurisdiction. Analogously, a functional approach to jurisdiction has the potential to resolve jurisdictional challenges relating to situations of remote migration control at sea.

In this vein, the Committee's decision in the *A.S.* case is of pivotal significance to the events in *S.S.* as it gives the opportunity to the Strasbourg Court to develop a functional test of jurisdiction. If the ECtHR decides to follow a similar approach, this will mean that Italy is most likely to be found to have jurisdiction over the migrants in distress as, to use the Committee's words, 'a relationship of dependency' could be said to have arisen in the specific circumstances. In particular, the normative considerations triggering such jurisdiction would be the following (based on the Committee's reasoning in *A.S.*): 1) initial contact made by the vessel and Italy's MRCC; 2) ongoing involvement by Italy's MRCC 'facilitating the whole process' that led to the hand down of the rescue to LCGN, which accumulated the violations complained of – the authorities knew or ought to have known that the LCGN is incapable of carrying out a rescue operation given the alarming evidence of human rights violations manifested by its practices and incapacity to provide a safe place for disembarkation (not least the violence documented against migrants during

26 Moreno-Lax, 'The Architecture of Functional Jurisdiction' (n 14) 413.
27 Ibid 384, 414.

the rescue); and 3) the choice to hand over the operation to an incapable unit while better *alternatives* existed, including an NGO vessel that was in close proximity to carry out the rescue, without creating a further risk to migrants' lives (as well as operations *Sophia* and *Mare Sicuro* which could have safely completed the rescue).

Against this backdrop, an RCC that coordinates a SAR operation taking place outside its SAR zone 'should refrain from giving directions or advice which it knows or ought reasonably to know would have negative human rights implications for those requiring assistance'.[28] As such, the RCCs have a negative duty to refrain from directing shipmasters who are unsuitable to carry out a rescue. Adding to the above, rescue operations must end in a safe harbor or a 'place of safety', and Libya, as expounded in Chapter 1, is in no way considered a safe place to disembark shipwrecked persons rescued at sea.[29] While Libya now has its own SAR zone, numerous reports from NGOs and individuals strongly argue for a re-evaluation of the Libyan SAR zone classification until the LCGN demonstrates that it will conduct SAR operations in line with international obligations and without endangering migrants' lives.[30] As noted above, rescue operations must end in a safe harbor or a 'place of safety', and Libya is not considered a safe place to disembark shipwrecked persons rescued at sea. The Libyan declaration submitted in December 2017 is highly problematic and raises many legality issues since Libya is not a party

28 UNHCR, *General Legal Considerations: Search and Rescue Operations Involving Refugees and Migrants at Sea* (November 2017) para 20 <https://www.refworld.org/docid/5a2e9efd4.html>; Moreno-Lax, 'The Architecture of Functional Jurisdiction' (n 14) 407.

29 See Communication to the Office of the Prosecutor of the International Criminal Court Pursuant to the Article 15 of the Rome Statute: EU Migration Policies in the Central Mediterranean and Libya (2014–2019)' (Communication to the ICC) 163 <https://www.statewatch.org/media/documents/news/2019/jun/eu-icc-case-EU-Migration-Policies.pdf>; *Hirsi Jamaa and Others v Italy*, App no 27765/09 (ECtHR, 23 February 2012) (*Hirsi*); Also an abundant of reports by international bodies including UNHCR, IOM and the UN mission in Libya providing such evidence. See for instance, UN Support Mission in Libya, '"Detained and Dehumanised" Report on Human Rights Abuses against Migrants in Libya' (13 December 2016) <https://www.ohchr.org/Documents/Countries/LY/DetainedAndDehumanised_en.pdf>; Parliamentary Assembly of the Council of Europe, Resolution 2215 (2018) 'The Situation in Libya: Prospects and Role of the Council of Europe' <http://assembly.coe.int/nw/xml/XRef/Xref-XML2HTML-EN.asp?fileid=24738>; UNHCR, 'UNHCR Position on Returns to Libya' (Update II), September 2018 <https://www.refworld.org/docid/5b8d02314.html>; Council of Europe, 'Third Party Intervention by the Council of Europe Commissioner for Human Rights under Article 36, paragraph 3, of the ECtHR, App no 21660/18, *S.S. and others v. Italy*' (15 November 2019) CommDH (2019) 29 <https://rm.coe.int/third-party-intervention-before-the-european-court-of-human-rights-app/168098dd4d>.

30 This recommendation was put forth in Chapter 2. See also, Open Letter, 'Hundreds of NGOs and Individuals Call for Revocation of Libya's SAR Zone' (3 July 2020) <http://www.migreurop.org/article2997.html?lang=fr>.

to the UNCLOS.[31] Given that the Libyan SAR zone is still in place, it will be up to the ECtHR to condemn such rescue 'hand-overs' and develop its ruling from *Hirsi*. Moreover, the State's influence over the perpetrator was highlighted by the Court in the *Ilaşcu* case, where it concluded that Russia bore responsibility for the abuses committed by Moldovan separatists in Moldova. This conclusion was based on Russia's 'decisive influence' over the separatists.[32] However, the Court's reasoning in this instance was rather ambiguous as it did not clearly explain the significance of Russian influence – whether it serves as a basis for attribution of responsibility or triggers the obligation to protect.[33] Nonetheless it can be posited that Libya was (and still is) under the decisive influence of Italy as they have tried over the years to train the LCGN and revive its authority by providing material and financial support, allowing in this way the LCGN to exercise 'public powers' as a proxy for Italy.[34]

The circumstances that led to the unfolding of the case were not unintended or unforeseen, as Moreno-Lax argues, but were rather expected and resulted from a situation created by the States themselves: in this case, Italy's tight-knit cooperation with Libya reflected by the 2017 Memorandum of Understanding (MOU). Accordingly, border control policies are primarily an expression of State authority and all forms of this control should result in the exercise of the State's jurisdiction.[35] Amidst these underlying facts, Italy (and other States) should no longer, to use the Court's earlier words in *Hirsi*, 'evade its own responsibility by relying on its obligations arising out of bilateral agreements with Libya'.[36] It is hoped that the decision in *A.S.* and the recent developments in this area amidst the burgeoning avoidable shipwrecks could help build a positive finding in *S.S.* and make a critical contribution to narrow the gap in migrant protection in ***mare liberum***.

31 But Libya did accede to the SAR Convention on 28 April 2005 (entry into force for Libya on 28 May 2005), see IMO, SAR/Circ. 77 (17 May 2005) Ref. A1/W/2.03; See also Kristof Gombeer and Melanie Fink, 'Non-Governmental Organizations and Search and Rescue at Sea' (2018) 4 Maritime Safety and Security Law Journal 1.

32 *Ilaşcu and Others v Moldova and Russia*, App no 48787/99 (ECtHR, 8 July 2004) para 392.

33 For a thorough discussion on abuses committed by third parties see Monica Hakimi, 'State Bystander Responsibility' (2010) 21(2) EJIL 341–385.

34 See also discussion by Jesper Lindholm, 'Remote Migration Control at Sea: Jurisdiction Relating to Joint or Proxy Interception in Foreign Waters or Foreign Search and Rescue Regions' in Siig, Feldtmann and Billing (n 7) 159.

35 *M.A. and Others v Lithuania*, App no 59793/17 (ECtHR, 11 December 2018) Concurring Opinion of Judge Pinto de Albuquerque, para 5.

36 *Hirsi* (n 29) para 180; This has been repeated in the Court's most recent judgment in *M.A. and Z.R. v Cyprus*, App no 39090/20 (ECtHR, 8 October 2024) para 91: '. . . the Court reiterates that States, and Cyprus in the present case, cannot evade their own responsibility by relying on obligations arising out of bilateral agreements with other countries, in this case Lebanon'.

3. Implications of a Functional Understanding of Human Rights Jurisdiction

Following the above discussion, a functional concept of jurisdiction is capable of bridging the gap between territorial and extraterritorial concepts of jurisdiction that focused so far on control over persons or territory and places equal importance on control over strategic operations and policy measures performed or producing effects over the enjoyment of rights.[37] In this way, the normative relationship between the State and the individual(s) in distress *exists prior* to any potential ensuing violations. The Committee's decision in the *A.S. case* is a groundbreaking development; apart from underlining the relevance of this book, it provides a more coherent argument on reconciling the universalist ethos of international human rights with areas beyond national jurisdiction in a manner sensitive to real-world concerns. It is likely, of course, that if the ECtHR chooses to adopt the functional jurisdiction test developed by the HRC in the *A.S.* case, or an interpretation closer to my account and of the counsels of the *S.S.* case, it will face political backlash from the Council of Europe's States and to charges of illegitimate power grab on the part of international human rights institutions.[38] A worst-case scenario would be that Contracting States withdraw from the Convention. Nevertheless, it is posited that the Court still needs to condemn these contemporary manifestations of State power over transnational migration control policies.

It is also possible that espousing a functional model of jurisdiction might have a chilling effect on collaborative efforts to manage migration and on the willingness of States to cooperate more broadly at the international level. This is so because a conclusion that Italy, for example, had jurisdiction in this case will require the State to take into consideration the human rights implications of such action when planning (future) operations, and this will arguably overburden States.[39] Ergo, this could lead to less international collaboration between States. Nonetheless, Contracting States to the ECHR are precluded from 'enter[ing] into an agreement with another state which conflicts with [their] obligations under the Convention',[40] with the principle carrying great force in the case of non-derogable and absolute rights, especially those at stake in interceptions, pull-backs and abandonment at sea.

37 Moreno-Lax, 'The Architecture of Functional Jurisdiction' (n 14) 402.

38 Yuval Shany, 'Taking Universality Seriously: A Functional Approach to Extraterritoriality in International Human Rights Law' (2013) 7(1) Law & Ethics of Human Rights 51; On this see discussion by Suzanne Egan, 'Tackling the Rise of Child Labour in Europe: Homework for the European Court of Human Rights' (2015) 64 International and Comparative Law Quarterly 616–167, in particular see fn 119; See, Niko Krisch, 'The Open Architecture of European Human Rights Law' (2008) 71(2) The Modern Law Review 213.

39 Moreno-Lax, 'The Architecture of Functional Jurisdiction' (n 14) 414.

40 *Al-Saadoon and Mufdhi v the United Kingdom*, App no 61498/08 (ECtHR, 2 March 2010) para 138.

There exist, however, instances where judges at the ECtHR find themselves in a precarious state where they have to take political concerns seriously. That follows from Contracting States keen interest in maintaining influence over international decision-making where judges decide issues affecting their interests.[41] Or, there could also be judges at the Strasbourg Court that may have personal policy preferences that impact how they evaluate cases. Hence, the functional model of jurisdiction might not be as welcome to the ECtHR.[42] In fact, in trying to address political and policy failures in an increasingly challenging legal and political milieu, there may come a point of paralysis whereby the Strasbourg Court perceives an impasse, deeming the expectations placed upon it to be excessively burdensome for its role as a court. Acknowledging that condemning migration policies is a technically complex and legally and politically sensitive task to be left for the Court, this should still not stop our efforts – as researchers, advocators and human rights institutions – from doing so.

The Court could fill the gap in migrant protection by detaching the concept of jurisdiction from notions of nationality and citizenship and attaching it to personhood. As it has been maintained throughout this book, the realization of the right to be rescued at sea rests on a functional concept of jurisdiction, which arguably constitutes the most efficient means of guaranteeing that its parent right, the right to life, is genuinely safeguarded in both theory and practice. However, the Court might reject a functional understanding of extraterritorial human rights jurisdiction, given that it rejected the 'capacity' or 'impact' approach argued by the applicants in *Banković*.[43] It went on to say that the mere capacity to interfere with the enjoyment of a right will not suffice to entail jurisdiction over the right-holder.[44] Still, *Banković* was a different scenario to the present context of external border and migration management, albeit also featuring competing policy considerations.

At this juncture, the Court has recently reiterated this approach in its judgment in *H.F. and Others v France*[45] in the context of France's failure to repatriate children and their mothers detained in Syrian camps. In particular, in considering the issue of jurisdiction in relation to Article 3 of the Convention,

41 Hellen Keller, 'Editorial: How to Improve Independence and Impartiality of Judges of the European Court of Human Rights' (2023) 4 The European Convention on Human Rights Law Review 6; See also Samantha Besson, 'The Extraterritoriality of the European Convention on Human Rights: Why Human Rights Depend on Jurisdiction and What Jurisdiction Amounts to' (2012) 25 Leiden Journal of International Law 860.

42 Examining further though the impartiality and independence of international judges is beyond the scope of this book. For further discussion see, for example, Erik Voeten, 'The Impartiality of International Judges: Evidence from the European Court of Human Rights' (2008) 102(4) American Political Science Review 418.

43 *Banković v Belgium*, App no 52207/99 (ECtHR, 12 December 2001) 75.

44 Ibid 75; See also Shany (n 38).

45 *H.F. and Others v France*, App nos 24384/19 and 44234/20 (ECtHR, 14 September 2022).

the Court concluded that the mere fact of operational capacity of the State to repatriate does not constitute a 'special feature capable of triggering an extraterritorial jurisdictional link'.[46] Ostensibly, the Court's reasoning regarding jurisdiction is overtly narrow as it failed to encapsulate important factors relating to the rights of children to be protected in cross-border settings. Adding to this, the joint partly dissenting opinion of judges Yudkivska, Wojtyczek and Roosma expressly rejected the 'capacity-based model of jurisdiction' as they claim it 'undermines the entire concept' of jurisdiction.[47] They further added that the idea of France's *potential* to *place* the applicants' family members under their effective control is not accorded to any existing authority or control. It is thus apparent that the Court encounters difficulties in maneuvering through the intricate legal and political challenges that this case represents. Not only this, but the Court's reasoning significantly diverts from the Committee on the Rights of the Child (CRC) approach to jurisdiction which found in 2020 that France exercised jurisdiction over the children detained in the camps in Syria as it had competence *ratione personae* over them.[48] The CRC supported that since France, as the State of the children's nationality, *knew* about the situation and extreme vulnerability of the children, had therefore the *power* and *capability* to protect the rights of those children by repatriating them or providing other consular assistance; hence, France had jurisdiction over them. It needs to be noted that although this approach echoes a functional understanding of jurisdiction, it nonetheless does so by basing such finding on 'nationality' grounds. As a result, disparities in the interpretation of jurisdictional issues among human rights treaty bodies and courts give rise to questions about the coherence of international human rights law.

In conclusion, an observation is in order: the fact that important migration and asylum cases like the *Nivin* (examined in Chapter 2 and further below) and the *A.S.* are being brought before regional human rights courts and UN bodies is likely a strategic move by lawyers amidst fear that the case will be unsuccessful in the ECtHR, which is increasingly criticized for its 'non-friendly' approach to migrants' human rights.[49] In this light, Dembour acknowledges that the ECtHR's jurisprudence in the area of migration has proven to be less helpful when it comes to protecting the rights of migrants than one 'might

46 Sanna Mustasaari, 'The Issue of Extraterritorial Jurisdiction in the Repatriation of Children Detained in Syrian Camps: Shortcomings in the ECtHR Judgment in H.F. and Others v. France' (Strasbourg Observers, 1 November 2022) <https://strasbourgobservers.com/2022/11/01/the-issue-of-extraterritorial-jurisdiction-in-the-repatriation-of-children-detained-in-syrian-camps-shortcomings-in-the-ecthr-judgment-in-h-f-and-others-v-france%EF%BF%BC/>.

47 H.F. and Others v France (n 45) para 5 of the joint partly dissenting opinion of Judges Yudkivska, Wojtyczek and Roosma.

48 Committee on the Rights of the Child in *L.H. et al v France* (30 September 2020) and *F.B. et al v France* (CRC/C/86/D/R.77/2019) (4 February 2021).

49 Lea Raible, *Human Rights Unbound: A Theory of Extraterritoriality* (OUP 2020).

have hoped, given that protecting human rights is the raison d'etre of the Court'.[50] She wonders, 'will it always be like this? It does not have to be'.[51]

One can think of cases (albeit only a few) where the ECtHR adopted a *pro-homine approach* to migration cases, such as in *M.S.S. v Belgium*, in which the transfer of an asylum seeker from Belgium to Greece, in accordance with EU legislation, was found to violate multiple provisions of the ECHR,[52] similar to the *Hirsi* and *M.A. and Z.R.* cases in which Italy and Cyprus were condemned for their practices and cooperation agreements with third countries that exposed migrants to serious risks. Accordingly, European States need to take into account the foreseeable impact of border control on human rights and lives. Whilst recognizing the difficulties faced by vanguard States due to their geographic location at the gates of Europe, the ECtHR in *M.S.S.* made it clear that this cannot absolve States of responsibility for their serious shortcomings.[53] In the same spirit, the report by the Special Rapporteur of the Human Rights Council on Extrajudicial, Summary or Arbitrary Executions affirmed that, since the:

> European Union and its member States have put in place an extensive surveillance system focused on security and border patrol [and have] chosen to provide security in the Mediterranean, the States members of the European Union . . . are exercising sufficient functional control to be subject to the one obligation inextricably linked to ocean surveillance: an adequate and effective system of rescue. This includes the implementation of the principle of *non-refoulement*, including to unsafe third countries, the protection of refugees and migrants, including against preventable and foreseeable loss of lives and support to ships operated by non-governmental organizations.[54]

While the Strasbourg Court has been a source of hope for many, an increasingly polarized stance has been witnessed when it comes to issues on extraterritoriality that has utterly undermined the protection landscape and empowered States to scapegoat vulnerable people who need protection. This is particularly so as international human rights institutions have been facing increasing political pressure, especially regarding their 'active' involvement in migrant and refugee matters. As Gammeltoft-Hansen – rightly, I contend – argues, in the European context, we are witnessing the contours of a more cautious, or possibly even

50 Marie-Bénédicte Dembour, 'The Migrant Case Law of the European Court of Human Rights' in Başak Çali *et al.* (eds), *Migration and the European Convention on Human Rights* (Oxford: OUP 2021) 36.

51 Ibid.

52 *M.S.S. v Belgium and Greece*, App no 30696/09 (ECtHR 21 January 2011) para 251.

53 Dembour (n 50) 36.

54 UN Special Rapporteur on extrajudicial, arbitrary and summary executions, *Unlawful Deaths of Refugees and Migrants*, UN Doc. A/72/335, para 64.

regressive, approach to migrant and refugee rights.[55] Acknowledging the vast number of inadmissible cases before the Court and the rare findings that adopt a *pro-homine* reasoning that reach a fair equilibrium between the interests of migrants and those of the State, this book recognizes that the Court is now invited to decide a migrant case on the highest ethical grounds. It needs be stressed that a negative verdict might have far-reaching consequences, setting a dangerous precedent on the scope of State actions beyond their borders and undermining the protection for victims and vulnerable migrant populations, compromising established principles of international human rights law.

4. Some Final Considerations: Border Externalization and Human Rights Challenges

The belief that border externalization and surveillance technologies can assist in tackling migration movements is seemingly gaining momentum. Policy stratagem aimed at blocking migrant exits altogether is already evident amidst the increasing incorporation of technologies of control (like aerial surveillance drones) that allow States to manage their borders. Against this backdrop, technologies play an instrumental role in border management as evidenced in Chapters 1 and 2 as they afford significant power to State authorities to *remotely* control the passage and entry of irregular migrants.[56] Evidently, sea crossings are placed under substantial (if not total) surveillance *vis-à-vis* generating visual knowledge by their ability to detect and trace migration movements. It could legitimately be expected that increased situational awareness of sea migration routes would enhance SAR responses by providing early warnings of distress and sustained vigilance over the danger to life at sea.[57] However, the spiralling loss of life at sea along with the abuse of migrants' human rights when being unlawfully intercepted by and returned to unsafe countries has exposed the systematic obstruction of the humanitarian duty to render assistance to persons in distress. It has become clear that Europe treats the sea as a border to halt migration flows at

55 Thomas Gammeltoft-Hansen, 'Extraterritorial Human Rights Obligations in Regard to Refugees and Migrants' (2021) in Mark Gibney Gamze Erdem Türkelli, Markus Krajewski and Wouter Vandenhole (eds), *The Routledge Handbook on Extraterritorial Human Rights Obligations* (1st edn, Routledge, Routledge International Handbooks Series 2021) 163.

56 On exclusion see, Didier Bigo's 'banopticon' apparatus, for instance, Didier Bigo, 'Detention of Foreigners, States of Exception, and the Social Practices of Control of the Banopticon' in P Rajaram and C Grundy-Warr (eds), *Borderscapes Hidden Geographies and Politics at Territory's Edge* (1st edn, Univ of Minnesota Press 2007) 23; Terri Tomsky, 'Citizens of Nowhere: Cosmopolitanisation and Cultures of Securitisation in Dionne Brand's *Inventory*' (2019) 40(5) Journal of Intercultural Studies 564.

57 The vacuum of human rights protection has been specifically referred to in the jurisprudence of the ECtHR see for instance: *Cyprus v Turkey*, App no 25781/94 (ECtHR, 10 May 2001) para 78; *Banković* (n 43) para 80; *Al-Skeini and Others v the United Kingdom*, App no 55721/07 (ECtHR, 7 July 2011).

all costs by increasingly investing in and employing technologies of control and surveillance that have as the primary goal to tame migration in the Mediterranean.[58]

The notable operational shift of migration and border management to the digital realm reflects the strategic priorities of the Union and its Member States to drastically strengthen the control of external borders. Conversely, my contention is that the increasing (ab)use of AI technologies in the field of migration policies and border management lends further support to the argument for recognizing a right to be rescued at sea and of developing a functional model of jurisdiction as it can capture new modalities of State control that fall outside the physical power tenet. This raises a thought-provoking question: could aerial surveillance (or other forms of remote technology) and the chain of events unfolding because of such surveillance be enough to establish extraterritorial human rights jurisdiction?

The *Cutro* migrant shipwreck of 26 February 2023 as examined in Chapter 2 provides a paradigmatic example of the kind of policy control that portrays a functional understanding of jurisdiction as designed in this book.[59] In brief, while no distress call was placed from the migrants' boat to alert the Italian authorities of their need for assistance, the use of surveillance technology by Frontex alerted the relevant authorities of a strong likelihood of an emergency. It was also reported that the thermal signs indicated that not only was the boat overcrowded, but also that there 'might be people below the deck'.[60] The Italian Maritime Rescue Coordination Centre (MRCC) had access to the live-streaming sensors that were shared by Frontex by virtue of the boat being in its SAR region, but still did not classify the incident as an 'emergency', and thus did not launch a SAR operation.[61] Did the Italian authorities then put forth their best efforts in handling the *Cutro* incident, given the available information at hand that was generated by technologies?

In line with a functional reading of jurisdiction as supported herein, it can be argued that technologies currently being used and deployed at external borders could be conceptualized as ***knowledge generators*** that have the ability to activate the jurisdictional nexus because they afford States with significant capacity to affect the course of events by their decisions.

A final example reflecting these changes is the *Nivin* case that was exhibited in Chapter 2. To briefly recap, the incident led to the submission of an

58 Michel Foucault, *Discipline and Punish: The Birth of the Prison* (Vintage Books 1975) 318.

59 Chapter 2 analyses the incident in-depth, 21.

60 EU Observer, 'Crotone Shipwreck Triggers Police vs Coastguard Blame Game' (2 March 2023) <https://euobserver.com/migration/156776>.

61 For further discussion see Aphrodite Papachristodoulou, 'The Crotone Migrant Shipwreck: A Cat-and-Mouse Blame Game and the Role of Technologies at External Borders' (*EJIL:Talk!*, 12 April 2023) <https://www.ejiltalk.org/the-crotone-migrant-shipwreck-a-cat-and-mouse-blame-game-and-the-role-of-technologies-at-external-borders/>.

individual complaint, *SDG v Italy*, currently pending before the HRC.[62] In the unfolding of events, Italian authorities had acquired knowledge about the migrants' boat in distress by virtue of the data transmitted by a Spanish surveillance aircraft operating within the then Operation *Sophia*. This information was then communicated to the LCGN who boarded the vessel and allegedly injured a number of the rescued migrants and returned them all to detention centers. This practice illuminates the systematic pattern of EU aerial surveillance strategies that facilitate the push-back of migrants to Libya, impede access to protection and expose migrants to abuse and threats to life.[63] Clearly, technology has been very effective for EU leaders and played a key role in preventing migrants from reaching Europe and curtailing the right to seek asylum. Looking forward, migration policies and external border management, in particular, aerial surveillance conducted by Frontex, should be used in the proactive service of rescue, and unless requested for other emergencies, its aircrafts and drones should remain on-site when they detect boats to monitor the situation and document rescue or interception activities. In this way, the recognition of the right to be rescued at sea will advance the cause of the safety of life at sea and will promote the rule of law by strengthening State accountability in complying with international obligations when using technologies at external borders.

Given the increasing phenomena of abandonment at sea and contemporary push-back practices,[64] the Court needs to continue adjusting the parameters of human rights jurisdiction to ensure that the Convention remains a 'living instrument' that is 'interpreted in the light of present-day conditions'.[65] The urge to tie and address the unprecedented implications of technologies on the law and, in particular, on human rights is profound. Hence, this last section has sought to provide a research agenda for scholars, practitioners and judges alike to build upon.

5. Concluding Thoughts

Undeniably, human rights are more like a double-edged sword as violations need to first occur in order for change to come – and it is hoped that such change will follow amidst the pending cases that call for the denunciation of

62 'Communication to the United Nations Human Rights Committee In the Case of SDG against Italy (Anonymized Version) Submitted for Consideration under the Optional Protocol to the International Covenant on Civil and Political Rights to The United Nations Human Rights Committee' (GLAN 2019).

63 GLAN, 'Privatised Migrant Abuse by Italy and Libya' <https://www.glanlaw.org/nivincase>.

64 Nick Vaughan-Williams, *Europe's Border Crisis: Biopolitical Security and Beyond* (Oxford: OUP 2015) 60.

65 *Hirsi* (n 29) para 174; The 'living instrument' doctrine which upholds this interpretative task was first articulated in *Tyrer v the United Kingdom*, App no 5856/72 (ECtHR, 25 April 1978) para 31.

practices that hinder protection. Whilst acknowledging that the problem is primarily structural, as the normative structures of international law allow for such violations to occur, it is up to the courts, activists, adjudicators and us, the scholars, to rectify the pitfalls of the international legal system. As Mann elucidates, 'if these rights abuses are not usually prevented and implicitly accepted by powerful actors as normal', then we have a *de facto* situation of rightlessness.[66] One should not forget that the ECtHR's role is to protect the inalienable rights of *all* human beings. For migrants to be no longer marginalized, arbitrary practices such as this should not be left unchallenged.

In conclusion, this book was guided by optimism in the advances that the law can make in minimizing the gaps in migrant protection and developing the law in a manner compatible with current challenges posed by migration at sea. It has put an individual right to be rescued at sea on the legal map, mindful of evolving migration challenges and the need to be responsive to human rights crises. By doing so, it showed that irregular migration by sea necessitates normative change and activated an international dialogue on recognizing an 'extraterritorial' right that will challenge to the utmost the boundaries of rights beyond national borders. Recognizing the existence of this right will not solve all challenges that migrants face when asserting rights, but it will likely strengthen the SAR system in a way that operationalizes the protection and safety of life at sea. Surely mere formal recognition will not by any realistic means bring about an instant practical achievement in this area. In turn, this will provide the starting point from which a dynamic process of interpretation could unfold to make this right functional.

There is no single solution to the problem of irregular migration by sea. A combination of measures is needed, with a multiplicity of actors working together to step up to present realities. While international human rights law alone cannot, of course, guarantee that migrants are fully protected at sea, it nonetheless affords a means by which to challenge their perceived 'rightlessness' and a way to enhance their rights. I hope that this book's findings will eventually contribute towards better protection of human life at sea and will prove helpful for future litigation efforts and, ultimately, in courts' future jurisprudence.

Returning to the opening paragraph of this book, the mythical story of *Europa* reveals that Mediterranean migration movements are a fundamental component of the history and identity of Europe. However, Europe seeks to distance itself from its southern and eastern Mediterranean neighbors by treating the sea as a border to halt migration flows at all costs. In fact, such migrant intolerance reveals that today's Europe is no longer 'the cradle of human rights'.[67] What, then, can Europe's mythical counterpart teach us about

66 Itamar Mann, 'Maritime Legal Black Holes: Migration and Rightlessness in International Law' (2018) 29(2) The European Journal of International Law 364.
67 *Hirsi* (n 29) Concurring Opinion of Judge Pinto de Albuquerque.

how we perceive the continent's identity today? It teaches us that *we* should embrace migration and, at the same time, stop treating migrants as the 'others' by virtue of cultural nationality but rather as human beings. The cradle will be formulated if *we* stop seeing the act of migration as a threat and instead take the voices of migrant suffering seriously. The urge is profound; *we* should take human rights seriously, be held to account and become more understanding and receptive of the structural nature of migration, as well as of the precariousness and vulnerability experienced by the 120 million people who are forcefully displaced in the world today.

Bibliography

Books and Monographs

Albahari, M., *Crimes of Peace: Mediterranean Migrations at the World's Deadliest Border* (Philadelphia: University of Pennsylvania Press 2015).

Arendt, H., *The Origins of Totalitarianism* (Cleveland: The World Publishing Company 1951).

Attard, F.G., *The Duty of the Shipmaster to Render Assistance at Sea under International Law* (Queen Mary Studies in International Law, Brill Nijhoff 2020).

Balibar, É., *Politics and the Other Scene* (London: Verso 2002).

Barnes, R.A., and Barrett, J. (eds), *Law of the Sea: UNCLOS as a Living Treaty* (British Institute of International and Comparative Law 2016).

Becker, L.C., and Becker, C.B. (eds), *Encyclopedia of Ethics* (Routledge 2001).

Benhabib, S., *The Right of Others: Aliens, Residents, and Citizens* (CUP 2004).

Boyle A., and Chinkin, C., *The Making of International Law* (New York: OUP 2007).

Bulto, T.S., *The Extraterritorial Application of the Human Right to Water in Africa* (CUP 2003).

Butler, B., *Precarious Life: The Powers of Mourning and Violence* (Verso 2004).

Colombos, C.J., *The International Law of the Sea* (London: Longmans 1967).

Cuttitta, P., and Last, T. (eds), *Border Deaths: Causes, Dynamics and Consequences of Migration Related Mortality* (Amsterdam University Press 2020).

Delanty, G., *Inventing Europe* (London: Palgrave Macmillan 1995).

Dembour, M., *When Humans Become Migrants: Study of the European Court of Human Rights with an Inter-American Counterpoint* (OUP 2015).

Dembour, M., and Kelly, T. (eds), *Are Human Rights for Migrants? Critical Reflections on the Status of Irregular in Europe and the United States* (Routledge 2011).

Fink, M., *Frontex and Human Rights Responsibility in 'Multi-Actor Situations' under the ECHR and EU Public Liability Law* (Meijers Research Institute and Graduate School of the Leiden Law School 2017).

Foster, M., *International Refugee Law and Socio-Economic Rights: Refuge from Deprivation* (CUP 2007).

Foucault, M., *Discipline and Punish: The Birth of the Prison* (Vintage Books 1975).

Gammeltoft-Hansen, T., *Access to Asylum – International Refugee Law and the Globalisation of Migration Control* (CUP 2011).

Gibney, M., Türkelli, G.E., Krajewski, M., and Vandenhole, W. (eds), *The Routledge Handbook on Extraterritorial Human Rights Obligations* (1st edn, Routledge, Routledge International Handbooks Series 2021).

Goodwin-Gill, G., and McAdam, J., *The Refugee in International Law* (3rd edn, Oxford: OUP 2011).

Grear, A., and Gearty, C. (eds), *Choosing a Future: The Social and Legal Aspects of Climate Change* (Edward Elgar Publishing 2014).

Guilfoyle, D., *Shipping Interdiction and the Law of the Sea* (CUP 2009).
Halpin, A., *Rights and Law Analysis and Theory* (Hart Publishing 1997).
Hathaway, J., *The Law of Refugee Status* (Butterworths 1991).
Heijer, M.D., *Europe and Extraterritorial Asylum* (Hart Publishing 2012).
Kant, I., *The Metaphysical Principles of Virtue: Part II of the Metaphysics of Morals* (James Ellington trans., Indianapolis 1964).
Komp, L., *Border Deaths at Sea under the Right to Life in the European Convention on Human Rights* (Routledge: Taylor & Francis 2022).
Mann, I., *Humanity at Sea: Maritime Migration and the Foundations of International Law* (CUP 2016).
Monnheimer, M., *Due Diligence Obligations in International Human Rights Law* (CUP 2021).
Moreno-Lax, V., *Accessing Asylum in Europe: Extraterritorial Border Controls and Refugee Rights under EU Law* (Oxford Studies in European Union Law, OUP 2017).
Morsink, J., *The Universal Declaration of Human Rights: Origins, Drafting and Intent* (University of Pennsylvania Press 1999).
Nifosi-Sutton, I., *The Protection of Vulnerable Groups under International Human Rights Law* (Taylor & Francis 2017).
Nordquist, M.H. (ed), *The United Nations Convention on the Law of the Sea 1982: A Commentary, Vol VII* (The Hague: Martinus Nijhoff 2011).
Ollino, A., *Due Diligence Obligations in International Law* (CUP 2022).
O'Neill, O., *Towards Justice and Virtue* (CUP 1996).
Papanicolopulu, I., *International Law and the Protection of People at Sea* (Oxford: OUP 2018).
Peters, Anne, *Beyond Human Rights: The Legal Status of Individuals in International Law* (UK: CUP 2016).
Petrig, A., *Human Rights and Law Enforcement at Sea: Arrest, Detention and Transfer of Piracy Suspects* (Brill, Nijhoff 2014).
Provost, R., and Sheppard, C., *Dialogues on Human Rights and Legal Pluralism* (Springer 2013).
Raible, L., *Human Rights Unbound: A Theory of Extraterritoriality* (OUP 2020).
Ramcharan, B.G. (ed), *The Right to Life in International Law* (Martinus Nijhoff 1983).
Sachs, J. (trans.), *Aristotle's Metaphysics* (Santa Fe: Green Lion Press 1999).
Shin, Y.J., *A Transnational Human Rights Approach to Human Trafficking: Empowering the Powerless* (Brill 2017).
Sikkink, K., *Evidence for Hope: Making Human Rights Work in the 21st Century* (Princeton University Press 2017).
Silverburg, S., *International Law: Contemporary Issues and Future Developments* (Routledge 2018).
Skogly, S.I., *Beyond National Borders: States' Human Rights Obligations in International Cooperation* (1st edn, Intersentia 2006).
Stoyanova, V., *Positive Obligations under the European Convention on Human Rights: Within and Beyond Boundaries* (Oxford: OUP 2023).
Vattel, E., *The Law of Nations: Or, Principles of the Law of Nature, Applied to the Conduct and Affairs of Nations and Sovereigns, with Three Early Essays on the Origin and Nature of Natural Law and on Luxury* (Richard Whatmore and Béla Kapossy eds., Indianapolis: Liberty Fund 2008).
Vaughan-Williams, N., *Europe's Border Crisis: Biopolitical Security and Beyond* (Oxford: OUP 2015).
Venzke, I., *How Interpretation Makes International Law: On Semantic Change and Normative Twists* (OUP 2012).

Journal Articles, Research Papers, Doctoral Theses and Working Papers

Aalberts, T.E., and Gammeltoft-Hansen, T., 'Sovereignty at Sea: The Law and Politics of Saving Lives in Mare Liberum' (2014) 17 Journal of International Relations and Development.

Addo, M.K., 'Does Hohfeld Still Matter' (1997) 29 Bracton Law Journal.

Agnafors, M., 'On Disjunctive Rights' (2017) 55(2) The Southern Journal of Philosophy.

Ahmed, S., 'Home and Away: Narratives of Migration and Estrangement' (1999) 2(3) International Journal of Cultural Studies.

Altwicker, T., 'Transnationalizing Rights: International Human Rights Law in Cross-Border Contexts' (2018) 29(2) EJIL 582.

Amoore, L., Marmura, S., and Salter, M.B.B., 'Editorial: Smart Borders and Mobilities: Spaces, Zones, Enclosures' (2022) 5(2) Surveillance & Society.

Aoláin, F., 'The Evolving Jurisprudence of the European Convention Concerning the Right to Life' (2001) 19(1) Netherlands Quarterly Human Rights.

Bacon, L., 'To What Extent Can the Right to Asylum Be Limited by a State's Sovereign Right to Control Its Borders? A Comparative Assessment of the Lawfulness of European National Asylum Law and Procedure' (2016) 22 Auckland University Law Review.

Bailliet, C., 'The Tampa Case and Its Impact on Burden Sharing at Sea' (2003) 25(3) Human Rights Quarterly.

Barnes, R., 'Refugee Law at Sea' (2008) 53(1) International and Comparative Law Quarterly.

Basaran, I., 'The Evolution of the International Maritime Organization's Role in Shipping' (2016) 47(1) Journal of Maritime Law and Commerce.

Basaran, T., 'The Saved and the Drowned: Governing Indifference in the Name of Security' (2015) 46(3) Security Dialogue.

Beckman, R., and Sun, Z., 'The Relationship between UNCLOS and IMO Instruments' (2017) 2(2) Asia-Pacific Journal of Ocean Law and Policy.

Benhabib, S., 'Claiming Rights across Borders: International Human Rights and Democratic Sovereignty' (2009) 103(4) American Political Science Review.

Berbera, H.D., 'The Pro Personae Principle and Its Application by Mexican Courts' (2017) 4(1) Human Rights Review.

Besson, S., 'The Extraterritoriality of the European Convention on Human Rights: Why Human Rights Depend on Jurisdiction and What Jurisdiction Amounts to' (2012) 25 Leiden Journal of International Law.

Bevilacqua, G., 'The Right to Life at Sea Seventy Years after the Proclamation of the Universal Declaration of Human Rights' (2019) 76(3–4) Europa Ethnica.

Biasetti, P., 'Infinite Regress and Hohfeld: A Comment on Hillel Steiner's "Directed Duties and Inalienable Rights"'(2015) 126(1) Ethics.

Blutman, L., 'In the Trap of a Legal Metaphor: International Soft Law' (2010) 59(3) The International and Comparative Law Quarterly.

Bostock, C.M., 'Legal Obligations Owed to the Asylum Seekers on the MV Tampa' (2002) 14(2/3) International Journal of Refugee Law.

Brandstedt, E., and Bergman, A., 'Climate Rights: Feasible or Not?' (2013) 22(3) Environmental Politics.

Buergenthal, T., 'The U.N. Human Rights Committee' (2001) 5 Max Planck Yearbook of United Nations Law.

Bulto, T.S., 'The Emergence of the Human Right to Water in International Human Rights Law: Invention or Discovery?' (2011) 12 Melbourne Journal of International Law.

Cacciaguidi-Fahy, S., 'The Law of the Sea and Human Rights' (2007) 2(9) Panóptica, Vitória 1, 20.

Çali, B., and Koch, A., 'Foxes Guarding the Foxes? The Peer Review of Human Rights Judgments by the Committee of Ministers of the Council of Europe' (2014) 14(2) Human Rights Law Review.

Carrerra, S., 'The Strasbourg Court Judgement N.D. and N.T. v Spain. A Carte Blanche to Push Backs at EU External Borders?' (2020) Robert Schuman Centre for Advanced Studies, EUI Working Paper RSCAS 2020/21.

Cassarino, J., and Marin, L., 'The Pact on Migration and Asylum: Turning the European Territory into a Non-Territory?' (2022) 24 EJML.

'Considerations' (British Institute of International and Comparative Law, 24 November 2020).

Cook, W.W., 'Hohfeld's Contributions to the Science of Law' (1919) 28(8) YLJ.

Costello, C., 'Overcoming Refugee Containment and Crisis' (2020) 21(1) German Law Journal.

Cruft, R., 'Rights: Beyond Interest Theory and Will Theory?' (2003) 23(4) Law and Philosophy.

Cullison, A.D., 'A Review of Hohfeld's Fundamental Legal Concepts' (1967) 16(3) Marshall Law Review.

Cusumano, E., 'Migrant Rescue as Organized Hypocrisy: EU Maritime Missions Offshore Libya between Humanitarianism and Border Control' (2018) 54(1) Cooperation and Conflict.

Cusumano, E., and Pattison, J., 'The Non-Governmental Provision of Search and Rescue in the Mediterranean and the Abdication of State Responsibility' (2018) 31(1) Cambridge Review of International Affairs.

Dauvergne, C., 'Sovereignty, Migration and the Rule of Law in Global Times' (2004) 67(4) Modern Law Review.

Dimitrova, S., 'Rethinking "Jurisdiction" in International Human Rights Law in Rescue Operations at Sea in the Light of AS and Others v Italy and AS and Others v Malta: A New Right to be Rescued at Sea?' (2023) 56 Israel Law Review.

Ebert, F.C., and Sijniensky, R.I., 'Preventing Violations of the Right to Life in the European and the Inter-American Human Rights Systems: From the Osman Test to a Coherent Doctrine on Risk Prevention?' (2015) 15(2) Human Rights Law Review.

Egan, S., 'Tackling the Rise of Child Labour in Europe: Homework for the European Court of Human Rights' (2015) 64 International and Comparative Law Quarterly.

Egan, S., 'The Doctrinal Approach in International Human Rights Scholarship' (2017) UCD Working Papers in Law, Criminology & Socio-Legal Studies Research Paper No. 19/17, 12 <https://papers.ssrn.com/sol3/papers.cfm?abstract_id=3082194>.

Fiorito, L., and Vatiero, M., 'Beyond Legal Relations Wesley Newcomb Hohfeld's Influence on American Institutionalism' (2009) 45(1) Journal of Economic Issue.

Fischer-Lescano, A., Löhr, T., and Tohidipur, T., 'Border Controls at Sea: Requirements under International Human Rights and Refugee Law' (2009) 21 International Journal of Refugee Law.

FitzGerald, D.S., 'Remote Control of Migration: Theorising Territoriality, Shared Coercion and Deterrence' (2020) 46(1) Journal of Ethnic and Migration Studies.

Galani, S., 'Port Closures and Persons at Sea in International Law' (2021) 70(3) International and Comparative Law Quarterly.

Ghezelbash, D., Moreno-Lax, V., Klein, N., and Opeskin, B., 'Securitization of Search and Rescue at Sea: The Response to Boat Migration in the Mediterranean and Offshore Australia' (2018) 67(2) International and Comparative Law Quarterly.

Ghráinne, B., 'Left to Die at Sea: State Responsibility for the May 2015 Thai, Indonesian and Malaysian Pushback Operations' (2017) 10 Irish Yearbook of International Law.
Goddard, K.S., 'Rescuing Refugees and Migrants at Sea: Some Commercial Shipping Implications' (2015) 21(5) The Journal of International Maritime Law.
Gombeer, K., 'Human Rights Adrift? Enabling the Disembarkation of Migrants to a Place of Safety in the Mediterranean' (2017) 10 Irish Yearbook of International Law.
Gombeer, K., and Fink, M., 'Non-Governmental Organizations and Search and Rescue at Sea' (2018) 4 Maritime Safety and Security Law Journal.
Guild, E., 'The Borders of the European Union' (2004) 7 Tidsskriftet Politik.
Hakimi, M., 'State Bystander Responsibility' (2010) 21(2) EJIL 341–385.
Halpin, A., 'Choosing Axioms of Correlativity' (2019) 64(2) The American Journal of Jurisprudence.
Hathaway, J., and Gammeltoft-Hansen, T., 'Non-Refoulement in a World of Cooperative Deterrence' (2015) 53 Columbia Journal of Transnational Law 235.
Hayward, T., 'On Prepositional Duties' (2013) 123(2) Ethics.
Hohfeld, W.N., 'Some Fundamental Legal Conceptions as Applied in Judicial Reasoning' (1913) 23 Yale Law Journal.
Hohfeld, W.N., 'Fundamental Legal Conceptions as Applied in Judicial Reasoning' (1917) 26 YLJ.
Hudson, B., 'Migration in the Mediterranean: Exposing the Limits of Vulnerability at the European Court of Human Rights' (2018) 4 Maritime Safety and Security Law Journal.
Hurd, H.M., and Moore, M., 'The Hohfeldian Analysis of Rights' (2018) 63(2) American Journal of Jurisprudence.
Kannis, E., 'Pulling (Apart) the Triggers of Extraterritorial Jurisdiction' (2015) 40 The University of Western Australia Law Review.
Kapogianni, V., and Magugliani, N., 'When Aerial Surveillance Becomes the Sine Qua Non for Interceptions at Sea: Mapping the EU and Its Member States' Complicity in Border Violence' (2023) EYHR 475.
Keady-Tabbal, N., and Mann, I., 'Weaponizing Rescue: Law and the Materiality of Migration Management in the Aegean' (2022) 36 (1) LJIL 61–82.
Keller, H., 'Editorial: How to Improve Independence and Impartiality of Judges of the European Court of Human Rights' (2023) 4 The European Convention on Human Rights Law Review.
Klein, N., 'Geneva Declaration on Human Rights at Sea: An Endeavor to Connect Law of the Sea and International Human Rights Law' (2022) 53(2–3) Ocean Development & International Law.
Klepp, S., 'A Double Bind: Malta and the Rescue of Unwanted Migrants at Sea, a Legal Anthropological Perspective on the Humanitarian Law of the Sea' (2011) 23 International Journal of Refugee Law.
Könönen, J., 'Legal Geographies of Irregular Migration: An Outlook on Immigration Detention' (2020) 26(5) Population, Space and Place.
Kowalska, S., 'Pro Homine Principle: An Axiological Compass in Interpretation Norms in the Field of Human Rights' (2021) 16 The Age of Human Rights Journal.
Krisch, N., 'The Open Architecture of European Human Rights Law' (2008) 71(2) The Modern Law Review.
Lixinskim, Lucas, 'Treaty Interpretation by the Inter-American Court of Human Rights: Expansionism at the Service of the Unity of International Law' (2010) 21(3) European Journal of International Law 588.
Mann, I., 'Maritime Legal Black Holes: Migration and Rightlessness in International Law' (2018) 29(2) The European Journal of International Law.
Mann, I., 'The Right to Perform Rescue at Sea: Jurisprudence and Drowning' (2020) 21(3) German Law Journal.

Manners, I., 'Global Europa: Mythology of the European Union in World Politics' (2010) 48(1) Journal of Common Market Studies.

Markard, N., 'The Right to Leave by Sea: Legal Limits on EU Migration Control by Third Countries' (2016) 27 EJIL 591.

Markovich, R., 'Understanding Hohfeld and Formalizing Legal Rights: The Hohfeldian Conceptions and Their Conditional Consequences' (2019) 108 Studia Logica.

Mazzuoll, V.O., and Ribeiro, D., 'The Pro Homine Principle as an Enshrined Feature of International Human Rights Law' (2016) III The Indonesian Journal of International & Comparative Law.

McLachlan, C., 'The Principle of Systemic Integration and Article 31 (3)(c) of the Vienna Convention' (2005) 54(2) International and Comparative Law Quarterly.

Milanovic, M., 'From Compromise to Principle: Clarifying the Concept of State Jurisdiction in Human Rights Treaties' (2008) 8(3) Human Rights Law Review.

Miller, S., 'Revisiting Extraterritorial Jurisdiction: A Territorial Justification for Extraterritorial Jurisdiction under the European Convention' (2009) 20(4) European Journal of International Law.

Mills, A., 'Rethinking Jurisdiction in International Law' (2014) 84(1) British Yearbook of International Law.

Miltner, B., 'The Mediterranean Migration Crisis: A Clash of the Titans' Obligations?' (2015) 22(1) The Brown Journal of World Affairs.

Moreno-Lax, V., 'Seeking Asylum in the Mediterranean: Against a Fragmentary Reading of EU Member States' Obligations Accruing at Sea' (2011) 23(2) International Journal of Refugee Law.

Moreno-Lax, V., 'Hirsi Jamaa and Others v Italy or the Strasbourg Court versus Extraterritorial Migration Control?' (2012) 12(3) Human Rights Law Review.

Moreno-Lax, V., 'The EU Humanitarian Border and the Securitization of Human Rights: The "Rescue- Through-Interdiction/Rescue-Without-Protection" Paradigm' (2017) 56(1) Journal of Common Market Studies.

Moreno-Lax, V., 'The Architecture of Functional Jurisdiction: Unpacking Contactless Control – On Public Powers, S.S. and Others v Italy, and the "Operational Model"' (2020) 21(3) German Law Journal.

Moreno-Lax, V., Ghezelbash, D., and Klein, N., 'Between Life, Security and Rights: Framing the Interdiction of "Boat Migrants" in the Central Mediterranean and Australia' (2019) 32(4) LJIL.

Morss, J.R., 'The Legal Relations of Collectives: Belated Insights from Hohfeld' (2009) 22(2) LJIL.

Morss, J.R., 'Power and International Law: Hohfeld to the Rescue?' (2011) 3(2) The Western Australian Jurist.

Mullins, R., 'Moral Conflict and the Logic of Rights' (2018) 177(3) Philosophical Studies.

Neuman, G.L., 'The Extraterritorial Constitution after Boumediene v. Bush' (2009) 82 Southern California Law Review.

Nyquist, C., 'Teaching Wesley Hohfeld's Theory of Legal Relations' (2002) 52(1/2) Journal of Legal Education.

O'Brien, K.S., 'Refugees on the High Seas: International Refugee Law Solutions to a Law of the Sea Problem' (2001) 3(2) Goettingen Journal of International Law.

O'Neill, O., 'The Dark Side of Human Rights' (2005) 81(2) International Affairs.

Oxman, B., 'Human Rights and the United Nations Convention on the Law of the Sea' (1997) 36 Columbia Journal of Transnational Law.

Pallis, M., 'Obligations of States Towards Asylum Seekers at Sea: Interactions and Conflicts between Legal Regimes' (2002) 14 International Journal of Refugee Law.

Papachristodoulou, A., 'Migrants at Sea Amid the Coronavirus Pandemic: The Perfect Pretext for Endorsing Respect for Human Rights' (2021) European Yearbook of Human Rights 259.

Papachristodoulou, A., 'The Recognition of a Right to Be Rescued at Sea in International Law' (2022) 35 (2) Leiden Journal of International Law 1–20.

Papachristodoulou, A., 'The Exercise of State Power Over Migrants at Sea Through Technologies of Remote Control: Reconceptualizing Human Rights Jurisdiction' (2024) 73(4) International & Comparative Law Quarterly 931–961.

Papachristodoulou, A., 'MA and ZR v Cyprus "Pushing Back" on Pushbacks? Debunking Readmission Agreements and Upholding the Rights of Maritime Migrants' (2025) 1 EHRLR 97–105.

Papanicolopulu, I., 'The Law of the Sea Convention: No Place for Persons?' (2012) 27(4) International Journal of Marine and Coastal Law.

Papanicolopulu, I., 'The Duty to Rescue at Sea, in Peacetime and in War: A General Overview' (2016) 98(2) International Review of the Red Cross.

Papastavridis, E., 'The "Left-to-Die Boat" Incident of March 2011: Questions of International Responsibility Arising from the Failure to Save Refugees at Sea' (2013) Refugee Law Initiative Working Paper No. 10, 3 <http://sas-space.sas.ac.uk/4957/1/RLI_Working_Paper_No.10.pdf>.

Papastavridis, E., 'The European Convention of Human Rights and Migration at Sea: Reading the "Jurisdictional Threshold" of the Convention under the Law of the Sea Paradigm' (2020) 21 German Law Journal.

Pazartizs, F., and Merkouris, P., 'Preliminary Report on the Interpretative Practice of the Human Rights Committee and Other UN Human Rights Treaty Bodies' (2018) <https://papers.ssrn.com/sol3/papers.cfm?abstract_id=3797716>

Pijnenburg, A., 'From Italian Pushbacks to Libyan Pullbacks: Is Hirsi 2.0 in the Making in Strasbourg?' (2018) 20(4) European Journal of Migration and Law.

Pugh, M.C., 'Drowning Not Waving: Boat People and Humanitarianism at Sea' (2004) 17 Journal of Refugee Studies.

Ratkovich, M., 'International Law and the Rescue of Refugees at Sea' (PhD thesis, Sweden: Stockholm University 2019).

Raz, J., 'Legal Rights' (1984) 4(1) Oxford Journal of Legal Studies.

Renger, A., 'Tracing the Line of Europa: Migration, Genealogy, and the Power of Holy Origins in Ancient Greek Narrative Knowledge and Cultural Memory' (2014) 25(3) History and Anthropology.

Reyhani, A., 'Absolute Rightlessness Sur Place Through Excessive Externalisation – The Case of Libya' (2019) European Yearbook on Human Rights 133.

Rohloff, A., and Wright, S., 'Moral Panic and Social Theory: Beyond the Heuristic' (2020) 58(3) Current Sociology.

Ryngaert, C., 'EU Trade Agreements and Human Rights: From Extraterritorial to Territorial Obligations' (2018) 20 International Law Community Review.

Schlag, P., 'How to Do things with Hohfeld' (2015) 78(1&2) Law and Contemporary Problems 211.

Seeberg, P., 'EU Strategic Interests in Post-Qadhafi Libya: Perspectives for Cooperation' (2014) XXI(1) Middle East Policy.

Sen, A., 'Elements of a Theory of Human Rights' (2004) 32(4) Philosophy and Public Affairs.

Severance, A.A., 'The Duty to Render Assistance in the Satellite Age' (2006) 26(2) California Western International Law Journal.

Shany, Y., 'Taking Universality Seriously: A Functional Approach to Extraterritoriality in International Human Rights Law' (2013) 7(1) Law & Ethics of Human Rights.

Shany, Y., 'The Case of a New Right to a Human Decision under International Human Rights Law' (2023) SSRN Working Draft <http://doi.org/10.2139/ssrn.4592244>.
Shany, Y., 'Digital Rights and the Outer Limits of International Human Rights Law' (2023) 24 German Law Journal 467.
Spijkerboer, T., 'Moving Migrants, States, and Rights: Human Rights and Border Deaths' (2013) 7(2) Law and Ethics of Human Rights.
Spijkerboer, T., 'Wasted Lives: Borders and the Right to Life of People Crossing Them' (2017) 20 Nordic Journal of International Law.
Staden, A.,' The Democratic Legitimacy of Judicial Review Beyond the State: Normative Subsidiarity and Judicial Standards of Review' (2012) 10(4) International Journal of Constitutional Law.
Steinhilper, E., and Gruijters, R.J., 'A Contested Crisis: Policy Narratives and Empirical Evidence on Border Deaths in the Mediterranean' (2018) 52 Sociology.
Stemplowska, Z., 'On the Real World Duties Imposed on Us by Human Rights' (2009) 40(4) Journal of Social Philosophy.
Stoyanova, V., 'The Right to Life Under the EU Charter and Cooperation with Third States to Combat Human Smuggling' (2020) 21(3) German Law Journal.
Stoyanova, V., 'Correlativity Between Human Rights and Positive Obligations and Its Role for the Execution of Judgments Delivered by the European Court of Human Rights' (2024) 5(4) European Convention on Human Rights Law Review.
Sundra-Karean, V., 'In Defense of Soft Law and Public-Private Initiatives: A Means to an End? – The Malaysian Case' (2011)12(2) Theoretical Inquiries in Law.
Tasioulas, J., 'Saving Hunan Rights from Human Rights Law' (2019) 52 Vanderbilt Journal of Transnational Law.
Thompson, J.C., 'The Rights Network: 100 Years of the Hohfeldian Rights Analytic' (2018) 7(28) Laws.
Tigroudja, H., 'La Cour Interaméricaine des Droits de l' Homme au Service de l' "Humanisation du Droit International Public" – Propos Autour des Récents Arrêts et Avis' (2006) 52 AFDI.
Tomalty, J., 'The Force of the Claimability Objection to the Human Right to Subsistence' (2014) 44(1) Canadian Journal of Philosophy.
Tomsky, T., 'Citizens of Nowhere: Cosmopolitanisation and Cultures of Securitisation in Dionne Brand's Inventory' (2019) 40(5) Journal of Intercultural Studies.
Treves, T., 'Human Rights and the Law of the Sea' (2010) 28(1) Berkeley Journal of International Law.
Trevisanut, S., 'The Principle of Non-Refoulement at Sea and the Effectiveness of Asylum Protection' (2008) 12 Max Planck United Nation Yearbook.
Trevisanut, S., 'Search and Rescue Operations in the Mediterranean: Factor of Cooperation or Conflict?' (2010) 25 The International Journal of Marine and Coastal Law.
Tzevelekos, V.P., and Proukaki, E.K., 'Migrants at Sea: A Duty of Plural States to Protect (Extraterritorially)?' (2017) 86 Nordic Journal of International Law.
Vayena, E., and Tasioulas, J., 'The Dynamics of Big Data and Human Rights: The Case of Scientific Research' (2016) 374(2083) Philosophical Transactions of The Royal Society A Mathematical Physical and Engineering Sciences.
Velasco, A.C., 'The International Convention on Maritime Search and Rescue: Legal Mechanisms of Responsibility Sharing and Cooperation in the Context of Sea Migration?' (Symposium, 2015) 10 Irish Yearbook of International Law.
Voeten, E., 'The Impartiality of International Judges: Evidence from the European Court of Human Rights' (2008) 102(4) American Political Science Review.
Weiler, J.H.H., 'Van Gend en Loos: The Individual as Subject and Object and the Dilemma of European Legitimacy' (2014) 12(1) International Journal of Constitutional Law.

Wisks, E., 'The Meaning of "Life": Dignity and the Right to Life in International Human Rights Treaties' (2012) 12(2) Human Rights Law Review.

Wouters, K., and Heijer, M.D., 'The Marine I Case: A Comment' (2009) 22(1) International Journal of Refugee Law.

Chapters in Books

Barnes, R., 'The International Law of the Sea and Migration Control' in Mitsilegas, V., and Ryan, B. (eds), *Extraterritorial Immigration Control* (The Hague: Brill 2010).

Bigo, D., 'Detention of Foreigners, States of Exception, and the Social Practices of Control of the Banopticon' in Rajaram, P., and Grundy-Warr, C. (eds), *Borderscapes Hidden Geographies and Politics at Territory's Edge* (1st edn, University of Minnesota Press 2007).

Blanco-Bazan, A., 'The IMO: Working within the UNCLOS Framework and Global Ocean Governance' in Attard, D.J. (ed), *The IMLI Treatise on Ocean Global Governance Volume III: IMO and Global Ocean Governance* (OUP 2018).

Boot, E., 'Judging Rights by Their Duties: A Kantian Perspective on Human Rights' in Krasnoff, L., Madrid, N.S., and Satne, P. (eds), *Kant's Doctrine of Right in the 21st Century* (University of Wales Press 2018).

Button, R., 'International Law and Search and Rescue' in Schildknecht, J., Dickey, R., Fink, M., and Ferris, L. (eds), *Operational Law in International Straits and Current Maritime Security Challenges* (Springer 2018).

Chetail, V., 'The Transnational Movement of Persons under General International Law – Mapping the Customary Law Foundations of International Migration Law' (2014) in Chetail, V., and Bauloz, C. (eds), *Research Handbook of International Law and Migration* (Cheltenham: Edward Elgar Publishing 2014).

Churchill, R.R., 'The 1982 United Nations Convention on the Law of the Sea' in Rothwell, D.R., Elferink, A.G.O., Scott, K.N., and Stephens, T. (eds), *The Oxford Handbook of the Law of the Sea* (OUP 2015).

Collins, R., '"Outlaw Oceans" and "Lawless Sea"? Revisiting the High Seas as a Regulatory Space Under (and After) UNCLOS 1982' in Siig, K., Feldtmann, B., and Billing, F.M.W. (eds), *The United Nations Convention on the Law of the Sea: A System of Regulation* (1st edn, Routledge 2023).

Cranston, M., 'Human Rights, Real and Supposed' in Raphael, D.D. (ed), *Political Theory and the Rights of Man* (Bloomington: Indiana University Press 1967).

Decken, K., and Koch, N., 'Recognition of New Human Rights: Phases, Techniques and the Approach of "Differentiated Traditionalism"' in Arnauld, A., Decken, K., and Susi, M. (eds), *The Cambridge Handbook of New Human Rights: Recognition, Novelty and Rhetoric* (CUP 2020).

Dembour, M.B., 'The Migrant Case Law of the European Court of Human Rights' in Çali, B., et al. (eds), *Migration and the European Convention on Human Rights* (Oxford: OUP 2021).

Evans, M.D., 'Adjudicating Human Rights' in Green, J.A., and Waters, C.P.M. (eds), *Adjudicating International Human Rights: Essays in Honour of Sandy Ghandhi* (Brill Nijhoff 2015).

Fantinato, M., 'Governance of International Sea Borders: Regional Approaches and Sustainable Solutions for Maritime Surveillance in the Mediterranean Sea' in Carpenter, A., Johansson, T.M., and Skinner, J.A. (eds), *Sustainability in the Maritime Domain: Towards Ocean Governance and Beyond* (Springer International Publishing AG 2021).

Gallagher, A.T., 'Migrant Smuggling' in Boister, N. and Currie, R.J. (eds), *Routledge Handbook of Transnational Criminal Law* (London: Routledge, Taylor & Francis Group 2015).

Gammeltoft-Hansen, T., 'Extraterritorial Human Rights Obligations in Regard to Refugees and Migrants' (2021) in Türkelli, M.G.G.E., Krajewski, M., and Vandenhole, W. (eds), *The Routledge Handbook on Extraterritorial Human Rights Obligations* (1st edn, Routledge, Routledge International Handbooks Series 2021).

Gerards, J., 'A Right of Access to Law – or Rather a Right of Legality and Legal Aid?' in Arnauld, A., Decken, K., and Susi, M. (eds), *The Cambridge Handbook of New Human Rights: Recognition, Novelty and Rhetoric* (CUP 2020).

Guilfoyle, D., 'Transnational Crime and the Rule of Law at Sea: Responses to Maritime Migration and Piracy Compared' in Moreno-Lax, V., and Papastavridis, E. (eds), *'Boat Refugees' and Migrants at Sea: A Comprehensive Approach: Integrating Maritime Security with Human Rights* (Vol. 7, International Refugee Law Series, Brill Nijhoff 2016).

Hathaway, J.C., 'Refugees and Asylum' in Opeskin, B., Perruchoud, R., and Redpath-Cross, J. (eds), *Foundations of International Migration Law* (Cambridge: CUP 2012).

Joseph, S., and Dipnall, S., 'Scope of Application' in Moeckli, D., Shah, S., and Sivakumaran, S. (eds), *International Human Rights Law* (3rd edn, OUP 2017).

Komp, L.M., 'The Duty to Assist Persons in Distress: An Alternative Source of Protection Against the Return of Migrants and Asylum Seekers to the High Seas?' in Moreno-Lax, V., and Papastavridis, E. (eds), *'Boat Refugees' and Migrants at Sea: A Comprehensive Approach: Integrating Maritime Security with Human Rights* (Vol. 7, International Refugee Law Series, Brill Nijhoff 2016).

Lauterpacht, E., and Bethlehem, D., 'The Scope and Content of the Principle of Non-Refoulement: Opinion' in Feller, E., Türk, V., and Nicholson, F. (eds), *Refugee Protection in International Law: UNHCR's Global Consultations on International Protection* (CUP 2003).

Lindholm, J., 'Remote Migration Control at Sea: Jurisdiction Relating to Joint or Proxy Interception in Foreign Waters or Foreign Search and Rescue Regions' in Siig, K., Feldtmann, B., and Billing, F.M.W. (eds), *The United Nations Convention on the Law of the Sea: A System of Regulation* (1st edn, Routledge 2023).

McAdam, J., 'Interpretation of the 1951 Convention' in Zimmermann, A. (ed), *The 1951 Convention Relating to the Status of Refugees and Its 1967 Protocol: A Commentary* (OUP 2011).

Mégret, F., 'Nature of Obligations' in Moeckli, D., Shah, S., and Sivakumaran, S. (eds), *International Human Rights Law* (3rd edn, OUP 2017).

Moreno-Lax, V., and Costello, C., 'The Extraterritorial Application of the EU Charter of Fundamental Rights: From Territoriality to Facticity–the Effectiveness Model' in Peers, S., et al. (eds), *The EU Charter of Fundamental Rights: A Commentary* (Hart Publishing 2014).

Mullally, S., 'Migration, Gender, and the Limits of Rights' in Rubio-Marín, R. (ed), *Human Rights and Immigration* (Oxford University Press 2014).

Papanicolopulu, I., 'Human Rights and the Law of the Sea' in Attard, D.J., Fizmaurice, M., and Gutiérrez, N.A.M. (eds), *The IMLI Manual on International Maritime Law: Volume I: The Law of the Sea* (OUP 2014).

Papastavridis, E., 'European Convention of Human Rights and the Law of the Sea: The Strasbourg Court in Unchartered Waters?' in Fitzmaurice, M., and Merkouris, P. (eds), *The Interpretation and Application of the European Convention of Human Rights: Legal and Practical Implications* (Queen Mary Studies of International Law 2013).

Papastavridis, E., 'Rescuing Migrants at Sea: The Responsibility of States under International Law' in Goodwin-Gill, G.S., and Weckel, E. (eds), *Migration and Refugee Protection in the 21st Century. International Aspects, Hague Academy of International Law* (Leiden: Martinus Nijhoff 2015).

Papastavridis, E., 'Introduction: Tracing the Bases of an Integrated Paradigm for Maritime Security and Human Rights at Sea' in Moreno-Lax, V., and Papastavridis, E. (eds), *'Boat*

Refugees' and Migrants at Sea: A Comprehensive Approach: Integrating Maritime Security with Human Rights (Vol. 7, International Refugee Law Series, Brill Nijhoff 2016).

Papastavridis, E., 'Rescuing Migrants at Sea and the Law of International Responsibility' in Gammeltoft-Hansen, T., and Vedsted-Hansen, J. (eds), *Human Rights and the Dark Side of Globalisation: Transnational Law Enforcement and Migration Control* (Routledge: Taylor & Francis 2016).

Petrig, A., and Bo, M., 'The International Tribunal for the Law of the Sea and Human Rights' in Scheinin, M. (ed), *Human Rights Norms in 'Other' International Courts* (CUP 2019).

Rodley, N.S., 'Integrity of the Person' in Moeckli, D., Shah, S., and Sivakumaran, S. (eds), *International Human Rights Law* (3rd edn, OUP 2017).

Sheinin, M., 'Extraterritorial Effect of the International Covenant on Civil and Political Rights' in Coomans, F., et al. (eds), *Extraterritorial Application of Human Rights* (Antwerp: Intersentia 2004).

Tasioulas, J., 'The Moral Reality of Human Rights' in Pogge, T. (ed), *Freedom from Poverty as a Human Right: Who Owes What to the Very Poor?* (Oxford: Unesco 2007) 75, 101.

Tasioulas, J., 'On the Nature of Human Rights' in Ernst, G., and Heilinger, J.-C. (eds), *The Philosophy of Human Rights: Contemporary Controversies* (Berlin: De Gruyter 2012).

Tasioulas, J., and Vayena, E., 'Just Global Health: Integrating Human Rights and Common Goods' in Brooks, T. (ed), *The Oxford Handbook of Global Justice* (OUP 2020).

Trevisanut, S., 'Search and Rescue Operations at Sea' in Nollkaemper, A., and Plakokefalos, I. (eds), *The Practice of Shared Responsibility in International Law* (CUP 2016).

Venzke, I., 'Is Interpretation in International Law a Game?' in Bianchi, A., Peat, D., and Windsor, M. (eds), *Interpretation in International Law* (OUP 2015).

Waldron, J., 'Cosmopolitan Norms' in Benhabib, S. (ed), *Another Cosmopolitanism* (OUP 2006).

Table of Cases

Al-Jedda v United Kingdom, App no 27021/08 (ECtHR, 7 July 2011).

Al-Saadoon and Mufdhi v the United Kingdom, App No 61498/08 (ECtHR, 2 March 2010).

Al-Skeini and Others v the United Kingdom, App no 55721/07 (ECtHR, 7 July 2011)

Alkhatib and Others v. Greece, App no 3566/16 (ECtHR, 16 January 2024).

Amirov v Russian Federation, Communication No 1447/2006, 2 April 2009, UN Doc CCPR/C/95/D/1447/2006.

Amuur v France, App no 19776/92 (ECtHR, 25 June 1996).

Andreou v Turkey, App no. 45653/99 (ECtHR, 3 June 2008).

Armed Activities on the Territory of the Congo (*Congo v Uganda*), Judgment 19 December 2005.

Artico v Italy (1980) 3 EHRR 1.

Berü v Turkey, App no 47304/07 (ECtHR, 11 January 2011).

Boumediene v Bush, 128 Supreme Court 2229 (2008).

Bromilow & Edwards Ltd. v. Inland Revenue Commissioners [1969] 1 WLR 1180.

Budayeva and others v Russia, App nos. 15339/02, 21166/02, 20058/02, 11673/02 and 15343/02 (ECtHR, 20 March 2008).

Case 26/62, *N.V. Algemeine Transport- en Expeditie Onderneming van Gend & Loos v Netherlands Inland Revenue Administration*, 1963 E.C.R. 1.

Case C-413/99, *Baumbast and R v Secretary of State for the Home Department*, 17 September 2002.
Case C-724/17, *Vantaan Kaupunki v Skanska Industrial Solutions Oy and Others*, 6 February 2019.
Catan and Others v Moldova and Russia, App nos 43370/04, 8252/05, and 18454/06 (ECtHR, 19 October 2012).
CCPR, *A.S. and Others v Italy*, 27 January 2021, UN Doc CCPR/C/130/D/3042/2017.
CCPR, *A.S. and Others v Malta*, 27 January 2021, UN Doc CCPR/C/128/D/30423/2017.
CCPR, *Ioane Teitiota v New Zealand*, CCPR/C/127/D/2728/2016.
CCPR, *Lopez Burgos v Uruguay*, Communication No 52/1979, 29 July 1981, UN Doc CCPR/13/D/52/1979.
Cervioğlu v Turkey, App no 69546/12 (ECtHR, 4 October 2016).
Chahal v the United Kingdom, App No 22414/93 (ECtHR) 15 November 1996.
City Inn Ltd v Shepherd Construction Ltd [2006] ScotCS CSOH_94.
Commission v Hungary, Case C-808/18 [2020] 1029.
Committee on the Rights of the Child in L.H. et al v France (30 September 2020) and F.B. et al v France (CRC/C/86/D/R.77/2019) (4 February 2021).
Corfu Channel (*United Kingdom of Great Britain and Northern Ireland v Albania*) (Merits) [1949] ICJ Rep 4.
Banković v Belgium, App no 52207/99 (ECtHR, 12 December 2001).
Cyprus v Turkey, App No 25781/94 (ECtHR, 10 May 2001).
Demir and Baykara v Turkey, App no 34503/97 (ECtHR, 12 November 2008).
Eshenov v Uzbekistan, HRC, Comm. No. 1225/2003 (2010).
F.B. et al v France (CRC/C/86/D/R.77/2019) (4 February 2021).
Fadeyeva v Russia, 55723/00 (ECtHR, 9 June 2005).
Friends of the Irish Environment (FIE) v Ireland [2019] IEHC 747.
Georgia v Russia (No 2), App no 38263/08 (ECtHR, 21 January 2021).
Gökdemir v Turkey, App no 66309/09 (ECtHR, 19 May 2015).
H.F. and Others v France, Applications Nos 24384/19 and 44234/20 (ECtHR, 14 September 2022).
Hirsi Jamaa and Others v Italy, App no 27765/09 (ECtHR, 23 February 2012.
Ilaşçu and Others v Moldova and Russia, App no 48787/99 (ECHR, 8 July 2004).
Isaak and others v Turkey, App no 44587/98 (ECtHR, 28 September 2006).
Issa v Turkey, App no 31821/96 (ECtHR, 16 November 2004).
Jabari v Turkey, App No 40035/98 (ECtHR, 11 July 2000).
Kate A. Hoff Administratrix of the Estate of Samuel B Allisson, decease (USA) v United Mexican States (2 April 1929) 4 RIAA 444.
Kaya v Turkey, App no 22729/93 (ECtHR, 19 February 1998).
Kebe and Others v Ukraine, App no 12552/12 (ECtHR, 12 January 2017).
Keenan v United Kingdom, App no 27229/95 (ECtHR, 3 April 2001).
Kelly Pipelines Ltd v British Gas plc (1990) 48 BLR 126.
Kemaloglu v Turkey, App no 19986/06 (ECtHR, 10 April 2012).
Khlaifia and Others v Italy, App no 16483/12 (ECtHR, 15 December 2016).
Kingdom of the Netherlands v Russian Federation, Provisional Measures, Request for Provisional Measures Submitted by the Netherlands, 21 October 2013.
Legal Consequences of the Construction of a Wall in the Occupied Palestinian Territory (Advisory Opinion) [2004] ICJ Rep 136 para 109, 112 (The Wall case).
Leray v France, App no 44617/98 (ECtHR, 16 January 2001).
Loizidou v Turkey, App No 15318/89, (ECtHR, 18 December 1996).
Lonas v State (1871) 3 Heisk. (Tenn.).

M.A. and Others v Lithuania, App no 59793/17 (ECtHR, 11 December 2018).
M.A. and Z.R. v Cyprus (M.A. and Z.R.) App no 39090/20 (ECtHR, 8 October 2024).
M.S.S. v Belgium and Greece, App no 30696/09 (ECtHR, 21 January 2011).
Makaratzis v Greece, App no 50385/99 (ECtHR, 20 December 2004).
Mastromatteo v Italy, App no 37703/97 (ECtHR, 24 October 2002).
McCann and Others v the United Kingdom, App no 18984/91 (ECtHR, 27 September 1995).
Medvedyev and others v France, App no 3394/03 (ECtHR, 29 March 2010).
Military and Paramilitary Activities in and against Nicaragua (*Nicaragua v United States of America*) 1986 I.C.J. 14.
Minister for Immigration and Multicultural and Indigenous Affairs v Al Khafaji [2004] HCA 38; (2004) 219 CLR 664; (2004) 208 ALR 201; (2004) 78 ALJR 1156 (6 August 2004).
Molie v Romania, App no 13754/02 (ECtHR, 1 September 2009).
N.D. and N.T. v Spain, Applications nos 8675/15 and 8697/15 (ECtHR 13 February 2020).
Nishimura Ekiu v United States [1982] 142 U.S. 651, Gray J., 659.
Öcalan v Turkey, App no 46221/99 (ECtHR, 12 May 2005)
Öneryildiz v Turkey, App no 48939/99 (ECtHR, 30 November 2004).
Opuz v Turkey, App no 33401/02 (ECtHR, 9 June 2009).
Osman v the United Kingdom, App no 23452/94 (ECtHR, 28 October 1998).
Pad and Others v Turkey, App no 60167/00 (ECtHR, 28 June 2007).
Prilutskiy v Ukraine, App no 40429/08 (ECtHR, 2005).
Quinn v Leathem [1901] AC 495
Rainbow Warrior Affair Case (*New Zealand v France*) (1990) 20 RIAA 217.
Ruddock v Vadarlis [2001] FCA 1329; 110 RCR 491; 183 ALR.
S.S. and Others v Italy, App no 21660/18 (ECtHR, communicated on 26 June 2019).
Saadi v United Kingdom, App no 13229/03 (ECtHR, 29 January 2008).
Safi and Others v Greece, App No 5418/15 (ECtHR, 7 July 2022) para 166.
Sale v Haitian Centers Council, 113 S. Ct. 2549, 125 L. (92–344), 509 U.S. 155 (1993).
Scaramanga v Stamp (1880) 5 C.P.D. 295.
Sharifi and Others v Italy and Greece, App No 16643/09 (ECtHR, 21 October 2014).
Soering v United Kingdom (1989) 11 EHRR 43.
Szanyi v Hungary, App no 35493/13 (ECtHR, 8 November 2016).
The 'Enrica Lexie' Incident (*Italy v India*), PCA Case No. 2015–28.
The Eleanor, 165 English Reports 1058, 1068 (English High Court of Admiralty, 22 November 1809).
The M/V 'Louisa' (*Saint Vincent and the Grenadines v Kingdom of Spain*) 28 May 2013, ITLOS Reports (2013).
The M/V 'Saiga' (No 2) (*Saint Vincent and the Grenadines v Guinea*) (Judgment of 1 July 1999) ITLOS Reports 1999.
The MV Toledo [1995] 2 ILRM 30, 48–9.
The Republic of Philippines v The People's Republic of China, PCA case No. 2013–19.
Tyrer v the United Kingdom, App No 5856/72 (ECtHR 25 April 1978).
Velásquez-Rodríguez v Honduras, Series C No. 4 (29 July 1988).
Wagner v International Ry. Co., 232 N.Y. 176, 133 N.E. 437 (1921).
Wemhoff v Germany, App no 2122/64, A/7 (ECtHR, 27 June 1968).
Women on Waves and Others v Portugal, App No 31276/05 (ECtHR, 3 February 2009).
X and Y v The Netherlands (1986) 8 EHRR 235.
Xhavara and Others v Italy and Albania, App no 39473/98 (ECtHR, 11 January 2001).

Other Materials

'Over 50 NGOs pen eleventh-hour open letter to EU on human rights risks in Migration Pact' (18 December 2023) <https://picum.org/blog/open-letter-eu-human-rights-risks-migration-pact/> accessed 1 May 2024; See also, UNHCR 'Child immigration detention must be prohibited following adoption of EU migration and asylum pact, UN experts say' (2 May 2024) <https://www.ohchr.org/en/press-releases/2024/05/child-immigration-detention-must-be-prohibited-following-adoption-eu> accessed 2 May 2024.

'State Responsibility: Second Report on State Responsibility, by Mr. James Crawford, Special Rapporteur', UN Doc. A/CN.4/498 (19 July 1999) <https://legal.un.org/ilc/documentation/english/a_cn4_498.pdf>.

1969 Vienna Convention on the Law of Treaties 1155 UNTS 331, at Art. 31. See also Suzanne

AFP '"Nobody should be forcibly returned to Libya": HRW Chief' (18 January 2018) <https://www.rfi.fr/en/contenu/20180118-nobody-should-be-forcibly-returned-libya-hrw-chief>.

Alagna, F., 'From Sophia to Irini: EU Mediterranean Policies and the Urgency of "Doing Something"' (2020) <https://www.iai.it/en/pubblicazioni/sophia-irini-eu-mediterranean-policies-and-urgency-doing-something>.

AlarmPhone, 'Continuous landings, increasing violence and deaths at sea' (AlarmPhone, 31 July 2023) <https://alarmphone.org/en/2023/07/31/continuous-landings-increasing-violence-and-deaths-at-sea/>.

AllAfrica, 'Africa: International Law Experts Warn Europe's 'Pull-Back' of Migrants is Illegal – Part 2' <https://allafrica.com/stories/201809170625.html>.

Amnesty International, 'A perfect Storm: The Failure of the European Policies in the Central Mediterranean' (2017) <https://www.amnesty.ie/wp-content/uploads/2017/07/A-Perfect-Storm-EUR0366552017.pdf>.

Amnesty International, 'EU: Plans to 'close' sea border would lock refugees and migrants in horrendous conditions in Libya' (2 February 2017) <https://www.amnesty.ie/eu-plans-close-sea-border-lock-refugees-migrants-horrendous-conditions-libya/>.

Amnesty International, 'Europe: A perfect storm: The failure of European policies in the Central Mediterranean' (6 July 2017) 23 <https://www.amnesty.org/download/Documents/EUR0366552017ENGLISH.PDF>.

Amnesty International, 'Libya/EU: Conditions remain 'hellish' as EU marks 5 years of cooperation agreements' (2022) <https://www.amnesty.org/en/latest/news/2022/01/libya-eu-conditions-remain-hellish-as-eu-marks-5-years-of-cooperation-agreements/>.

Amnesty International, 'Universal Declaration of Human Rights' <https://www.amnesty.org/en/what-we-do/universal-declaration-of-human-rights/>.

BBC News, 'Migrant crisis: Malta seeks solutions to stem the tide' (21 April 2015) <https://www.bbc.com/news/world-europe-32389754>.

Blaming the Rescuers. Criminalising Solidarity, (Re)enforcing Deterrence (2017) <http://blamingtherescuers.org/>.

Bob-Milliar, G., 'Rescuing Migrants in Libya: The Political Economy of State Responses to Migration Crises – The Case of Ghana' (DIIS Report, 2012:16) <https://pure.diis.dk/ws/files/56074/WP2012_16_Rescuing_migrants_in_Libya_web.pdf>.

Bredeloup, S., and Pliez, O., 'The Libyan Migration Corridor' (European University Institute, Research Report, Case Study, EU-US Immigration Systems 2011/03) <https://cadmus.eui.eu/bitstream/handle/1814/16213/EU-US%20Immigration%20Systems%202011%20-%2003.pdf?sequence=1&isAllowed=y>.

Busco, P., 'Not All That Glitters Is Gold: The Human Rights Committee's Test for the Extraterritorial Application of the ICCPR in the Context of Search and Rescue Operations' (OpinioJuris, 2 March 2021) <https://opiniojuris.

org/2021/03/02/not-all-that-glitters-is-gold-the-human-rights-committees-test-for-the-extraterritorial-application-of-the-iccpr-in-the-context-of-search-and-rescue-operations/>.

Chouliaraki, L., and Georgiou, G., 'Migration – the crisis imaginary' (LSE, 14 July2023)<https://blogs.lse.ac.uk/europpblog/2023/07/14/migration-the-crisis-imaginary/>.

Communication to the Office of the Prosecutor of the International Criminal Court Pursuant to the Article 15 of the Rome Statute: EU Migration Policies in the Central Mediterranean and Libya (2014–2019) <https://www.statewatch.org/media/documents/news/2019/jun/eu-icc-case-EU-Migration-Policies.pdf>.

Communication to the United Nations Human Rights Committee In the Case of SDG against Italy (Anonymized Version) Submitted for Consideration under the Optional Protocol to the International Covenant on Civil and Political Rights to The United Nations Human Rights Committee (GLAN 2019).

Council of Europe, 'Third party intervention by the Council of Europe Commissioner for Human Rights under Article 36 of the ECtHR, App No 21660/18, S.S. and others v. Italy' (15 November 2019) CommDH (2019) 29 <https://rm.coe.int/third-party-intervention-before-the-european-court-of-human-rights-app/168098dd4d>.

Council of Europe, European Court of Human Rights, 'COURTalks disCOURs' (2016) <https://www.echr.coe.int/documents/d/echr/COURTalks_Asyl_Talk_ENG>.

Council of Europe: Parliamentary Assembly, 'Lives lost in the Mediterranean Sea: Who is responsible?' (2012) <http://www.unhcr.org/refworld/docid/4f7be86b2.html>.

Council of the EU, 'EU launches Operation IRINI to enforce Libya arms embargo' (31 March 2020) <https://www.consilium.europa.eu/en/press/press-releases/2020/03/31/eu-launches-operation-irini-to-enforce-libya-arms-embargo/>.

Council of the European Union, 'EUNAVFOR MED Operation Sophia: mandate extended until 30 September 2019' (29 March 2019) <https://www.consilium.europa.eu/en/press/press-releases/2019/03/29/eunavfor-med-operation-sophia-mandate-extended-until-30-september-2019/>.

Court of Auditors, 'Frontex's support to external border management: not sufficiently effective to date' (2021) <https://www.eca.europa.eu/Lists/ECADocuments/SR21_08/SR_

Cuttitta, P., 'Pushing Migrants Back to Libya, Persecuting Rescue NGOs: The End of the Humanitarian Turn (Part I)' (BorderCriminologies, 18 April 2018) <https://www.law.ox.ac.uk/research-subject-groups/centre-criminology/centreborder-criminologies/blog/2018/04/pushing-migrants>.

Data from IOM, 'Missing Migrants Project Global Data Overview, January 2022-December 2022' (21 June 2023) <https://missingmigrants.iom.int/sites/g/files/tmzbdl601/files/publication/file/MMP%20global%20data%20briefing%20 2022.pdf>.

Denti, A., 'Hundreds drown off Libya, EU leaders forced to reconsider migrant crisis' (19 April 2015) <https://www.reuters.com/article/us-europe-migrants/hundreds-drown-off-libya-eu-leaders-forced-to-reconsider-migrant-crisis-idUSKBN-0NA07020150419>; BBC News, 'Mediterranean migrants: Hundreds feared dead after boat capsizes (19 April 2015) <https://www.bbc.com/news/world-europe-32371348>.

ECtHR, Guide on Article 2 of the European Convention on Human Rights, (2018) <https://fln.dk/-/media/FLN/Publikationer-og-notater/EMRK/Guide-on-Article-2-of-the-European-Convention-on-Human-Rights.pdf?la=da&hash=90AF97C1CA74479FFED7012EBC0C91479D0686CF>.

Eroukhmanoff, C., 'Securitisation Theory: An Introduction' (E-International Relations, 14 January 2018) <https://www.e-ir.info/2018/01/14/securitisation-theory-an-introduction/>.

EU Observer, 'Crotone shipwreck triggers police vs coastguard blame game' (2 March 2023) <https://euobserver.com/migration/156776>.

EUBAM Libya, 'About EU Border Assistance Mission in Libya (EUBAM)' (2016) <https://eeas.europa.eu/csdp-missions-operations/eubam-libya/3859/about-eu-border-assistance-mission-libya-eubam_en>.

European Anti Fraud Office, Final Report <https://cdn.prod.www.spiegel.de/media/00847a5e-8604-45dc-a0fe-37d920056673/Directorate_A_redacted-2.pdf>.

European Commission, 'A European Agenda on Migration' (2015) <https://eur-lex.europa.eu/legal-content/EN/TXT/?uri=CELEX%3A52015DC0240>.

European Commission, 'Communication from the Commission to the European Parliament, the Council, the European Economic and Social Committee and the Committee of the Regions on a New Pact on Migration and Asylum' (European Commission, 23 September 2020) COM (2020) 609 final (Communication 2020) <https://ec.europa.eu/info/sites/default/files/1_en_act_part1_v7_1.pdf>; Philippe De Bruycker, The New Pact on Migration and Asylum: What it is not and what it could have been (2020) <https://eumigrationlawblog.eu/the-new-pact-on-migration-and-asylum-what-it-is-not-and-what-it-could-have-been/>.

European Commission, 'Communication from the Commission to The European Parliament, The Council, The European Economic and Social Committee and The Committee Of The Regions, EU Action Plan Against Migrant Smuggling (2015–2020)' (27May2015)<https://eur-lex.europa.eu/legal-content/EN/TXT/?uri=celex:52015DC0285>.

European Commission, 'Managing migration better in all aspects: A European Agenda on Migration' (13 May 2015) <https://ec.europa.eu/commission/presscorner/detail/en/IP_15_4956>.

European Council (EC), 'EUNAVFORMED Operation Sophia: Mandate Extended Until 31 March 2019' (21 December 2018) <https://www.consilium.europa.eu/en/press/press-releases/2018/12/21/eunavfor-med-operation-sophia-mandate-extended-until-31-march-2019/>.

European Council, Council Conclusions (EUCO 22/15) of 26 June 2015, at para 3 <https://data.consilium.europa.eu/doc/document/ST-22–2015-INIT/en/pdf>.

European External Action Service (EEAS), 'European Union Naval Force – Mediterranean Operation Sophia' (10 April 2018) <https://www.operationsophia.eu/wp-content/uploads/2018/04/Mission.pdf>.

European Ombudsman, 'Decision on how the European Border and Coast Guard Agency (Frontex) complies with its fundamental rights obligations with regard to search and rescue in the context of its maritime surveillance activities, in particular the Adriana shipwreck (26 February 2024) OI/3/2023/MHZ <https://www.ombudsman.europa.eu/fr/decision/en/182665#_ftn24>.

European Parliament, 'Resolution on the need for EU action on search and rescue in the Mediterranean' (13 July 2023) 2023/2787 (RSP) <https://oeil.secure.europarl.europa.eu/oeil/popups/ficheprocedure.do?lang=en&reference=2023/2787(RSP)>.

Executive Committee of the High Commissioner's Programme (excom), 'Interception of Asylum-Seekers and Refugees: The International Framework and Recommendations for a Comprehensive Approach' 9 June 2000 EC/50/SC/CPR.17 3 <http://www.unhcr.org/4963237411.pdf>.

Forensic Architecture, 'Privatized Push-Back of the Nivin' (18.12.2019) <https://forensic-architecture.org/investigation/nivin>.

FRA, 'Fundamental rights considerations: NGO ships involved in search and rescue in the Mediterranean and criminal investigations – Tables and figures' (FRA, 1 October 2018) <https://fra.europa.eu/en/publication/2018/ngos-sar-activities>.

FRA, 'Fundamental rights of refugees, asylum applicants and migrants at the European borders' <https://fra.europa.eu/sites/default/files/fra_uploads/fra-coe-2020-european-law-land-borders_en.pdf>.

Fremaux, P.V., and Attard, F., 'Navigating the Human Rights Trajectory of the EU Migration and Asylum Pact in Search and Rescue Operations (Part Two)' (opiniojuris, 17.09.2024) <https://opiniojuris.org/2024/09/17/navigating-the-human-rights-trajectory-of-the-eu-migration-and-asylum-pact-in-search-and-rescue-operations-part-two/>.

Fremeaux, P.V., and Attard, F.G., 'Rescue at Sea and the Establishment of Jurisdiction: New Direction from the Human Rights Committee? Part I' (OpinioJuris, 3 March 2021) <http://opiniojuris.org/2021/03/03/rescue-at-sea-and-the-establishment-of-jurisdiction-new-direction-from-the-human-rights-committee-part-i/>.

French, P., 'Rescue a Refugee: Get Charged with Trafficking?' (The New Republic, 5 March 2019) <https://newrepublic.com/article/153216/rescue-refugee-get-charged-trafficking>.

Front-LEX, 'For the First Time, a "Pushback" Victim Sues Frontex for Half a Million Euro' (2024) <https://www.front-lex.eu/alaa-hamoudi>.

Frontex, 'Frontex Situation Centre: Multipurpose Aerial Surveillance' (2018) <https://op.europa.eu/en/publication-detail/-/publication/b96286e0–1aa8–11e8-ac73–01aa75ed71a1>.

Galani, S., '"Human Rights At Sea" Challenges For Shipping' (2018) <https://safety4sea.com/human-rights-sea-challenges-shipping/>.

Gauci, J.P., 'When Private Vessels Rescue Migrants and Refugees: A mapping of Legal Considerations' (British Institute of International and Comparative Law, 24 November 2020) <https://www.biicl.org/documents/124_private_vessels_research.pdf>.

Gkliati, M., Angeli, D., Mavropoulou, E., and Vavoula, N., 'Greece Boat Disaster: Questions of International Law' (OpinioJuris, 5 August 2023) <http://opiniojuris.org/2023/08/05/greece-boat-disaster-questions-of-international-law/>.

GLAN <https://www.glanlaw.org/migrationandborders>.

GLAN, 'Privatised Migrant Abuse by Italy and Libya' <https://www.glanlaw.org/nivincase>.

Goodwin-Gill, g., 'Drowning in the Mediterranean: Time to think and act regionally' (EJIL: Talk!, 12 April 2021)<https://www.ejiltalk.org/drowning-in-the-mediterranean-time-to-think-and-act-regionally/>.

Hayden, J., 'EU finalizes migrant deal with Tunisia' (16 July 2013, Politico) <https://www.politico.eu/article/eu-migration-deal-tunisia-migrants-africa-european-commission/>.

Heller, C., and Pezzani, L., 'Death by rescue. Forensic Architecture Agency' (2016) <https://deathbyrescue.org/report/narrative/>.

Heller, C., Pezzani, L., and SITU Research, 'Case: "Left-to-die boat"' (2014) <https://www.forensic-architecture.org/case/left-die-boat/>.

Herbert, M., 'Losing Hope: Why Tunisians are leading the surge in irregular migration to Europe' (Global Initiative, January 2022) <https://globalinitiative.net/wp-content/uploads/2022/01/GI-TOC-Losing-Hope_Tunisia-Report–2021.pdf>.

Heyns, C., and Probert, T., 'Securing the Right to Life: A cornerstone of the human rights system' (EJIL:Talk!, 11 May 2016) <https://www.ejiltalk.org/securing-the-right-to-life-a-cornerstone-of-the-human-rights-system/>.

Hugues, E.A., 'Waiting for Godot No More: The Climate Crisis and the New European Asylum Pact' (Oxford Human Rights Hub, 18 April 2024) < https://

ohrh.law.ox.ac.uk/waiting-for-godot-no-more-the-climate-crisis-and-the-new-european-asylum-pact>.

Human Rights at Sea, 'Geneva Declaration on Human Rights at Sea (Version 1, 5 April 2019)' <https://gdhras.com/wp-content/uploads/2019/07/HRAS_GENEVA_DECLARATION_ON_HUMAN_RIGHTS_AT_SEA_April_2019-Version1-FINAL-LOCKED.pdf>.

Human Rights at Sea, 'The Right to Life: Italy found by UN in violation of the right to life of Migrants at Sea' (28 January 2021) <https://www.humanrightsatsea.org/2021/01/28/the-right-to-life-italy-found-by-un-in-violation-of-the-right-to-life-of-migrants-at-sea/>.

Human Rights at Sea, Geneva Declaration on Human Rights at Sea (launched 1 March 2022) <https://www.humanrightsatsea.org/GDHRAS>.

Human Rights Council, 'Report of the Independent Fact-Finding Mission on Libya' (2023) A/HRC/52/83; Human Rights Watch, 'No Escape from Hell: EU Policies Contribute to Abuse of Migrants in Libya' (21 January 2019) <https://www.hrw.org/report/2019/01/21/no-escape-hell/eu-policies-contribute-abuse-migrants-libya>.

Human Rights Watch, 'EU: Frontex Complicit in Abuse in Libya: Aerial Surveillance Is Enabling Interceptions Return of Migrants to Harm' (HRW, 12 December 2023) <https://www.hrw.org/news/2022/12/12/eu-frontex-complicit-abuse-libya>.

Human Rights Watch, 'EU: Shifting Rescue to Libya Risks Lives' (19 June 2017) <https://www.hrw.org/news/2017/06/19/eu-shifting-rescue-libya-risks-lives>.

Infographics, 'Lives saved in EU Mediterranean operations (2015–2021)' (2021) <http://www.consilium.europa.eu/en/infographics/saving-lives-sea-february-2018/>.

International Law Association, 'Protection of People at Sea' < https://www.ila-hq.org/en_GB/committees/protection-of-people-at-sea>.

International Law Commission, 'Draft articles on the expulsion of aliens, with commentaries' (2014) UN Doc. A/69/10 <https://legal.un.org/ilc/texts/instruments/english/commentaries/9_12_2014.pdf>.

International Organization for Migration, 'IOM Applauds Italy's Life-Saving Mare Nostrum Operation: "Not a Migrant Pull Factor"' (IOM, 31 October 2014) <https://www.iom.int/news/iom-applauds-italys-life-saving-mare-nostrum-operation-not-migrant-pull-factor>.

International Organization for Migration, 'International Migration Law No 34, Glossary on Migration' (IOM, 2019) <https://publications.iom.int/system/files/pdf/iml_34_glossary.pdf>.

Jeannerod, B., 'France Gifts Boats to Abusive Libyan Coast Guard' (Human Rights Watch, 13 March 2019) <https://www.hrw.org/news/2019/03/13/france-gifts-boats-abusive-libyan-coast-guard>.

Jeppesen, F., 'New decree obstructs lifesaving rescue efforts at sea and will cause more deaths' (MSF, 5 January 2023) <https://reliefweb.int/report/italy/new-decree-obstructs-lifesaving-rescue-efforts-sea-and-will-cause-more-deaths>.

Katz, H., and Mann, I., 'From Farmakonisi to Pylos at the ECtHR' (EJIL:Talk!, 12 July 2023) <https://www.ejiltalk.org/from-farmakonisi-to-pylos-at-the-ecthr/>.

Keady-Tabbal, N., & Cennabháin, E., 'Detention, Deportation & Drowning: Ireland's Embrace of Fortress Europe' (Rebel News, 26 June 2024) <https://www.rebelnews.ie/2024/06/26/detention-deportation-and-drowning-irelands-embrace-of-fortress-europe/>.

Kelly, P.W., 'What is Hope for?' (7 July 2018) <https://lareviewofbooks.org/article/what-is-hope-for/>.

Lazarus, L., Goold, B., Desai, R., and Rasheed, Q., 'The relationship between rights and responsibilities' (2009) 18/09 Ministry of Justice Research Paper Series <https://commons.allard.ubc.ca/fac_pubs/153/>.

Liempt, V., 'Tunisia deal unlikely to reduce illegal migration, say experts' (Dutch News, 20 July 2023) <https://www.dutchnews.nl/2023/07/tunisia-deal-unlikely-to-reduce-illegal-migration-say-experts/>.

MacGregor, M., 'Migrants rescued by "Lady Sham" detained in Libya' (23 January 2019) <https://www.infomigrants.net/en/post/14678/migrants-rescued-by-lady-sham-detained-in-libya>.

Madjidian, N., 'In Search of (Ir)Responsibility: The Crotone Shipwreck and the Quest For the Legally Responsible' (12 June 2023) <https://verfassungsblog.de/in-search-of-irresponsibility/>.

Mallia, P., 'The MV Salamis and the State of Disembarkation at International Law: The Undefinable Goal' (2014) 18 (11) American Society of International Law <http://www.asil.org/insights/volume/18/issue/11/mv-salamis-and-state-disembarkation-international-law-undefinable-goal>.

Mangiapane, G., 'Italian political standoff keeps rescued migrants stranded at sea' (Reuters, 19 December 2019) <https://www.euronews.com/2019/08/16/italian-political-standoff-keeps-rescued-migrants-stranded-at-sea>.

Markard, N., 'A Hole of Unclear Dimensions: Reading ND and NT v. Spain' (EU Migration law blog, 1 April 2020) <https://eumigrationlawblog.eu/a-hole-of-unclear-dimensions-reading-nd-and-nt-v-spain/>.

Memorandum of understanding on cooperation in the fields of development, the fight against illegal immigration, human trafficking and fuel smuggling and on reinforcing the security of borders between the State of Libya and the Italian Republic (2017) <https://eumigrationlawblog.eu/wp-content/uploads/2017/10/MEMORANDUM_translation_finalversion.doc.pdf>.

Milanovic, M., 'European Court Decides Al-Skeini and Al-Jeeda' (EJIL:Talk!, 7 July 2011) <https://www.ejiltalk.org/european-court-decides-al-skeini-and-al-jedda/>.

Milanovic, M., 'Drowning Migrants, the Human Rights Committee, and Extraterritorial Human Rights Obligations' (EJIL:Talk!, 16 March 2021) <https://www.ejiltalk.org/drowning-migrants-the-human-rights-committee-and-extraterritorial-human-rights-obligations/>.

Milanovic, M., 'Georgia v. Russia No. 2: The European Court's Resurrection of Bankovic in the Contexts of Chaos' (EJIL:Talk!, 25 January 2021) <www.ejiltalk.org/georgia-v-russia-no-2-the-european-courts-resurrection-of-bankovic-in-the-contexts-of-chaos/>.

Minestero della Difesa, 'Mare Nostrum Operation' <http://www.marina.difesa.it/EN/operations/Pagine/MareNostrum.aspx>.

Moreno-Lax, V., 'A New Common European Approach to Search and Rescue? Entrenching Proactive Containment' (EU Migration Law Blog, 2021) <https://eumigrationlawblog.eu/a-new-common-european-approach-to-search-and-rescue-entrenching-proactive-containment/>.

Mullally, S., 'A Crisis of Protection in Europe: Migrants at Sea' (2016) 110 Proceedings of the ASIL Annual Meeting 175, <https://www.cambridge.org/core/journals/proceedings-of-the-asil-annual-meeting/article/abs/crisis-of-protection-in-europe-migrants-at-sea/A664A0B464DEA0EDF45EFC595BBC5A00>

Mullally, S., 'Migrant crisis: It's a question of human rights – not charity' (Irish Times, 3 September 2015) <https://www.irishtimes.com/opinion/migrant-crisis-it-s-a-question-of-human-rights-not-charity-1.2339237>.

Mustasaari, S., 'The issue of extraterritorial jurisdiction in the repatriation of children detained in Syrian camps: Shortcomings in the ECtHR judgment in H.F. and Others v. France' (Strasbourg Observers, 1 November 2022) <https://strasbourgobservers.com/2022/11/01/the-issue-of-extraterritorial-jurisdiction-in-the-repatriation-of-children-detained-in-syrian-camps-shortcomings-in-the-ecthr-judgment-in-h-f-and-others-v-france%EF%BF%BC/>.

Natalino Ronzitti, The Treaty on Friendship, Partnership and Cooperation between Italy and Libya: New prospects for cooperation in the Mediterranean? (Rome: Istituto Aff ari Internazionali, 2009) <http://www.iai.it/pdf/DocIAI/IAI0909.pdf>.

Natter, K., 'Reinventing a Broken Wheel: What the EU-Tunisia Deal Reveals over Europe's Migration Cooperation' (5 September 2023, Verfassungsblog) <https://verfassungsblog.de/reinventing-a-broken-wheel/>.

OHCHR, 'Europe/Migrants: "Let them die, this is a good deterrence" – UN human rights expert' (30 October 2014) <https://www.ohchr.org/EN/NewsEvents/Pages/DisplayNews.aspx?NewsID=15239&LangID=E>.

OHCHR, 'Migration' (Foreword) <https://www2.ohchr.org/english/issues/migration/taskforce/docs/foreword.pdf>.

OHCHR, 'Statement by Mr. Zeid Ra'ad Al Hussein, United Nations High Commissioner for Human Rights, at the International Law Commission' (OHCHR, 21 July 2015) <https://www.ohchr.org/EN/NewsEvents/Pages/DisplayNews.aspx?NewsID=16254&LangID=E>.

OHCHR, 'Statement of Mr Craig Mokhiber, IMO High-Level Meeting to Address Unsafe Mixed Migration by Sea' (2015) <https://www.ohchr.org/EN/NewsEvents/Pages/DisplayNews.aspx?NewsID=15696&LangID=E>.

OHCHR, 'UN human rights chief: Suffering of migrants in Libya outrage to conscience of humanity' (14 November 2017) <https://www.ohchr.org/en/NewsEvents/Pages/DisplayNews.aspx?NewsID=22393>.

Open Letter, 'Hundreds of NGOs and individuals call for revocation of Libya's SAR Zone' (3 July 2020) <http://www.migreurop.org/article2997.html?lang=fr>.

Palm, A., 'The Italy-Libya Memorandum of Understanding: The baseline of a policy approach aimed at closing all doors to Europe?'(EU migration Law Blog, 2017) <http://eumigrationlawblog.eu/the-italy-libya-memorandum-of-understanding-the-baseline-of-a-policy-approach-aimed-at-closing-all-doors-to-europe/>.

Papachristodoulou, A, 'Shipwreck after Shipwreck: Frontex Emergency Signals and the Integration of AI systems' (Verfassungsblog, 11 March 2024) <https://verfassungsblog.de/shipwreck-after-shipwreck/>.

Papachristodoulou, A., 'The Crotone Migrant Shipwreck: A Cat-and-Mouse Blame Game and the Role of Technologies at External Borders' (EJIL:Talk!, 12 April 2023) <https://www.ejiltalk.org/the-crotone-migrant-shipwreck-a-cat-and-mouse-blame-game-and-the-role-of-technologies-at-external-borders/>.

Papachristodoulou, A., 'The Principle of Saving Lives at Sea: Just a Fool's Hope' (International Law Blog, 27 June 2019) <https://internationallaw.blog/2019/06/27/the-principle-of-saving-lives-at-sea-just-a-fools-hope/>.

Papachristodoulou, A., and Collins, R., 'Pulling Back Navies and Pushing Back Migrants: Questioning the EU's Legal Responsibility in the Mediterranean Sea' (2018) UCD Working Papers in Law, Criminology & Socio-Legal Studies, Research Paper No. 01/2020 <https://papers.ssrn.com/sol3/papers.cfm?abstract_id=3548637>.

Papastavridis, E., 'Is there a right to be rescued at sea? A Skeptical View' (Questions of International Law, Zoom-In, 23 June 2014) <http://www.qil-qdi.org/is-there-a-right-to-be-rescued-at-sea-a-constructive-view/>.

Parliamentary Assembly of the Council of Europe, Resolution 2215 (2018) 'The Situation in Libya: Prospects and Role of the Council of Europe' <http://assembly.coe.int/nw/xml/XRef/Xref-XML2HTML-EN.asp?fileid=24738>.

Pellet, A., Tenth report on reservations to treaties, Addendum, International Law Commission, Fifty-seventh session, UN Doc A/CN.4/558/Add 1 <https://legal.un.org/ilc/documentation/english/a_cn4_558.pdf>.

Pijnenburg, A., 'Team Europe's Deal: What's Wrong with the EU-Tunisia Migration Agreement?' (Verfassungsblog, 21 August 2023) < https://verfassungsblog.de/team-europes-deal/>.

Raible, L., 'Extraterritoriality between a rock and hard place' (Question of International Law, Zoom-in, 30 June 2021) <http://www.qil-qdi.org/extraterritoriality-between-a-rock-and-hard-place/#_ftn1>.

Report of the Special Rapporteur on the Human Rights Council on Extrajudicial, Summary or Arbitrary Executions, UN Doc. A/72/335, 15 August 2017.

Riegert, B., 'Libya takes over from Italy on Rescuing Shipwrecked Migrants' (DW, 5 July 2018) <https://p.dw.com/p/30ue2>.

Ronzitti, N., The Treaty on Friendship, Partnership and Cooperation between Italy and Libya: New prospects for cooperation in the Mediterranean? (Rome: Istituto Aff ari Internazionali, 2009) <http://www.iai.it/pdf/DocIAI/IAI0909.pdf>.

Secretary-General of the International Maritime Organization, 'The United Nations Convention on the Law of the Sea and the International Maritime Organization Address by Mr. Koji Sekimizu' (18 March 2014) <https://www.imo.org/en/MediaCentre/SecretaryGeneral/Pages/itlos.aspx>.

Sitaropoulos, N., 'States Are Bound to Consider the UN Human Rights Committee's Views in Good Faith' (Oxford Human Rights Hub, 11 March 2015) <https://ohrh.law.ox.ac.uk/states-are-bound-to-consider-the-un-human-rights-committees-view s-in-good-faith/>.

The National, 'Malta denounced after assisting Libyan coastguard to intercept migrant boat' (2019) <https://www.thenational.ae/world/europe/malta-denounced-after-assisting-libyan-coastguard-to-intercept-migrant-boat–1.856853>.

The United Kingdom Parliament (2014) Written answers <https://publications.parliament.uk/pa/ld201415/ldhansrd/text/141015w0001.htm>.

Trevisanut, S., 'Is there a right to be rescued at sea? A constructive view' (Questions of International Law, Zoom-In, 23 June 2014) <http://www.qil-qdi.org/is-there-a-right-to-be-rescued-at-sea-a-constructive-view/>.

UN Human Rights Council, Report of the Independent Fact-Finding Mission on Libya (27 March 2023), A/HRC/52/83 <https://reliefweb.int/report/libya/report-independent-fact-finding-mission-libya-ahrc5283-advance-edited-version-enar>.

UN Support Mission in Libya, '"Detained and Dehumanised" Report on Human Rights Abuses against Migrants in Libya' (13 December 2016) <https://www.ohchr.org/Documents/Countries/LY/DetainedAndDehumanised_en.pdf>.

UN, 'Europe and the Refugee Crisis: A Challenge to Our Civilization' <https://www.un.org/en/academic-impact/europe-and-refugee-crisis-challenge-our-civilization>.

UNCHR, 'UNHCR and IOM appeal to European leaders to tackle Mediterranean deaths' (2018) <https://www.unhcr.org/cy/2018/10/17/unhcr-and-iom-appeal-to-european-leaders-to-tackle-mediterranean-deaths/>.

UNDOC, 'Issue Paper: Smuggling of Migrants by Sea' (2011) <https://www.unodc.org/documents/human-trafficking/Migrant-Smuggling/Issue-Papers/Issue_Paper_-_Smuggling_of_Migrants_by_Sea.pdf>.

UNGA, New York Declaration for Refugees and Migrants, A/RES71/1 (3 October 2016).

UNHCR, 'Libya: UN experts alarmed at reports of trafficking in persons, arbitrary detention, enforced disappearances and torture of migrants and refugees' (UNHCR, Special Procedures, 21 July 2023) <https://www.ohchr.org/en/press-releases/2023/07/libya-un-experts-alarmed-reports-trafficking-persons-arbitrary-detention>.

UNHCR, 'Towards a Human Rights-Based Approach to Migration'. See here < https://www.ohchr.org/sites/default/files/documents/publications/Towards-Human-Rights-Based-Approach-Migration-Training-Guide.pdf>.

UNHCR, 'UNHCR Position on returns to Libya' (Update II), September 2018 <https://www.refworld.org/docid/5b8d02314.html>.

UNHCR, General legal considerations: search and rescue operations involving refugees and migrants at sea (November 2017) <https://www.refworld.org/docid/5a2e9efd4.html>.

UNHCR, The treatment of persons rescued at sea: conclusions and recommendations from recent meetings and expert round tables convened by the Office of the United Nations High Commissioner for Refugees: report of the Office of the United Nations High Commissioner for Refugees (11 April 2008) A/AC.259/17 <www.unhcr.org/refworld/docid/49997aeb27.html>.

United Nations General Assembly, 'Contemporary Forms of Racism, Racial Discrimination, Xenophobia and Related Intolerance', 10.11.2020, A/75/590, <https://digitallibrary.un.org/record/3893019?ln=en>.

Urbina, I., 'Lawless Ocean: The Link Between Human Rights Abuses and Overfishing' (Yale Environment 360, 20 November 2019) <https://e360.yale.edu/features/lawless-ocean-the-link-between-human-rights-abuses-and-overfishing>.

Urbina, I., 'Stowaways and Crimes Aboard a Scofflaw Ship' New York Times (New York, 17 July 2015) <https://www.nytimes.com/2015/07/19/world/stowaway-crime-scofflaw-ship.html>.

Vasques, E., 'EU to pay Tunisia €785m in 2023 as part of "cash for migrants" deal' (EURACTIV, 17 July 2023) <https://www.euractiv.com/section/global-europe/news/eu-to-pay-tunisia-e675m-in-2023-as-part-of-cash-for-migrants-deal>.

Villa, M., 'Outsourcing European Border Control: Recent Trends in Departure, Deaths and Search and Rescue Activities in the Central Mediterranean' (Border Criminologies, 11 September 2018) <https://www.law.ox.ac.uk/research-subject-groups/centre-criminology/centreborder-criminologies/blog/2018/09/outsourcing>.

Warin, C., 'Individual rights in EU migration and asylum law' (EU migration blog 2020) <http://eumigrationlawblog.eu/individual-rights-in-eu-migration-and-asylum-law/>.

Written Submission on behalf of the AIRE CENTRE (Advise on Individual Rights in Europe), The Dutch Refugee Council (DCR), the European Council on Refugees and Exiles (ECRE) and the International Commission of Jurists (ICJ) S.S. and Others v. Italy (11 November 2019) 4 <https://www.icj.org/wp-content/uploads/2019/11/ECtHR-SS_v_Italy_final-JointTPI-ICJECREAIREDCR-English-2019.pdf>.

Index

Note: Page numbers followed by 'n' indicate a footnote on the corresponding page.

FSC
www.fsc.org
MIX
Papier | Fördert gute Waldnutzung
FSC® C083411

Kolibri 360 GmbH
Ferdinand-Jühlke-Straße 7
99095 Erfurt, Deutschland
produktsicherheit@kolibri360.de